MW00488718

The Life and Teachings of Sai Baba of Shirdi

72

SUNY Series in
Religious Studies

Harold Coward, Editor

The Life and Teachings of Sai Baba of Shirdi

Antonio Rigopoulos

STATE UNIVERSITY OF NEW YORK PRESS

Production by Ruth Fisher
Marketing by Theresa A. Swierzowski

Published by
State University of New York Press, Albany

Printed in the United States of America

For information, address State University of New York Press, State University Plaza, Albany, NY 12246

Library of Congress Cataloging-in-Publication Data

Rigopoulos, Antonio, 1962–
The life and teachings of Sai Baba of Shirdi / Antonio Rigopoulos.
p. cm. — (SUNY series in religious studies)
Includes bibliographical references and index.
ISBN 0–7914–1267–9 (hard : alk. paper). — ISBN 0–7914–1268–7 (pbk. : alk. paper)
1. Sri Sai Baba, 1836–1918. 2. Hindus—India—Biography.
I. Title. II. Series.
BL1175.S7R54 1993
294.5'092—dc20
[B] 91–40880
CIP

10 9 8 7 6 5 4 3

To my dear parents

Mātaraṃ pitarañcaiva sākṣāt pratyakṣadevatām
matvā gṛhī niṣeveta sadā sarvaprayatnataḥ

Regarding his father and mother as visible incarnate deities, he should ever and by every means in his power serve them.

Mahānirvāṇa Tantra 8, 25

Contents

Foreword

It is both a pleasure and an honor for the writer of these lines to be asked to open, as it were, the gates of Antonio Rigopoulos' outstanding endeavor. The reader has in his or her hands a work of scholarly depth that is also highly readable: a comparatively uncommon achievement. The book grew from its original format of doctorate thesis (discussed at the University of Venice, Italy, in 1987) into the present comprehensive monography through years of dedicated bibliographical exploration and field-research. The whole scope of the available material concerning the fascinating and elusive figure of the *Sai Baba* (roughly "Holy Father": an epithet usually applied to respected Muslim ascetics, but here identifying a purposely no-label spiritual teacher) of the village of Shirdi has been utilized. The result is a rich fresco of Indian religious life between the end of the nineteenth and the beginning of the twentieth century.

As will be seen, the protagonist of the book, widely known and well-loved in India today, was possessed of a sharp wit and we find him more than once deliberately misleading his devotees by paradoxical gestures and teachings. There is, in the Sai's occasional antics, something of a village Socrates' irony, an anticlimax to his clamorous miracle-working which truly endears him to the Indian (and non-Indian) public. Several Muslim and Hindu tesserae of the incredibly complex mosaic of the *Sai*'s background and theatre of operations are introduced in due order by Rigopoulos, so that even those unfamiliar with such a scene are enabled to follow that mysterious man's often perplexing behavior in the light of the culture of the people with whom he was interacting.

To learn about the *Sai* through a study full of color and details like the one here available for the first time to the Western reader, means to possess a precious key to India's soul so as to approach the capital question: "What actually does meeting a *guru* feel like?" For every spiritual teacher is *the Guru*, but also *a guru*: side by side with his divine or quasi-divine role, he has idiosyncrasies and characteristic features both in his way of teaching and in his daily life persona. Eventually, the former may subside and the simple *presence* of the latter will afford a prop to devotees' search for liberating experience.

Rigopoulos has taken pains to find witnesses recalling the *Sai*'s teachings, which were certainly imparted in traditional fashion, even as commentaries to spiritual texts: the collective memory of Shirdi has maintained just their barest outlines, whereas a full-fledged account of many a curious happening is still available. The *Sai* himself encouraged such a somewhat sloppy approach—at least to Western eyes—on the part of the local people. He endorsed the importance of abandonment without much ado (*prapatti*) to divine Grace through his medium, which is, of course, a perfectly legitimate and time-honored quietistic dimension of *bhakti* in Indian outlook. The result is not only the aforementioned emphasis on his own life's incidents, but a decisive identification of himself with the Supreme God, whatever his identity be held to be, as well as with the Transcendent Absolute itself, the *Brahman* of Vedāntic teachings. For every spiritual teacher is *a guru,* but also *the Guru.*

Nothing helps us to understand how these two valences coexist, in Indian eyes, in the very same figure, better than the literary materials pertaining to the cult of deceased *guravas* (if a plural is to be used, the Sanskritic one is perhaps more in order than the 'barbaric' semi-English form "*guru*-s"). Rigopoulos has brought to the present writer's attention an interesting invocation of the Shirdi *Sai Baba* by his epithets, in the frequently adopted form of repeated *namovākas.* This hymn, in its happy syncretistic fashion, is eloquent as a full treatise: the whole field of religious experiences—either Vaishnavite or Shaivite, either centered on the personal aspect of Divinity or following the Advaitic line of approach to the Supreme Self—is employed by the Hindu devotees of our personage (different texts, no doubt, would be adopted for his worship by Muslim ones). The reader may be interested to peruse it. Here follows a translation.

The Garland of One Hundred and Eight Names of the Venerable Sai Baba

"*Om*, to the Venerable Lord *Sai*, prostration (*namaḥ*; the term stands for worship, but also for meditation directed to the Divine Figure to whom it is addressed)!

Om, to (Vishnu as the Sleeping God lying on waters in the interval between destruction and re-manifestation of universes) Narayana (accompanied by Fortune Goddess) Lakshmi, prostration!

Om, to Him whose forms Krishna and Rama (the well-known descents of Vishnu in the world), Shiva (Hanumat, considered as His descent) the Son of Wind and so on are, prostration!

Om, to Vishnu (in His aforementioned form) laying on (the Divine Serpent) Shesha, prostration!

Om, to (Rama) who has His abode near the shores of (the Holy She-river) Godāvarī, prostration!

Om, to Him whose seat (His) devotees' hearts are, prostration!

Om, to Him whose abode the hearts of all (beings) are, prostration!

Om, to Him in whom the beings dwell, prostration!

Om, to Him who is bereft of past, future and present, prostration!

Om, to Him who transcends time (and/or death), prostration!

Om, to (Krishna in his cosmic aspect shown to Arjuna in the *Bhagavadgītā*) who is Time (and/or Death), prostration!

Om, to (Shiva as Savior of His devotee Markandeya menaced by Yama) the Death of Time (and/or Death), prostration!

Om, to (Shiva in His aforementioned form) the Subduer of the pride of Time (and/or Death), prostration!

Om, to (Shiva in His aforementioned form) the Death-winner, prostration!

Om, to the Deathless One, prostration!

Om, to Him who gives mortals immortality, prostration!

Om, to Him who substains the living (beings), prostration!

Om, to Him who substains all, prostration!

Om, to Him able to grant favors to (His) devotees, prostration!

Om, to Him who promises to grant favors (whenever asked by them) to (His) devotees, prostration!

Om, to Him who grants food and clothing, prostration!

Om, to Him who grants health and patience, prostration!

Om, to Him who freely gives wealth and fortune, prostration!

Om, to Him who grants (yogic) powers and realization, prostration!

Om, to Him who grants sons, friends, wives and kin, prostration!

Om, to Him who brings forth yogic accomplishment, prostration!

Om, to Him who washes away misfortunes, prostration!

Om, to (Shiva as sung in a celebrated hymn by the mystic, philosopher, and literate Appayya Dikshita) the Friend along the path, prostration!

Om, to Him who grants fruitions, liberation, heaven and abandonment of rebirth, prostration!

Om, to the Beloved One, prostration!

Om, to Him who increases love, prostration!

Om, to (the Absolute as *Paramātman*, the Supreme Self) the Inner Ruler, prostration!

Om, to (*Paramātman*) whose self Being and Consciousness are, prostration!

Om, to (*Paramātman*) who is Eternal Bliss, prostration!

Om, to Him who grants supreme ease, prostration!

Om, to (*Paramātman*) the Supreme Lord, prostration!

Om, to (*Paramātman*) the Supreme *Brahman*, prostration!

Om, to the Supreme Self, prostration!

Om, to (*Paramātman*) whose very nature gnosis is, prostration!

Om, to (Brahmā) the Father of the universe, prostration!

Om, to (Brahmā) who is a mother for (His) devotees, the Bearer (of universe) and the Great Sire, prostration!

Om, to Him who freely gives to (His) devotees fearlessness, prostration!

Om, to Him who cares for (His) devotees, prostration!

Om, to Him who is very gracious to (His) devotees, prostration!

Om, to Him who loves (like a cow her calf) those who seek refuge (in Him), prostration!

Om, to Him who freely gives devotion and power, prostration!

Om, to Him who grants gnosis and detachment, prostration!

Om, to Him who freely gives love, prostration!

Om, to Him who causes obliteration of doubts, heart feebleness, sins, *karman* (of present and past lives) and the traces (thereof), prostration!

Om, to Him who cuts off the heart knot (a well-known Upanishadic metaphor for ultimate realization), prostration!

Om, to the Destroyer of *karman* (of present and past lives), prostration!

Om, to Him who stays in pure minds, prostration!

Om, to (*Paramātman*) who transcends attributes and (yet) is the very self of attributes, prostration!

Om, to (Vishnu as worshipped by the Pañcarātra tradition) who is possessed of infinite auspicious attributes, prostration!

Om, to Him whose strength is unmeasurable, prostration!

Om, to the Conqueror, prostration!

Om, to the Unconquerable and Unshakable One, prostration!

Om, to the Invincible One, prostration!

Om, to (Vishnu in His descent in the world as the Brahmin Dwarf, Vamana) whose going is unimpeded in the three worlds (earth, intermediate space, and heaven), prostration!

Om, to Him for whom nothing is impossible, prostration!

Om, to Him who is All-Powerful, prostration!

Om, to the Handsome and Beautiful One, prostration!

Om, to Him with beautiful (or far-seeing) eyes, prostration!

Om, to Him of many shapes, having all forms, prostration!

Om, to (*Paramātman*) the Formless and Unmanifest One, prostration!

Om, to (*Paramātman*) the Unthinkable One, prostration!

Om, to (*Paramātman*) the Subtle One, prostration!

Om, to (*Paramātman*) who is everybody's Inner Ruler, prostration!

Om, to (*Paramātman*) who transcends mind and speech, prostration!

Om, to Him whose face Love (as the ultimate mystic experience) is, prostration!

Om, to Him easy to reach (yet) difficult to approach, prostration!

Om, to the Assistant without assistant, prostration!

Om, to the Protector of those without protector, the Friend of the poor, prostration!

Om, to Him who takes upon Himself everyone's burden, prostration!

Om, to Him who well accomplishes the unsavory tasks, prostration!

Om, to Him the hearing of whose glorification is purifying, prostration!

Om, to the (holy) Ford, prostration!

Om, to (Krishna) Vasudeva's Son, prostration!

Om, to the Ultimate Resort of the good, prostration!

Om, to the Final End of the good, prostration!

Om, to the Lord of the worlds, prostration!

Om, to the Purifier Immaculate, prostration!

Om, to (the Moon identified with the Holy Plant Soma) whose filaments give forth the juice of immortality, prostration!

Om, to the Sun of shining halo, prostration!

Om, to Him whose vows are chastity, asceticism and so on, prostration!

Om, to Him who is the ultimate resort of truthfulness, prostration!

Om, to the Lord of the Realized Ones (the immortal *yogin* Dattatreya), prostration!

Om, to Him whose resolutions are (immediately) realized, prostration!

Om, to (Shiva) the Lord of *yoga*, prostration!

Om, to the Possessor of Divine Glory (*Bhagavat*, an epithet referred to Shiva as well as to Vishnu, but also employed for a respectful designation of the *Guru*, e.g. the *Buddha* in Buddhist texts), prostration!

Om, to Him who loves (like a cow her calf) His devotees, prostration!

Om, to (Vishnu as the Sacrifice, the Primordial Makranthropos from the portions of whose sacrificed body the universe was made according to a celebrated Vedic Hymn) the True Male (*Puruṣa*), prostration!

Om, to (Vishnu in His aforementioned aspect) the Supreme Male (*Puruṣa*), prostration!

Om, to (the *Guru*) who awakens (His disciples) to the Principle of Reality, prostration!

Om, to the Destroyer of the Six Foes beginning with Desire (Desire, Anger, Greed, Hatred, Pride, and Envy), prostration!

Om, to Him who freely gives the actual experience of Undivided Bliss, prostration!

Om, to (the *Sai* himself, here presented in a characteristic feature of His teaching) who approves all religious persuasions (*matāni*) as equal, prostration!

Om, to the Venerable (Shiva as Teacher of Absolute Truth through silence) with His face to the South (the direction of Death, as identified with one of the Fires in Vedic sacrifice), prostration!

Om, to the Lord of the Venkata Hill (Vishnu as Tirupati, a Tamil epithet denoting Him as Husband of Fortune Goddess Shri), prostration!

Om, to Him of wonderful and blissful deeds, prostration!

Om, to Him who takes away the pains of those who yield themselves (to Him), prostration!

Om, to the Cause of the obliteration of every suffering of the Round of Rebirth, prostration!

Om, to the Omniscient One, whose face is turned everywhere, prostration!

Om, to Him who stays inside and outside all (beings), prostration!

Om, to the Cause of all auspiciousness, prostration!

Om, to Him who freely gives all things wished for, prostration!

Om, to Him who consolidates the True Path along which all experience (for the mystic) has the same taste, prostration!

Om, to the Venerable Efficacious True *Guru*, the Lord *Sai*, prostration!"

Mario Piantelli,
Turin, Italy

Acknowledgments

My special thanks go to Prof. Franco Michelini-Tocci of the University of Venice and Prof. Mario Piantelli of the University of Turin, who, with their advice and encouragement, have patiently guided my research. Without their inspiration and support this work could have never been accomplished.

It also gives me great pleasure to thank all those who helped and assisted me during my sojourn and field-research in India, in Autumn 1985.

In general, to the Shirdi and Puttaparthi Sansthans for their hospitality and encouragement, and to all Sai Baba devotees, who have proved so kind, generous, and supportive.

In particular, I wish to thank the Agraval family, for offering me hospitality in their homes in Bombay and Khamgaon, providing me with transportation and introducing me to several *āśrams* and holy men.

My gratitude goes to my guide and translator during my permanence in Shirdi, the *Svāmin* Shekar Rao. Indeed an ascetic, he patiently and earnestly accompanied me for two weeks around the village, as well as to Sakuri, introducing me to innumerable old devotees of Baba.

Thanks are also due to Mr. Tipnis, who introduced me to Sati Godavari Mataji, of whose blessings I am unworthy of, and to Mr. Baldev Girme and his wife of Kopergaon. The latter couple helped me interview people in the Shirdi area, and made possible my encounter with the *Svāmin* Ram Baba in Bombay.

Finally, my thoughts turn with deep reverence to the *Svāmin* Satya Sai Baba, who, through his touch, blessed the package containing all my tapes, casting a benign glance upon me.

In Venice, Italy, my thanks go to my dear mother Sally, who read, reread, and corrected my English, always giving useful suggestions along the way.

A. R.
Venice, Italy

Guide to Pronunciation

Sanskrit and Marathi vowels are pronounced as in Italian, except for the short *a*, which is pronounced like the *u* in the English word *but*; the long *a* is pronounced like the *a* in *father*; *e* and *o* are always long; *ṛ* in Sanskrit is a vowel and should be pronounced like the *ri* in *ring*.

Consonants are pronounced as in English, with the following cases being noted: *c* is pronounced as in *church*; *j* is pronounced as in *joy*; *ś* and *ṣ* are similar to the sound *sh* in *shine*.

The aspirated consonants should be pronounced distinctly: *th* as in *hothouse*; *ph* as in *top hat*; *gh* as in *doghouse*; and *bh* as in *clubhouse*.

Underdotted consonants—*ṭ, ṭh, ḍ, ḍh, ṇ,* and *ṣ*—are not common phonemes in English and are produced by curling the tongue slightly backward toward the roof of the mouth.*

The letter *w* is sometimes found as the incorrect transliteration of Sanskrit and Marathi *v*.

In the few Hindi words, there is usually a final syllable (the *a* sound) dropped.

Perso-Arabic words are transliterated according to standard rules.

The names of Hindu deities as well as proper names, the names of places, and those of texts are generally used without diacritical marks and follow commonly recognized spelling (e.g., Ganesha rather than Gaṇeśa, Sai Baba rather than Sāī Bābā, Shirdi rather than Śirḍī, Upanishad rather than Upaniṣad, etc.).

*The underdotted *ṃ* as well as the overdotted *ṁ* and *ṅ* are all nasals.

Prologue

Sai Baba, the celebrated saint of Shirdi from the Ahmednagar district of Maharashtra State, though almost unknown to the public in the West, is an extremely popular figure all across the Indian subcontinent. Millions of people revere and worship him as a god, an *avatāra*, and as a teacher of tolerance and mutual harmony between Hinduism and Islam.

His ever-expanding fame is due, in the first place, to his alleged powers as a miracle worker and a healer. According to devotees, his acts of healing have not only continued but actually increased in number since the holy man's death in October 1918.

Besides this fundamental characteristic of the saint of Shirdi, his personality remains, overall, enigmatic and obscure. His birthplace and religious affiliation are a mystery to all, and today people still debate whether he was a Hindu or a Muslim.

What is certain is that a young ascetic, identified by villagers as a Muslim, reached the hamlet of Shirdi one day in the last century; that he was attributed the name of Sai Baba; and that he lived in the village till the end of his days, dwelling in a dilapidated mosque.

Even an approach to his teachings is not simple. Sai Baba disliked theorizing on religious matters, and he never gave spiritual discourses. He told stories and parables on occasion, and his language was then allusive, metaphoric, or paradoxical.

Of unpredictable moods, devotees remember him as both loving and harsh. When he got angry, often for no apparent reason, he would scream or abuse people, sometimes for hours on end, at times even tearing off his clothes.

What the old villagers in Shirdi emphasize, however, was Sai Baba's overall spiritual charisma: simply being in his presence gave one the feeling of being in the presence of God. His words pierced hearts, and his prolonged silences expressed extraordinary power. Apparently, Sai Baba's whole persona, his movements, words, and glances, conveyed a tangible and immediate experience of the sacred.

This study of the life and teachings of Sai Baba of Shirdi is intended as a general introduction to this fascinating, eclectic religious figure, firmly rooted in Maharashtrian spirituality.

The first part of this book attempts a chronological reconstruction of the saint's legendary life, trying to detect possible historical traces within the multifarious hagiographic material of the available sources. The presentation of Sai Baba's life includes an overview of many of the miraculous deeds attributed to him. These deeds are indeed so predominant in all sources that to underestimate them would mean losing sight of a fundamental aspect of Sai Baba's persona and the devotional cult surrounding him.

The second part deals with the holy man's teachings or "path philosophy," from within a triple perspective: that of Hindu *advaita-bhakti* mysticism, that of Sufism, and that of the teachings of the medieval *Sant* Kabir, Sai Baba's exemplary model.

The following is an outline of the main sources upon which the study has been conducted. In chronological order:

1. *Shri Sai Satcharita* by Govindrao Raghunath Dabholkar. Translated from the original Marathi into many Indian languages, it was rendered into English by Nagesh V. Gunaji in 1944. The writing of the *Shri Sai Satcharita* began while Sai Baba was still alive, Dabholkar having obtained Baba's permission to produce an account of his life. The author lived in Shirdi intermittantly from 1910 to 1916, becoming a permanent resident after 1916.

Devotees revere this work as a sacred text, that is, as the most authoritative repository of the life and teachings of their beloved saint.

The fifty chapters of the *Shri Sai Satcharita,* not arranged according to chronological order, offer a rich and detailed hagiographic account of Sai Baba's life and deeds. Despite its emphasis on the miraculous, the text constitutes an invaluable source for an understanding of Sai Baba and the movement surrounding him.

2. *Shri Sai Baba of Shirdi* by Rao Bahadur M. W. Pradhan (ex-member of the legislative council, Bombay Government). The first edition, with an introduction by G. S. Khaparde, dates back to 1933. This work is the English rendering of the Marathi memos of

Hari Sitaram Dikshit, one of Baba's closest devotees from 1909 onward. It furnishes valuable details concerning Sai Baba's daily life and activities.

3. The article "Hazrat Sai Baba" in *The Meher Baba Journal*, vol. 1 (Ahmednagar, 1938–39) of Abdul Ghani Munsiff. The importance of this article is twofold: (a) It furnishes an English summary of Das Ganu's work *Bhaktalīlāmrita* (offering, within a Hindu framework, the most widely accepted reconstruction of Sai Baba's life before his arrival in Shirdi) and (b) It presents Sai Baba in the light of Sufism, Abdul Ghani Munsiff being an Indian Muslim, pupil of Meher Baba (an important figure within the later Sai Baba movement).

4. *Sri Sai Baba's Charters and Sayings* by B. V. Narasimhaswami (with foreword by M. B. Rege). The fourth edition was published in Madras in 1942. Presented in the form of dialogues between Sai Baba and his devotees, this is the only source available for many of the sayings attributed to Sai Baba. We have reorganized this material under thematical headings in alphabetical order.

5. *Devotees' Experiences of Sai Baba* by B. V. Narasimhaswami (3 volumes). This was published in Madras in 1942. A detailed presentation of alleged miraculous phenomena witnessed and experienced by Sai Baba's devotees, while the saint was living, as well as after his death. The intent of the work is clearly hagiographic, aiming at the expansion of Sai Baba's popularity among the public at large.

6. *Life of Sai Baba* by B. V. Narasimhaswami (4 volumes). The first edition of volume 1 was published in Madras in 1955 (2,000 copies). It is the most accurate and thorough presentation of the life and teachings of Sai Baba. Volume 1 is chiefly dedicated to a biography of the saint. Volumes 2 and 3 present the life and personality of Baba's closest devotees. Volume 4 deals with Sai Baba's teachings and the future of the devotional movement inspired by him. Though the author presents a Hinduized version of Sai Baba's life, overshadowing the Islamic influence and background, this work, for its comprehensiveness, stands as the most important contribution to an understanding of the Shirdi saint and the entourage of his Hindu devotees.

7. *Ambrosia in Shirdi* by Ramalingaswami. The first edition was published in Shirdi in 1984 (2,000 copies). It gives information about the sacred sites of Shirdi and the ritual activities promoted

by the Sai Baba Organization (Sansthan). It presents, within a hagiographic mold, about two hundred episodes of Sai Baba's miraculous feats: one hundred are set during Baba's life and one hundred are said to have occurred after the saint's death in 1918.

With one or two exceptions, the biographies that have been written about Sai Baba have drawn from the *Shri Sai Satcharita* and Narasimhaswami's sources. The principal works include:

1. *Sai Baba: The Saint of Shirdi* by Mani Sahukar. First published in August 1952 with a foreword by Narasimhaswami. The author utilizes Narasimhaswami's *Charters and Sayings* and the *Shri Sai Satcharita* as her main sources. The last two chapters offer a brief presentation of the life and teachings of Upasani Baba and Sati Godavari Mataji, two important figures in the Sai Baba movement. In the third edition, published in 1983, Mani Sahukar added another chapter on the charismatic figure of the living saint Satya Sai Baba.

2. *The Incredible Sai Baba* by Arthur Osborne. First published in December 1957 (reprinted May 1970). The author principally drew on two of Narasimhaswami's sources: the *Charters and Sayings* and the *Devotees' Experiences of Sai Baba*. This is an excellent biography, with interesting comparisons between Sai Baba and Ramana Maharshi, the famous Vedāntin sage of Arunachala. Osborne's chapters on Hinduism and Islam and on Sai Baba's use of symbolism are noteworthy. This is perhaps the only biography of the saint of Shirdi that has been accessible to the Western public until recently.

3. *Understanding Shirdi Sai* by S. Gopalakrishna Murthy. First published in 1977 (1,000 copies). The author, formerly chief professor of physics at Presidency College, Madras, presents a thematical survey of Sai Baba's life and teachings, based upon all major sources. The biography is couched within an overall Vedāntic perspective.

4. *Sai Baba of Shirdi* by Perin S. Bharucha. First published by the *Shri Sai Sansthan* of Shirdi in 1980. This Parsi author utilizes the *Shri Sai Satcharita* as her main source. In the preface, she declares her work to be a "distillate" of the anecdotes about Sai Baba contained in Nagesh Gunaji's English rendition of the *Shri Sai Satcharita*. This is a fine portrait of the saint of Shirdi using a rare economy of words.

5. *Sai Baba the Master* by Acharya E. Bharadwaja. First published in Ongole (Andhra Pradesh) in 1983 (2,000 copies), it contains some previously unpublished stories and testimonies. The author gives space to experiences had by devotees after Sai Baba's death, as well as to the presentation of other saints and holy men connected with Sai Baba. This work contains original interpretative hypotheses.

6. *Gurus Rediscovered: Biographies of Sai Baba of Shirdi and Upasni Maharaj of Sakori* by Kevin Shepherd. First published in 1985 in Cambridge, Great Britain. A ground-breaking work presenting Sai Baba as a Muslim and a Sufi adept (possibly of the *majzūb* variety), thus countering the 'Hinduizing' tendency of all past Indian authors. Underplaying the miraculous element present in the sources, and focusing on the saint's teachings, Shepherd is particularly critical of Narasimhaswami's works, in his opinion heavily marked by hagiographic and apologetic concerns (though he surprisingly seems to ignore the existence of the latter's major contribution, i. e., the four volumes of the *Life of Sai Baba,* which he never mentions). Shepherd's portrayal of Sai Baba as a Sufi owes much to the views of Meher Baba and his devotional milieu.

7. *Sai Baba of Shirdi. A Unique Saint* by M. V. Kamath and V. B. Kher. Published in 1991, this book is a thoughtful and detailed account of Sai Baba's life and times, based on the research papers of V. B. Kher (previously published in the monthly *Shri Sai Leela* between 1976 and 1990). The authors attribute great value to the testimony of the *Svāmin* Shri Sai Sharan Anand, who first met Sai Baba in December 1911.

The few Marathi texts and pamphlets which have not been translated into English are secondary sources, that is, elaborations drawn from the *Shri Sai Satcharita.*

I have been greatly benefited from the memories and oral testimony gathered from old Shirdi villagers during my field research in the region in October 1985. Not knowing the Marathi language, I conducted all conversations in English with a local interpreter present, my remarkable guide the *Svāmin* Shekar Rao, who has lived in Shirdi for many years. All the interviews were taped.

In translation, some of the richness and nuances of the original Marathi language may have been somewhat lost. In Italy, my friend Mahesh Jaisval, late Prof. of Hindi Literature at the Venice University, kindly agreed to listen to the tapes. He found the translation from Marathi to be reasonably accurate and reliable, though in some circumstances the translator tended to synthesize the exact words, omitting the details. For reasons of clarity, I have rendered incomplete phrases with complete sentences.

Part 1

THE LIFE

1

Sai Baba's Background

The life of Sai Baba before his final settlement in the village of Shirdi,[1] in the Ahmednagar district, Kopergaon *tālukā*, is basically unknown. No historical evidence is available concerning the time and place of his birth, the identity of his parents, or his religious affiliation and training.

Even his very name is unknown, since Sai Baba is not an appellation in the usual sense. *Sāī* is a term of Persian origin, usually attributed to Muslim ascetics, meaning "holy one" or "saint."[2] *Bābā*, on the other hand, is a Hindi term attributed to respected seniors and holy men, and literally means "father."[3] The Sai Baba appellative thus comes to mean "holy father," "saintly father."

The *Shri Sai Satcharita*[4] refers to the occasion in which this "name" was supposedly attached to him. Mhalsapati,[5] the *pujārī* of the small temple of Khandoba,[6] situated on the outskirts of the village, seeing the young man coming to Shirdi with a marriage party, addressed him with the words *Yā Sāī*,[7] "Welcome, saint." Following Mhalsapati's example, others also addressed him so, to the extent that he became generally known as Sai.[8] The term *Bābā* was probably added later on, as he grew older. Possibly this was after 1890, when his fame started spreading, although some of his closest devotees at Shirdi might have called him Sai Baba from early times as a sign of respect.

Such a casual and generic naming (since he never revealed his true name, if indeed he had one), indicates that Sai Baba never attributed importance to such mundane matters, nor did he appreciate speculations concerning his earlier life. In fact, he always discouraged his devotees from investigating his origins, whether he was born a Hindu or a Muslim, and so forth, considering all these to be mere distractions and even obstacles along the spiritual path.

Temporality is a mere accident within the flux of *saṃsāra*[9] and is absolutely irrelevant. Thus, the Indian mind tends to devalue history and to emphasize rather those nontemporal elements which myth, with its power of symbolization, best illuminates. Along the path leading to liberation (*mokṣa*), the whole complex of *nāma-rūpa* (names and forms) represents a hindrance, and the wise one tries not to identify himself/herself with it. The soul (*ātman*) alone constitutes what truly *is*, being the only permanent reality.

Viewed from this perspective, the real Sai Baba (i.e., his true nature, which is the *ātman*) never had an origin, a starting point, being one with the qualityless Absolute. This condition is of course shared by all individual souls (*jīvātmas*), though very few have realized it in their own life experience. Baba constantly taught this lesson to his devotees, often expressing himself in paradoxical ways.

To the question "Baba, who are you? From where did you come?" he replied: "I am the Attributeless, Absolute, Nirguna. I have no name, no residence."[10]

He would also say the following: "I am Parvardigar[11] (God). I live at Shirdi and everywhere. My age is lakhs of years. My business is to give blessings. All things are mine. I give everything to everyone. I am in Gangapur,[12] Pandharpur,[13] and in all places. I am in every bit of the globe. All the universe is in me."[14]

From a dualistic standpoint, he would say: "I got embroiled by Karma,[15] and came into a body. So I got a name and an abode. The Dehi, that is, the embodied, is my name; and the world is my abode. Brahman[16] is my father, and Maya,[17] my mother. As they interlocked, I got this body. The world is evanescent, mutable."[18]

With these and other utterances, typical of a nondualistic approach, Baba underlined the radical uselessness of any speculation concerning his earthly identity. Often, when pressed with questions concerning his origins or his Hindu or Muslim affiliations, Sai Baba would become angry, cursing and abusing people, even for hours at length. At other times, he would answer these questions in provocatory and ambiguous terms or refer to a previous birth, enjoying the bewildered reactions of his devotees.

The *Shri Sai Satcharita*, considering the understanding of the mysterious ways of saints to be an impossible task, and in accordance with its hagiographic character, opts for a miraculous interpretation of Sai Baba's origins. Thus, it says: "Namadev and Kabir were not born like ordinary mortals. They were found as infants in mother-of-pearls, Namadev being found in Bhimrathi River by Gonayee and Kabir in Bhagirathi River by Tamal.[19] Similar was the case with Sai Baba. He first manifested Himself as a young lad of sixteen under a Neem tree in Shirdi for the sake of bhaktas."[20]

There are, however, some important elements which should be noted. First of all, Sai Baba, from his very first appearance in the village of Shirdi and throughout his life, was commonly identified as a Muslim. The appellation *Sāī*, in this regard, is highly indicative.

The biography by Charles B. Purdom on the life of Meher Baba[21] (1894–1969), written in 1937, states clearly: "Thousands of Sai Baba's devotees were Hindus, and, though he was a Mahommedan, they performed the ceremony of arti in his honour."[22]

The main reasons for Sai's identification as a Muslim ascetic, at least in the beginning, were two: his dress style and the few words he uttered, which were not Hindi or Marathi but apparently Persian or Arabic. The sources tell us that he used to wear a long white robe, that is, a *kafnī* (*kaphan*) and a white cloth around his head,[23] a style of dress typical of Muslim ascetics. Moreover, the term Sai Baba used for referring to himself was, almost invariably, that of *faqīr*. This word, which literally means "a poor man," is commonly applied to Muslim mendicants who wander about subsisting on alms.[24] Such *faqīrs* and ecstatics of the *dervish* variety[25] are found all over India.[26] Since *faqīrs* stem from heterodox Sufi brotherhoods, it seems plausible to argue that Sai Baba received some kind of training from one or more Sufi adepts and that he himself belonged to some Sufi school.[27]

The influence of the Madari order, possibly the most prominent among heterodox Sufi brotherhoods, seems not to be applicable to Sai Baba's persona, however.[28] On the Madarian, the Indian traveler Mohsan Fani (d. 1670) remarked:

> Among the most celebrated of [unorthodox Sufis] are, in the first line, the Madarian, who, like the Sanyasis Avadhuts, wear the hair entangled; and the ashes which they and the Sanyasis rub upon their bodies are called bhasma; besides, they carry iron chains on their heads and necks, and have black flags and black turbans; they know neither prayers nor fasts; they are always sitting at a fire; they drink a great deal of bang; and the most perfect among them go without any dress.[29]

As we shall see, the only element of this description applicable to Sai Baba is his habit of sitting at a fire.

It is well known that Islamic kingdoms were established in the Deccan area during medieval times, and Sufi activities have been prominent in places like Ahmednagar, Aurangabad, Khuldabad, Hyderabad, and Bijapur. Recently, Kevin Shepherd has proposed linking Sai Baba with those unorthodox Sufis known as *majzūbs*, "someone 'attracted' to God." It usually denotes a person who has abandoned the path of strict Islamic orthodoxy in favor of the life of a wandering beggar absorbed in love of God.[30] The inspiration for this identification is drawn from the work of Richard Maxwell Eaton on the Sufis of the kingdom of Bijapur, situated south of Ahmednagar.[31] We know that most *majzūbs* lived in the late seventeenth century or early eighteenth century, their number increasing in the period of the kingdom's decline. As a matter of fact, they appeared at this time in reaction to the values and life-styles of the urban and landed Sufis, who, in their opinion, had become corrupted. Apparently, many of these unorthodox Sufis were linked to the Chishti order of Shahpur Hillock, by either spiritual or family ties.[32] Most *majzūbs,* who never left any writings, held the heretical position that man and God are identical, and they often ignored even procedural exercises, such as the practice of remembering Allah (*dhikr*). Their most startling feature, however, is represented by their bizarre and eccentric behavior. They are often described as cursing and abusing people, even hurling stones at them, or exercising their power of prophecy while dancing in ecstatic moods. As Eaton remarks: "Being a majzūb necessarily involved embracing doctrines that were heretical from the standpoint of Islamic orthodoxy, adopting practices like drinking bhang or wine that were condemned by the orthodox, and flaunting behavioral eccentricities such as nakedness that were offensive to the 'worldly people'."[33]

Though some aspects of the teachings and eccentric behavior of *majzūbs* match Sai Baba's personality, it is not possible to establish any certain identification. The term *majzūb* never occurs in our sources on the *faqīr*'s life. Anyhow, it seems reasonable to suggest that Sai Baba belonged to or was strongly influenced by some Deccani Sufi brotherhood or teacher, possibly of Chishti background.

The earliest Sufis came to the Deccan around the end of the thirteenth century. They established themselves around Devagiri, renamed Daulatabad[34] by the Muslim rulers, which is in the vicinity of Paithan, then the center of religion and learning. A most prominent Sufi figure was that of Muntajab-ud-din Jarjaribaksha, who, together with seven hundred fellow Sufis, established himself in the area of Khuldabad,[35] near Devagiri. This community developed remarkably liberal and even pro-Hindu tendencies, bringing about a peculiar blend of Islamic features and *advaita-bhakti* teachings. This kind of Hindu-Muslim cross-fertilization is one of the characteristic features of Maharashtrian spirituality.[36]

The emblematic proof of this eclecticism is offered by the study of Marathi Muslim saint-poets. One of the most well known is Sheikh Mahammad (1560–1650) of Shrigonde in the Ahmednagar district. The son of Raje Mahammad, a Kādrī Sufi, he was initiated by one of the latter's disciples, that is, Chanda Bodhale, who also happened to be the teacher of Janardana, the guru of the celebrated saint-poet Eknath (1533–99). It is interesting to note that Chanda Bodhale, although a Hindu, was a follower of the Sufi line and used to dress as a *faqīr,* proof of how fuzzy the boundaries between Hindus and Sufis can sometimes be in the Deccani milieu. In one of his poems, Sheikh Mahammad sings:

> Through the grace of (god) Gopāḷa,
> I have transgressed all notions of purity and impurity.
> The jack-fruit has a thorny skin, but inside it are lumps of sugar.
> The bee-hive with all its humming bees contains the very nectar inside.
> (So also) Sheikh Mahammad may be an avindha, but in his heart he has the very Govinda.[37]

Thus, criticizing both Hinduism and Islam, he proclaims his faith in the one God, his language and style clearly showing the influence of Kabir's poetry and teachings.[38]

The fusion of the Sufi and Bhakti cults is also well reflected in other Muslim saint-poets, such as Latif Shah (sixteenth century), Shah Muntoji Bahamani (1575–1650), Husain Ambar Khan (1602–?), Shah Muni (c. 1756–1807).[39] As Shankar Gopal Tulpule aptly states: "Actually they (i.e., the Muslim poets) belonged to the cult of the Sufis which was close to devotional Hinduism and were trying to merge into the cult of Bhakti as propounded by the Marathi poet-saints. Their writings are an indication of this trend."[40]

Bijapuri Chishtis also drew from the *bhakti* tradition to illustrate their doctrines. For example, their depiction of God as Lover or Friend finds a parallel in the *bhakti* ideal of a personal deity actively concerned with his devotees. Burhan al-Din (one of the Chishti Literati) frequently used Sanskrit technical terms in expressing Sufi concepts. For instance, he designated God as *Śuddha Brahman* (Pure Being) and the phenomenal world as *māyā*.[41] As we have seen, such Vedāntic terminology was employed by Sai Baba himself.

Besides the Sufi element, the depth of Shirdi Baba's knowledge of the Hindu tradition and the breadth of his *advaita-bhakti* sayings are indicative of a strong Hindu influence upon his formative years.[42] Apparently, he often referred to a Hindu guru of his, whom he called "Venkusha."

I now come to a presentation of the various hypotheses concerning Baba's origins as found in the sources.

Mhalsapati, perhaps Sai Baba's closest disciple in the early days, stated that Baba had told him he was a *brāhmaṇ* from the village of Pathri who had been entrusted to a *faqīr* in his infancy. When Baba told him this, some people had just come to Shirdi from Pathri, and Baba asked them about certain people who lived there.[43] At that time, Pathri was located in the Parbhani district, in the Aurangabad Division of Hyderabad State,[44] and was the headquarters of the Pathri *tālukā*, which included an area of 784 square miles.[45]

On another occasion, during the first days of October 1918, that is, about two weeks before his death, Baba supposedly said: "My fakir's wife left me with 'Venkusa' at Selu. I stayed with him 12 years, and left Selu. This brick (which Baba always lovingly used to support his arm or head) is my Guru's gift, my life companion. It is not the brick that is broken now—but my Karma (prarabdha) that has snapped. I cannot survive the breaking of the brick."[46]

Sai Baba mentioned Venkusa or Venkusha on other occasions also. Once, when talking to a devotee, he said: "Nana, I am not angry with you. You, my children, can be angry with me. If Venkusha were alive, I could be angry with him."[47]

Thus, according to this reconstruction, Sai Baba was born into a *brāhmaṇ* family and subsequently entrusted to a *faqīr* and his wife. The motif of the Hindu birth of reputed Muslim figures is often attested to in Indian hagiographic literature (for example, in the legendary tales concerning Kabir). It is also a useful device to explain Sai Baba's eclectic personality, although of course one cannot rule out the possibility that such were the historical facts. The most important datum of the account, however, is that Sai Baba's earliest religious education came from a *faqīr,* perhaps a Sufi belonging to some major brotherhood. Baba's habit of referring to God as *Faqīr,* may be due to his influence.[48] Narasimhaswami thinks that Sai Baba's stay with this *faqīr* and his wife did not exceed five years.[49] That such a short estimate could be correct seems quite improbable, however. Sai Baba must have remained under direct Sufi influence for a longer period of time, perhaps ten years or even more. Observing, listening to, and following the ways of his preceptor, young Sai received a basic education in Sufi tenets, the substance of which, unfortunately, eludes us completely.

V. B. Kher, a trustee of the Shirdi Sansthan from 1984 to 1989 and author of several research papers on Sai Baba, recently stated that Sai, at the tender age of eight, left his *brāhmaṇ* family in Pathri in the company of a Sufi *faqīr*. This would have taken place between 1846 and 1850. The boy would have come to Paithan and afterwards wandered all over Marathvada from the age of eight to the age of twenty-five or thirty.[50]

According to Narasimhaswami's account, the *faqīr*, just before dying, directed his wife to take the young boy to Selu, which was the political center of the Jintur *parganā*.[51] Here she was to leave him with a Hindu guru, namely Venkusha.

More information on this period of Sai's life was supposedly gathered in 1903 by Ganapat Rao Dattatreya Sahasrabuddhe, one of Baba's closest devotees, popularly known as Das Ganu Maharaj (1868–1962).[52] In 1901 he went on a field-research trip to Selu, where he discovered many interesting details connecting Venkusha with the military and administrative system of the *peśvās*.[53] Venkusha was the pseudonym under which one Gopalrao Deshmukh was known when he was the provincial governor of the Jintur province.[54]

Selu was the capital of the province, and Gopalrao resided in its fort. He was able to maintain political control over the region and was thus feared by the Islamic Nizām, to whom he was opposed.[55] Because of his devotion to his chosen deity (*iṣṭadevatā*) of Tirupati Venkatesha,[56] he was also known as Venkusha, which is a contraction of the term *Venkatesha*.[57]

During his research on Sai Baba's early years, Das Ganu is said to have had access to a collection of family papers and legends referring to Gopalrao's life. From these reports we learn that Gopalrao or Venkusha spent much time in pilgrimages and the performance of sacred rituals. He was rich and liberal and he encouraged righteousness, piety, and study. Unlike the majority of *deshmukhs* and *zamindārs* of his times, who were known for their cruelty and lack of moral values, he is here pictured as a very pious man animated by an intense devotion for his *iṣṭadevatā*. The sources describe his purity, his self-control, his virtues, and his powers (*siddhis*).[58] Celebrated as a saint, the papers also describe his moments of identification with Venkatesha, when "he spoke words which were Venkatesha's words."[59]

One of these family papers reports a curious story. Once, when Gopalrao was in Ahmedabad, he approached the tomb of Suvag Shah, a celebrated Muslim saint. The tomb (*dargāh*) then began to 'perspire' out of joy and spoke to him. It said that he,

Gopalrao, had been the famous Ramananda of Kashi in a previous birth,[60] and that he had now become a householder (*gṛhastha*) and a governor. All the same, his former devotee Kabir would be coming to him soon.[61] Thus, the identity of Ramananda as Venkusha and Kabir as Sai Baba would be established. It was apparently after this "revelation," that the young boy was brought to Gopalrao by the *faqīr*'s widow. Venkusha, having recognized him as Kabir, enthusiastically accepted him as his *śiṣya*.

Young Sai would have then practiced a second period of spiritual training, this time within the framework of Vaiṣṇava *bhakti*. Such a training with a Hindu *ācārya* must have lasted a fairly long time. Sai Baba himself, in a tribute of love and devotion to his guru, is reported to have said:

> For 12 years I waited on my Guru who is peerless and loving. How can I describe his love for me? When he was Dhyanastha (i.e., in love-trance), I sat and gazed at him. We were both filled with Bliss. I cared not to turn my eye upon anything else. Night and day I pored upon his face with an ardor of love that banished hunger and thirst.
>
> The Guru's absence, even for a second, made me restless. I meditated on nothing but the Guru, and had no goal, or object, other than the Guru. Unceasingly fixed upon him was my mind. Wonderful indeed, the art of my Guru! I wanted nothing but the Guru and he wanted nothing but this intense love from me.
>
> Apparently inactive, he never neglected me, but always protected me by his glance. That Guru never blew any mantra into my ear. By his grace, I attained my present state.[62]

The *bhakti* element is here expressed in all its intensity. In Sai's formative years, the themes of devotion and surrender to the teacher's will may indeed have constituted the backbone of his religious upbringing. We shall later see how other themes relate to this central core of *bhakti* and *śaraṇāgati*.[63]

The Selu manuscripts describe in some detail the transfer of spiritual authority from Venkusha to the boy (*guru-paramparā*), Venkusha's death, and the boy's departure from the town. This story will play a considerable role in the tradition of Sai Baba's cult, and thus it is important to relate it in full:

> Baba's[64] being favoured by the master evoked considerable jealousy amongst the Guru's retainers and some of them

resolved to kill young Baba by hurling brickbats at him. During a "chaturmasya" (August to November) Gopal Rao was in a garden, and young Baba was attending upon him. The villains hurled bricks at Baba. One of the bricks came very near Baba's head, but the Guru saw it, and by his order it stood still in mid air, unable to proceed further or hit Baba. Another man threw a second brick to hurt Baba. But Gopal Rao got up and got the brick on his head. This led to profuse bleeding. Baba was moved to tears, and he begged his master to send him away, as the master was getting harmed from his unfortunate company. But the master declined to send him away. As for the injury, the master bandaged it with a shred torn from his own cloth, and then suddenly he said: "I see that the time has come for me to part with you. Tomorrow at 4 P.M. I shall leave this body, not as a result of this injury, but by my own yoga power of Svecchha Marana.[65] Therefore, I shall now vest my full spiritual personality in you. For that purpose, bring milk from yonder black cow." Young Baba went to Hulla the lambadi (herdsman) in charge of the cow, who pointed out that the cow was barren, had not calved and could not, therefore, yield milk. All the same, he came with the cow to the chieftain Gopal Rao who just touched it from horns to tail and told the lambadi: "Now pull at the teats." The lambadi's pull drew out plenty of milk, and this milk was given to Baba with Gopal Rao's blessings that the full power and grace of the Guru should pass on to young Baba.

This was the Diksha, the investiture, of the Guru's personality which young Baba underwent.... The villain whose brickbat had hit Gopal Rao, the chieftain, fell down dead, the moment Gopal Rao was hit. His companions were horrified and they came with repentance to Gopal Rao's feet and prayed for pardon not only for themselves but also for their dead companion whom they begged Gopal Rao to revive. The chieftain pointed out that the power of revival now rested in the young man, and that they should appeal to him.[66] They accordingly appealed, and Baba took some of the dust of his Guru's feet and placed it on the corpse. The dead boy rose at once. The Guru's declaration that he would pass away from this life the next day...was fulfilled. After making the fullest preparations for settling all his temporal affairs, Gopal Rao with his full consciousness sat up in the midst of a religious group carrying on puja, bhajan, namasmarana, etc., in the presence of his Ishta Devata Sri Venkatesha and at the solemn hour he had

> himself fixed for departure, his soul left in perfect peace and happiness like Parikshit in Srimad Bhagavata. Before leaving the body, the master waved his hand westward to the young boy and bade him leave Selu...and Baba by slow degrees moved on from place to place and arrived at Shirdi and after some time made it his permanent residence.[67]

Such is the reconstruction of Sai Baba's early period which Narasimhaswami upholds.[68]

At first sight the details of this story, clearly couched within a hagiographic framework, appear unrealistic. It seems hard to believe that a pious Muslim would ask his wife to entrust his young disciple to a Hindu, who, among other considerations, represented a political and military threat to his coreligionists within the Nizām. Moreover, to accept Gopalrao as guru and also as military and political chief doesn't seem very plausible.

The first objection might be countered by positing the high degree of religious tolerance of this *faqīr*, possibly a Sufi of high spiritual attainment. The syncretistic, blending milieu of the Deccan might in fact have contributed to a kind of vision in which there is, so to speak, "no more Hindu nor Muslim," all being but expressions of one same reality. Illustrious examples of Islamic openness to Hinduism are historically represented by Akbar[69] (1556–1605) and Dārā Shikōh's (1615–59) syncretistic mysticism.[70]

With regard to the second objection, one could argue that there have been numerous examples of reconcilability, within Indian history, of the religious and political spheres. Numerous ministers, as the famous Sayana and his brother Madhava of the Vijayanagara Empire, combined spiritual life with administrative and political duties.[71] In more recent times, the figure of Mohandas Karamchand Gandhi (1869–1948) comes immediately to mind.[72] Other examples could be added, though perhaps not so famous.[73] After all, such an effort, striving to reconcile active and contemplative life, is typically Indian from the time of the *Bhagavadgītā*.

Let us now consider the more "realistic" aspects of Das Ganu's reconstruction, notwithstanding its hagiographic character. In the first place, Sai Baba's exposure to both the Sufi and Hindu traditions would account for his eclectic persona and teachings. His early training under a *faqīr*, and afterwards under the Hindu guru Venkusha at Selu, seems to have been confirmed by Baba himself. Moreover, it would not be methodologically correct to reject Narasimhaswami's testimony *in toto*. Thus, the hypothesis of a sort of "double-phased" spiritual biography appears plausible.

The description of Sai Baba's *brāhmaṇ* origin and subsequent tutelage by a Muslim couple, follows a traditional hagiographic pattern that aims at the Hinduization of the *faqīr*. We find the same in legends concerning Kabir's life.[74] It appears, however, that Sai Baba himself affirmed his *brāhmaṇ* origin. He would say: "This is a Brahmin's mosque."[75]

And again (referring to himself): "This is a Brahmin, a pure Brahmin, a white Brahmin, who will carry thousands on to Subhra Marga."[76]

Arthur Osborne has proposed taking Sai Baba's use of the term *Brahmin* as symbolical, however, expressing a state of spiritual election.[77] I agree.

Sai Baba's birth at Pathri is not historically proven, though Baba himself seems to have "revealed" this to his *bhakta* Mhalsapati.[78] The claim of Baba's birth at Pathri and of his *brāhmaṇ* origin is also found in two more recent accounts that I shall shortly examine.

All in all, the hagiographic character of Das Ganu's reconstruction does not eliminate the possible historicity of some of the structural elements of the narrative.

In more recent times, however, the *ācārya* E. Bharadwaja in his biography *Sai Baba the Master*, has questioned the credibility of Das Ganu's reconstruction: "He [Das Ganu] admits that he does not even remember which facts of Baba's life were conveyed to him by which native of Selu."[79]

He adds: "All that he could gather was that a hundred years earlier, there lived an old man in Selu; that a fakir came and stayed with him; that some people had killed the old mahatma for some grouse which they had against him; that the fakir had finally escaped."[80]

Bharadwaja points out the vagueness of Das Ganu's findings. It may be observed, however, that if the "old mahatma" lived in Selu a century prior to Das Ganu's researches (i.e., around 1801), this would not necessarily contradict Narasimhaswami's report, which says that Gopalrao was nominated *deshmukh* of Selu between 1800 and 1825.[81] Young Sai could have then known Gopalrao, since the *Shri Sai Satcharita* argues that Baba was probably born around 1838.[82]

This argument was nonetheless rejected by Lakshmikant Malharrao Subhedar of Selu, apparently one of Gopalrao's sixth-generation descendants, who told V. B. Kher that Gopalrao was born in 1715 and died in 1802 (Subhedar is said to have produced documentary evidence in support of his statement).[83] Of course, if this is true, Sai Baba could never have been Gopalrao's disciple.

If one accepts Bharadwaja's and Kher's rejection of Das Ganu's report, we are left with a missing link in regard to Sai Baba's allusions to Selu and Venkusha.

Bharadwaja further argues: "When I was gathering information about the life of Hazrat Tajuddin Baba of Nagpur, one of his disciples told me that a fakir came to the Baba for instructions, and that he was Sai Baba. I found a similar claim from the devotees of Sri Svami Samarth of Akalkot. His devotees claim that Sai Baba was his disciple. I found that the source of all this confusion is the custom of referring to fakirs as Sai (a saint)."[84]

Bharadwaja aptly remarks about the generic quality of the *Sāī* name and the tendency present among other religious groups of "appropriating" Baba's persona. Evidencing the ambiguity of many of Sai Baba's statements concerning his guru, he says: "Sai Baba told his early devotees of Shirdi that his guru's tomb was underneath the local neem tree. He told Svami Sai Sarananandaji, that Roshan Shah was his guru. On another occasion, he told Hemadpant[85] that he met his guru in a forest."[86]

These allusive statements of Baba, however, seem not comparable with the persistence of the references to Selu and Venkusha.

The first testimony concerning his guru's tomb refers almost certainly to one of his previous births.[87] We shall get back to it shortly. The second testimony, which makes one Roshan Shah, obviously a Muslim, Sai Baba's teacher, is not attested to in any of our chief sources. Such a reference might be purely symbolical, since Bharadwaja himself notes how Baba often mentioned the term *Roshan* in his parables.[88] The third testimony, relating how Baba met his guru in a forest, is a well-known one. This story, however, is almost certainly allegorical. No historical value is attached to it by any of our sources, with the exception of A. Osborne, who posits that this anonimous guru might be identified with Venkusha.[89]

Indeed, Baba loved indulging in allusive as well as paradoxical talk. Instances of his incomprehensible and bizarre speech are numerous. In one curious dialogue, we read:

> One devotee: Baba, what is your native place?
>
> B.: I came here from Aurangabad. My maternal uncle (Mama) brought me down here.
>
> Devotee: What is the name of that Mama? Where is he now?

> B.: (laughing) He was a mad man, having no name. He must be living somewhere now.[90]

The *Shri Sai Satcharita* reports this same dialogue, adding however that Baba said that his uncle's name was Nasatya.[91] The Nasatya, according to Hindu mythology, are the twin Ashvins, the gods' divine physicians.[92]

It seems that Sai Baba's first intention was that of disconcerting his listeners. The name Nasatya is not at all common among humans![93] Thus, to follow each of these allusions as possible autobiographic hints would certainly lead us astray.

The fact remains that the references to Selu and Venkusha, although within a fragmentary frame, are the only recurring elements within the majority of the hagiographies.

The story of the brick that hit Gopalrao finds a correspondance with another statement Sai Baba seems to have made just a few days before his death: "This brick...is my Guru's gift, my life companion. It is not the brick that is broken now, but my Karma.... I cannot survive the breaking of the brick."[94]

Moreover, on another occasion, when asked by a magistrate: "Your Guru's name?" Sai Baba apparently replied, "Venkusa."[95]

Texts report various utterances attributed to Baba, in which he connects and sometimes identifies himself with Kabir.[96]

Kabir,[97] the fifteenth-century[98] Muslim weaver (*julāhā*) of Benares, was certainly the greatest poet-singer of the North Indian *Sant* tradition.[99] Considered a Sufi by the Muslims and a *bhakta* of the Ramananda school by the Hindus, he represented a peculiar blending of traditional Hinduism, the Vaiṣṇava *bhakti* of the great reformers, and the yogic Nātha schools.[100] His iconoclastic monism might be classified as *nirguṇi bhakti,* of which he was the initiator; a *bhakti* directed to the qualityless (*nirguṇa*) aspect of the supreme Reality, which he called "Rām."

The *Bhakta-mālā* of Nabhaji, a Vaiṣṇava poet who lived c. 1600, gives us a valuable description of Kabir:

> Kabir refused to acknowledge caste distinctions or to recognize the authority of the six Hindu schools of philosophy, nor did he set any store by the four divisions of life (*āśramas*) prescribed for Brahmans. He held that religion (*dharma*) without devotion (*bhakti*) was no religion at all (*adharma*), and that asceticism, fasting, and alms-giving had no value if not accompanied by adoration (*bhajana*). By means of *ramainīs,*

> *śabdīs*, and *sākhīs*,[101] he imparted religious instruction to Hindus and Turks alike. He showed no partiality to either but gave teaching beneficial to all. With determination he spoke and never tried to please the world.[102]

The Maharashtrian *Sant* tradition of the *Vārakarī saṃpradāya*[103] is surely anterior to Kabir. Its foremost saint-poet, Namdev (1270–1350), together with Jaydev[104], is mentioned by Kabir as a great saint of the *Kali* age and as his "predecessor." Namdev, like Kabir, magnified the greatness of the *sadguru* and similarly never named his own human guru. On the religious plane, there are striking similarities between Kabir and the *Sants* of Maharashtra. As Charlotte Vaudeville puts it:

> Though immersed in a hopelessly corrupt world, the "Sant"... alone remains unsullied by it: through the Satguru's grace, he is able to resist the lures of the all-powerful Māyā and the enticements of "woman and gold." Through the constant invocation and inner contemplation of the divine Name, he is able to bring into subjection passions of the flesh and to control the fickle Mind. Thus, firmly clinging to the "Name of Rām," he crosses over the Ocean of Existence and reaches personal salvation, whilst the whole world goes to its doom.[105]

Kabir's stature within Maharashtra's culture is considerable and reflects the typical blending of this region, of Muslim and Hindu components. An important hagiographic treatment on Kabir's life is found in the *Bhaktavijaya* of Mahipati (1715–90), written in 1762.[106] Through such literature, one can acquire valuable insight into how Kabir was and still is perceived at a popular level.[107] The allusive and often paradoxical poetic style of many of the saint-poets (Muslim as well as Hindus; cf. Tukaram), also reveals the depth of Kabir's influence.[108] Sai Baba's understanding of Kabir's *persona* certainly reflected the Deccani characterization of it.

Baba's choice of Kabir as an exemplary model is attested to in the following dialogue with a magistrate:

> Commissioner: What is your name?
>
> Baba: They call me Sai Baba.
>
> Com.: Your father's name?

B.: Also Sai Baba.

Com.: Your Guru's name?

B.: Venkusa.

Com.: Creed or Religion?

B.: Kabir.

Com.: Caste or race?

B.: Parvardigar (i.e., God).

Com.: Age, please?

B.: Lakhs of years.[109]

Sai Baba's statement of belonging to "the religion of Kabir" is an important point. It could imply his connection to the vast movement of the Kabīrpanthīs or even his being a member of it.[110] Indeed, many Baba devotees consider him an emanation from the vast spiritual movement which Kabir originated. During my research in India, the first word uttered by N. Kasturi, late biographer of the present Satya Sai Baba,[111] when asked about Shirdi Sai Baba's origins, was "Kabīrpanthī."

Apparently, Baba also claimed to have been Kabir in a previous birth: "I was Kabir and used to spin yarn."[112]

On other occasions, Baba spoke of himself as a weaver, perhaps on analogy with Kabir, the weaver (*julāhā*).

In the *Charters and Sayings*, we read: "As a boy I was weaving shawls, and my father was once so pleased with my work that he gave me a present of Rs. 5 or so."[113]

And again, "Once I wove cloths, turbans, pitambar,[114] rugs, etc. but still I could not get enough to satisfy my hunger."[115]

Of course, such statements could refer to a previous birth of Baba's, not necessarily identifiable with that of Kabir. Some of these allusions do not, in fact, strictly coincide with a *julāhā*'s job.

It is also reported that Sai Baba stated that Kabir had been his guru: "At the foot of the Margosa tree[116] is the tomb of Kabir. Thus, Kabir's body became flowers.[117] Kabir was my Guru. I put up at that tree foot, for that reason. God will bless those who burn incense here, on Thursdays and Fridays."[118]

Such an utterance might signify either a past identity as Kabir's disciple or the belonging to some kind of Kabīrpanthī circle.

Such statements all seem to imply that Sai Baba viewed Kabir's life and teachings as exemplary: his *imitatio* of Kabir grows to the point of identifying with him. Due to Baba's link with Kabir, many devotees, as well as some scholars, are of the opinion that he might have been connected to the vast pan-Indian movement of the Nātha yogis of Gorakhnath.[119]

To be sure, the presence of Nātha yogis in Maharashtra, with a center at Tryambak, is attested to from the thirteenth century. Jñāndev, the founder of the Marathi *bhakti* movement, is said to have been initiated into the Nātha cult by his elder brother Nivṛtti, who was himself a disciple of Gahininatha, the fourth Nātha in the legendary Marathi lineage. As Charlotte Vaudeville puts it:

> Concerning the Marathi branch of this sect of northern origin, it seems to have first established itself in the region of Tryambak, near the Godavari source, probably around the 12th or 13th century. From Tryambak, the Nath Yogis spread all over Maharashtra: thus, from the "Gazetteer" of the Satara district (Southern Maharashtra), we learn about the existence of a mountain named "Macchendragadh" and of a tamarind tree named "Gorakh-chincha," sacred to the memory of Gorakhnath. According to the Nath tradition of Maharashtra, Matsyendra himself instructed Gorakhnath while on the "Saptasringi" mountain, north of Nasik,[120] where a famous sanctuary sacred to the Devi is located.[121]

Nātha brotherhoods are present in the Ahmednagar district, and images of Nātha gurus are even seen inside the Shirdi temple (*mandir*) where Sai Baba's *samādhi* (tomb) is located. In particular, the sacred fire (*dhunī*) that Baba always kept burning is often considered a Nātha influence. The most important characteristic of a Nāthapanthī monastic center is indeed the *dhunī* (perhaps from a Sanskrit root *dhū*, "to kindle"), that is, the continuous fire. The use of keeping a burning fire, however, is not a prerogative of Nāthas alone: we find it widely attested to among Sufi orders and *faqīrs*.[122]

Another popular belief identifies Sai Baba with an *avatāra* of Dattatreya.[123] Thus, in the prologue the *Shri Sai Satcharita* notes:

> The well-known Marathi work viz. Gurucharitra is familiar to all the people of Maharashtra. It is read and studied daily by all the devotees of the God Dattatreya all over the country. The author Sarasvati-Gangadhar describes in this book the miracles and teachings of Shri Shripad Shrivallabha and Shri Narasinha Sarasvati Swami, the two prominent Incarnations

> of the God Dattatreya. According to the opinion of an expert Marathi scholar, Mr. L. R. Pangarkar, these two Incarnations flourished in the 14th and 15th centuries.... There were other later Incarnations of Dattatreya: prominent amongst them were Shri Manikprabhu in the Nizam's dominions and Shri Akalkot Maharaj in the Sholapur district, and lastly, Shri Sai Baba of Shirdi in the Ahmednagar district, who took his samadhi in 1918. Shri Sai Baba is believed by some devotees to be the Continuation-Avatar of Shri Akalkot Maharaj.[124]

The process of identification of Sai Baba with Dattatreya is such, that the *Shri Sai Satcharita* is often called "the modern *Gurucharitra*."[125] Such popular belief is not confined to Maharashtra, being present in other parts of India as well.[126]

Indeed, Sai Baba himself is reported to have claimed such an identity. One day, he told a devotee: "Are you puffed up? Where was male progeny in your destiny? (In answer to the prayer you offered before Datta at Gangapur) I tore up this body and gave you a son."[127]

Baba apparently manifested himself in Datta form on occasion.[128] We read:

> In 1911, on Datta Jayanti day,[129] Mr. Balawant Kohojkar went to Baba at Shirdi.
>
> At 5 P.M. Baba said: "I am having pangs of labour and cannot bear the pain." So saying, he drove everyone out of the mosque.
>
> He was evidently identifying himself with Anasuya. A little later, Baba called all people in. Kohojkar went first, and on Baba's gadi[130] saw not Baba, but a small charming three-headed baby, i.e., Datta. In a moment, Datta disappeared and Baba was seen instead.[131]

Like Datta, Sai Baba came to be identified by many as an *avadhūta*, that is, a yogin who has attained the highest realization, free from all ties.[132] Sai Baba's love of dogs, with whom he often identified,[133] may be another reason why he is viewed as an *avatāra* of Datta. Though dogs are generally considered impure animals in India (and are thus not household pets!), they are also believed to be an incarnation of the deity Khandoba. He, like Datta, is surrounded by dogs both in myth and iconography. In many Dattatreya temples, dogs are regularly worshipped.[134]

I must stress, however, that Baba is reported to have identified himself with almost every deity of the Hindu pantheon, thus impressing on his *bhaktas* the unity of God. On various occasions, he declared he was Mahalakshmi,[135] Vithoba of Pandhari,[136] Maruti,[137] Ganapati,[138] Krishna,[139] and so forth.

In the same way, he would tell his Muslim followers, "I am God (Allah)."[140]

Sai Baba's appearance in the form of other gurus or Sufi adepts is also reported. Indeed, the sources abound in the description of such wonders.[141]

To be sure, Sai Baba never gave preference to any particular form of Hindu God over others. He preferred describing God in terms of *nirguṇa Brahman*, the attributeless Absolute. Throughout Baba's life, the name of Allah remained his favorite expression. Also, he would sometimes describe himself as just a poor *faqīr*, with normal limbs and organs.[142]

Thus, there was no particular preference on Baba's part for Dattatreya's form. Such a specific identification, rather, was attached to him by his devoted *bhaktas*, particularly after his death. As Mani Sahukar aptly puts it: "The Hindus thought him to be an Avatar of some God-head; the Muslims said he was a Pir[143] sent by Allah to liberate men. To one man he was the Avatar of Dattatreya, to another he was Akalkot Maharaj re-incarnated. Each individual saw in this unique Saint a personification of his own favourite deity, an incarnation of his own chosen ideal, and worshipped him as such."[144]

We now come to the presentation of two more recent reconstructions of Baba's origins, ones certainly unknown to Das Ganu, Narasimhaswami, Osborne, and others.

The first one, proposed by one Sri Mittha Lakshmi Narasaiyya, a popular lawyer of Hyderabad, is quite disconcerting and can hardly be applicable to the habits of the *brāhmaṇic* caste in last-century India. It is summarized thus:

> Baba was born in Jaffa Gate, the old city of Jerusalem, on the 11th of March at 9 P.M. in the year 1836. His parents, Nandlal and Jamunabai, were Vaishnav Brahmins who lived in Gujarat in the later half of the 19th century. Having no issue, they were visiting all the holy places, during which they happened to come in contact with a Muslim Fakir who took them to Mecca. After visiting all the holy places in and around Mecca, they eventually came to Jerusalem where at Jaffa Gate Jamunabai gave birth to a male child.... They returned to India and lived for a while at Pathri village in Aurangabad district in the Nizam State which is now in Maharashtra.[145]

No explanation is offered concerning the sources of this story. Such a bizarre elaboration clearly aims at the brāhmaṇization of Baba's origins, while at the same time framing it within the sacred geography of Islam. The apologetic concern is evident. The reference to the village of Pathri is again utilized, perhaps in hopes of linking the birth story to attested data.

The second recent reconstruction of Sai Baba's early life bears more interest. Not many years ago, the living saint Satya Sai Baba, who claims to be the reincarnation of the Baba of Shirdi,[146] offered a lengthy narration relative to his "previous birth." Such narration is so informative and evocative of the atmosphere of Indian village life, it seems useful to review it in detail:

> Ganga Bhavadia[147] was a poor boatman, who used to ferry his passengers across a river flowing placidly by the little hamlet of Pathri, near Manmad. His wife Devagiriamma[148] was a kind devout soul, who after completing her domestic chores, devoted her time worshipping God in the form of Parvati. Her husband paid his homage to the form of God he loved most, which was Shiva, consort of Parvati. They were a devoted but childless couple. One evening when Ganga Bhavadia had returned home from work, he noticed the gathering clouds on the horizon.... That night, a furious storm broke over Pathri and the normally placid waters of the river were surging wildly, sweeping everything away in a rushing torrent. Ganga Bhavadia hurried to the river bank to strengthen the moorings of his boats and look after their safety during the storm.
>
> After a while an old man took refuge from the storm into the verandah of Ganga Bhavadia's house. He requested Devagiriamma to provide him with food and shelter for the night. She served some food to the old man and permitted him to rest on the verandah. After some time, the old man knocked on the door and complained to Devagiriamma that he could not sleep and wanted a lady to maalish (massage) his legs. The lady of the house was taken aback at this strange request from a strange man, particularly as she was all by herself in the house. Nevertheless she did not wish to disappoint the old man. So she left the house by the back door to visit the houses of a couple of courtesans, who might help her out of this peculiar situation. However no courtesans were available.... She was in a state of confusion and began to cry. Interspersed with bitter sobbing, she prayed to Parvati for help...[149] Just then she heard a knock on the back door.... She opened the door

and found a woman standing there. She had come to offer her services to Devagiriamma. This woman was from one of the houses visited earlier by her. That is what the woman told Devagiriamma.... She took this woman to the old man in the verandah and firmly bolted the door behind them. No sooner had she thought of settling down for the night when a tap was heard on the front door. As Devagiriamma opened the door, she was absolutely amazed by the vision she beheld. In speechless wonder she knelt and bowed low before the Divine Pair. God had manifested before her in the form of Lord Shiva and Parvati, to bless her. Parvati said: "Let us bless her together." Shiva replied that as He had come here specifically to test her, He would bless her separately. Parvati blessed her with two children[150] and Shiva announced that He Himself would be born to her as her third child, a Son. With her eyes brimful of tears, Devagiriamma looked up. The Divine Pair had vanished.[151]

The storm had abated, and Ganga Bhavadia returned home in the early hours of the morning. When his wife related to him her experiences of the previous night, he thought they were hysterical utterances of a woman left by herself on a stormy night and promptly dismissed the matter. However, subsequent events proved otherwise.

The childless couple bore two children. Years rolled by and it was apparent that a third child was on the way. In the meantime Ganga Bhavadia began to lose all interest in his everyday work and domestic life. He developed an intense yearning to see God face to face. Just as Devagiriamma was approaching full term with her third child, his craving for Ishvara Darshan[152] became so intense that he decided to leave his family and home. Devagiriamma argued that all that had been told by Shiva and Parvati had been fulfilled, and as Shiva Himself was due to take birth as her next child, what was the necessity of leaving home in search of God. Ganga Bhavadia replied that he was not going to be satisfied with the vision of God through the human body of his son. He wanted to see the pure splendour of Divinity without the agency of a human mask.[153] And so he set forth on his quest. The dictates of dharma[154] left no choice to Devagiriamma, except to follow her husband. The two children were sent to her mother's house and she followed her husband into the wilderness.

Very soon Devagiriamma experienced the first symptoms of her impending delivery and she asked her husband to wait for her, but he just hurried on. She stopped exhausted beneath a banyan tree[155] and prepared herself for the delivery of her child. A son was born to Devagiriamma, in fulfillment of her vision. She prepared a bed of leaves and covered the child with some more leaves. She was in such haste to follow her husband, that she did not even wipe the blood stains off the new born child.

Now it so happened, that Mr. Patil, a Moslem, was returning to his village in a tonga with his wife. She had gone to visit her mother in a nearby hamlet. As the tonga approached the banyan tree, Shrimati Patil decided to answer a call of nature. She alighted from the tonga and went in the direction of the banyan tree. There she heard the cry of a baby and discovered a child under the leaves.... With great excitement she called her husband from the tonga and showed him the baby. They looked around for the mother of the child, but they looked in vain.... Finally, they decided to take the child home. The Patils had no children of their own, so they considered this child as God's gift to them and brought Him up as their own son.[156] They named him Babu.[157]

By the time Babu grew into boyhood His foster father had died and Shrimati Patil was left alone to take care of Him. However, Baba was no ordinary boy of His age and His activities caused her great concern. He not only installed and worshipped a stone lingam[158] in a mosque, but also recited passages from the Koran in all the Hindu temples He visited. Thus He upset both communities. By these acts, Babu tried to show the unity of both the religions to the people of that village. However, the whole neighbourhood was in an uproar and bitter complaints about His activities began pouring into Shrimati Patil. Not knowing Babu's antecedents, she did not know how to handle Him.

One day Baba[159] or the future Shri Sai Baba of Shirdi, declared His Divinity to a shaukar's (a wealthy landlord) wife. While playing a game, the shaukar's son lost all his marbles to Baba. The boy wanted to win back his marbles but as he had lost them all, what could he stake or play with? Suddenly, he remembered the Saligram[160] (black globular stone used for worship) in his mother's puja room and decided to stake that to win back his marbles. Very soon he lost even the Saligram to Baba. However, the boy felt that Baba had cheated him and he demanded it back from Baba. But Baba refused to part with it and promptly put it in His mouth. Then the shaukar's son was frightened and made a clean breast of his foolish activities to his mother. When he told her about taking the Saligram from the puja room and losing it to Baba, the horrified shaukar's wife came rushing to Baba and demanded the Saligram back from him. But she found a tight stubborn Boy, Who refused to return it. No amount of coaxing or pleading worked with Baba. Finally, she compelled Him to open His mouth and she saw a vision of the Cosmic Person in place of the Saligram! The same Visvasvarup[161] of the Lord, which Yashoda had seen in Krishna's mouth! Baba laughed and told her to look for the Saligram in the puja room. She found that the Saligram had miraculously arrived back in its place in the puja room. Realizing the significance of this Lila, the shaukar's wife prostrated herself at Baba's feet. From that day onwards she used to visit Baba's house everyday and touch His feet, until ignorant people criticised her which made her stop this outward act of homage to Baba. Thereafter, she worshipped Him mentally.

By now, Shrimati Patil was a thoroughly confused woman, and she felt utterly helpless trying to curb Baba's activities. She decided to take Him to an ashram for orphans run by a sadhu called Venkusha. The ashram was situated some distance away at Selu and the foster mother felt that Baba would be safe in that place, away from various distractions and "mischief." The night before the arrival of Baba at the ashram, Venkusha had a dream in which Lord Shiva told him that He, Shiva Himself, would come to him tomorrow at 10 AM. The next morning, a slightly puzzled Venkusha expectantly awaited events. Around ten o'clock Shrimati Patil arrived with Baba at the ashram.[162] She told Venkusha about Baba's behaviour in the village, praying him to accept Baba as an inmate of the ashram. Venkusha instinctively recognized the young Baba as none other than an incarnation of the Lord, and with great delight and due reverence, he accepted Him into the ashram. Venkusha said that the very pupil for whom he had been waiting a long time had at last arrived. A happy foster mother turned back towards her village.

Very soon the other boys in the ashram grew jealous of Baba, as Venkusha was very fond of Him, or appeared to be so in their minds. They began to persecute Baba. The climax came when Venkusha sent Baba in the woods to fetch some Bilva leaves[163] for worship one day. A group of boys followed Him and at the appropriate time, they overpowered Him and beat Him mercilessly. One of them threw a brick at Baba which inflicted a deep wound on His forehead. He bled profusely all the way back to Venkusha. Baba did not utter a single word of complaint, only showed the brick to Venkusha. Seeing Baba in this condition, Venkusha was deeply grieved and moved to tears. He quickly tore a part of his dress and bandaged Baba's wound. He shed tears over the brick which was now stained with the Lord's blood.

When Baba left Selu, this brick was given to Him by Venkusha as Guru-Diksha.[164] What a strange situation! The young Lord received a brick stained with His own blood, as a token of love and reverence towards Him from Venkusha. The brick was almost as dear to Venkusha as Baba Himself, and Baba having received it from Venkusha as Guru-Diksha, it was equally dear to Him as well. What a bond! Is it any wonder that Baba carried the brick with Him when He arrived in Shirdi with Patil's marriage party from Kirkee (near Pune).[165] It was always by His side. When He took up his abode in the dilapidated Masjid (Dwarkamayi) the brick went with Him, and it amazed many a devotee to witness Baba's strange behaviour towards that brick. He used to lean against it, or rest His hand on it or sometimes at night used it as a pillow.[166]

Thus ends the long and detailed account. Its most noticeable feature is the presentation of young Baba as *avatāra* of Shiva. The episode of the divine couple visiting Devagiriamma, testing her piety and chastity, and granting her children, with the promise that Shiva himself would be born as the third of them, calls to mind the Purāṇic figure of Atri's wife, Anasuya, paradigm of the dutiful and chaste Hindu wife and mother of Dattatreya.[167] Shiva also takes Kabir's place in the episode of Venkusha's forewarning dream.

Baba is presented as an enlightened soul beyond all religious barriers, proclaiming God's unity. He profusely manifests his powers (*siddhis*), which are an expression of his divine nature.

The ways in which this account harmonizes with B. V. Narasimhaswami's presentation are numerous: (1) Baba's birth at Pathri (2) first tutelage under a Muslim couple (3) Baba being taken to Venkusha at Selu by the Muslim widow (4) second period of tutelage at Venkusha's *āśram*, and (5) final departure with *guru-dīkṣā*.

The whole perspective is a Hindu one. No word is said relative to a possible Sufi or Islamic training of young Baba with the Patil couple.

In this account, Venkusha, from a rich and pious Vaiṣṇava, respected governor of a district, is transformed into the Śaivite guru of an *āśram*, strongly recalling the ambience of numerous Purāṇic scenes.

The theme of the disciples' envy and of the hurling of the brick is here modified. Whereas in Narasimhaswami's version Venkusha was the one who got wounded (in Baba's place), in Satya Sai Baba's rendition it was Baba himself who received the injury.

The hagiographic character of the narration, offering a new and more detailed version of Sai Baba's origins, places the whole event in a nontemporal atmosphere, which characterizes the moments of great spiritual awakenings. Possible historical elements are here integrated within a mythical "Purāṇic" framework. This story clearly utilizes Das Ganu's reconstruction as its guiding line, which is indicative of that version's popularity and persistence.

As recently as September 1990, Satya Sai Baba has offered further "details" relative to Shirdi Baba's origins. He stated that Shirdi Baba was born on September 28, 1835. Moreover:

> There was in the same village (Pathri) a Sufi Fakir. As he was also childless, he took charge of this child and brought him up in his home (1835 to 1839). The Fakir passed away in the tide of time. The Fakir's wife, who had lavished great affection on the child, was grief-stricken. To add to her worries, the boy was behaving in a troublesome manner. In those days, Hindu-Muslim differences in that area were growing alarmingly. There was considerable bitterness between members of the two communities. What the boy used to do was to visit a Hindu temple and sing songs in praise of Allah. "Mein Allah hoo!" (I am God). "Allah Malik hai!" (Allah is the Supreme Lord). He used to declaim in this manner in the temple. The Hindus used to chastise the boy in various ways for his misbehaviour. Nor was that all. He would enter a mosque and declare: "Rama is God," "Shiva is Allah." His behaviour in singing about Allah in a Hindu temple and about Rama and Shiva in a mosque was a puzzle to the public. Members belonging to both the communities went to the Fakir's wife and complained about the boy's behaviour. Unable to deal with the situation the Fakir's wife handed over the boy to a high-souled, pious scholar named Venkusha, who was living near her house. The boy stayed in Venkusha's ashram for 12 years from 1839 to 1851. Venkusha was extremely fond of the

> boy. In every matter, he used to give priority to the young Baba's views. Seeing this, in course of time, members of the ashram developed envy towards the boy. One night in 1851, the boy left the ashram.[168]

Apart from the interesting details concerning dates and chronology, that is, Sai Baba's exact birth date, the four years spent with the Muslim couple, and the twelve spent with Venkusha (confirming the traditional account), this story presents two variants.

First of all, the Muslim who adopted Sai is identified as a Sufi *faqīr*. Only a four year's tutelage is allowed, however. The boy would have been just four years old when demonstrating, through words and deeds, his precocious vision of religious universalism.

Secondly, Venkusha, who is said to be living near the house of the *faqīr*'s widow, is described as a pious scholar, and no mention is made of Selu as the site of his *āśram* or of the story relative to his premonitory dream or the brick.

It seems appropriate to close this presentation of the various hagiographic reconstructions by quoting Sai Baba's own words:

> I am formless and everywhere. I am in everything. I am in everything and beyond. I fill all space. All that you see, taken together, is Myself. I do not shake or move.
>
> All that is seen is my form: ant, fly, prince, pauper.
>
> I am in the water, in dry places, in woods, amidst crowds, and in the solitary wilderness. I am in the fire and in ether. I am not limited to any place.[169]

Notes

1. The Marathi term *shirdi* (a corrupt form of *shiladhi* or *shailadhi*) is said to mean "sugarcane." The village probably came to be known by this name because of its location in the heart of Maharashtra's sugarcane belt. Cf. P. S. Bharucha, *Sai Baba of Shirdi*, Shri Sai Sansthan, Shirdi, 1980, 2n.

2. The *ī* letter of the word *sāī* is nasalized. In Hindi, the term can also mean "god," "master," "husband." It may be pointed out that the Arabic term *sā'il* identifies a beggar and that the term *sā'ih* was used to designate itinerant ascetics of Islamic background in the early Medieval era of Islam. Many Hindus, on the other hand, consider this term as a contracted form of *svāmin* (lord, teacher) as is the case with the term *gosāī* (Skt. *gosvāmin*). *Gosāī*, originally a yogic title, was later assumed by Vaiṣṇava *ācāryas*. In

Maharashtra, the Gosāvīs are Śaiva mendicants. The derivation of *sāī* from *svāmin* is, however, doubtful.

3. It carries an endearing connotation, as in the English "dad."

4. The term *charita* or *charitra* (story) refers to a genre of poetical biography concerning the lives of saints.

5. A name of Khandoba, meaning "lord or husband of Mhalsa." According to the mythology of the *Mallāri Māhātmya*, Mhalsa (= Parvati) was the first wife of the god Khandoba, from the Liṅgāyat *vāṇī* community.

6. Also known as Malhari, Mailar, and Martand Bhairav, Khandoba is one of the most widely worshipped gods in the Deccan, with more than six hundred temples dedicated to him. Originally a mountain-top deity connected with pastoral environments, Khandoba has now become a complex amalgam of gods of several communities and regions. He is the premier god of *sakāma bhakti* (wish-granting devotion) and one of the most powerful deities responsive to *navas* (vows). Khandoba is the most popular *avatāra* (descent) of Shiva, particularly among low-caste Maharashtrians. According to the mythology of the cult (cf. the *Mallāri Māhātmya*), Shiva assumed the Khandoba *avatāra* in ancient times to destroy the two demons Mani and Malla. After defeating them, he was persuaded by his devotees to remain at the ancient city of Prempur, now usually identified as Jejuri in the Pune district, from whence his cult has spread. On the *Mallāri Māhātmya*, cf. Gunther D. Sontheimer, "God as the King for All: The Sanskrit *Mallāri Māhātmya* and its Context," in Hans Bakker, ed., *Panels of the VIIth World Sanskrit Conference,* vol. 3, *The History of Sacred Places in India as Reflected in Traditional Literature* (E. J. Brill, Leiden, 1990), 103–30. On Khandoba, see G. D. Sontheimer, *Pastoral Deities in Western India* (Oxford University Press, 1989). Cf. also John M. Stanley, "The Capitulation of *Maṇi*: A Conversion Myth in the Cult of Khaṇḍobā," in A. Hiltebeitel, ed., *Criminal Gods and Demon Devotees: Essays on the Guardians of Popular Hinduism* (SUNY Press, 1989), 271–98, and G. D. Sontheimer, "Between Ghost and God: A Folk Deity of the Deccan," comprised in Hiltebeitel, 299–337.

7. The particle *Yā* is an exclamatory one.

8. See N. V. Gunaji, *Shri Sai Satcharita,* 10th ed. (Shirdi Sansthan Publication, Shirdi, 1982), 23.

9. The endless and painful wheel of transmigration on which deluded men are caught through ignorance.

10. See B. V. Narasimhaswami, *Sri Sai Baba's Charters and Sayings* (Madras, 1942), 10.

11. This was apparently a favorite expression of Baba's. The term

Parvardigar seems to be of Persian origin, and sources translate it as "God-Almighty-Sustainer."

12. Gangapur or Ganagapur, in northern Karnataka, has become in modern times the most important pilgrimage place in the Dattatreya cult. Narasimha Sarasvati (1378–1458), a *brāhmaṇ* of Karanjangar (Akola district) who spent twenty-three years at Gangapur, is considered by the highly revered Marathi text *Gurucharitra* (c. 1550) as one of the prominent incarnations of Datta, together with Shripad Shrivallabha (1320–50). The chief center of attraction in Gangapur is represented by a set of footprints (*pādukās*), which are believed to be the ones of Narasimha Sarasvati. On Gangapur, see M. S. Mate, *Temples and Legends of Maharashtra* (Bombay, Bharatiya Vidya Bhavan, 1962), 79–101. Also, H. S. Joshi, *Origin and Development of Dattātreya Worship in India* (Baroda, Maharaja Sayajirao University of Baroda, 1965), 201–3.

13. Pandharpur is perhaps the most important religious center of Maharashtra, being the focal point of devotion for the poet-saints from Jñāndev (1271–96) onwards. Vithoba or Vitthala is the deity presiding over the city. He is identified as a form of Vishnu, though the icon (*mūrti*) manifests Śaiva tracts also. The folk etymology connects the deity with the Marathi term *vīṭṭh* (brick). The story goes as follows: A saintly person by the name of Pundarika lived in the area at the time of Krishna. He was known for his intense devotion to his parents, on whom he attended night and day. When Krishna came to visit him, Pundarika was busy serving his parents (*mātāpitṛ-bhakti*), and so asked the Lord to wait until his filial duties were completed. Thus he threw a brick to Krishna, so that he could rest on it while waiting. Pundarika's filial piety impressed Krishna so much that he commanded later generations to worship him as standing on a brick. On the legend of Pundarika, see E. R. Sand, "The Legend of Puṇḍarīka: The Founder of Pandharpur," *History of Sacred Places* in Bakker, 33–61. On the city of Pandharpur, the meeting place of all saints open to all castes, see Charlotte Vaudeville, "Pandharpur: The City of Saints," in *Structural Approaches to South Asian Studies*, ed. Buck and Yocum (Chambersburg, Pennsylvania, 1974), 137–61. See also G. A. Deleury, *The Cult of Viṭhobā* (Pune, Deccan College Post-graduate and Research Institute, 1960).

14. Narasimhaswami, *Charters and Sayings*, 10–11.

15. Derived from the verbal root *kṛ*, meaning to do, to make, to perform, the neuter noun *karman* has the general meaning of work or action, result of an action. For an exhaustive overview on this fundamental and yet difficult notion, see W. D. O'Flaherty, *Karma and Rebirth in Classical Indian Traditions* (Berkeley and Los Angeles: University of California Press, 1980).

16. The absolute, cosmic, transcendent principle; the supreme soul of the universe. It most probably derives from root *brh* (to grow, to become

strong, to increase). On the notion of *Brahman,* see K. Vatsyayan, *Kalātattvakośa: A Lexicon of Fundamental Concepts of the Indian Arts* (Delhi: Indira Gandhi National Centre for the Arts; Motilal Banarsidass, 1988), 1–22.

17. The power of illusion, by which what is unreal, i.e., the world and its trappings, lacking any ontological status, appears as if it were the Real. The term was used as early as the *Rig Veda* (10.54.2) with the meaning of a mysterious power. It appears only once in the older Upanishads, however (cf. *Prashna Upanishad*). Among the later Upanishads, we find it used in the *Maitri* and the *Shvetāshvatara.* Shankara (788–820) rarely used the term. In post-Shankara Kevalādvaitavedānta, however, *māyā* became a very common technical term. On the concept of *māyā,* see J. Gonda, *Change and Continuity in Indian Religion* (New Delhi: Munshiram Manoharlal, 1985), 164–97. First published in 1965 as vol. 9 in *Disputationes Rheno-Trajectinae,* Berlin.

18. Narasimhaswami, *Charters and Sayings,* 10.

19. For such hagiographic representations in Marathi devotional literature, see *Stories of Indian Saints: Translation of Mahipati's Marathi "Bhaktavijaya,"* trans. Justin E. Abbott and Narhar R. Godbole (Pune, 1933; reprint, New Delhi: Motilal Banarsidass, 1982), 57ff.

20. Gunaji, *Shri Sai Satcharita* 19–20.

21. A Parsi ascetic whose birth-name was Mervan Sheriar Irani and who was an important figure of the Sai Baba movement. He met Sai Baba for the first time in December 1915, after which he became a disciple of Upasani Maharaj (1870–1941), the most prominent spiritual figure among Sai Baba's disciples. On both Upasani Maharaj and Meher Baba, see chapters 7 and 8.

22. Charles B. Purdom, *The Perfect Master: The Early Life of Meher Baba,* 2d ed. (North Myrtle Beach: Sheriar Press, 1976), 26. This statement can be referred to Sai Baba's last years, when his fame had spread.

23. This attire of Baba may not have been typical in the earliest days of his life in Shirdi, though it apparently became so soon afterward. On this issue, see chapters 2 and 3.

24. Poverty (*faqr*) is held in high esteem within Islam, particularly among mystics. The saying ascribed to Muhammad, *al-faḳr fakhrī,* "poverty is my pride" has encouraged this. *Faqr* has thus come to indicate need in relation to Allah and dependence of every kind upon Allah. The term is opposed to *ghanī* (one who is independent, rich).

25. Any Muslim mystic or Sufi, as used in Persian sources. The term carries the connotation of one who stresses ecstasy over knowledge, even at the risk of violating Islamic Law.

26. At the beginning of our century, the distinguished ethnologist of Indian folklore William Crooke, reported: "It is practically impossible to discover from the Census returns the numbers...of the persons classed under the general head of Fakir. Out of the 5,000,000 beggars in India 700,000 are religious mendicants or inmates of monasteries, but the wandering Friars, if they may be so designated, must be far more numerous." See W. Crooke, *Things Indian: Being Discursive Notes on Various Subjects Connected with India* (London: John Murray, Albemarle Street, 1906), 200.

27. The exact etymology of the term Sufi has not yet been determined with certainty. Commonly, the Sufis themselves believed that it came from the Arabic word *safa* (purity). Some denigrators, however, liked to point to a different origin, that is, that the poorest members of the early Arab community resorted to the benches (*suffa*) in front of the mosque for their bed and shelter. The most probable meaning of the word, however, is to be derived from *ṣūf*, the woolen garments worn by the Sufis.

28. The Madari order was founded by Badi al-zaman Shah Madar, a Syrian of Jewish origin who came to India in the fifteenth century.

29. Mohsan Fani, *Dabistan or School of Manners*, trans. D. Shea and A. Troyer (Paris, 1843), vol. 2, 223. For more interesting observations on the Madari order and *faqīrs* in general, see M. Gaborieau, "On Traditional Patterns of Dominance among South Asian Muslims," in *Colloques Internationaux du C. N. R. S.*, no. 582 (*Asie du Sud: Traditions et Changements*), 189–95.

30. See Kevin Shepherd, *Gurus Rediscovered: Biographies of Sai Baba of Shirdi and Upasni Maharaj of Sakori* (Cambridge: Anthropographia Publications, 1985), 19ff.

31. It was bounded on the north by the Balaghat Range, on the west by the Western Ghats, on the south by the Tungabhadra River, and on the east by the seventy-eighth meridian, there being no natural barrier between the Kingdom of Bijapur and the neighboring Kingdom of Golconda to the east. See Richard Maxwell Eaton, *Sufis of Bijapur, 1300–1700: Social Roles of Sufis in Medieval India* (Princeton: Princeton University Press, 1978).

32. The Chishtiya order is the largest Sufi brotherhood in India. According to some, it was founded by one Abu Ishak, descended in the ninth generation from Ali, who, migrating from Asia Minor, settled at Chisht, a village of Khurasan, or, in another account, settled in Syria and was buried at Acre. Tradition, however, says that the order was founded by Khwadja Ahmad Abdal of Chisht (d. 965) and brought to India by Mu 'īn al-Dīn Chishti of Sistan, born in 1142. In 1193 he came to Delhi, but almost immediately he moved to Ajmer, where he died in 1236. His tomb soon became a very popular place of pilgrimage, and the great emperor Akbar is said to have made a pilgrimage to it on foot. The order lays special

stress on the words *illa'llāh,* uses vocal music in religious services, and wears colored clothes, dyed with ochre or the bark of the acacia tree. The neophyte is given instructions that he should observe poverty, contentment, the mention and remembrance of Allah, and austerity. Drugs and liquors are strictly forbidden. For a presentation of the Chishti order, see S. A. A. Rizvi, *A History of Sufism in India* (New Delhi: Munshiram Manoharlal, 1983), vol. 2, 264–318.

33. Eaton, *Sufis of Bijapur,* 276.

34. Located 14 km from Aurangabad, its name "town of good fortune," was bestowed in 1338 by Muhammad Tughluq, Sultan of Delhi, who made the town his capital.

35. Khuldabad, 26 km from Aurangabad and only 3 km from the Ellora Caves, contains, among other things, the tomb of Aurangzeb, decorated with an openwork marble screen on the lower part or the west side.

36. For a presentation of Sufism within the Deccani milieu, see K. A. Nizami, "Sufi Movement in the Deccan," in H. K. Sherwani and P. M. Joshi, *History of Medieval Deccan (1295–1724)* (Hyderabad: The Government of Andhra Pradesh, 1974), vol. 2, 173–99.

37. V. S. Bendre, *Sheikh Mahammadkṛta Kavitāsaṅgraha* (1961), 55. Sheikh Mahammad is traditionally taken to be an *avatāra* of Kabir (1440–1518).

38. On Kabir, the celebrated *Sant* who Sai Baba himself viewed as exemplary model, see 15ff.

39. See Narayan H. Kulkarnee, "Medieval Maharashtra and Muslim Saint-Poets," in N. N. Bhattacharyya, *Medieval Bhakti Movements in India: Sri Caitanya Quincentenary Commemoration Volume* (New Delhi: Munshiram Manoharlal, 1989), 198–231. For a general presentation of the Muslim Saint-Poets, see R. C. Dhere, *Musalmān Marāṭhī Santakavi* (Pune, 1967).

40. See S. G. Tulpule, *Classical Marāṭhī Literature: From the Beginning to* A.D. *1818* (Wiesbaden: Otto Harrassowitz, 1979), 378.

41. See Mohammad Hafiz Syed, *Suk-Sahela of Shah Burhan-uddin Janam,* Allahabad University Studies, 6 (Allahabad, 1930), pt. 1, 508.

42. Though the sources clearly emphasize the Hindu factor in Sai Baba's life, wanting to Hinduize him as much as possible, still the Hindu element is so strong and articulate that one must consider it fundamental for the comprehension of Baba's persona.

43. See Gunaji, *Shri Sai Satcharita,* 39n.

44. The percentage of Muslims in the Aurangabad district testifies to

considerable conversion activity: this area counts 7 percent of its population as Muslim, a higher percentage than in the Ahmednagar district.

45. Pathri town is situated at 19° 15' north latitude and 76° 27' east longitude. Its population in 1901 was 5,828. Pathri and Manvat (population 7,395 in 1901) were the only two towns of the *tālukā*.

46. Narasimhaswami, *Charters and Sayings,* 61.

47. Ibid., 62.

48. For three cases of Baba referring to God as *Faqīr,* see ibid., 17, 269–70.

49. Because of Baba's supposed twelve-year stay in Selu, and the tradition of the *Shri Sai Satcharita* that Sai Baba first arrived at the village of Shirdi at the age of sixteen. The number twelve, however, might have a purely symbolic function, meaning a period of fullness and perfection. See on this issue Arthur Osborne, *The Incredible Sai Baba* (Delhi: Orient Longmans, 1970), 6.

50. M. V. Kamath and V. B. Kher, *Sai Baba of Shirdi: A Unique Saint* (Bombay: Jaico Publishing House, 1991), 6.

51. A *parganā* is a province. This Jintur *parganā* was politically under the control of the descendants of the *peśvās:* Jintur, partly situated on the plateau south of the Sahyadri Range, is one of the *tālukā* of Parbhani district, 798 square miles, comprising 260 villages. It may be noted that Pathri and Selu are separated by a distance of only fifteen miles.

52. Although the correct transliteration of his name would be Dasaganu, I shall adopt the popular rendering. He published his findings in the work *Bhaktalīlāmrita.* A summary of it was given by Abdul Ghani Munsiff in his article "Hazrat Sai Baba," which appeared in *The Meher Baba Journal* (Ahmednagar) 1 (1938–39).

53. Das Ganu's trip to Selu in 1901 seems to indicate that Baba made some allusions to Venkusha and Selu even before the last years of his life. In the Maratha administration after Shivaji (1627–80), the second ministers were called *peśvās* (the *pratinīdhi* being the prime minister). The power of the *peśvā,* however, soon overshadowed that of the *rāja.* In fact, after Shahu (d. 1749), the descendants of Shivaji sank into a purely ornamental position. The *peśvā* leadership lasted from 1714 to 1818, starting with Balaji Vishvanath (d. 1720). The battle of Panipat on January 14, 1761, in which the Maratha army was defeated by the army of the Afghan chief Ahmad Shah Durrani, marked the beginning of the *peśvās'* gradual decline. For a presentation of the *peśvā* period, see Vincent A. Smith, *The Oxford History of India,* 4th ed. (New Delhi: Oxford University Press, 1985), 434ff.

54. The title of *deshmukh* identifies a hereditary native officer exercising chief police and revenue authority over a district. Apparently, Gopalrao received this concession (*sanad*) from the descendants of the *peśvās* in recognition of his military qualities, through which he and his army were able to place the Jintur territory under control. He is not to be confused with the Pune *brāhmaṇ* Gopalrao Hari Deshmukh (1823–92), popularly known as Lokahitavadi (literally, "well-wisher of the people"), who was the pioneer of an all-sided reformism in Maharashtra. He is the author of the famous *Shatapatra* (100 epistles), in which he attacked the British economic policy and the damaging predominance of *brāhmaṇs* in Indian society.

55. Nizām was the State which the Muslim ruler Nizam-ul-Mulk created in 1724, with Hyderabad as capital. His territory comprised the six southern *subah* of the Moghul empire, that is, the whole region of western and central India south of the Narbadā River. The Maratha power always represented a major threat to the Nizām because of its military and economic superiority. Numerous were the wars and battles between these two neighboring powers. What possibly saved the Nizām from collapsing was the defeat suffered by the Maratha army in 1761 against Ahmad Shah Durrani. Hyderabad State survived until 1948, playing a vital role in the preservation and development of Islamic culture. It may be noted that the Ahmednagar district was the seat of the Nizām Shāhi government.

56. Tirupati is the site of the most sacred Vaiṣṇava center of Andhra Pradesh. It lies in the midst of seven peaks or groups of hills in the Eastern Ghats Range. The sacred area is dedicated to Vishnu as Shri Venkateshvara (literally, "Lord of the Venkata hill"). The deity is worshipped also by north Indian pilgrims under the name of "Balaji." In the *Tirumālāī* temple, which appears to be the oldest, Vishnu is represented by a standing stone two m high.

57. Half a mile away from Selu station is a Venkatesha *mandir* with a tall *gopuram*. The temple was built around 1808; see Kamath and V. B. Kher, *Sai Baba*, 28.

58. See B. V. Narasimhaswami, *Life of Sai Baba*, 3rd ed. (Madras: All India Sai Samaj, 1980), vol. 1, 13–16.

59. Ibid., 16. The unitive state of Gopalrao with Venkatesha is very much emphasized.

60. The Vaiṣṇava reformer Ramananda is generally said to have been a Rāmānujīya ascetic, the fifth in descent from Ramanuja (ca. 1050–1137). According to the *Agastya-saṃhitā*, Ramananda was born in Prayag (Allahabad) in the year 1400 of the *Kali* age, corresponding to 1299 C.E. By the Hindu tradition, however, he is unanimously regarded as the teacher of Kabir, and thus placed between 1400 and 1470.

61. Narasimhaswami, *Life of Sai Baba,* 1:14.

62. Narasimhaswami, *Charters and Sayings,* 60–61.

63. A term that indicates perfect surrender to God. It bears the meaning of "getting close to someone for the purpose of protection, refuge, shelter."

64. Narasimhaswami refers to the boy as Baba, though, of course, the Selu story does not.

65. The yogic power of *svecchā-maraṇa* is the power of dying at one's own will, choosing the time of death.

66. On a few occasions, Sai Baba was reported to have the power of restoring a dead body to life. See Narasimhaswami, *Charters and Sayings,* 16.

67. Narasimhaswami, *Life of Sai Baba,* 1:16–18. The *samādhi* of Gopalrao Deshmukh stands just behind the Venkateshvara temple of Selu; see Kamath and Kher, *Sai Baba,* 28.

68. There is a discrepancy in K. Shepherd's account relative to Das Ganu's findings. The former places Baba's birthplace at Selu instead of Pathri, and posits Shelvadi and not Selu as the locale of Venkusha's *āśram.*

69. For a general presentation of Akbar's peculiar kind of monotheism, see P. Tacchi Venturi, *Storia delle Religioni* (Torino, 1971), vol. 5, 254ff.

70. On the fascinating figure of Prince Dārā Shikōh, see Bikrama Jit Hasrat, *Dārā Shikūh: Life and Works* (Calcutta, 1953).

71. Vijayanagara, the last indigenous monarchy of some importance in Indian history, was founded by the *rājas* Harihara and Bukka. Madhava, brother of the Vedic commentator Sayana, turned to ascetic life around 1368 or 1391, and took the name of Vidyaranya. His major works, include the celebrated compendium of all philosophical views, known as *Sarvadarshanasaṃgraha,* and the popular poem *Pañcadashī.*

72. An insightful and thorough introduction to M. K. Gandhi's thought may be found in Raghavan Iyer, *The Moral and Political Thought of Mahatma Gandhi,* 2d ed. (Santa Barbara: Concord Grove Press, 1983).

73. See, for instance, guru Lahiri Mahasaya, an important figure of early twentieth-century Bengal. For an introduction, see Paramahansa Yogananda, *Autobiography of a Yogi,* 12th ed. (Los Angeles: Self-Realization Fellowship, 1981) chaps. 9, 35.

74. In late biographies (after the time of Priya-das) and popular Kabīrpanthī texts, Kabir is represented as the son of a *brāhmaṇ* virgin

widow, born without a human father as a result of a blessing of saint Ramananda. The infant was later abandoned on a lake and picked up by a Muslim *julāhā* couple, Niru and Nima, who became Kabir's foster parents.

75. See Narasimhaswami, *Charters and Sayings,* 212.

76. Ibid.

77. See A. Osborne, *Incredible Sai Baba,* 58.

78. On the thesis of Pathri being Sai Baba's birthplace, see the account of V. B. Kher's researches in Kamath and Kher, *Sai Baba,* 16f. Kher suggests that Sai Baba's original name might have been Shri Haribhau Bhusari.

79. A. E. Bharadwaja, *Sai Baba the Master* (Ongole, Sai Master Publications, 1983), 248.

80. Ibid., 248–49.

81. See Narasimhaswami, *Life of Sai Baba,* 1:12. Moreover, if one takes into consideration the fact that the *peśvās'* power lasted until 1818, is reasonable to argue that he was nominated *deshmukh* prior to this date.

82. The *Shri Sai Satcharita* argues that Baba first appeared in Shirdi in 1854, at the apparent age of sixteen. On this whole issue, see chapter 2.

83. Kamath and Kher, *Sai Baba,* 29.

84. Bharadwaja, *Sai Baba,* 249.

85. The nickname Baba attributed to G. R. Dabholkar, author of the *Shri Sai Satcharita.*

86. Bharadwaja, *Sai Baba,* 249.

87. Cf. Narasimhaswami, *Charters and Sayings,* 62.

88. Cf. Bharadwaja, *Sai Baba,* 12.

89. For an examination of this narrative, see Osborne, *Incredible Sai Baba,* 3–5. For my commentary on this episode, see chapter 7.

90. Narasimhaswami, *Charters and Sayings,* 207.

91. Cf. Gunaji, *Shri Sai Satcharita,* xxiii.

92. The Ashvins appear in the sky just before sunrise on a golden chariot, led by horses or birds. They are associated to light and the sun, Surya. On the Ashvins, see A. A. Macdonell, *Vedic Mythology* (reprint, Delhi: Motilal Banarsidass, 1974), 49–54.

93. This name, in any case, would indicate his Hindu origin.

94. Narasimhaswami, *Charters and Sayings,* 61.

95. Ibid., 256.

96. Though we know of the existence of several Kabirs in the Indian tradition, when Sai Baba referred to Kabir he most certainly had in mind the celebrated medieval mystic, not an anonymous Sufi or guru bearing that same name.

97. The name is indisputably Muhammedan, meaning "great" in Arabic. *Al-Kabīr,* i.e., "the Great," is the thirty-eighth name in the traditional list of ninety-nine names applied to Allah in the Koran. It seems that Kabir and not Kabir-das was his real name. In the few instances where the two words *Kabīr* and *dās* (literally, "servant") are found together in his verses, the more probable meaning seems to be: "Kabir, who is a servant of Ram."

98. The question of dates is a controversial matter. The available material does not allow one to draw definite conclusions. Chaturvedi has proposed 1398 as Kabir's birth date and 1448 as the year of his death. If this is correct, Kabir would have lived under the Sayyed dynasty at Delhi and the independent Sharqi dynasty at Jaunpur, the capital of the eastern Muslim kingdom, which included the ancient city of Kashi (Benares).

99. The term *sant* (present participle of the verbal root *as,* "to be") is a synonym of *sādhu,* meaning "saint." The *Sant* are neither itinerant ascetics (*saṃnyāsis*), nor monks. Though generally leading an austere life, they are laymen. Most of them are Hindus, although a few are of Muslim origin. Nearly all are low-caste *śūdras.* Their most characteristic religious feature is the singing of the names of God. There is no historical "founder" of the so-called *Sant-paramparā,* though in northern India this honor is usually attributed to Ramananda and, in Maharashtra, to Jñāndev. Both groups, however, recognize Kabir and Namdev as their ancestors.

100. The Nātha schools belong to a lineage within Śaiva Tantrism. The origins of Nāthism are obscure. It has been described as a particular phase of the Siddha cult, whose members aspired to bodily immortality (*kāya-sādhanā*). *Haṭha-yoga* (literally, the yoga of exertion) came to be developed within Nāthism. Its two most outstanding adepts (possibly legendary figures) were Matsyendra and his disciple Goraksha. Northern India knows of a tradition of nine Nāthas. On the Nātha schools, see the classic monographic work of George Weston Briggs, *Gorakhnāth and the Kānphaṭa Yogīs* (Calcutta: Motilal Banarsidass, 1938). See also S. Dasgupta, *Obscure Religious Cults* (Calcutta, 1962), 191–255, 367–98.

101. Different kinds of Kabir's poetical compositions.

102. See S. B. Rupkala, *Bhakta-mālā* with *Bhaktisudhāsvād ṭīkā,* 2d ed. (Lukhnow, 1962), *chappay* 60, 479.

103. The Maharashtrian Vaiṣṇavas, whose devotion centers on the god Vitthala of Pandharpur, are called *Vārakāris,* i.e., "makers of a *vāra,*" "a regular trip to a holy spot."

104. Kabir never mentions Jaydev alone, but always brackets him with Nama, i.e., Namdev. It could be possible that Kabir, by saying Jaydev, really referred to Jñāndev, the great Marathi saint who, according to tradition (cf. *Bhakta-mālā, chappay* 166) had been Namdev's guru. Namdev, however, must have lived one century after the author of the *Jñāneshvarī.*

105. Charlotte Vaudeville, *Kabīr* (Oxford University Press, 1974), vol. 1, 105.

106. Mahipati was certainly the most prominent among Marathi hagiographers. He lived at Taharabad in the Ahmednagar district and, as a *Bhāgavata,* devoted his whole life to the performance of *kīrtans.* According to legend, he was inspired by Tukaram (1598–1649), who appeared in his dream and asked him to write the lives of the saints as he himself had obeyed the dictate of Namdev to compose *abhaṅgas.* He produced four major collections: the *Bhaktavijaya* in 1762, the *Santalīlāmrita* in 1767, the *Bhaktalīlāmrita* in 1774, and the *Santavijaya,* which was, however, left incomplete at his death in 1790.

107. See Abbott and Godbole, *Stories of Indian Saints,* 78–122, 177–186, 386–400.

108. On Kabir's influence on particularly Muslim saint-poets, see S. G. Tulpule, *Classical Marāṭhī Literature,* 377–78.

109. See Narasimhaswami, *Charters and Sayings,* 256.

110. The Kabīrpanthī is a large sect that originated soon after Kabir's death. It is divided into two branches, the Hindu and the Muslim. Usually, the *panth* is joined by people of low caste. The ascetics of this sect keep on roaming all the year round and depend on alms for their maintenance. Some members of the *panth,* however, remain attached to their families even after their initiation, which is quite long and elaborate. Kabīrpanthīs greet their *mahant* (head of a monastery) with the words: *Saheb Bandagi.* According to some recent estimates, their number amounts to about one million. For a sociological view of the Kabīrpanthīs, see David N. Lorenzen, "Traditions of non-caste Hinduism: The Kabīr Panth," *Contributions to Indian Sociology,* n. s., 21:2 (1987), 263–83.

111. The living saint Ratnakaram Satyanarayana Raju, better known as Satya Sai Baba, was born in the village of Puttaparthi, Andhra Pradesh, Anantapur district, on November 23, 1926. He is venerated by millions of people as *avatāra* and reincarnation of Shirdi Sai Baba. His biographer, N. Kasturi, died on August 14, 1987, at the age of eighty-nine. Born in Cochin, Kerala, in 1897, he was a noted poet and humorist. He was

a recipient of the State Sahitya Academy Award in 1981 for his contributions to Kaṇṇāda literature.

112. Narasimhaswami, *Charters and Sayings,* 207.

113. Ibid., 208.

114. An ochre-colored garment, such as the one worn by Krishna-Gopal, often worn by ascetics.

115. Narasimhaswami, *Charters and Sayings,* 210.

116. This margosa or nīm tree was the one under which young Baba lived for some time on his first sojourn in Shirdi. On this issue, see chapter 2.

117. The theme of Kabir's body being transmuted into flowers is celebrated in the legends concerning Kabir's death. The legend says that, soon after Kabir's death, his Muslim and Hindu disciples disputed the possession of his body. The Muslims wished to bury it, the Hindus to burn it. As they argued, Kabir himself appeared before them, and told them to lift the shroud and look at that which lay beneath. On doing so, they found a heap of flowers in place of the corpse; half of the flowers were buried by the Muslims at Maghar, and half were carried by the Hindus to the city of Benares to be cremated.

118. Narasimhaswami, *Charters and Sayings,* 62.

119. See Charles S. J. White, "The Sai Baba Movement: Approaches to the Study of Indian Saints," in *Journal of Asian Studies,* vol. 31, no. 4 (1972), 866ff. Also, D. A. Swallow, "Ashes and Powers: Myth, Rite and Miracle in an Indian God-Man's Cult," *Modern Asian Studies,* 16, no. 1 (1982), 131ff. On Gorakhnath and his teachings, see the excellent work of Akshaya Kumar Banerjea, *Philosophy of Gorakhnath with Goraksha-Vacana-Sangraha* (Gorakhpur: Mahant Dig Vijai Nath Trust, 1961).

120. Nasik lies 185 km northeast of Bombay. The town is laid out in terraces on the banks of the sacred Godāvarī River (see *MBh.* 3.88.2; *Ram.* 3.13.13 and 21), the Ganges of Maharashtrians, the source of which is 29 km away at Tryambak. The sacred river, also known as *Gautamī,* is celebrated in the *Gautamī-māhātmya* of the *Brahma Purāṇa.* See *BrP.* 70–175; see also P. V. Kane, *History of Dharmaśāstra* (Pune: Bhandarkar Oriental Research Institute, 1973 [2d ed.]), vol. 4, 707–11. Nasik, one of the great holy cities of India, is known as "the Benares of the west." Every twelve years, the festival of *Kumbha Melā* attracts hundreds of thousands of pilgrims.

121. Charlotte Vaudeville, *L'Invocation: Le Haripāṭh de Dñyāndev* (Paris, École Française d'Extrême-Orient, 1969), 10n. My translation.

122. As M. Gaborieau observes: "Nowadays the popular stories of

fakirs, as those which I have collected in Nepal, present them living like Hindu ascetics, meditating, as the latter do, near a sacred fire, i.e., a dhuni." See M. Gaborieau, "Les ordres mystiques dans le sous-continent Indien: Un point de vue ethnologique," in A. Popovic and G. Veinstein, *Les ordres mystiques dans l'Islam: Cheminements et situation actuelle* (Paris: Éditions de l'École des Hautes Études en Sciences Sociales, 1986), 118. My translation.

123. According to Hindu mythology, Dattatreya is the son of the Vedic sage Atri and his wife Anasuya. In the course of time, he came to be considered an *avatāra* of Vishnu (the sixth in a list of twenty-two, according to the *Bhāgavata Purāṇa*), though he combines both Vaiṣṇava and Śaiva aspects. In modern times, i.e., from the time of the *Gurucharitra* onwards, he is regarded as an incarnation of the *trimūrti* (cf. the three-headed Datta) and as the exemplary type of the *avadhūta*. In fact, he combines three figures in a paradigmatic fashion: the renunciant, the guru and the *avatāra*. The image of Datta most frequently depicted throughout western India shows not only the three heads of the three gods attached to one body, but also six hands that hold the emblems of the three gods: the trident and *damaru* of Shiva, the water pot and lotus or rosary of Brahmā, and the conch and *cakra* of Vishnu. Moreover, Dattatreya is dressed as a Śaiva ascetic and is accompanied by a cow, which is a Vaiṣṇava symbol representing mother earth. He is also surrounded by four dogs, which are said to represent the four Vedas and are thus connected with Brahmā the Creator. At the same time, dogs are a symbol of pollution and are thus associated with the antinomian Shiva. Dattatreya's multifaceted nature appeals to a wide variety of social strata, including low castes and outcastes, prostitutes, thieves, and also Muslims. The belief that Datta may incarnate in *faqīrs* is well known. According to legend, Janardana brought the young Eknath into spiritual realization through invoking an appearance of Datta, who came in the form of a Muslim *faqīr*. For a presentation of this fascinating deity and of a detailed Datta *paramparā*, see Joshi, *Origin and Development*. On Sai Baba as *avatāra* of Datta, see pp. 158–59 of this same work.

124. Gunaji, *Shri Sai Satcharita*, xx. On the *Svāmin* of Akalkot (d. 1878), considered as one of the most famous *avatārs* of Dattatreya for his miraculous powers and his "childlike" (*bala*) and "mad" (*unmatta*) aspects, see Joshi, *Origin and Development*, 136–42.

125. See Gunaji, *Shri Sai Satcharita*, xvii.

126. For instance in Andhra Pradesh, where the charismatic figure of Satya Sai Baba is also identified with Dattatreya. Several episodes are reported of his giving *darśan* in the form of Datta. N. Kasturi underlined this identification during a conversation we had in Puttaparthi in November 1985.

127. Narasimhaswami, *Charters and Sayings*, 9.

128. Such miraculous happenings, which are reported in all of the

saint's literature, are referred to as *camatkārs* (miracle, wonder, strange happening).

129. The day on which the birth of Dattatreya is celebrated. It falls on the fourteenth day of the month of Mārgaśīrṣa.

130. Baba's seat.

131. Narasimhaswami, *Charters and Sayings,* 153–54.

132. The term *avadhūta* comes from the root *dhū* + *ava,* with the meaning of "shaking off, removing all impediments." The *avadhūta* ascetics are usually depicted as roaming about naked from place to place. On the *avadhūta* as the perfect yogin, see the short poem *Avadhūtagītā,* which is attributed to Dattatreya and relates the deity to the philosophy of nondualism (*advaita*). Cf. Swami Ashokananda, *Avadhūta Gītā of Dattātreya* (Madras: Sri Ramakrishna Math, 1988).

133. See Narasimhaswami, *Charters and Sayings,* 155. Baba's identification with dogs is viewed as a powerful device to stress the notion of God's oneness.

134. See R. E. Enthoven, *The Folklore of Bombay* (Oxford, 1924), 216.

135. Vishnu's consort, goddess of wealth and prosperity.

136. Other name of Vitthala, whose major cult center is located in Pandharpur, i.e., Pandhari.

137. Other name for Hanuman, son of Pavana, the wind. His form as monkey-god is extremely popular all over India. In most villages in the Deccan, he is the chief god. Maruti is supposed to guard the village against evils of all kind. Therefore, care is usually taken to build his temple at the outskirts of a village, so as to prevent evil forces from crossing its boundaries. On Maruti, cf. R. E. Enthoven, *Folklore of Bombay,* 188–92.

138. Literally, "Lord of the *gaṇas*" or Ganesha. The elephant-headed god, second son of Shiva and Parvati. He is the auspicious one (*maṅgalam*), the remover (*vināyaka*) of obstacles. On Ganesha, see the comprehensive study of P. B. Courtright, *Gaṇeśa: Lord of Obstacles, Lord of Beginnings* (New York: Oxford University Press, 1985). See also Regina Nava, *Aspetti dell'Iconografia di Gaṇeśa* (Venezia: Arsenale Editrice, 1988).

139. Son of Vasudeva and Devaki. The most celebrated hero of Hindu mythology, eighth *avatāra* of Vishnu.

140. On all these various identifications, see Narasimhaswami, *Charters and Sayings,* 9.

141. Cf. ibid., 9–15.

142. Ibid., 121.

143. A Muslim saint in the Sufi tradition.

144. M. Sahukar, *Sai Baba: The Saint of Shirdi,* 3d ed. (Bombay: Somaiya Publications, 1983), 24.

145. See the booklet *Sri Sai Vani,* no. 18 (July–Aug. 1981), ed. Sri Narayana Baba (Thane, Maharashtra: Sri Bhagawati Sai Sansthan), 8.

146. The question concerning the relationship between the two Babas will be discussed in chapter 8.

147. It might perhaps be read Ganga Bhavadiya, i.e., Your Honor the Ganges, indeed an appropriate name for a river boatman!

148. Literally, "the mother of the divine hill." Devagiri is also another name of Daulatabad (situated between mountains).

149. There is here a conflict with the host's duties. The guest is sacred in the Hindu tradition and must be given all he/she needs. A married woman, however, cannot massage the legs of a man other than her husband. Thus, the need to request a prostitute's help, a realistic element within the overall hagiographic tone of the episode.

150. In a more recent account, which will be examined later in some of its most interesting details, Satya Sai Baba reported: "Parvati then blessed her: 'I grant you a son to maintain the lineage and a daughter for kanyakadana [a girl to be offered in marriage].'" See Satya Sai Baba's monthly journal *Sanathana Sarathi,* printed and published by P. K. Suri at Sri Sathya Sai Books and Publications Press, Prasanthi Nilayam, 33, no. 11 (Nov. 1990): 295.

151. Some typical motifs of Hindu spirituality are here presented in a sequence: the barenness that is miraculously cured, the appearance of a deity incognito, and the announcement of Shiva's birth in human form.

152. Literally, the vision of Ishvara, which means "lord" and is a title of Shiva.

153. Such a conception is interestingly modern.

154. The term *dharma* stands here for duty. In this case, the duty of a traditional Hindu wife is to follow her husband.

155. *Ficus indica.* At the foot of this tree, Shiva traditionally manifests himself in the form of Dakshinamurti, who teaches through silence. The term *dakṣiṇāmūrti* literally means "having one's face turned to the South," so as to conquer death, which comes from the southern direction.

156. We witness here the classic theme of the abandoned child, who is divine, and of the raising of that child by foster parents.

157. Quite a common name for an Indian Muslim.

158. The *liṅga* is the phallic symbol employed in Shiva's anichonic worship. It is not necessarily made of stone. *Liṅga* worship, which most probably reflects an archaic autochthonous cult, is unknown to the Vedas. We find it textually attested from the times of the *Mahābhārata* epic.

159. From this moment on, the text refers to Babu as Baba, i.e., Shirdi Sai Baba.

160. The *śālagrāma* is an ammonite stone held sacred by the Vaiṣṇavas because its spirals are supposed to contain, or to be typical of, Vishnu. It is valued more or less highly according to the number of its spirals and perforations. On the *śālagrāma* stone, G. Oppert, *On the Original Inhabitants of Bhāratavarśa or India* (1983; reprint, New York: Arno Press, 1978), 337–59.

161. A title applied to both Vishnu and Shiva. It literally means "One who has the universe as its very form." Again, this episode follows a classic pattern.

162. The device of a forewarning dream is typical of Hindu lore.

163. The leaves of the *bel* tree (*Aegle marmelos*) are an indespensable ingredient in Shiva's cult. Their trifoliate shape symbolically represents Shiva's three eyes as well as the three functions of God: creation, preservation, and destruction.

164. The initiation into religious life performed by a guru. Evidently, the brick is here identified as a concrete symbol of spiritual transmission.

165. On this episode, see chapter 2.

166. E. B. Fanibunda, *Vision of the Divine* (Prasanthi Nilayam, Sri Sathya Sai Books and Publications, 1987), 1–2. See also V. K. Gokak, *Sai Chandana* (Bangalore, 1985), where the thesis of Venkusha being Sai Baba's guru is emphasized.

167. For a presentation of the most popular version of Dattatreya's birth and other variants, cf. the introduction by S. M. Punekar in Sri Purohit Swami, *Avadhoota Gita* (Delhi: Munshiram Manoharlal, 1979), 30–31.

168. *Sanathana Sarathi*, 33, no. 11 (Nov. 1990): 290. The quote is taken from a discourse on Shirdi Sai, which Satya Sai Baba delivered at Puttaparthi on Sept. 28, 1990.

169. Narasimhaswami, *Charters and Sayings*, 11.

2

Arrival in Shirdi, Departure, and Final Reentry

Having left Venkusha and Selu, young Sai Baba is said to have wandered from place to place for an indefinite period of time. This phase marked perhaps a time of inwardness and solitude spent in the performance of spiritual exercises.

We thus come to an examination of Baba's first arrival in Shirdi, which the *Shri Sai Satcharita* assigns to the year 1854. Other accounts, depending on this source, are generally in agreement with this date.[1] A woman of the village, mother of one Nana Chopdar, is said to have been witness to Sai Baba's first arrival: "This young lad, fair, smart and very handsome, was first seen under the Neem tree seated in an Asan."[2]

Most sources report that Baba, on his first arrival at Shirdi, was a lad of sixteen.[3] He apparently stayed in Shirdi for about three years, then he left the village for a year, making his definite return in 1858. According to this reconstruction, Sai Baba was born around 1838.

As previously reported, Satya Sai Baba has recently claimed that Shirdi Baba was born in 1835. He also stated that Sai reached the village in 1851, that is, at the age of sixteen, resided there for barely two months, and then went wandering from place to place. Moreover, Satya Sai Baba has said, "After strolling for many years, he reached a place called Dhupkheda. When he was residing there, the marriage of Chand Patil's brother's son was celebrated there. Baba joined the marriage party and reached Shirdi again. That was in the year 1858. From that day, till 1918, he did not move out of Shirdi. He remained there for 60 years."[4]

Satya Sai Baba confirms the *Shri Sai Satcharita* version in positing the year 1858 as the one in which young Baba made his final return to Shirdi. The date he gives for Sai Baba's birth (1835) also comes close to that offered in the *Shri Sai Satcharita* (1838). Contrary to G. R. Dabholkar's thesis, he assigns only a two-month stay to Baba's first visit to the village and "many years" to his itinerant phase before returning to Shirdi, at least six (1852–58) according to his report. Sai Baba would have finally established himself in Shirdi at the age of twenty-three.

According to a second hypothesis sustained by Narasimhaswami, however, Baba's final return to Shirdi was in the year 1872. Confronting this date with the one proposed by the *Shri Sai Satcharita*, that is, 1858, we have a difference of fourteen years! For Narasimhaswami and all other accounts that follow this tradition, Sai Baba would have been born around 1852.[5]

A third hypothesis that attempts a kind of conciliation of the *Shri Sai Satcharita* and Narasimhaswami's versions was recently upheld by V. B. Kher. He places Sai Baba's birth at Pathri from a *brāhmaṇ* family between the years 1838 and 1842, and his first arrival in Shirdi between 1868 and 1872 with the marriage party of Chand Patil. After a few days, Sai Baba and Chand Patil left for Aurangabad. After a two-month period, however, Sai Baba would have returned alone to Shirdi. Thus, when Sai Baba arrived to the village he would have been between twenty-five and thirty years old.[6]

According to the *Shri Sai Satcharita* version, Sai Baba lived in Shirdi for full sixty years, dying at the age of eighty (Baba's *mahāsamādhi*[7] dating to 1918), whereas according to Narasimhaswami he lived in the village for no more than forty-six years, dying at the age of sixty-six.

I would be inclined to favor a solution closer to the first version. The people I interviewed in Shirdi also supported the thesis of an older Baba.[8]

The *Shri Sai Satcharita* recounts the villagers' amazement in observing young Sai's peculiar behavior on his arrival in Shirdi: "The people of the village were wonder-struck to see such a young lad practicing hard penance, not minding heat and cold. By day he associated with none, by night he was afraid of nobody.... He went to nobody's door, always sat near the Neem tree.... He was the embodiment of dispassion and was an enigma to all."[9]

Perin S. Bharucha also reports: "The inhabitants of Shirdi recalled being surprised to see so young a man practicing difficult yogic exercises. It had also been apparent that he had no interest in worldly possessions."[10]

Sai Baba's introversion and aloofness are presented as characteristic traits of his early years, not unusual in Muslim and Hindu ascetics. An interesting point upon which sources insist (with the exception of Narasimhaswami) is Baba's habit of practicing complicated yogic exercises and postures (*āsanas*).[11] The *Shri Sai Satcharita* notes:

> *Dhauti* or cleaning process. Baba used to go to the well near a Banyan tree at a considerable distance from the masjid every third day, wash his mouth and have a bath. On one occasion, he was seen to vomit out his intestines, clean them inside and outside and place them on a Jamb tree[12] for drying. There are persons in Shirdi who have actually seen that and who have testified to this fact. Ordinary *Dhauti* is done by a moistened piece of linen, 3 inches broad and 22 and a half ft. long. This piece is gulped down the throat and allowed to remain in the stomach for about half an hour for being reacted there and then taken out. But Baba's *Dhauti* was quite unique and extraordinary.
>
> *Khanda Yoga*. In this practice Baba severed the various limbs from his body and strew them separately at different places in the masjid. Once a gentleman went to the masjid and saw the limbs of Baba lying here and there. He was much terrified and he first thought of running to the village officers and informing them about Baba having been hacked to pieces and murdered. He thought that he would be held responsible as he was the first informant and knew something of the affair. So he kept quiet. But next day when he went to the masjid, he was very surprised to see Baba, hale and hearty, and sound as before. He thought that what he had seen the previous day was only a dream.
>
> Baba practised Yoga since his infancy and nobody knew or guessed the proficiency he attained.[13]

The hagiographic character of the narrative when it indulges in such details (following a typical scheme, as in the case of great yogins) does not diminish the general impression of an assiduous practice of *haṭha-yoga* on Baba's part, reproposing the hypothesis of a training in which Nātha influences might have played a role.

The performance of *khaṇḍa-yoga,* interestingly, finds an analogous Sufi counterpart. As A. Schimmel remarks: "A miracle which I have not found anywhere outside India is that some saints (in Sind, the Punjab, and South India) were seen during the dhikr[14] when their limbs got separated from their body, each limb performing its own dhikr."[15]

Apparently, the most interesting episode reported for Baba's early period was the possession of a villager by the god Khandoba,[16] during which the reason why that young man had come to Shirdi was made known.[17] Ecstatic possession by a god, *pīr* (master), or saint is known as *angāt yeṇe* in Maharashtra, and it is a common and almost institutionalized feature in rural India, especially among low-caste people.[18] The *Shri Sai Satcharita* reports:

> One day it so happened that God Khandoba possessed the body of some devotee[19] and people began to ask him: "Deva (God), you please enquire what blessed father's son is this lad and whence did he come." God Khandoba asked them to bring a pick-axe and dig in a particular place.[20] When it was dug, bricks were found and underneath, a flat stone. When the stone was removed, a corridor was seen, in which four Samayis (Lights) were burning.[21] The corridor led to a cellar where cow-mouth-shaped structures, wooden boards, and necklaces were seen. Khandoba said: "This lad practised penance here for 12 years."[22] Then the people began to question the lad about the same. He put them off the scent by telling them that it was his Guru's place,[23] his holy Vatan[24] and requested them to guard it well. The people then closed the corridor as before.... Mhalsapati and other Shirdi devotees regard this site as the resting place (Samadhi-sthana) of Baba's Guru and prostrate before it.[25]

B. V. Narasimhaswami doesn't even mention this episode, probably considering it a pious invention. Concluding his remarks on Sai Baba's early period, he says: "This is all the history of the early years of Baba. There might have been an incident or two remembered by some of the villagers about his early years, but they do not deserve mention in a serious biography."[26]

Relying on the possession story, many devotees claimed that the presence of his guru's tomb was indeed the reason why Sai Baba lived his whole life in Shirdi. Such a belief is still very strong and has become a kind of dogma encouraged by the Shirdi Sansthan. In this way, a long-standing connection can be established between Baba and the village, dating back to one of his previous lives.

Sai Baba himself seems to have encouraged such belief. Once, he is reported to have said, "I was here eight or ten thousand years ago."[27]

The *nīm* tree[28] and the area surrounding it must have represented an important site for Baba. He lived at the foot of this tree for a considerable period of time, making it his resting place and the consecrated spot for his meditative exercises. After his daily wanderings around Shirdi, he found his way back to this particular margosa tree,[29] which he possibly envisioned as especially sacred, charged with spiritual energy. We know that the *nīm*, probably because of the bitterness of its leaves, is associated with purification and the godlings of disease. In Bombay, it is said to have sprung from the *amṛta* or nectar of the gods.[30]

Baba's connection with trees mirrors the Hindu typology of the human yogin (cf. the Buddha) as well as the divine one (cf. Shiva Dakshinamurti). The *nīm* becomes an *axis mundi*, symbolically connecting the celestial realms (through its branches) to the netherworld (through its roots). In future years, Sai Baba would ask his devotees to burn incense by the tree on Thursdays and Fridays as a means for deriving blessings.[31] Religious tolerance again emerges here, Thursdays being particularly sacred to Hindus and Fridays to Muslims. Today the practice of burning incense there is still very much in vogue, the tree being one of the most important sacred spots in the village, goal of pious circumambulations (*pradakṣiṇā*).

Young Sai's appearance in Shirdi and his peculiar behavior must have aroused the curiosity of the local people, especially that of the religiously inclined. Apparently, Mhalsapati, together with some of his friends, that is, Appa Jogle and Kashinatha, a tailor, used to go see him.[32]

The majority of the people, however, judged the young lad to be quite strange and used to call him *pāgal*, "the crazy one." Baba, for his part, seems to have kept to himself, avoiding social interaction.

Concerning his early clothing style we have no clues. He probably did not wear a beard or mustache yet.[33] His possessions, if indeed he had any, must have consisted of a worn out garment, a begging bowl, and a staff.

All of a sudden, Baba is said to have disappeared from the village. Various hypotheses have been made concerning this period of his life. Bharadwaja reports, "One Khusal Bhav said that Baba lived in a chavadi[34] (now in ruins) at Rahata[35] for some months; that previously he lived with a Muslim saint named Ali (Akbar Ali perhaps) whose portrait is still kept in Rahatekar's gin[36] near Vadia Park at Ahmednagar; that one Daulu Sait had seen him with the saint there; that Baba came thence to Rahata and then to Shirdi."[37]

One Abdul Karim Abdulla (also known as Ramjoo Abdulla) reports that in 1952 Meher Baba, in the vicinity of Khuldabad, pinpointed the exact location of a cave occupied by young Sai.[38] Meher Baba also stated that Muntajab-ud-din Jarjaribaksha, a Sufi who emigrated from Delhi to the Khuldabad locale around the thirteenth century, was Sai Baba's master, evidently referring to a previous life of the *faqīr*.[39]

Moreover, K. Shepherd advances the following conjecture:

> In the Khuldabad cave, Sai Baba appears to have experienced the activation process associated with the *lataif*, the "subtle organs" of perception.... This activation process is rendered more complex by the two-fold occurrence of what is known in Sufi terminology as *fanā* (absorption) and *baqā* (permanence).... Suffice it to say here that Sai Baba appears to have undergone an intense *fanā* at the Khuldabad cave, and was subsequently helped to achieve a due equilibrium in *baqā* involving the "normalization" of his consciousness in relation to the external world.[40]

Das Ganu, in his account, tells us that young Baba lived an itinerant life until he retired for a while in a mountain cave in the Aurangabad area. Here, he was given to severe ascetic practices. Before coming back to Shirdi, he is said to have contacted the *Svāmin* Samarth of Akalkot.[41]

It may be noted that V. B. Kher, though arguing that Baba left the village for just a two-month period, claims that young Sai, before reaching Shirdi between 1868 and 1872, stayed for twelve years in Aurangabad, instructing a *faqīr* by the name of Bade Baba.[42]

The *Shri Sai Satcharita* refers to Sai Baba's return at length:

> There lived in the Aurangabad district (Nizam State), in a village called Dhup, a well-to-do Mahomedan gentleman by name Chand Patil.[43] While he was making a trip to Aurangabad, he lost a mare. For two long months, he made a diligent search but could get no trace of the lost mare. Disappointed, he was returning from Aurangabad with the saddle on his back.
>
> After travelling four Kos and a half,[44] he came to a mango tree at the foot of which sat a ratna (queer fellow).[45] He had a cap on his head, wore kafni (long robe) and had a "satka" (short stick) under his arm-pit and he was preparing to smoke a chilim (clay pipe).[46]
>
> Seeing Chand Patil pass by the way, he called out to him and asked him to have a smoke and rest a little. The queer fellow or Fakir[47] asked him about the saddle. Chand Patil replied that it was of his lost mare. The Fakir asked him to make a search in the Nala[48] close by. He went and wonder of wonders! He found the mare! He thought that this Fakir was not an ordinary man but an Avalia (a great saint).[49] He returned to the Fakir with the mare.
>
> The chilim was ready to be smoked, but two things were wanting: (1) fire to light the pipe, and (2) water to wet the

chhapi (piece of cloth through which smoke is sucked). The Fakir took his prong and thrust it forcibly into the ground and out came a live coal, which he put on the pipe.[50] Then he dashed the satka on the ground, and water began to ooze. The chhapi was wet with that water, it was wrung out and wrapped round the pipe. Thus everything being complete, the Fakir smoked the chilim and gave a smoke also to Chand Patil.

Seeing all that, Chand Patil was wonder-struck. He requested the Fakir to come to his home and accept his hospitality. Next day the Fakir went to the Patil's house and stayed there for some time. The Patil was a village-officer of Dhup. His wife's brother's son was to be married, and the selected bride was from Shirdi.[51] So Patil made preparations to start for Shirdi for the marriage. The Fakir also accompanied the marriage-party.

...When the marriage-party came to Shirdi, it alighted at the foot of a Banyan tree in Bhagat[52] Mhalsapati's field near Khandoba's temple. The carts were unharnessed in the open court-yard of Khandoba's temple and the members of the party descended one by one and the Fakir also got down. Bhagat Mhalsapati saw the young Fakir getting down and accosted him with the words "*Ya Sai*" (Welcome, Sai)... The marriage concluded without any hitch, the party returned to Dhup, but the Fakir alone remained in Shirdi and remained there forever.[53]

As we have above stated, the *Shri Sai Satcharita* places this episode in 1858; while Narasimhaswami sets it in 1872. How these different "oral traditions" came to be developed we do not know.

The hagiographic character of the whole story is evident, though we cannot rule out the possibility that historical facts might be intertwined with such material.

In particular, the episodes of the lost horse and of the marriage party bear rich allegorical potential. The horse is often symbolic of the mind or the senses, constantly restless and hard to tame. The theme of marriage is also recurrent in mystical symbology. In this case, the "marriage" between young Sai and the village of Shirdi might be subtly alluded to.

In the story's description, Sai Baba's possessions are limited to a short stick (*satka*) and a clay pipe (*cilīm*). Not even a sack or small bag are mentioned.

Young Baba's dress is presented in some detail. In his meeting with Chand Patil, he is described as wearing a *kafnī* and a cap.

Such attire, typical of a Muslim ascetic, must be assumed as a realistic tract (within the Hinduized context of the *Shri Sai Satcharita* account).[54] Iconography and the testimony of Shirdi villagers present a similar description of Baba's dress: he wore white clothes and a peculiar white turban with a long hanging pending on his left side. He maintained such an attire all his life.[55]

The Muslim Chand Patil identifies the young man with a *faqīr* and an *avaliā*. Sai Baba's meeting with Patil at this crucial juncture and his stay with his family are also significative of his Muslim affiliation.[56] No wonder Mhalsapati addressed him as "Sai" upon the arrival of the Muslim marriage party! The fact that the *Shri Sai Satcharita* could not but preserve these traits enhances the possible historical reliability of at least parts of the narrative.

Thus, from the beginning, Sai Baba came to be identified as a *faqīr* by the Shirdi villagers precisely because of his attire. Certainly, the presence of a Muslim in their midst did not thrill the local people. According to our sources, Sai Baba's return to Shirdi took place in an atmosphere of general indifference. Mhalsapati, *pujārī* of Khandoba's temple, was perhaps one of the very few who approached the strange *faqīr* with a mix of curiosity and sympathy.

Finally, it is worth noting that, although the various sources are in agreement in describing Baba's first arrival in Shirdi, his leaving the village, and his final reentry, the question of Sai Baba's identification is not free of difficulty. In other words, we have no proof that the young lad said to have been seen for the first time under the *nīm* tree by Nana Chopdar's mother was the same person whom Mhalsapati greeted later on.

Notes

1. The discrepancies are limited within two or three years before 1854. For instance, the *Guide to Holy Shirdi* of the Shri Sai Baba Sansthan, places Baba's arrival in 1852.

2. Gunaji, 20. According to Narasimhaswami, she rendered this testimony in 1900; cf. *Life of Sai Baba*, 1:10. *Āsana* literally means "seat." In Yoga, it indicates various sitting postures (up to eighty-four). The manner of sitting forms part of the eightfold observances of ascetics.

3. The number sixteen could well be purely symbolical, representing the time of spiritual awakening. Epic heroes as well as saints are often reported to manifest their splendor at this crucial age.

4. *Sanathana Sarathi*, 33, no. 11 (Nov. 1990): 290. On Sai Baba's

final return to Shirdi in 1858 with the marriage party of Chand Patil, compare the episode contained in the *Shri Sai Satcharita* referred to below.

5. A. G. Munsiff, in his article "Hazrat Sai Baba," dated Sai Baba's birth at 1856, apparently on the basis of Das Ganu's account. Kevin Shepherd refers Sai Baba's birth-date to circa 1850; see Shepherd, *Gurus Rediscovered,* 76 n. 21.

6. See Kamath and Kher, *Sai Baba,* 6. Kher also reports the testimony of the devotee Ramgir Bua, who said that Sai Baba appeared to be about twenty-five or thirty years old when he first arrived in Shirdi; cf. ibid., 77.

7. Literally, "great absorption." The moment of a saint's death, on which he enters definite union with God or *Brahman.* The term *samādhi* is also used to refer to the sanctuary or tomb of a saint.

8. Devotees tend to exaggerate the age of their masters, so as to emphasize their sanctity. This notwithstanding, it still seems more likely that Baba was older than sixty-six when he died.

9. Gunaji, *Shri Sai Satcharita,* 20.

10. P. S. Bharucha, *Sai Baba of Shirdi* (Shirdi: Shri Sai Sansthan, 1980), 2–3.

11. Though the hagiographic Hindu imput is overall dominant, the insistence on this point calls for our attention.

12. The *jambu* tree (*Eugenia jambos*) is the rose-apple. The name *jambu* is applied in some parts of India to the exotic guava, as well as to other species of *Eugenia.*

13. Gunaji, *Shri Sai Satcharita,* 41. These specific instances of *dhautī* and *khaṇḍa-yoga* are to be referred to a later period, when Baba had already established himself at the mosque.

14. Literally, "remembrance." The impetus for the practice of *dhikr* is derived from those Koranic verses that enjoin the faithful to remember God. Most *dhikr* techniques involve the rhythmic repetition of one of the ninety-nine traditional names of Allah. Methods of *dhikr* usually involve breath control. The goal is to move from a kind of vocal remembrance to a silent *dhikr,* in which the formula is perfectly internalized. At the highest stage, each limb of the body "performs" the *dhikr*: every distinction between subject and object is then lost. On the issue of *dhikr,* see chapter 9.

15. A. Schimmel, *Islām in the Indian Subcontinent* (Leiden: E. J. Brill, 1980), 132.

16. The villager who was possessed is to be identified with Mhalsapati, priest of Khandoba's small temple located just at the outskirts of the village.

17. Unfortunately, the date of this episode is not specified.

18. Not all Maharashtrian gods possess their devotees. For instance, Khandoba, Kal Bhairav, Dattatreya do possess but not Ganesha, Rama, Shiva, Krishna, Vithoba, Hanuman, or Vishnu. The list of Hindu gods who do possess, corresponds closely to those ancient non-Aryan local gods who were gradually assimilated into the *brāhmaṇic* tradition. On possession in Maharashtra, see the article of J. M. Stanley, "Gods, Ghosts, and Possession," in E. Zelliot and M. Berntsen, eds., *The Experience of Hinduism: Essays on Religion in Maharashtra* (Albany, N.Y.: SUNY Press), 26–59.

19. On the places where possession phenomena occur, J. M. Stanley observes: "Khandoba possession seems to be especially dependent on certain locations. Most of the Khandoba *angāt ālelī* (possessed ones) interviewed, said they were possessed only at or near a Khandoba temple or during a procession while close to the *pālkhī* (palanquin)"; ibid., 42.

20. Most probably under the *nīm* tree that Baba selected as his temporary abode.

21. One may usefully compare this narration with a similar one of Harihara (fifteenth century). Allamaprabhu, Liṅgāyat guru, discovers a subterranean temple where he finds a yogin, lighted lamps, and a *liṅga* which he receives. See A. K. Ramanujan, *Speaking of Śiva* (Harmondsworth: Penguin, 1973), 143–44.

22. Again, we find a reference to a twelve-year period. The symbolical meaning, expressing a totality or fullness of time, is evident.

23. Almost certainly, Baba is here referring to the guru of one of his previous births. On this issue, cf. P. S. Bharucha, *Sai Baba of Shirdi,* 3.

24. Burial place.

25. N. V. Gunaji, *Shri Sai Satcharita,* 20.

26. Narasimhaswami, *Life of Sai Baba,* 1:21.

27. Narasimhaswami, *Charters and Sayings,* 209.

28. This particular *nīm* tree is also known as *gode nīm* (sweet margosa), since the leaves of one of its two big branches are not so bitter as margosa leaves. In *Observations on the Mussulmauns of India* (1917; reprint, Oxford University Press, 1973), Meer Hassan Ali thus describes the tree:

> The neam-tree is cultivated near the houses of Natives generally, in the Upper Provinces, because, as they affirm, it is very conducive to health, to breathe the air through the neam-trees. This tree is not very quick of growth, but reaches a good size. When it has attained its full height, the branches spread out as luxuriantly

as the oak, and it supplies an agreeable shelter from the sun. The bark is rough; the leaves long, narrow, curved, pointed, and with saw teeth edges; both the wood and leaves partake of the same disagreeable bitter flavour. The green leaves are used medicinally as a remedy for biles; after being pounded they are mixed with water and taken as a draught; they are also esteemed efficacious as poultices and fomentations for tumours, etc. The young twigs are preferred by all classes of the Natives for tooth-brushes. (309–10)

29. This point is confirmed by all sources.

30. In Ahmednagar, when a man is bitten by a snake, he is taken to Bahiroba's temple, crushed *nīm* leaves mixed with chillies are applied, and the branches are waved over his head. W. Crooke, *Religion and Folklore of Northern India* (Oxford University Press, 1926), 410.

31. The tree came also to be connected with particular forms of worship. Consider Baba's footprints (*pādukās*), which were installed nearby the tree and came to be magnified by the poetic verses of Upasani Maharaj; see Gunaji, *Shri Sai Satcharita,* 24–25. Although *pādukā* worship is a devotional practice found throughout India, it is a particularly relevant feature within the Dattatreya cult. On Datta's *pādukās,* see Joshi, *Origin and Development,* 189–90.

32. See Bharadwaja, *Sai Baba,* 6.

33. Narasimhaswami confirms this; see *Life of Sai Baba,* 1:10. We know, however, that Muslims are supposed to wear a beard, according to the prophetic tradition that "the beard is the light of God."

34. A rural assembly hall. Also, the official room of the head of a village (*pāṭīl*).

35. A town located just few miles away from Shirdi.

36. A meeting hall.

37. Bharadwaja, *Sai Baba,* 7.

38. Khuldabad (literally, "the perpetual city") was situated on the periphery of the Nizām's territory, about twenty miles northwest of Aurangabad. The presence of Sufi shrines is a noticeable feature of this area; cf. the *dargāh* of the famous Chishti saint Sayyid Muhammad Gesu Daraz (d. 1422). A legend reports how the saints of Allah descended upon the Khuldabad hills in fourteen hundred celestial palanquins. As Schimmel remarks: "Khuldabad is a place emanating a somewhat unearthly atmosphere, and the hill the small town is leaning upon has been a place of mystic meditation for ages. Next to the small mosque on top of the hill, one still sees the cave in which the Sufis of Khuldabad spent their *chillā,* their forty days' retreat." See A. Schimmel, "Deccani Art and Culture," in A. L.

Dallapiccola, ed., *Vijayanagara-City and Empire: New Currents of Research* (Steiner Verlag Wiesbaden GMBH: Stuttgart, 1985), 177.

39. Abdulla, however, gave the impression that Sai was the literal disciple of Jarjaribaksha. See Ramjoo Abdulla, *Meher Baba's Fiery Life and External Activities* (Pt. 3), *The Awakener*, New York, 1953, 1(2): 22–5, 23. Shepherd observes that: "One might take it that Meher Baba had tapped something of the eclipsed Muslim repertory at Shirdi"; Sheperd, *Gurus Rediscovered*, 12.

40. Shepherd, *Gurus Rediscovered*, 23–24.

41. See Das Ganu's *Bhaktalīlāmrita*, and the references quoted in Shepherd, *Gurus Rediscovered*, 11, 24.

42. Also known as Faqir Baba and as Faqir Pir Mohammad Yasinmia. See Kamath and Kher, *Sai Baba*, 6.

43. The name Chand (*cāṇḍ*) means angry.

44. *Kos* (*Skt: krośa*) is a measure of distance. The term is not used with exactness but can be taken to mean approximately two and one half miles. Four and a half *kos* would thus correspond to about eleven and a half miles.

45. The term *ratna* literally means a "gem" or "precious stone." It also comes to mean the most outstanding individual of a class.

46. Sai Baba was always fond of smoking the pipe. The common tobacco pipe consists of three parts: the bowl (*cilam*) containing the tobacco, the stem with the "snake" (*naicā*) on which the pipe head is fixed, and the bowl containing water or rose water. In the Deccan, tobacco is called *gudākū* or *gurākū* (from *gur*, "raw sugar," and the Telugu word *āku*, "leaf").

47. This is the first "early" text that identifies Sai Baba as a *faqīr*.

48. Stream.

49. *Avaliā* commonly refers to Muslim saints. It literally means "one who is a friend (*valī*) of God."

50. For lighting the tobacco, specially prepared balls of charcoal (*gul*) are generally used. They are made of tamarind or *Ficus religiosa* (*pipal*) charcoal, mixed with acacia gum, molasses, and rice gruel.

51. V. B. Kher, however, claims that the marriage was between Chand Patil's *sister* with Hamid, the *son* of one Aminbhai of Shirdi; Kamath and Kher, *Sai Baba*, 6, 76–77.

52. Equivalent to the term *bhakta*, "devotee." As the words *karma* and *dharma* are often pronounced *karam* and *dharam*, so *bhakta* is often changed into *bhagat*, the *g* supplanting the *k*.

53. Gunaji, *Shri Sai Satcharita*, 22–23. K. Shepherd, M. Sahukar,

and V. B. Kher relate this episode to Baba's first visit to Shirdi. This interpretation, however, appears incorrect, since both the *Shri Sai Satcharita* and the works of B. V. Narasimhaswami refer the story to Sai Baba's final return to the village. See Narasimhaswami, *Life of Sai Baba,* 1:10–1.

54. A robe or a shirt and wide trousers and a cap were the essential features of a Muslim man's dress. The normal headgear in olden times was the turban, from whose shape, material, and style of tying one could recognize the person's descent, profession, and place of origin.

55. Sai's style of dress is confirmed by several photographs showing Baba in the first years of our century.

56. The recurrence of the name Patil, even in Satya Sai Baba's accounts concerning Baba's origins, is noticeable.

3

The Village of Shirdi. Sai Baba's Habits and Daily Life in the Early Years. First Miracles and the Beginning of Worship

Once back in Shirdi, Sai Baba, with the exception of brief wandering periods, is said to have resided therein till the end of his life.[1] Thus it becomes important to examine what the village looked like in those years and to understand its human and social configurations.

Shirdi, around the middle of the nineteenth century, was very different from the sacred pilgrimage place it has become nowadays. The village is located in the heart of the Upper Godāvarī-Pravarā Basin,[2] which, at the beginning of our century, became the site of intense sugarcane cultivation through the introduction of canal irrigation.[3] Even today, when approaching the village along the roads that border the fields, one is overpowered by the pungent and penetrating smell that emanates from the canes.[4] In Sai Baba's time, however, at least until 1910, Shirdi's soil was quite unproductive. Yet, the majority of the village population was engaged in farming and agricultural activities.

Around the middle of the nineteenth century, Shirdi, which is about twelve miles south of Kopergaon, was an obscure hamlet of the Ahmednagar district.[5] A tightly nucleated village with its habitations clearly separated from the surrounding cultivated fields, Shirdi consisted of a cluster of perhaps two hundred individual houses,[6] connected by narrow alleys.[7] Possibly, the village population did not amount to more than a thousand inhabitants. It encompassed an area of 3.3 square miles.[8] Shirdi's closest town-center was the village of Rahata, which covers an area of 8.7 square miles and, at least since 1884, has been the site of a permanent market.[9]

Shirdi, like most rural hamlets, had just a few shops providing the inhabitants with their day-to-day needs.[10] Water was brought from a nearby well, which served the entire community. There existed two small *cāvaḍīs* which, among other functions,

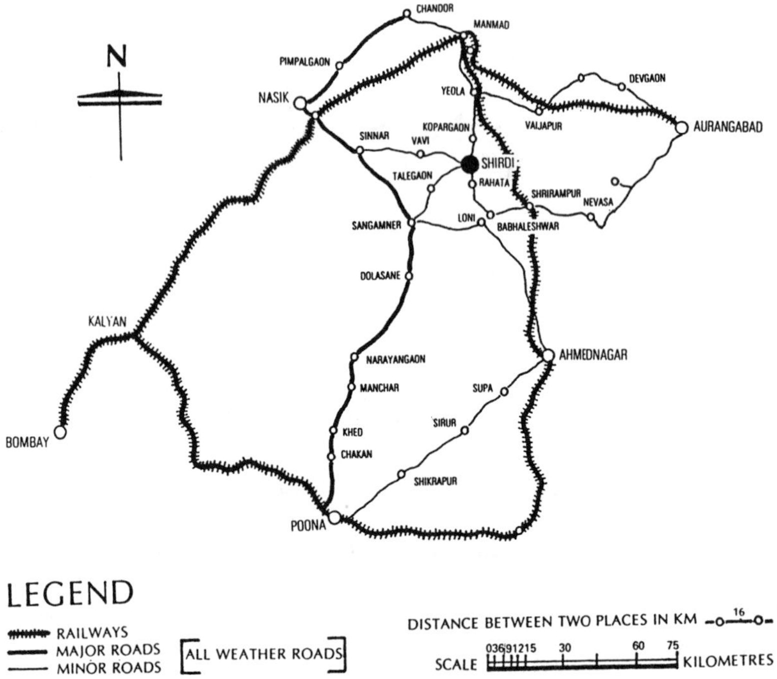

Map of Maharashtra showing the location of Shirdi.

served as schools and as resting places for visitors. The weekly bazaar,[11] constituted one of the few attractions.

The majority of the population was Hindu. The Muslims, comprising perhaps 10 percent, worked mainly as artisans or fields laborers. The hereditary chief of the village, that is, the *pāṭīl,* was Ganapat Rao Patil Kote.[12] Upon his death, his brother or cousin inherited the appointment.

The two main Hindu temples, as in all Maharashtrian villages, were those of Maruti and Khandoba. Maruti's temple, a small construction of about four square meters, was situated near the *masjid.*[13] The Khandoba temple, of which Mhalsapati was priest, was located just outside the village and was a bigger edifice. There was also a small Vitthala temple right in the village.[14] The *masjid* stood in a very precarious condition. The various sources describe it as being in a dilapidated state.

This is how Shirdi and its environs appeared when Sai Baba apparently took up residence once again beneath the *nīm* tree, and continued his daily wanderings around the area. The *Shri Sai Satcharita* reports: "By day he always sat under the Neem tree, or sometimes under the shade of a branch of a Babhul tree near the stream at the outskirts of the village. In the afternoon he used to walk at random and go at times to Nimgaon."[15]

V. B. Kher suggests that Sai Baba initially stayed on the outskirts of the village in a *bābhūḷ* forest for about two and a half years, then under a *nīm* tree for four to five years.[16]

On one occasion, young Sai is said to have come to the Khandoba temple. Noticing what a solitary and placid place it was, he exclaimed, "What a nice place this is, for ascetics like me to live in!"[17]

Mhalsapati, however, objected to Sai Baba's wish to reside there and told him that no Mohammedan would be allowed to set foot in the Khandoba temple.[18] It was possibly the same Mhalsapati who later invited Baba to take residence at the mosque, logically the most fitting place for a *faqīr*. Meanwhile, Sai Baba made his way back to the *nīm* tree.

The *Shri Sai Satcharita* narrates how the *pāṭīl* and his wife, Bayajibai, once went to see Baba. Baba greeted them warmly, adding that Bayajibai was his "sister." Apparently, Bayajibai was so favorably impressed during this first visit to the young *faqīr* that she promised to herself that she would not take any food before having fed Baba first. Often, in order to find him, she had to wander around the groves where she would discover him absorbed in ecstatic trances. She would then place the food in front of him and silently leave. We are told that Sai Baba always accepted the woman's offerings, knowing her devotion. Bayajibai continued rendering such service for many years, and Baba himself once told her that he would never forget her many acts of charity, which first she had offered him.[19]

Gradually, Baba must have reduced his roamings through the woods. Starting to move through the streets and narrow lanes of Shirdi more frequently, he came in closer contact with the local people. Most of them, however, continued ignoring him, considering the young lad to be a bizarre character, if not mad (*pāgal*). The sources report that the villagers would often see him muttering to himself, or even yelling and getting angry for no apparent reason.

Within religious circles, the madness of the saint is often compared to the "madness" of God himself: God, as the madman, is free, transcendent, not bound to the world and its ways. The *pāgal*'s life, as well as that of God, is then described as pure *līlā*, that is, play.[20]

Soon, Baba got in the habit of visiting four or five houses of Shirdi daily, begging his food there. V. B. Kher reports, "Sai Baba would go for alms every morning and stand before the houses of Bayajibai Kote Patil, Patilbua Gondkar, Nandram Savairam, Appaji

Kote, and Narayan Teli, who would dutifully give him food."[21]

He would gather solid foods in his *jholī*[22] and liquids such as drinks and soups in a tumbler or tin. Begging is indeed the rule among *faqīrs*. This is also the typical habit of the renunciant (*saṃnyāsin*). According to traditional Hindu customs, begging must adhere to precise norms: it must be started after householders have presented their offerings to the gods and have themselves eaten. The renunciant is allowed to beg from fellow ascetics and at *brāhmaṇ* houses: only in such cases is he allowed to enter a village. The maximum number of houses from which he can beg is fixed at seven, and the time for doing so must be the same as that necessary for the milking of a cow (*godohanakāla*).[23]

Sai Baba reportedly had the habit of sharing his food with the poor as well as with animals such as dogs, birds, insects, and so forth. Often, he would eat only after having left his dish outside the *masjid* at the disposal of anybody who wanted food. According to traditional rules, the *saṃnyāsin* should place the food received in a consecrated spot, wash his hands and feet, and announce to the sun what has been offered him. Before eating, he should give some of his food to animals and sprinkle it with water. The renunciant can take only up to eight mouthfuls of food.[24]

Sai Baba's decision to install himself at the *masjid* probably developed in this early period. He did so with no objection on the villagers' part, not long after Mhalsapati refused to allow him to establish himself at the Khandoba temple. Thus the sources present Baba's decision to live at the mosque as a secondary decision. Baba's primary desire of settling at Khandoba's temple need not be necessarily interpreted as a Hindu hagiographic input. In fact, Muslim devotion to Khandoba is a common feature in the Deccan. As G. D. Sontheimer remarks:

> Khaṇḍobā's affiliation with the Muslims is visible in the style of his temples (as in Jejuri or in Andur, Osmanabad district). He (Khaṇḍobā) appears as a Paṭhān on horseback, one of his wives is Muslim, and the keeper of the god's horses and his kotvāl is a Muslim in Jejuri. In the *Mārtaṇḍa Vijaya* (24. 30–31) Muslims are expressly said to be his bhaktas. A typical instance of this mutual appreciation is a special order issued by the Sultan of Bijapur, Ibrahim II in 1614, in which he assured the right of pilgrims to perform rituals to Khaṇḍerāo or Mallāri at Naldurg and the reinstatement of the annual jātrā.[25]

Sai Baba, even at the *masjid,* seems to have led a solitary life. From time to time he probably enjoyed the company of other ascetics, both Hindu and Muslim, who either resided in the village or passed by it. Most of these visitors were directed towards pilgrimage places such as Pandharpur and Rameshvar.

The *Shri Sai Satcharita* furnishes some accounts concerning such meetings. We are told that Baba liked the company of one Devidas,[26] a young Hindu ascetic who had been living in Shirdi for many years.[27] They would meet at the Maruti temple, where Devidas usually resided, or at one of the two small *cāvaḍīs*. Apparently, there was another Hindu ascetic named Jankidas,[28] with whom Baba also liked to meet.

The *Shri Sai Satcharita* mentions how once an ascetic named Gangagiri,[29] passing through Shirdi coming from Puntambe,[30] saw Baba and exclaimed: "Blessed is Shirdi, that it got this precious Jewel! This man is carrying water today[31] but he is not an ordinary fellow. As this land (Shirdi) was lucky and meritorious, it secured this Jewel."[32]

Another saint, one Anandanath[33] of the Yeola *maṭha,*[34] disciple of the *Svāmin* of Akalkot, also saw Baba at Shirdi and is said to have exclaimed: "This is a precious Diamond in reality. Though he looks like an ordinary man, he is not a 'gar' (ordinary stone) but a Diamond. You will realize this in the near future."[35]

Sai Baba was frugal in his speech. He usually spoke only if questioned.[36] The local people reported how they would sometimes hear him speaking to himself or even with an unknown interlocutor in a low tone. One Madhavrao Deshpande, a teacher in the primary school of the village, who accepted Baba as his guru in 1881, recalled how he could hear Sai speaking at night, inside the mosque, in many different languages: Hindi, English, and others unknown to him. Such facts amazed him.[37]

At other times, Baba was heard speaking aloud to himself or murmuring the names of God according to Hindu custom. He was also heard reciting the *namāz,* the ritual Muslim prayer,[38] and sacred phrases in Urdu. But this happened only occasionally, without any regularity.[39]

Sai Baba, probably from these early years, practiced the repetition of his favorite phrase *Allāh Mālik* as a constant reminder of Allah's glory and sovereignty. The term *mālik* designates a king and is one of the ninety-nine traditional names of God in the Islamic tradition.[40]

As Narasimhaswami aptly remarks: "Generally speaking his worship was mostly mental; he went through no external forms. He seldom performed the five Namazes and never was bending on the knees and rising, as most Moslems do. He was an adept in concentration and had reached the perfection of Manolaya on the Atman (Merger of the self in the Self). That is why he could say, as he did: 'Maim Alla hum', 'I am God'."[41]

Such total identification with Allah is a feature of some extreme forms of Sufism, as is seen in the case of the celebrated al-Ḥallāj (857–922), who in his ecstatic moods would sing the phrase *anā al-Ḥaqq,* I am God.[42] Sai Baba's self-identification with the Absolute was one of the reasons why he was envisioned by Hindus as an *avatāra.*

The sources inform us that Baba enjoyed music and dance. Contrary to his usual reserve, at night he sometimes went to the so-called *takiyā,* a resting place for Muslim visitors.[43] Here he sang devotional hymns, among which figured some popular motives attributed to Kabir. He apparently also sang in Persian or Arabic, languages that the local people could not understand.[44] He is described tying bells (*ghungūr*) to his ankles and dancing, enraptured in ecstatic joy.[45]

In such activities, Sai Baba expressed his devotion to the various forms and attributes of God: Krishna, *al-Rahīm,*[46] and so forth, though always bearing in mind the formless character of the Absolute (*nirākāra*). Indeed, it is typical of a Hindu or Muslim ascetic to experience one's unitive state both in the depths of impenetrable silence and in devotional rapture, when the heart's emotion bursts out, the bliss of divine love intoxicating the mind.

Baba himself, later in life, remarked how the *sākāra* (the anthropomorphic form of God) bears a strong emotional impact on most people, especially the young, and should never be disdained or rejected.[47] The sources inform us that Baba continued to sing and dance more or less regularly until 1890.[48]

We can relate Sai Baba's habit of singing and dancing to the Sufi ritual practice of *samā* (audition). This involves the listening to music and the singing of Koranic chants and musical poetry. The recital is intended to favor mystical absorption. Those most affected by *samā* rise up to dance in unison with the music. Depending on the Sufi group, the dance can be a marvel of esthetic movement or the frenetic writhings of the seemingly possessed. From its inception, the issue of *samā* has been controversial among Sufis. The Chishti brotherhood, however, encouraged the practice, exported it to India, and effected what might be termed the Indianization of *samā* . Bruce B. Lawrence has emphasized the importance Chishti groups came to attribute to *tawājud,* that is, the graceful movement that voluntarily emanates from the listener when he is overcome by *samā* . For the Chishtis, every participant in sacred musical gatherings was obliged to experience *tawājud* prior to attaining ecstasy (*wajd*) and the "unity of existence" (*wujūd*).[49]

Sai Baba's abode in the *masjid* brought him in closer contact with the local people. Sources inform us about some healing acts performed by the young *faqīr*. He would collect herbs and inexpensive drugs from the local shops and apply them to the sick. He is said to have cured snake bite, leprosy by using snake poison, and "rotting eyes" with *bibā*,[50] (washermen's marking-nut) as an alkaline aseptic. Many started calling him *hakīm*, "doctor."[51] Such medicinal knowledge, coupled with his mastery of yogic practices, already suggest the connotation of a knower of the secrets of human physiology and of a thaumaturge. Though Baba never wrote anything and was almost certainly lacking formal education, to his devotees he was a *sarvajña*, an omniscient person.[52]

The Khandoba temple where Sai Baba, according to the Shri Sai Satcharita, first wanted to settle down. Mhalsapati, the pujārī of the temple (later to become one of Baba's most ardent devotees), objected to his wish having identified the young ascetic as a Muslim.

Sai Baba had a passion for horticulture. The *Shri Sai Satcharita* tells us that one day, coming from Rahata, he brought different kinds of seeds, small plants of *zendu, jai,* and *juī,*[53] and, after having marked and levelled an open space, he planted and watered them. Daily, Vaman Tatya, a villager who became one of his devotees, furnished him with two water jars. Baba would get water from the well, balancing the jars on his shoulders. At night, these jars were kept at the foot of the *nīm* tree. Being made of earthen clay, they could break very easily. Thus, it was necessary to have two earthen jars ready every day. Such work was carried on for about three years, and a nice garden grew. It is on this piece of land that the *samādhi-mandir*[54] of Baba was later built.[55] Sources report that he used to distribute flowers from his garden in the Hindu temples and the *masjid.*

Sai Baba possibly wore a beard and mustache by this time. Concerning the attire of young Sai, the *Shri Sai Satcharita* reports that "in the early days, He wore a white turban, a clean dhoti and a shirt."[56] It also states that "He dressed like an athlete."[57] This would perhaps imply that he wore a loincloth on occasion. With reference to Baba's "athletic" dress, the *Shri Sai Satcharita* narrates:

> There was a wrestler in Shirdi, by name Mohidden Tamboli.[58] Baba and he did not agree on some items and they had a fight in which Baba was defeated. Thenceforth, Baba changed his dress and mode of living. He donned kafni, wore a langot (waist band) and covered his head with a piece of cloth. He took a piece of sack-cloth for his seat, sack-cloth for his bed and was content with wearing torn and worn out rags. He always said: "Poverty is better than Kingship, far better than lordship. The Lord is always brother (befriender) of the poor."[59]

This interesting episode, which the *Shri Sai Satcharita* alone mentions,[60] may possibly be ascribed to the year 1885. The reason given for Baba's change in dress and "mode of living" does not, however, tally with what the same source had previously narrated: Baba's presentation as a *faqīr* already wearing a *kafnī* at the time of his first meeting with Chand Patil.

This story, nonetheless, shows some credible tracts. Wrestling is one of the most popular forms of Indian athletics, particularly in villages where there is generally an arena in which the youths contend amid the excitement of the assembled crowd. William Crooke offers a nice description of it:

> The North Indian wrestler, before entering the arena, smears his body with clay, and struts about with inflated chest and solemn gait. The crouching position, head to head, is adopted, and each combatant uses every art to secure a favorable grip, in the intervals slapping his arms and thighs with his open hand. A fair fall consists in being thrown flat on the back, both shoulders touching the ground.[61]

In the *Shri Sai Satcharita,* the ascetic Gangagiri himself is said to have been a wrestler before converting to religious life.[62] In our text, Sai Baba adopts the *kafnī* in a spirit of humility and identification with the poor. The color of it is not specified. Baba's praise of poverty brings to mind once again the saying ascribed to Mohammad: *al-faḳr fakhrī* (poverty is my pride).

Interestingly, this same story, but with the roles of winner and loser reversed, was presented in a new version by Satya Sai Baba. On March 4, 1962, during a speech held on occasion of the *Mahāshivarātri* festival, he said:

> I am reminded now of past events, events in my previous body. Even then, I had Sathya or Truth as my Support. A wrestler challenged Me then for a fight and he was defeated before a large gathering of villagers. Pained by the insult, he invited Baba for a second tussle the next day, so that he might win back his lost reputation. The man swore that if defeated again, he would wear a long rough kafni and move about with his head covered in cloth. He dared Baba too to swear likewise. Baba was in no mood to enter the arena again and he was quite prepared to concede the fellow the victory he craved. So he accepted defeat and himself donned the kafni and the kerchief. The wrestler felt great remorse and his insolence melted away. He appealed to Baba to resume his usual style of dress and released him from the obligation. But Baba stuck to his word. He was Sathya Itself. Then, as He is now, He wore the new attire.[63]

The hagiographic molding of such a version presents Sai Baba as truthful to his given word. His donning a *kafnī* is motivated by his spirit of submission and equanimity.

Baba apparently wore no sandals, always walking barefooted. Such custom is typical among rural Muslims and low-caste Hindus even today.

At this time the dilapidated mosque became the center

around which Baba's life revolved.[64] Inside, Sai Baba built a *dhunī*, that is, a sacred wood-fire that he kept perpetually burning.[65] A. Osborne has traced such custom to Parsi influence.[66] The habit of keeping a *dhunī*, however, is typical of the Hindu Nātha sect[67] and is attested to as common practice in Sufi circles as well.[68]

Sai Baba is described as sitting in front of the fire, facing south,[69] keeping his left hand on a wooden support, a typical aid used by Indian ascetics. The local villagers reported seeing him seated in front of the fire for hours, absorbed in the practice of repeating sacred formulas or rapt in silent contemplation. The use of fire as one's focus of attention is a typical feature of Indian yogic techniques.[70] Similarly, light plays a crucial function in Sufi cosmology and mysticism, often in relation to the effects of *dhikr* practice.[71] The "mysticism of light" of Shihaboddin Yahya Sohrawardi (1155–91), with his description of the events originating in the *Malakūt* sphere,[72] is paradigmatic in this regard.[73]

As the *Shri Sai Satcharita* notes, the *dhunī* represented the seat of the sacrificial oblation, the purificatory fire at which Sai Baba offered his whole being. At the *dhunī* he would intercede for his devotees, offering them the sacred ash or *udī*[74] drawn from the fire, which he administered as a tangible sign of his grace (*prasād*). (I will soon return to the *udī* and its supposed healing power.)

Sai Baba seems to have been very fond of lights. Besides tending the *dhunī*, he used to beg oil from the local shopkeepers and kept earthen dishes with wicks burning the whole night in the mosque.[75]

Inside the *masjid*, near one of the walls, was a large flat stone[76] on which Baba used to sit for hours in his typical posture, perhaps the most well known image of the saint: his right arm resting on his right thigh or lap, the foot or the ankle on the opposite knee, and the head slightly inclined in an attitude of contemplation or reflection. The left hand lies on the foot or the ankle of the crossed leg. Such posture in Indian iconography represents sovereignty and is the prerogative of gods and *rājas* alone.[77] Baba's adoption of such posture appears to be intentional, perhaps in an attempt to signify the true royalty of *faqīri* life (reflection of God's absolute sovereignty) versus the false one of human lordship.

Although villagers at that time had different opinions on Sai Baba, some considering him an ecstatic, to the majority he was only a mad *faqīr*. His equanimity and detachment (*vairāgya*), however, must have been apparent to all.

The *Shri Sai Satcharita* reports perhaps the earliest testimony of Sai Baba's alleged miraculous powers:

> In the afternoon he used to walk at random and go at times to Nimgaon. There he frequented the house of Trimbakji Dengle. Shri Sai Baba loved Mr. Babasaheb Dengle. His younger brother, named Nanasaheb, had no son though he married a second wife. Babasaheb sent Nanasaheb for taking darshan of Sai Baba and after some time, with His grace, Nanasaheb got a son. From that time people began to come in numbers to see Sai Baba and his fame began to spread and reached Ahmednagar; from where Nanasaheb Chandorkar and Keshav Chidambar and many others began to come to Shirdi.[78]

Many other instances of Sai Baba granting offspring to childless couples are recorded in the sources. Baba's touch, words such as *Allāh karegā* (Allah will do) or *that Faqīr is good,* and even glance were thought to be powerful enough to produce the desired effect.

The request for progeny, especially male, has always been one of the most common graces (*prasād*) that Indians seek from holy men. Living saints as well as tombs of *sādhus* and *faqīrs* often become famous for their reputation for granting offspring.[79] In India, having no progeny is viewed as a terrible family disgrace, not only due to obvious economic reasons, but also because of religious tabus. Indeed, a childless couple is considered to be cursed, not being able to fulfill its obligations towards the *pitṛs* (ancestors).[80] Such bad fate is responsible for social discrimination, the couple (especially the woman) being viewed as bearing an evil influence.[81]

Due to these and other "miraculous" occurrences, Baba's prestige increased significantly, to the point that several people started revering him as a saint possessing special powers (*siddhis*): V. B. Kher reports that by 1878 Mhalsapati, Appa Kulkarni, Jagle, and Nanasaheb Dengle had accepted Sai Baba as their *sadguru*. One Chidambar Keshav Gadgil, a *māmlātdār,* is said to have been the first government official to consider Sai Baba a *jñānin* and call on him.[82]

A few Hindus began offering him some kind of worship inside the *masjid,* though Sai Baba strongly disapproved. The Muslims of the village protested against such practice, in their eyes an obvious case of impiety and idolatry. Indeed, Sai Baba must have perceived the incongruity of Hindu devotees offering him *pūjā* inside the *masjid.*

Narasimhaswami reports how, even as late as 1913, one Muslim, Abdul Rahim Rangari of Thana, noticing that sandal paste was being applied to Baba's forehead,[83] asked him: "What is this? The Hindus are applying sandal paste to your forehead. This is not the custom among the Muslims.' Baba had to appease him by pointing out that he had to bend to circumstances. Baba's words were: 'Jaisa Desh Aiysa Vesh', meaning: 'When in Rome do as the Romans do'. Baba also told Rangari that he (Baba) himself was a devotee of Allah."[84]

To other similar objections, Baba pointed out that if the Hindus wished to please themselves by worshipping him (identified by all as a Muslim) inside a mosque, this was no loss to Islam but only to Hinduism.

The more Sai Baba's fame grew, however, the more accentuated became the rivalry between the two communities. Baba himself maintained an ambiguous profile, unwilling to identify with either of the two religions. His Muslim devotees were fully convinced that he belonged to their fold, identifying him as an *avaliā*. The Hindu *bhaktas* also viewed him as one of them, since he often identified himself with their gods and customs.

Sai Baba wanted to belong to all and be shared by all. He apparently found himself at ease in this paradoxical situation. When pressed on whether he was Hindu or Muslim, he would often get very angry and abuse people. Once he told a devotee: "You have been with me for eighteen years now. Does Sai mean for you only these three and a half cubits of height?"[85]

Certainly, Sai Baba never encouraged his own worship, though in the last years he gave up resistance and accepted the cult which the Hindus tributed to him, often in a quite ostentatious form.

Sai Baba was able to avoid clashes between the two communities, and, in fact, succeeded in unifying them in an atmosphere of general harmony. In a verse of the midday *ārtī*, devotees sing: "In essence or basic principle, there is no difference whatever between Hindu and Muslim. You took birth in human body to point out this. You look with affection on both Hindus and Muslims. This, Sai, who pervades all, as the soul of all, shows."[86]

At this early period, Hindu worship of Baba was purely individual. A devotee would bring flowers, bow to him, ask for a blessing, and leave. Mhalsapati was apparently the only one who honored him with a sandal-paste *pūjā*.

Baba would often talk about the Hindu gods, quoting from sacred texts or even commenting upon passages of the *Bhagavadgītā*, the *Īsha Upanishad*, and so forth. The names of Krishna and Rama seem to have been particularly dear to him.

With his Muslim followers, Baba would always talk of Allah and the Koran, often quoting Persian verses.[87] Apparently, one of his favorite expressions was *Allāh rakhegā vaiśa rahena*, that is,

"Let us be content with what we have, and submit our will to Allah."[88] On several occasions, Sai reassured his listeners by saying that he, like them, was but a devotee of Allah, a humble *faqīr* with two arms and two legs.[89]

In later years, Parsis and even a few Christians would come to Shirdi. Sai Baba respected all creeds, true to his conviction that all religions are but particular paths leading to one ineffable goal.

All had free access to the *masjid*: outcastes, lepers, dogs, birds, and so on. Baba particularly enjoyed the company of untouchables and the ill. One Bhagoji Shinde, a leper, came to be one of Sai's closest devotees.[90]

This was the reason why the *masjid* came to be known by the Hindu name of Dvārakāmāī "the many-gated mother": *Dvārakā*[91] literally means "many-gated," and *māī* means "mother."[92] Another definition of *Dvārakā* is found in the *Skanda Purāṇa*, where it is said to be a place open to people of all four castes (*brāhmaṇs, kṣatriyas, vaiśyas,* and *śūdras*), so as to promote the realization of the four legitimate aims (*puruṣārthas*) of human existence: *kāma, artha, dharma,* and *mokṣa*.[93]

The *masjid* or Dvārakāmāī gradually attracted more and more people, who came from nearby villages. From the young *faqīr*, most asked for blessings of a material kind (progeny, jobs, cures from illness, etc.); very few requested spiritual guidance.

Notes

1. We know from the sources that, from time to time, he went to Rahata and Nimgaon. Rahata is located south of Shirdi, about four miles away. Nimgaon (literally, "village of the *nīm* trees"), is located about two miles north. V. B. Kher claims that Sai Baba "toyed with the idea of taking up his residence in Rahata...but finally decided in favor of Shirdi for his abode"; Kamath and Kher, *Sai Baba*, 6–7.

2. Part of the Desh region, also comprising the Ahmednagar-Balaghat Plateau, the Bhima Basin and the Krishna Valley.

3. The first two decades of this century witnessed events that radically changed the economy of the Ahmednagar district, which until then had been a famine stricken area of dry infertile land. The events were related to the construction of the Godāvarī and Pravarā irrigation canals. The choice of sugarcane cultivation was somewhat forced. As N. G. Bapat remarks: "The main problem for the irrigation authorities was to develop such crops which would demand water supply at regular intervals, would consume water to the maximum extent and in concentrated area, and at the same

time bear high water charges. It was found that sugarcane was the only crop which satisfied these conditions. This explains the Government's positive interest in the extension of cane cultivation on the canals." See N. G. Bapat, *Economic Development of Ahmednagar District 1881–1960* (Bombay: Progressive Corporation Private, 1973), 307. Thus, the region which was popularly known as the Famine-Belt until the first decade of 1900, later came to be known as the Sugar-Belt. To the present day, the economic landscape of the Kopergaon-Shrirampur tract stands out like an island in the parched hinterland of subsistence agriculture.

4. I have experienced this myself.

5. Kopergaon or Kopargaon, literally "corner" (*koprā*) or "elbow" (*kopar*) village (*gāon*), was and still is the headquarters of its *tālukā*. In 1961, the *tālukā* had a population of 173,748. See *Census of India, 1961,* vol. 10. *Maharashtra,* pt. 7–C "Weekly Markets in Maharashtra" (Bombay, 1968), 16.

6. As Iravati Karve notes: "In the tightly packed Deccan villages one loses sight of the individual houses which are but vaguely felt as parts of a big conglomerate." See I. Karve, ed., "The Indian Village," in A. R. Desai, ed., *Rural Sociology in India* (Bombay: Popular Prakashan, 1969), 188.

7. A whole series of words denotes types of roads: *alī* is a row of houses of one caste or profession, *gallī* is a narrow street, and so forth. See ibid., 189.

8. This calculation is based on the assumption that a medium-size family comprised five members. We know, for example, that the average number of persons per household in the rural areas of Pune district from 1921 to 1951, was between 4. 7 and 5. 5; see H. Orenstein, *Gaon: Conflict and Cohesion in an Indian Village* (Princeton: Princeton University Press, 1965), 40. In 1961, Shirdi had a population of 5,239; see *Census of India, 1961,* vol. 10, *Maharashtra,* pt. 7–C, 67. Such increase is to be partly attributed to Shirdi's fame as a pilgrimage center.

9. See *Census of India, 1961,* vol. 10, *Maharashtra,* pt. 7–C, Appendix I (*Ahmednagar District Gazetteer,* 1884). Every village in Maharashtra is within the reach of one or more bazaars held on different days of the week. In 1961, Rahata had a population of 8,661.

10. The articles sold in these shops are various kinds of grains, salt, oil, sugar, soap, tea, tobacco, betel-nuts, and so forth. The shopkeepers are generally Gujaratis, Marvaris, Kutchies (popularly known as *vāṇīs*), and local communities of merchants (*vaiśyas*). See *Census of India, 1961,* vol. 10, *Maharashtra,* pt. 7–C, 2.

11. In 1961, it used to be held on Sundays.

12. The *pāṭīl* is usually the biggest land holder in a village, where the

majority of the houses belong to his clan. The pāṭīlship is generally the privilege of Maratha families.

13. In most villages in the Deccan the chief village god is Maruti or Hanuman, whose temple is situated at the entrance of the village. Maruti is considered to be an *avatāra* of Shiva and is held in great reverence by all classes. A festival is held in his honor in the bright half of the month of Caitra (March–April). His sacred day is Saturday: fresh oil and red lead are offered to him by the devotees. The priests in most of Maruti's temples are Guravs, Ghadis, Marathas, or Gosavis.

14. These temples are preserved in good condition, having been restored in course of time. Also to be noted are some small shrines dedicated to Ganapati, Shankara, and Shani, i.e., Saturn. The latter's influence is an evil one, and must be appeased through offerings and magic spells.

15. Gunaji, *Shri Sai Satcharita,* 27.

16. Kamath and Kher, *Sai Baba,* 7.

17. Narasimhaswami, *Life of Sai Baba,* 1:19.

18. Ibid. Evidently, Mhalsapati thought that Sai might profane the sacred space, or even break the images in a iconoclastic fit.

19. See Gunaji, *Shri Sai Satcharita,* 48. Bayajibai's great devotion to Baba is confirmed by all sources.

20. On the crucial connection between sainthood and "pāgalness" in the Indian context, see David R. Kinsley, "Through the Looking Glass: Divine Madness in the Hindu Religious Tradition," in *History of Religions* 13, no. 1 (May 1974), 270–305. See also the excellent work of June McDaniel, *The Madness of the Saints: Ecstatic Religion in Bengal* (Chicago: University of Chicago Press, 1989). On the theme of the holy fool, see the valuable monograph of Lee Siegel, *Laughing Matters: Comic Tradition in India* (Chicago: University of Chicago Press, 1987; Delhi: Motilal Banarsidass, 1989), 260–70. For a presentation of holy madness within the Maharashtrian sect of the Mahānubhāvas, see A. Feldhaus, "God and Madman: Guṇḍam Rāuḷ," in *School of Oriental and African Studies* 45 (1982): 74–83. Also A. Feldhaus, *The Deeds of God in Ṛddhipur* (New York: Oxford University Press, 1984).

21. Kamath and Kher, *Sai Baba,* 7.

22. The begging bag in which are also often kept the magic turmeric powder (*bhaṇḍār*) and ashes (*vibhūti*).

23. On *saṃnyāsa* begging rules, see Kane, *History of Dharmaśāstra,* vol. 2, pt. 2, 933ff.

24. A famous verse declares "An ascetic should take only eight morsels of food, a forest hermit sixteen, a householder thirty-two and a Vedic student an unlimited number." See *Āpastambha Dharmasūtra* 2.4.9.13.

25. See Sontheimer, *Between Ghost and God,* 326–27.

26. The name literally means "the slave or servant of the Goddess (*Devī*)." It possibly identifies a Śākta. Some details on Devidas are offered in Gunaji, *Shri Sai Satcharita,* 29.

27. Kher reports that he had come to Shirdi as a lad of ten or eleven and had been living in Shirdi for twelve years; see Kamath and Kher, *Sai Baba,* 7.

28. Literally, "the slave or servant of Jan(a)ki," a patronymic of Sita, Rama's wife and paradigm of the virtuous wife according to *strī-dharma.* This Jankidas is reported being a member of the Mahānubhāva sect; see Kamath and Kher, *Sai Baba,* 7.

29. Literally, "the mountain of the Ganges," i.e., the Himalaya. Said to be a Vaiṣṇava holy man (though the name might well identify a Śaiva ascetic), Gangagiri was quite fond of wrestling. The *Shri Sai Satcharita* describes his conversion to religious life thus: "While he was once wrestling, a...feeling of dispassion came over him and at the proper time he heard the voice of an adept, saying that he should wear out his body, plying with God. So he too gave up Samsara and turned towards God-realization. He established a Math on the banks of the river near Puntambe and lived there with disciples"; cf. Gunaji, *Shri Sai Satcharita,* 26–27.

30. A locale situated about ten or fifteen miles east of Shirdi. Puntambe covers an area of 26.9 miles; in 1961 its population was 14,448. See *Census of India, 1961,* vol. 10, *Maharashtra* pt. 7–C, 67.

31. Baba was carrying water jars for watering some trees and plants.

32. Gunaji, *Shri Sai Satcharita,* 23. V. B. Kher also reports that Gangagiri told Nanasaheb Dengle of Nimgaon that Sai Baba was a *cintāmaṇi,* i.e., a "jewel." On hearing that, Nanasaheb went to the *bābhūḷ* forest, where Sai was residing, and bowed at his feet. See Kamath and Kher, *Sai Baba,* 7.

33. Literally, "lord of bliss." The *nātha* ending most probably designates a Nāthapanthī Śaiva ascetic.

34. The hermitage or monastery of Yeola, a town not far from Shirdi. Headquarters of the *tālukā* of the same name in the Nasik district, Yeola is situated on the Dhond-Manmad line, thirteen miles south of Manmad station. In 1901, the town had a population of 16,559. See *The Imperial Gazetteer of India,* vol. 24 (Oxford: Clarendon Press, 1908), 422.

35. Gunaji, *Shri Sai Satcharita,* 23. Such a statement was supposedly made around 1885. On that same page, Gunaji refers to Baba's encounters with Devidas and Jankidas.

36. Such habit is typical among all ascetics and renouncers. *Saṃnyāsins* should observe silence at all times, except when repeating Vedic texts.

37. Bharadwaja, *Sai Baba,* 18.

38. Prayer (*namāz*) is a devotional service whose performance is obligatory for every Muslim of age, at least five times a day; namely dawn, noon, afternoon, evening, and night. These prayers, to be said in Arabic, are always preceded by the ablution of the face, hands, and feet; this is done whether they are offered individually or in a congregation.

39. Osborne, *Incredible Sai Baba,* 2.

40. On Baba's use of repeating the phrase *Allāh Mālik,* see chapter 9, where the practice of *dhikr* is discussed.

41. Narasimhaswami, *Life of Sai Baba,* 1:20.

42. The declarations by Ḥusayn ibn-Manṣūr, also called al-Ḥallāj, of being one with God, were the reason for his arrest in 915. Beheaded in 922, his last words, according to some witnesses, were the following: "What matters to the ecstatic is that the One might 'reduce' him to Unity." On al-Ḥallāj, see the classic work of L. Massignon, *La Passion d'al-Ḥusayn-ibn-Manṣūr al-Ḥallāj, martyr mystique de l'Islam, exécuté à Bagdad le 26 Mars 922,* 2 vols. (Paris, 1922).

43. *Takiyā* is probably derived from Arabic *ittikā,* and was first employed in the sense of "refectory." In Marathi, the term *takyā* means "bolster," or "cushion."

44. Bharadwaja, *Sai Baba,* 16.

45. G. S. Khaparde, an important figure among Baba's devotees, wrote in his diary notes of 1911 and 1912 that he sometimes saw Baba skipping and dancing. See Narasimhaswami, *Life of Sai Baba,* 1:20n.

46. Literally, "The Compassionate One," one of Allah's attributes.

47. See Narasimhaswami, *Life of Sai Baba,* 1:20.

48. Ibid., 19.

49. See B. B. Lawrence, "The Early Chishti Approach to Samā," in M. Israel and N. K. Wagle, *Islamic Society and Culture: Essays in Honour of Professor Aziz Ahmad* (Manohar, 1983), 69–93. For a general presentation of *samā,* see M. Molé, *La danse extatique en Islam* (Paris: Sources Orientales 6, 1963).

50. *Semecarpus anacardium.*

51. The Muslim term *hakīm* designates the doctor as well as the philosopher. Compare the case of the Iranian Hosayn Tirmidhi (d. 898), who came to be known as al-Hakīm, that is, the philosopher, being the first Sufi to follow Hellenistic philosophy.

52. Many followers viewed his habit of administering herbs and medicines as a mere symbolic device, believing that Sai's power did not need other instrument than his divine will (*saṃkalpa*).

53. Varieties of jasmines and marigolds.

54. The temple (*mandir*) where Baba's tomb is located.

55. Gunaji, *Shri Sai Satcharita,* 24.

56. Ibid., 40.

57. Ibid., 24.

58. Such name identifies a Muslim.

59. Ibid., 26. The expression "friend of the poor," *dīnabandhu,* is typically Hindu.

60. Contrary to the *Shri Sai Satcharita* version, V. B. Kher reports that the villager Ramgir Bua stated that Sai Baba did not wrestle but rather had a quarrel with Mohidden's son-in-law, a *māntrika,* as a result of which Baba retreated to the jungle, a mile or two away from Shirdi. See Kamath and Kher, *Sai Baba,* 79.

61. Crooke, *Things Indian,* 530.

62. See Gunaji, *Shri Sai Satcharita,* 26–27.

63. See Satya Sai Baba, *Sathya Sai Speaks: Discourses given by Bhagavan Sri Sathya Sai Baba.* Compiled by N. Kasturi, 4th ed. (Prasanthi Nilayam, 1981), 2:158–59.

64. The edifice was restored only in 1912.

65. The term *dhunī* derives most probably from the Sanskrit root *dhū* (to fan or kindle). G. S. Ghurye, however, derives it from the Sanskrit root *dhun* (to waft); see G. S. Ghurye, *Indian Sādhus* (Bombay: Popular Prakashan, 1964), 137. A devotee named Appa Bhil periodically furnished Baba with fresh wood.

66. See Osborne, *Incredible Sai Baba,* 2.

67. The chief characteristic of a Nāthapanthī monastic center (*akāṛā*), is certainly represented by the ever-burning fire (*dhunī*).

68. For example, as W. Crooke mentions: "In the city of Gorakhpur the representative of a famous Musalman Shi'a Faqir keeps a fire continually burning in the court of the Imambara, and this is said to have lasted for more than a century and a half; the ashes are reputed to cure fever in children." See Crooke, *Religion and Folklore,* 338.

69. One may usefully compare such posture with that kept by Shiva Dakshinamurti, who faces death and the demons which come from the South to threaten the sacrifice.

70. Light meditation (*jyotir dhyāna*) is one of three kinds of meditation described in the *Gheraṇḍa Saṃhitā* (6:1). Since ancient times, the transcendental Reality has been described as unimaginably luminous. The *Bhagavadgītā* (13:17) calls it "light of lights beyond darkness" (*jyotiṣām api taj jyotis tamasaḥ param ucyate*). Most Hindu scriptures make reference to the light aspect of the Self.

71. See for example the description of light phenomena that characterize the *dhikr* practice in the *Kubrawiyya* school. On this issue, see H. Corbin, *L'Homme de lumière dans le soufisme iranien,* 2d ed. (Paris: 1971).

72. One of the four worlds according to Sohrawardi's cosmology, it is the abode of the celestial and human souls.

73. On Sohrawardi's thought, influenced by both the Mazdean tradition and Neoplatonic theosophism, see H. Corbin, *En Islam iranien,* vol. 2, *Sohrawardi et les platoniciens de Perse* (Paris, 1971).

74. *Udī* is also referred to as frankincense, that is, a gum resin containing volatile oil obtained from various East African or Arabian trees of the genus *Boswellia.* Valued for embalming and fumigation, it is an important incense resin.

75. Such practice calls to mind the popular Hindu festival of *Dīpāvālī,* which is celebrated on the new moon of the months of either Āśvin or Kārttika (between mid-October and mid-November).

76. The stone is still there, an object of veneration for all devotees. Hanging above it, is an impressive life-size portrait of Sai Baba seated on the stone, realized by a devotee in Baba's times.

77. For interesting details on the "pensive attitude" in Buddhist iconography, see E. D. Saunders, *Mudrā: A Study of Symbolic Gestures in Japanese Buddhist Sculpture,* reprint, Bollingen Series, 58 (Princeton: Princeton University Press, 1985), 130–31.

78. Gunaji, *Shri Sai Satcharita,* 27. V. B. Kher notes that Nanasaheb Dengle knew many government officials and contributed significantly in the expansion of Baba's reknown. See Kamath and Kher, *Sai Baba,* 7.

79. As Ja'far Sharif, a native of the Deccan, reports: "The tomb of

Shaikh Salīm Chishtī at Fathpur Sīkrī, by whose intercession Akbar believed that he had been blessed with a son, is even at the present day visited by childless Hindu and Musalmān women who tie threads or rags on the lovely screen which surrounds it"; Ja'far Sharif, *Islam in India or the Qānūn-I-Islām,* composed under the direction of and translated by G. A. Herklots [1921; reprint, London and Dublin: Curzon Press, 1972], 18.

80. Such belief goes back to Vedic times. A barren woman, at death, is believed to become a ghost (*preta*), causing great trouble to the living in her anger as failed mother. The themes of childlessness and desire for fulfillment are recurrent in the typology of disease goddesses, such as in the case of Sitala and Mariammai, India's smallpox goddess; see on this issue Pauline Kolenda, "Pox and the Terror of Childlessness: Images and Ideas of the Smallpox Goddess in a North Indian Village," in P. Kolenda, *Caste, Cult and Hierarchy: Essays on the Culture of India* (New Delhi: Folklore Institute, 1983), 198–221.

81. A childless woman is suspected of having an evil eye. Thus, she should never praise another woman's child, lest she betray her own envy. An evil eye is believed to possess the power to kill.

82. Kamath and Kher, *Sai Baba,* 7.

83. Sandal paste is used to signify the presence of the divine. Three horizontal lines are representative of Shiva, three vertical lines are representative of Vishnu.

84. Narasimhaswami, *Life of Sai Baba,* 1:24. On Abdul Rahim Rangari, see ibid., vol. 3, 177–79.

85. Narasimhaswami, *Charters and Sayings,* 12. A cubit is an ancient unit of linear measure, approximately seventeen to twenty-two inches. Thus, Baba would have been about six feet high, quite tall for his times.

86. "Bheda Na Tatvim Hindu Yavananca Kahim / Davayasi Jhale Punarapi Nara Dehi / Pahasi Premane Tu Hindu Yavananhi / Davisi Atmatvane Vyapaka Ha Sai"; Narasimhaswami, *Life of Sai Baba,* 1:63.

87. See ibid., 4:107.

88. Narasimhaswami, *Charters and Sayings,* 106–7.

89. Ibid., 119–21.

90. Gunaji, *Shri Sai Satcharita,* 42–43.

91. Name of the capital of lord Krishna on the western point of Gujarat (Saurashtra), supposed to have been submerged by the sea; see *Mahābhārata, Mausala-parvan* (sixteenth book), where the death of Krishna and his brother Balarama, the submersion of *Dvārakā* by the sea, and the mutual destruction of the Yādavas in a fight with clubs (*musala*) of miraculous origin are narrated.

92. See Bharucha, *Sai Baba,* 12.

93. See Gunaji, *Shri Sai Satcharita,* 18n. The verse runs as follows: *caturṇāmapi vargāṇām yatra dvārāṇi sarvataḥ / ato dvārāvatītyuktā vidvadbhistattvavedibhiḥ* (*kāma* designates sensual pleasure, *artha* material advantage or gain, *dharma* righteousness, and *mokṣa* the highest aim, emancipation from the round of births and deaths [*saṃsāra*]). According to tradition, *kāma* represents the focal aim of *śūdras, artha* the focal aim of *vaiśyas, dharma* the focal aim of *kṣatriyas,* and *mokṣa* the focal aim of *brāhmaṇs.*

4

Sai Baba's Daily Routine. His "Death" and "Resurrection" in 1886

Regarding this early period the sources are vague, lacking any dates. In fact, it is only from the beginning of 1900 that more attention is paid to chronological order. This general lack of data makes a hypothetical reconstruction problematic.

The only date on which most biographical accounts agree is that of 1886. In this year, Baba is said to have "died" and to have come back to life after three days.[1] We will later analyze this significant episode in detail.

As already mentioned, appreciation for Baba expanded slowly. It was only after 1890 that Sai Baba's fame spread with increasing speed, bringing to Shirdi tens and sometimes hundreds of people daily (even coming from "distant" places, such as Bombay, Nagpur, etc.). Narasimhaswami holds that, before 1886, Baba's main interest was directed toward the people who were physically close to him (in Shirdi and nearby villages); this was due to *rīṇānubandha* connections.[2]

In dealing with this time period, we must consider the terrible famine of 1876, perhaps one of the worst in the Ahmednagar district, caused, as usual, by the shortage of rainfall. This famine, resulting in high mortality, devastated the whole economy of the district, and the distress was so severe that it flared into riots in the rural areas, generally known as "Deccan riots." The *tālukās* of Karjat, Rahuri, and Shrigonde suffered worst from the effects of this famine.[3]

Available sources provide enough material for a tentative reconstruction of Sai Baba's daily routine at Shirdi.

Apparently, even when he performed some extraordinary feat or found himself the focus of popular attention, his humble life-rhythms remained unchanged. Sai Baba would get up early in the morning and go sit in front of his sacred fireplace (*dhunī*) facing south. He would remain there for quite some time, absorbed in contemplation. Now and then people would hear him murmuring sacred formulas.[4] After a few hours, he would wash his hands, feet, and face. Sai Baba, like most *faqīrs,* was not known to have a daily bath. Often, somebody would massage his legs. This was a service highly sought by the devotees, a sign of their closeness and intimacy with the master. Baba would reward a disciple's devotion by letting him massage his limbs. Sometimes, he would call a barber to shave his head and trim his beard, paying for the service with a few metallic coins.

Around eight o'clock Baba left the *masjid* and went begging for his food from door to door, visiting no more than four or five houses. As an old villager of Shirdi, Shri Uddhao Madhavrao Deshpande, told me: "Baba used to go out for his round of begging around 8 A.M.. He would go to certain houses.... When doing this, Baba cried, 'Māe bhākrīān,' which means 'Mother, give me some food.'"[5]

In one hand Sai Baba kept a tin pot and in the other a *jholī,* a rectangular piece of cloth also called *cūpadarī.* Liquid or semiliquid eatables as soups, vegetables, milk, or curds he received in his tin pot, whereas boiled rice, bread, and other solid foodstuffs he kept inside his *jholī.*

When he got back to the *masjid,* he would offer a *roṭī* and some boiled rice to the fire of the *dhunī,* and the rest of the food he would put in an earthen pot (*kuṇḍī*), kept just outside of the mosque. Cats and dogs, crows, beggars and untouchables, all could partake of it freely. Then, Sai would mix together the leftover food and eat a few handfuls. The *Shri Sai Satcharita* emphasizes that Baba didn't care at all about the taste of the food, having perfect control over his palate. He ate whatever people offered him.[6]

Around half past eight, Baba sat and met with visitors for an hour or so. During this time, Sai's behavior was, as usual, unpredictable. He often remained silent or simply whispered some words in God's praise. Sometimes, he had a very serious and grim expression; other times he manifested a joyful and loquacious mood. If the latter was the case, he would talk with whomever was present on the most varied subjects. During these conversations, Sai Baba would often give proof of his *antarajñāna,* his knowledge of past and future events, and showered his blessings on people.

Almost everybody asked Sai to grant some special grace, usually a very material one. Then Baba would say: "Allah will bestow..." or "Hari is good..." and this meant that the blessing was granted. In *Sufi* terminology, such power of blessing is known as *barakat,* identifying the spiritual power inherent in a saint. After his death, it is transferable to his tomb and to his descendants.

Often, when performing an act of power through his determined will (*saṃkalpa*), he would impose his hands on the person's head, forehead, or shoulders. Other times, however, he would not touch the person at all, simply glancing at him/her. The intensity of these glances were the prelude, in the devotees' interpretation, to Baba's healing intervention. It is fairly certain that each of these different acts was not casual but had its particular significance, which Baba, however, never cared to explain.

Around half past nine or ten o'clock, Sai Baba used to walk down to the *Leṇḍī*[7] stream and the gardens surrounding it. Here he roamed in solitude or sat behind the enclosed *Nanda Dīpa*[8] for about an hour. He would then return from the *Leṇḍī* to the *masjid*. Between eleven o'clock and noon, Baba would hold a second sitting and meet with visitors.

Around noon, Sai Baba again left the *masjid* for begging his meal. As usual, he would stop at four or five houses of the village, calling out loud. Sometimes, he would also leave the mosque earlier and make two or more rounds of begging. When he came back, he distributed a part of the food among all the devotees present. Often, seated on the floor for his meal, he would take a fruit, for example, a mango, taste it, and distribute it to the people as a token of communion and intimacy.

Baba probably had the habit of eating with some close devotees or with occasional visitors. In later years, he would sometimes prepare and cook the food at the *masjid*, doing everything by himself and inviting lots of people to eat wih him. He cooked large quantities of rice, vegetables, *roṭī*, sweets, and so forth. As Uddhao Madhavrao Deshpande reported to me:

> When Baba liked to cook, vessels were brought inside the masjid. There is a fire there, you must have seen it...
>
> A fellow called Madhav Phasle poured water into the vessels and helped Baba. Then Baba would cook the food.
>
> After having helped Baba to wash and cut the vegetables, Baba would place them inside the vessels. Then he would mix the vegetables with the rice. Vegetables and rice together...for cooking.
>
> Baba also used to put "sugar candies" inside the vessels. He himself would put his hand in the vessel for mixing the food.

After finishing his meal, between one and two o'clock, Baba would remain alone for a while. He often sat on the large flat stone in the mosque, keeping his typical posture. Apparently, he never took a nap.

Around two o'clock, he would leave the *masjid* and go take a

Sai Baba on his daily round of begging in the marketplace of the village.

walk in the *Leṇḍī* area, where he remained alone for some time, often sitting in some isolated spot. His love for the vegetation of the *Leṇḍī*, for the animals and for the woods around the village, indicates that Sai Baba, as many ascetics, cultivated a close relationship with nature.

At three o'clock he came back to the mosque, and around five o'clock devotees again assembled to see him and speak to him.

Sources inform us that he would never rest his back against the wall. On the contrary, he would stay at a distance from it, keeping his back straight. This observation is of importance, since all yogic schools require the adept to keep a straight posture.

Around half past six he went out again. Sometimes, he went back to the gardens, but usually he would go out for his evening round of begging. Then, he would shout his beloved formula *Allāh Mālik* or call *Ammā*[9] or cry out sentences in unknown languages. He never entered the other small temples of the village. Nonetheless, he took care of their upkeep, especially in later years.

After these walks, Sai Baba returned to the *Dvārakāmāī*. He might leave the mosque many other times but usually returned to it before or soon after sunset. Then Baba faced the sacred fire of the *dhunī* for hours, absorbed in contemplation.

Thus, there were three main occasions during which people

would daily gather around Sai. In the morning after breakfast (half past eight to half past nine), after his wandering at the *Leṇḍī* (eleven o'clock to noon), and before supper (five o'clock to half past six). These meetings came to be known as *darbār*.[10]

Of course, Baba, unpredictable as he was, modified all activities at will. Many of the people now considered him a *bolte cālte dev*, that is, a "speaking and walking god."[11]

In the evening, he would often listen to the recitation of devotional music, performed by either Hindu or Muslim adepts. Baba himself would sometimes sing along with the others, breaking into ecstatic dances which could go on for several hours.[12]

For years he used to sleep on the ground or on rags. It seems that, from an early period, Baba developed the habit of sleeping one night at the *masjid* and the other night at the *cāvaḍī*. Often, Mhalsapati and Tatya Kote Patil slept by his side at the *masjid*.

The *Shri Sai Satcharita* offers an interesting description of how these three used to sleep. Unfortunately, we have no chronological reference for this account:

> Blessed are the saints in whose heart Lord Vasudev[13] dwells, and fortunate indeed are the devotees who get the benefit of the company of such saints. Two such fortunate fellows, Tatya Kote Patil and Bhagat Mhalsapati, equally shared the company of Sai Baba. Baba also loved them equally. These three persons slept in the masjid with their heads towards the east, west and north and with their feet touching one another at the centre. Stretching their beds, they lay on them, chitchatting and gossiping about many things till late at night. If any one of them showed any signs of sleep, the others would wake him up. For instance, if Tatya began to snore, Baba at once got up and shook him from side to side and pressed his head, or with Mhalsapati hugged him close, stroked his legs and kneaded his back. In this way for full fourteen years Tatya, leaving his parents at home, slept in the masjid on account of his love for Baba.[14]

The impression that Sai Baba did not sleep at all or slept very little is found in other biographical accounts. On occasion, Baba said that his vigils were passed in the remembrance of the divine name (*nāmasmaraṇa*).[15]

It is interesting to note the men's habit of sleeping facing cardinal directions, though unfortunately the text is not clear on the direction faced by Baba. The southern direction is not mentioned. This omission could have been intentional since, as previously noted, death (in the form of the god Yama) comes from the south. The three men's positions probably symbolized the all-pervading reality of spiritual potency. The center, represented by Sai's, Mhalsapati's and Tatya Kote's feet, might have also constituted an *axis mundi* of a sort.

Of course Sai Baba gave spiritual lessons. He recommended the reading of Hindu sacred texts along with the Koran,[16] and especially insisted on the unbroken remembrance of God's name (*dhikr, nāmasmaraṇa*). When teaching, Baba often expressed himself cryptically through parables, allegories, and symbols, forcing his listeners to gain an intuitive comprehension.[17] His relationship with devotees and visitors was very personal and direct, heart to heart.

Baba conveyed his teaching more through his own way of life than through his words; that is, his life was his message. Maybe for this reason, he disliked discourses and theorizing about the spiritual path.

The *Shri Sai Satcharita* mentions a notable case of Sai Baba's "concrete" *upadeśa*:

> Once Mrs. Tarkhad was staying in a certain house in Shirdi. At noon, meals were ready and dishes were being served, when a hungry dog turned up there and began to cry. Mrs. Tarkhad got up at once and threw a piece of bread, which the dog gulped with great relish. In the afternoon when she went to the masjid and sat at some distance, Sai Baba said to her: "Mother, you have fed me sumptuously up to my throat, my afflicted pranas (life-forces) have been satisfied. Always act like this, and this will stand you in good stead. Sitting in this masjid I shall never, never speak untruth. Take pity on me like this. First give bread to the hungry and then eat yourself. Note this well." She could not at first understand the meaning of what Baba said. So she replied: "Baba, how could I feed you? I am myself dependent on others and take my food from them on payment." Then Baba replied: "Eating that lovely bread I am heartily contented and I am still belching. The dog which you saw before meals and to which you gave the piece of bread is one with me, so also other creatures (cats, pigs, flies, cows, etc.) are one with me. I am roaming in their forms. He who sees me in all these creatures is my beloved. So abandon the sense of duality and distinction and serve me as you did today."
>
> Drinking these nectar-like words, she was moved, her eyes were filled with tears, her throat was choked and her joy knew no bounds.[18]

In Narasimhaswami's *Charters and Sayings* we also read:

> I am still belching with the heavy feeding you gave the dog this morning. I am also in the mire-besmirched pig (that you did not feed, though it came to you). To serve me, give up differentiation.
>
> Sometimes I come as dog, sometimes as pig. The devotee who recognizes me in each form and treats me adequately is blessed.[19]

Thus, Baba expressed the Indian Sufi ideal of *waḥdat al-wujūd*, the unity of all beings, divine and human. As the Turk says in verse 11 of Eknath's *Hindu-Turk Saṃvād*, "Allah, you exist everywhere...you are the seeing and the seen...the knower and the known...you are life and the giver of life...you are the alms that fill the stomach and take away sin."[20]

Sai Baba's experience of oneness exemplifies equally well the metaphysical principles of *advaita-vedānta*, that is, the identity *ātman-Brahman* of the Upanishads.[21] Sai left no space for theories: the dog is Baba and Baba is the dog.

On other occasions, he is reported to have demonstrated his all-pervading nature in even more startling ways, for example, by vomiting the same food that had been offered to a domestic animal, or by showing the bruises and wounds he had on his back, when a dog had been cruelly beaten by a local villager. To again quote Uddhao Madhavrao Deshpande:

> One day, when Mhalsapati was taking his lunch meal, a dog came to his house, wailing and crying. But Mhalsapati didn't feed the dog; instead he beat it with a stick, wounding it on its head and mouth.
>
> The same day, in the evening, devotees went to the masjid to meet Baba and saw he was wounded. They asked him what had happened. Mhalsapati was present and Baba told him: "I came to your house today to beg and you beat me like this." Mhalsapati protested: "But when did you come? I didn't see you." Then Baba said: "Didn't that dog come to your door?" Thus Mhalsapati understood the lesson.[22]

Sai Baba showed deep concern with the material and physical problems of his devotees. He often said that such difficulties should be welcomed, since they functioned as bait, attracting people to Shirdi. Here, the discovery of religious values would initiate them along the path of purification (*viśuddhi mārga*).

Shri Uddhao Madhavrao Deshpande and his wife outside their home in Shirdi. Uddhao, son of Shyama Deshpande, was 79 years old in 1985.

He apparently continued the cure of illnesses through his knowledge of medicinal plants, herbs, and so forth. It is probable, however, that even prior to 1886 he began to distribute *udī* along with, or in place of, the herbs. In fact, Baba is once reported to have said that he went on with the repetition of Hari's name till Hari appeared to him. After that, he stopped giving medicines and gave only blessings and *udī*. This was enough.[23]

Interestingly, the *bhagat* Ravidas (fl. 1450?), in the *Ādi Granth* of the Sikhs, mentions Kabir as well as Namdev in connection with the redeeming power of Hari's name: "Through the name of Hari,

Kabir became renowned and the accounts of his sins of many births were torn up."[24]

Baba distributed ash as a tangible sign of his grace (*kṛpā*) when visitors left the village. He would take handfuls of *udī* out of the *dhunī* and put them into the devotees' hands. At times, he himself would apply some to their foreheads. Baba often recommended drinking the *udī* in water daily, assuring that diseases and pain would be healed.

The *Shri Sai Satcharita* narrates that, when Baba was in a good mood, he sang a little song concerning *udī*, while distributing it:

Ramte Rām āojī āojī
Udiyāṅ kī goniyāṅ lāojī

which means: "Come, come oh playful Rām, and bring with You sacks of *udī*."[25]

Udī had a symbolic meaning, underlined by Sai, representing the transitory nature of all things, which inevitably change, decay, and die.

Ash is traditionally identified with the *semen virile* (*vīrya*) of Shiva. The connection between sperm and ash is evident in the iconographic representations of Shiva's body. The ash (*bhasman* or *vibhūti*) which Shiva smeared on himself, symbolizes the life principle and, at the same time, the dissoving principle (*laya*).

The use of smearing the body with ash goes back to Vedic times. The belief is that substances burnt by fire return to their pure and primeval condition. Ash conveys the idea of a perfectly pure substance. Among the many properties that are attributed to it, we find that of reviving the dead. An exemplary illustration is the legend of the young *brāhmaṇ* Candrasvāmin, whose dead wife was on the verge of being cremated. At the crucial point, a Kāpālika ascetic[26] placed some ash on the woman's corpse. Immediately she rose from the pyre, untouched by fire.[27]

It is also believed that ash has the power of fertility as well as of turning away evil forces. The rubbing of ash is done by the yogin following precise traditional rules.[28]

With reference to *udī*, Baba insisted on the lesson of impermanence. Nothing really belongs to us in this world, said Sai: not our properties nor our children or relatives. Through *udī*, the *faqīr* taught his devotees the use of discrimination (*viveka*) between what is real and what is unreal, what is transitory and what is eternal, that is, the all-pervading Power devoid of attributes.

People in general, however, were primarily interested in the alleged healing powers of Baba's ash. When a devotee regained his health, Sai would always exhort him to thank God alone. All sources narrate episodes about the *udī*'s miraculous powers. The *Shri Sai Satcharita* offers a typical example:

> Shama's younger brother, Bapaji, was staying near the Savul well. Once his wife was attacked by bubonic plague. She had a high fever and two bubos in her groin. Bapaji ran to Shama at Shirdi and asked him to come and help. Shama was frightened but...he went to Baba, prostrated himself before Him, invoked His aid, and requested Him to cure the case. He also asked His permission to go to his brother's house.[29] Then Baba said: "Don't go there at this late hour (night); send her Udi. Why worry for the fever and the bubos? God is our father and master; she will be all right easily. Do not go now, but go there in the morning and return immediately." Shama had full faith in Baba's Udi. It was sent with Bapaji. It was applied on the bubos and some of it was mixed with water and given to the patient for drinking. No sooner was it taken in, than perspiration set in profusely, the fever abated and the patient had good sleep. Next morning Bapaji was surprised to see his wife all right and refreshed, with no fever and no bubos. When Shama went there the next morning with Baba's permission, he was also surprised to see her at the hearth and preparing tea. On questioning his brother, he learnt that Baba's Udi cured her completely in one night. Then Shama realized the significance of Baba's words: "Go there in the morning and return immediately."[30]

Here, Baba intervenes by helping the sister-in-law of a village devotee, Shyama,[31] connected with Sai by *rīṇānubandha*.[32] Later I shall return to the subject of miracles related to the assumption of *udī*.

Sai Baba, at the *masjid*, cultivated a very informal and brotherly atmosphere. He often lit his earthen pipe and smoked. Sometimes, a devotee would prepare the *cilīm* for Baba. When pleased, Sai passed the pipe around, so that everyone could take a puff and share the pleasure. In this way, the intimacy between Sai Baba and his devotees and friends grew. Mhalsapati, Shyama, Bayajibai, Tukaram Darji, Appa Jogle, Tatya Kote, Kashinatha and others would sit around him and listen to his stories. Often, the villagers would hear hearty laughs coming from the mosque. Apparently,

Baba loved the company of children. He often encouraged them to play and held them in his lap.

Other times, however, Baba got angry or simply, out of the blue, would start shouting and abusing people. Often he would punish a visitor, scolding him severely or even beating him with his stick, the *satka* he always kept nearby.

We know that in these years Sai had not yet developed the habit of requesting the *dakṣiṇā*[33] from his devotees. Even when somebody wanted to make an offering, Baba very seldom accepted it. When he did, it consisted of a few coins of the lowest value.[34] He probably received these small amounts so as to purchase small quantities of oil and tobacco, two things that he used daily.[35] We will come back to the subject of *dakṣiṇā* later.[36]

With regard to the worship offered him by Hindus, the use of celebrating the *ārtī* (at dawn, at noon, at sunset) evolved much later, certainly after 1890.

It is reported that, after Mhalsapati, Baba gave permission to Bapu, the son of Nanasaheb Chandorkar, to smear his forehead with sandal paste. He permitted this because the child used to place sandal paste on the forehead of his family *iṣṭadevatā,* whom he worshiped at home. Similarly, an old person who used to worship his guru by placing sandal paste on his forehead did the same to Baba, whom he considered the same as his guru.

Other people were encouraged to worship him with sandal paste; in this way they identified themselves as "children" of Sai. This *pūjā,* however, remained nonsystematic and silent and was generally opposed by Baba.

I now come to the consideration of the all-important 1886 episode, concerning which I shall quote two different versions.

The *Shri Sai Satcharita,* which entitles the event "Seventy-two hours of Samadhi," narrates:

> In 1886, Baba made an attempt to cross the border line. On a Margasirsa Purnima (Full moon) day, Baba suffered from a severe attack of asthma. To get rid of it, Baba decided to take His prana high up and to go into samadhi. He said to Bhagat Mhalsapati: "Protect My body for three days. If I return, it will be all right; if I do not, bury My body in that open land (pointing to it) and fix two flags there as a mark." Saying so, Baba fell down at about 10 P.M. His breathing stopped, as well as His pulse. It seemed as if His prana left the body. All the...villagers came there and wanted to hold an inquest and bury the body in the place pointed out by Baba. But Mhalsap-

ati prevented that. With Baba's body on his lap he sat full three days guarding it. After three days had passed, Baba showed signs of life at 3 A.M. His breathing commenced, the abdomen began to move. His eyes opened and stretching His limbs, Baba returned to consciousness (life) again.[37]

Narasimhaswami, in his biography, presents a different account (and a more detailed aftermath):

> One day in 1886 Baba told Mhalsapati, who was by his side: "Arre[38] Bhagat, I am going to Allah. You better guard this body for three days. If I return thereafter, I will look after the body. If I do not, you may have this body interred in that place (pointing somewhere near the sweet Nim tree)." After saying that, Baba reclined on Mhalsapati and was soon a corpse. Breathing stopped. The bodily heat disappeared. The colour of the body also turned livid. Soon the rumour got round that Baba was dead. The village officers came and also the police. An inquest was held. An inquest report was drawn up wherein it was said that Baba was dead. The Police Officers wanted Mhalsapati to bury the corpse as it should not remain in the Mosque.[39] But Mhalsapati quoted to them Baba's own words saying that he might return in three days. The Police Officers and others who obviously did not believe revival possible, tried to induce Mhalsapati to change his mind. But he stuck to his guns and pointed out that Baba was a Yogi of wonderful powers and that it was possible for such persons to return to life after three days. The Police thought ultimately that it was safer to leave the responsibility of keeping the body for three days with Mhalsapati and other devotees of Baba. The body remained there for three days, a perfect corpse, no sign of life at all being seen. But after three days suddenly a finger of Baba's began to move. Then his eyes opened. Then he sat up with breath and all. After this, for thirty-two years, he led a normal life, and it was only in 1918 that his life finally passed out of his body. His body was thereafter interred in its present place (by the Buti vada). What did the passing away from earthly life and the return to it in 1886 mean? Baba evidently returned to the world because more of the "prarabda" of the Sai body, i.e. His mission, remained unfulfilled, and therefore, he had to get back into the same body to work out the remaining portion of his life.[40]

By comparing these two versions, it is surprising to see how the *Shri Sai Satcharita* presents the episode in such a plain and unsentimental form, that is, with no miraculous overtones. Baba is said to manifest his extraordinary powers simply for ridding himself of an acute asthmatic attack. Indeed, Sai Baba suffered from asthmatic attacks on occasions. His biographers mention this illness, but only peripherally. For instance, the *Charters and Sayings* reports of an asthmatic crisis which Baba suffered in 1915.[41]

Narasimhaswami, on the other hand, develops a suggestive theory, interpreting the "death" and "resurrection" of Baba as a turning point, as the event that launched the expansion of the master's mission. It may be noted that a similar occurrence can be found in the career of another famous Indian master, Ramana Maharshi (1879–1950), a contemporary of Sai Baba's.[42]

Even mythical figures, such as the hero Rama, show stage developments in their *avatāric* career. Thus Rama, after his marriage with Sita, was empowered of the fullness of Vishnu's presence soon after his triumph in a duel with the previous *avatāra* Parashuram. Rama rid him of almost all his power. Even so, Rama did not become fully aware of his own divine identity until many years later, when he rescued his beloved wife Sita from the demon Ravana, whom he killed after having had a dialogue with the god Brahmā.

Narasimhaswami's conjectures are of interest from a theological and devotional perspective, relating Sai Baba's life to an *avatāric* plan (or, more generally, to a divine mission) developing through subsequent stages. Such a point of view is, of course, shared by many devotees.

To be sure, the diagnosed "death" of Baba and his coming back to life three days later are disconcerting to say the least.[43] We must remember, however, that in India, phemomenon of apparent death with the suspension of heart and breathing activities is renowned and somewhat familiar in yogic circles. *Prāṇāyāma,* "breath control," is the fourth "limb" (*aṅga*) of the eightfold path taught by Patañjali in the early post-Christian centuries. It is recognized as one of the chief means of rejuvenating and immortalizing the body and plays a crucial role in the practices of Nātha adepts, who are striving to attain an incorruptible body (*kāya-sādhanā*). Properly executed, *prāṇāyāma* has great curative value, and the texts mention cough, asthma, and pain in head, ears, and eyes as being among the diseases that can effectively be healed through breath control. The powers (*siddhis*) which can be attained through yogic exercises, are mentioned in a multitude of texts and have a secular tradition.[44]

Certain *faqīrs*, for example, are said to possess the power of remaining completely buried underground for a considerable time without detriment to their health.[45] Indeed, this is a common theme in legends concerning heterodox Sufis, as in the case of Shah Madar.[46]

Mhalsapati himself proves to be a clear example of the belief in *siddhis*, through his obstinacy in guarding Baba's body, in obedience to his master's last instructions.

Despite the amazement of the villagers and his devotees, Baba did not offer any explanation regarding this event and simply resumed his modest life-style.

Notes

1. V. B. Kher, however, refers this episode to the year 1885; see Kamath and Kher, *Sai Baba*, 8.

2. *Rīṇānubandha* connections are Karmic ties contracted in previous births. People who were physically close to Baba were thought to be related to him by prenatal links.

3. On the famine of 1876, see N. G. Bapat, *Economic Development of Ahmednagar District 1881–1960*, 146ff.

4. For example *Yāde Ḥaq*, an Arabic formula meaning "Remember Reality"; see Bharadwaja, *Sai Baba*, 56.

5. *Bhākrī* is millet pancake, the staple food of rural Maharashtra.

6. See Gunaji, *Shri Sai Satcharita*, 47–48.

7. The term *leṇḍī* literally means "turd," "piece of dung."

8. Also known as *Akhaṇḍa Dīpa* (the perpetually burning lamp).

9. Literally, "mother." Baba would usually address women in this manner. Men he would address with nicknames used for elder brothers such as *dādā, annā, tātyā, bāpū, bhāu*. In some cases, Baba used some actual kinship terms such as *kākā* (father's brother) as a nickname. With the addition of the suffix *saheb* applied to the names, the familiarity is lost but nevertheless a vague kinship feeling is indicated.

10. See M. V. Pradhan, *Shri Sai Baba of Shirdi*, 8th ed. (Bombay: Shri Sai Baba Sansthan, 1982), 50. See also Kamath and Kher, *Sai Baba*, 282–84. The term *darbār* designates the assembly of a king's court. Here, it refers to the assembly of devotees surrounding Baba, who is regarded as a *mahārāja* (great king).

11. See Narasimhaswami, *Life of Sai Baba,* 1:31.

12. Even in 1910, Baba is reported to have been "abused" because of the length and frenzy of the music; see Narasimhaswami, *Charters and Sayings,* 76–77.

13. A name of Krishna, derived from that of his father Vasudeva son of Sura, of the Yadava branch of the Lunar race.

14. Gunaji, *Shri Sai Satcharita,* 48–49.

15. See Narasimhaswami, *Charters and Sayings,* 115–16.

16. For a detailed examination of these texts, see chapter 9, in which I discuss Baba's teachings.

17. On Baba's use of symbolism and allegory, see chapter 12.

18. Gunaji, *Shri Sai Satcharita,* 55–56.

19. Narasimhaswami, *Charters and Sayings,* 12.

20. E. Zelliot, "A Medieval Encounter Between Hindu and Muslim: Eknāth's Drama-Poem *Hindu-Turk Saṃvād,*" in F. W. Clothey, ed., *Images of Man: Religion and Historical Process in South Asia* (Madras: New Era Publications, 1982), 179–80.

21. Compare the famous Upanishadic sayings *Tat Tvam Asi* (Thou art That; *Chānd.Up.* 6.8f.), *Aham Brahmāsmi* (I am *Brahman*; *Bṛhad.Up.* I.4.10), and so on.

22. The episodes of Baba's identification with animals are frequent in the sources. See Narasimhaswami, *Life of Sai Baba,* 4:163–64.

23. Cf. ibid., 1:48n.

24. *Ādi Granth, asa* 5, quoted in Charlotte Vaudeville, *Kabīr,* 1 :29.

25. Gunaji, *Shri Sai Satcharita,* 181. The term *Rāma* is a generic term designating God, with no necessary reference to Vishnu's *avatāra.*

26. The Kāpālika is a Tantric medieval sect that originated in South India. It represents a secondary branch of the wider Śaiva cult of the Pāśupata. On the Kāpālikas, see the classic work of David N. Lorenzen, *The Kāpālikas and Kālāmukhas: Two Lost Śaivite Sects* (Berkeley and Los Angeles: University of California Press, 1972). From the same author, see also "New Data on the Kāpālikas," in A. Hiltebeitel, *Criminal Gods,* 231–38.

27. *Kathāsaritsāgara,* 2d ed., vol. 2 (Delhi, 1968), 611ff.

28. As an example, see the rules described in the *Bhasmajābālopanishad,* Srinivasa T. R. Ayyangar, trans., *Śaiva Upaniṣads* (Madras: Adyar, 1953), 165–92.

29. The devotee ready to leave Shirdi always had to ask permission of Baba.

30. Gunaji, *Shri Sai Satcharita,* 190–91.

31. Literally, "black," "of dark color." Name of a form of Durga, Shiva's consort.

32. Baba himself seems to have confirmed this on several occasions; see Narasimhaswami, *Charters and Sayings,* 211.

33. Sacrificial salary in Vedic times. Later, it became the salary due to priests and *ācāryas.*

34. Probably the equivalent of a few *pices* or *āṇās.* A *pice* was a small copper coin which, under the Anglo-Indian system of currency, was worth 1/4 of an *āṇā* and 1/64 of a rupee. An *āṇā* corresponded to 1/16 of a rupee. It is reported that one Kashiram succeeded in having Baba accept his small offerings.

35. There were devotees, however, who would supply Baba freely almost every day.

36. See chapter 6.

37. Gunaji, *Shri Sai Satcharita,* 238.

38. *Are,* which is spelled "arre" in Narasimhaswami's text, is an exclamatory particle like "hey!" calling a person's attention, used in an informal situation. *Arere,* on the other hand, is an exclamation of distress.

39. In India, due to climatic conditions, a corpse must be either buried or cremated twenty-four hours after death.

40. Narasimhaswami, *Life of Sai Baba,* 1:182–83.

41. Baba is reported to have said during his 1915 asthmatic crisis, "Allah has given me this illness and He will make me alright" (Narasimhaswami, *Charters and Sayings,* 213–14).

42. See T. M. P. Mahadevan, *Rāmaṇa Maharṣi: The Sage of Aruṇācala* (London, 1977), 16–19.

43. The symbolism of number three is of course open to a wide set of interpretations: perfection, completion, totality, and so forth. On this issue, see Jan Gonda, *Triads in the Veda* (Amsterdam: North-Holland Publishing, 1973).

44. On supernormal powers, see the entire third section (*Vibhūti pāda*) in Patañjali's *Yogasūtra;* cf. Swami Hariharānanda Āraṇya, *Yoga Philosophy of Patañjali* (Albany, N.Y.: SUNY Press, 1983), 249–345. Among the eight traditional attainments, we find *prāpti,* that is, the ability to expand

infinitely, and *īśitva,* that is, sovereignty over nature, allowing the adept to create, rearrange, or even destroy the material elements (*bhūta*).

45. W. Crooke observed: "Cases of this kind have been reported from the Panjab by travellers like Dr. Honigberger, Lieutenant Boileau, and Captain Osborne. Some of these are obviously impostures, some, as in a case reported from Bengal in 1868, the acts of ignorant fanatics. Others, again, like that of a Guru at Dehra Dun, are possibly cases of hypnotic trance. This man is said to have possessed the power of dying at will, and returning to life after a concerted interval. In the end he mistook his reckoning, was not awaked at the proper time, and never revived" (Crooke, *Things Indian,* 202).

46. Gaborieau, *Les ordres mystiques,* 118.

5

Expansion of Sai Baba's Fame (1886–1900)

The fourteen year period between 1886 and 1900 witnessed a sensible growth in Sai Baba's renown. Beginning in 1890, pilgrims from quite distant areas found their way to Shirdi, attracted by Sai's fame as miracle worker.

It is also in these years, that the already mentioned Das Ganu Maharaj and one Narayan Govind Chandorkar,[1] came to Baba.[2] These two figures would play significant roles in the expansion of Baba's cult.

Narasimhaswami, for example, viewed Chandorkar as Baba's "Saint Paul," because of his missionary zeal. Chandorkar was perhaps the only person whom Sai Baba searched for, requesting him to come to Shirdi, as if perceiving in him a man necessary for his work. A *brāhmaṇ* by birth, Chandorkar attained the position of deputy collector at a young age. He was respected as a pious and learned man, having graduated in philosophy and having supplemented his college studies by careful examination of Vedāntic Shastras. He was possibly in his thirties when he first met Baba.[3]

Also among local villagers we find important figures of *bhaktas*. Apart from the well-known Mhalsapati, Tatya Kote, Bayajibai, and so on, another significant devotee was Madhavrao Deshpande (d. 1940), better known as Shyama. He lived in close contact with Sai Baba, often acting as intermediary between Baba and the devotees. Many of the episodes contained in the sources see him as coprotagonist.[4]

Sai Baba maintained his usual life-style right up until his death. With the progressive increase of visitors, his *darbārs* increased in length, probably inspiring him to be more articulate in his teachings (*upadeśa*). The sources report an intensification in Baba's miraculous activities, which present a remarkable variety in their typology.

Sai Baba's periods of *dhunī* contemplation and solitary vagaries must have necessarily been abbreviated. Once, he is reported to have been disturbed during the night by noisy visitors, while praying to Allah in the *masjid* in order to prevent the death from plague of the wife of one Nigoj Patil.[5]

Concerning worship of him, Sai Baba's systematic *pūjā* was inaugurated only in 1908.

For an examination of the years 1886–1900, I will limit myself to the consideration of those relevant episodes for which available sources furnish an approximate date.

The first one is a prediction about Shirdi's glorious future:

> Long before N. G. Chandorkar and others arrived, i.e., in the eighties of the last century, Baba spoke of the future of Shirdi. Baba told Bhagat and others who were with him at the chavadi: "In this place (Shirdi) there will be huge storeyed buildings rising. Big fairs will be held, and big men, Subhedars, and others will be coming. My Brahmins will gather, and elephants, horses and Shankar Nana[6] will also come. Guns will be fired (Dhadanga Dishe Udenga)." People hearing this began to smile. They thought: "What, all this for this worthless nook of an insignificant hamlet." But some decades later, every one of Baba's statements came true.[7]

If not an hagiographic interpolation, this story would indicate Baba's awareness of future events, when Shirdi became an important pilgrimage center.

A second episode, dated around 1888, is presented in the text *Ambrosia in Shirdi,* a collection of narratives:

> Shri Prangondji and his wife Manigouri came to Baba for His darshan. Baba blessed them. Afterwards, His Holiness Shri Sai Sharan Anand was born to them on 5–4–1889 [April 5, 1889] at Mota village, Bardoli Taluka in Surat district and named by them Shri Vaman Rao Prana Govind Patel. When he was three years of age, he fell sick.... At that time, Baba disguised as a Fakir had gone to his house and given His Udi. He asked the mother to give it to her son, mixing it with water, and told her that, since there was a scar on the child's right side of the back, he would become a Satpurusha. The Udi was administered to him and the child was miraculously saved by Baba.[8]

Granting offspring to childless couples and operating cures through *udī* are frequently attested to by sources. Again, Baba is presented as a miracle worker and a doctor (*hakīm*). The belief that Sai Baba may manifest himself under disguise is a common hagiographic feature up to this day.

The belief that highly developed souls have particular bodily

My interpreter in Shirdi, the Svāmin Shekar Rao, proudly displays a sack which Sai Baba gave his devotee Tatya Kote Patil, as a blessing to cure barrenness. The sack is symbolical of pregnancy and maternity.

signs, such as scars, moles, or birthmarks, is a recurrent theme within Indian spirituality. For instance, Uddhao Madhavrao Deshpande, son of Shyama, told me that Sai Baba had "a very big mole on his shoulder," evidently in order to emphasize Baba's extraordinary nature. Another peculiar bodily characteristic attributed to Sai Baba was recounted to me both by Uddhao and another old villager known as "Bappa Baba." The latter stated: "Sai Baba had very long arms: the ends of his fingers reached down to his knees. This is called 'jānubāhu' in Hindi."

This characteristic figures as the eighteenth in the traditional Buddhist list of the thirty-two bodily signs of a great man (*mahāpuruṣa lakṣaṇāni*). The French scholar M. E. Burnouf commented, "We know that such a quality is one of those with which Brahman poets especially like to honor their Indian heroes."[9]

A third story is based on the testimony which Dabholkar got from old Mhalsapati, and is entitled "The Pseudo-guru Javhar Ali."[10] V. B. Kher dates the episode around 1890.[11]

> Five years after the wrestling bout mentioned above, one Fakir from Ahmednagar, by name Javhar Ali, came to Rahata with his disciple and stayed in a Bakhal (open space) near Virabhadra[12] temple. The Fakir was learned, could repeat the whole Koran and had a sweet tongue. Many religious and devout people of the village came to him and began to respect him. With the help of the people, he started to build an Idga[13] (a wall before which Mahomedans pray on Idga day) near the Virabhadra temple. There was some quarrel about this affair, on account of which Javhar Ali had to leave Rahata. Then he came to Shirdi and lived in the masjid with Baba. People were captured by his sweet talk. He also bewitched Baba and began to call him his disciple. Baba did not object and consented to be his chela. Then both Guru and chela decided to return to Rahata and live there.[14] The Guru never knew his disciple's worth, but the disciple knew the defects of the Guru, still he never disrespected him, observing carefully his duties. He even served the master in various ways.[15] They used to come to Shirdi occasionally but their main stay was in Rahata. The loving devotees of Baba in Shirdi did not like that Baba should stay away from them in Rahata. So they went...to take Baba back to Shirdi. When they met Baba near the Idga and told the purpose for which they came, Baba said that the Fakir was an ill-tempered fellow. He would not leave him and added that they should return to Shirdi without him before the Fakir returned. While they were thus talking, the Fakir turned up and was very angry with them for trying to take away his disciple. There was some discussion and it was finally decided that both the Guru and the chela should return to Shirdi.[16] And so they returned and lived in Shirdi. But after a few days the Guru was tested by Devidas and found wanting. Twelve years before Baba arrived in Shirdi with the marriage-party, this Devidas, aged about 10 or 11, came to Shirdi and lived in the Maruti temple. Devidas had fine features and brilliant eyes.

> He was dispassion incarnate, and a Jnani. Many persons, namely Tatya Kote, Kashinath, and others regarded him as their Guru. They brought Javhar Ali in his presence and in the discussion that followed, Javhar was worsted and fled from Shirdi. He went and stayed in Vaijapur and returned after many years to Shirdi and prostrated himself before Sai Baba. The delusion that he was Guru and Sai Baba his chela was cleared away and, as he repented, Sai Baba treated him with respect. In this case Sai Baba showed by actual conduct how one should get rid of egoism and do the duties of a disciple to attain the highest end, viz., self-realization.[17]

Though such a glorious ending inscribes the whole narrative within a hagiographic frame, this episode presents some interesting facets. In the first place, the idea that Sai Baba accepted the role as disciple of an unknown *faqīr* said to be a knower of the holy Koran, confirms his Muslim background. Narasimhaswami's version tells us that when Javhar Ali (here identified as a *maulānā*) came to Shirdi, he noted that Baba had a Hindu following worshipping him at the *masjid*. Thus, he called upon Baba, and asked him whether he knew the Koran and the *sharī'at*. But Baba had learned neither. Thus, the *maulānā* ordered him to accompany him to Rahata, evidently for some kind of religious training.[18]

Sai Baba's acceptance of Javhar Ali as his teacher at this particular juncture (when his Hindu devotees were already rendering him *pūjā*), serves the function of emphasizing Baba's exemplary virtues of equanimity and humility. Moreover, Baba's supposed decision to reside for some time with a *maulānā* could not but gladden the Muslim minority of Shirdi, who needed to receive some assurances relative to his orthodoxy.

The fact that his Hindu devotees went to Rahata in order to convince him to come back to Shirdi, if true, would indeed constitute an example of Sai Baba's growing popularity.

The account of public debate in which Devidas defeats Javhar Ali reflects a hagiographic typology: the superiority of Hindu *jñāna* over Muslim doctrine. The custom of holding philosophical and religious debates, however, is not uncommon in village India.

A fourth story sees Baba involved in a young man's marriage preparations. The *Charters and Sayings* reports:

> Lakshman Govind Munge went in 1890 to Rahata and there met Sai Baba.[19]
>
> Baba—Come child, I was thinking of you yesterday. Come,

eat this mango and shampoo my leg. What have you come for?

Munge—My marriage is settled. I have no jewels. I have come to borrow jewels (from my relations).

Baba—Who is whose? Who gives? Who receives? None will give timely help. If you need 1,000 Rupees or 2,000 Rupees (worth of ornaments), receive it from me.

Munge (thinks)—How is this poor Fakir to give me 2,000 Rupees of jewels?

His relatives (as foretold by Baba) refused to help. Then a Gujarati Sovcar,[20] at Sinner, was induced by Munge's friend to lend him 2,000 Rupees worth of jewels, for a payment of 25 Rupees cash. Thus, the marriage was celebrated.[21]

There are numerous episodes in which Baba is said to allow or inspire marriage plans. He advised most of his devotees to lead a normal family life, discouraging "mystical flights" and condemning ascetic excesses.[22] Indeed, very few were the persons whom he encouraged to take the path of renunciation (*saṃnyāsa*).

In the above episode, Sai Baba is very cordial with the young man. Indeed, his words: "If you need 1,000 or 2,000 Rupees receive it from me" appear disconcerting, implying that material as well as spiritual riches are at his disposal.

The questions that Baba poses are the seeds of important teachings that aim at awakening the mind to crucial existential issues. "Who is whose? Who gives? Who receives?" are the classic interrogations which a wise person must consider. The last part of the first verse of the *Īsha Upanishad*[23] (which Baba, almost certainly, knew) comes to mind: *Kasya svid dhanam*, "Of whom, indeed, is wealth?"[24]

In other circumstances, we read that Baba requested his devotees to meditate on the fundamental questions "Who am I? Who are we?"[25] Such a call to tread the path of knowledge (*jñāna-mārga*), reminds us of the teachings and meditative practices of Ramana Maharshi.[26] We shall later notice how in Baba's *upadeśa* various orientations intertwine and are fused in a perspective which nonetheless exalts the prominence of the *bhakti* element.

Interestingly, the *Charters and Sayings* reports an incident in which Baba refuses to accept money: "In 1890 Nana Saheb Nimonkar voluntarily offered a ten rupee note. [Baba responded,] 'I will not take this. I am a fakir.'"[27]

Baba's "faqīrness" and spirit of nonacceptance (*aparigraha*) are confirmed here. The request for *dakṣiṇā* would be inaugurated only in 1908, the same year in which formal *pūjā* was started.[28]

Around 1889 or 1890, Abdul Baḇa, then aged about twenty, came to Shirdi from Nanded. The story goes that Sai Baba appeared in a dream to Amiruddin, Abdul's *faqīr,* and gave him two mangoes, telling him to give the fruits to Abdul and send him to Shirdi. When he arrived at the village, Baba welcomed Abdul with the curious words: *Merā kāvā āyā,* that is, "My crow has come."

Abdul lived in a stable near the mosque, his main job being to feed five perpetually burning oil lamps, such as those at the *Leṇḍī, cāvaḍī, masjid,* and so forth. An interesting story is told about the lamp he kept at the *Leṇḍī* (*Nanda Dīpa*). Naraṣimhaswami reports:

> There was nothing above to protect it, and on its four sides 20 pieces of cloth were tied and the hole was covered with a zinc sheet. Baba used to sit behind that lamp and order Abdul to fill up two pots with water and place them near him. Baba would pour out water in various directions from those pots. Why that was done, Abdul could not say, nor whether any mantra accompanied the action. Except Abdul, no one else would be present when Baba scattered the water.[29]

Abdul often read the Koran at the mosque. Sometimes, Baba himself would open the Koran and make him recite some passages. We are told that Sai Baba would occasionally utter words, which Abdul wrote down in Marathi, and they became his main source of inspiration. About this notebook, Narasimhaswami says:

> There are prayers in it to Maruti from Baba. There are recitals of Avatars of Gods dovetailing Mohamed and the Dasa Avatars.... Maruti temple is next to the Dvaraka Mayi and on his way from the mosque to the chavadi, Baba had to pass in front of Maruti (some 20 yards off). Baba would then get Avesa[30] and 4 men could not keep him in check. When asked the reason, Baba said that his parents had dedicated him to Maruti, and so he was telling Maruti: "I am your brother."[31]

Abdul seems to have used his precious notebook not merely for daily reading but also for prophecy. He died in April 1954.

Bharadwaja's book refers to an event I already mentioned, which, nonetheless, may be useful to recall:

> He used to go to the Takia (the public resting place for Moslem visitors) at night and, in the company of sojourning

> fakirs, he would dance and sing melodiously, with small trinklets tied around his ankles. He sang mostly Persian or Arabic songs and sometimes, the more popular songs of Kabir. This went on till 1890. Subsequently too, he was fond of listening to Kavvalis and Kirtans and the chanting of the attributes of God.[32]

Thus, Sai Baba's habitual dances and chants stopped around 1890. After this date, perhaps due to his age, he simply listened to music, developing a more pensive attitude.[33]

The circumstance that Narasimhaswami and other sources view as a turning point in Sai Baba's relationship with the villagers, was his act of turning water into oil. The biography by M. V. Kamath and V. B. Kher assigns this episode to the year 1892.[34] In the evening, Baba would usually beg oil from the local shopkeepers, in order to illuminate the interior of the mosque. Indeed, both Hindu and Muslim temples are required to be illumined at night, so as to be accessible to pilgrims at all times. Thus, one night, Baba stepped out of the *masjid* in order to beg for his oil.

Narasimhaswami relates this episode in detail:

> So, he went round begging for oil from the vanis (oil mongers). There were only two such shops and they supplied him with oil, gratis. The oil pressman also (ganamdar or chakkiwala) supplied him with oil. One day it struck these people either that they should make Baba realize their importance or that they should have some fun at his expense and they told him mockingly that they had no oil. Baba had to return to his mosque with his oil tin pot (tumbler) empty. It was already dusk. The vanis and ganamdar came behind him to see what he was going to do in the darkness, i.e., to have some fun. Baba took some water from the water jar (water jars are always kept in the mosques for people to wash their feet before entering the sacred precincts) in the tumbler, and shaking up the little bit of oil sticking to the tin, drank it up. Then he took pure water from the water pot and filled his four earthen lamps with it. He placed in each of them a cotton wick and struck up a match and lighted it. The spectators thought at first that cotton soaked in water could not possibly be lit up. But to their great surprise, the lamps were lit up and went on burning the whole night. After a little time, consternation seized the guilty vanis and ganamdar, and being terribly afraid that Baba, having shown himself to be a man of mystic

power, might curse them..., fell at his feet and prayed that he should not curse them.[35]

Baba reproached them for not having told the truth, since falsehood offends God, who is truth (*satya*). Moreover, he pointed out how mean and asocial their refusal of giving oil had been, since light was necessary to allow people inside the mosque. He also scolded them for having followed him with the aim of making fun of him.

According to Narasimhaswami, this was the first "public" miracle performed by Baba. The young *faqīr* came at that point to be regarded as a magician of great powers. The miracle of changing water into oil appears to be a prodigy often attributed to heterodox Sufis. The reformist Sufi Abu'l-Hasan Qadiri (d. 1635), warning of the dangerous tendencies of these *majzūbs,* said:

> ...They are involved with various kinds of magic,
> like jugglers.
> They change water to oil.
> They indulge in giving out prophecy;
> Within a moment they change into a boy, or disappear.[36]

Narasimhaswami reports an interesting episode of how some Muslims, led by a *qāzi*[37] of Sangamner, tried to oppose Sai Baba's worship in the *masjid.* V. B. Kher refers this episode to the year 1894:

> But some (Muslims) were still dissatisfied with the puja that was being done to Baba, and some of the more vigorous opponents of his puja went to consult the Sangamner Kazi for finding a remedy. That Kazi found that the only chance of obstructing this heterodox (*haram*) puja was by threat of force. The Hindus were no doubt the majority in the village, but the actual worshippers were only a handful, and a few muscular Muslims, standing at the entrance to the Mosque, and threatening force could stop this *haram*. Accordingly a very stout, muscular, powerful and well built Muslim, by name Tambuli,[38] and four or five others went up to the entrance to the Mosque and stood there with clubs one morning. The chief worshipper, Mhalsapati, was a very slim, meek, and apparently cowardly sort of person, and they hoped to stop his puja by their threats. Tambuli went and explained to Mhalsapati the exact situation, namely, that he ran the risk of being clubbed by the Muslims if he entered the Mosque and applied sandal paste to Baba. Mhalsapati, in his great shock and grief,

> prayed to Khandoba and hit upon an alternative. He went up to the compound wall of the Mosque and without entering into the Mosque, used all the puja articles (that he had brought on a plate) for worshipping a part of the compound wall itself into which he invoked Baba. After such invocation or Avahana, he went on applying water, flowers, scents, etc. to the wall. Baba...asked him what he was doing. Mhalsapati explained that the Muslims there threatened to beat any one who would enter into the Mosque and worship Baba with sandal paste, etc. Then Baba judged the situation very correctly and said: "Come in. Go on doing your puja. Apply your sandal paste here, there and anywhere. Let me see who will beat you."[39] So saying he dashed his satka, a short club,...on the ground with such thunderous sound that the few Muslims at the entrance trembled. They found that they would have to reckon with Baba himself if they wished to pursue their plan, and Baba, individually and physically, would be more than a match for them.[40] Besides, Baba was a weird personality who could turn water into oil, and they had therefore greater fear in trying to oppose Baba. So they considered discretion the better part of valour and retreated quietly. Mhalsapati entered and carried on the worship. Mhalsapati feared that they might attack him on his way back home, and told Baba of his fears. Baba then gave him the assurance that not merely these, but any others who would come to attack him, not merely at that time but at any time in any other place, and not merely in this janma, but in future janmas also, could do him no harm and Baba would see to it. Thus assured, Mhalsapati finished his puja and was not molested. Thus all joined in Baba's worship.[41]

Sai Baba seems to have encouraged the aspirations of all persons, disregarding barriers of sex, caste, and so forth, as long as they were motivated by pure and loving intentions. Since Mhalsapati was moved by sincere *bhakti*, Baba rewarded him.[42] The acceptance of the *pūjā* on Baba's part, however, appears not to be the true issue. Here what really stands out is the Muslims' violent disposition, which he angrily condemns. Paradoxically, in the Muslim determination of violently stopping the *haram* and Baba's reaction to it, Hindus found new encouragement for their *pūjā* practice.

The orthodox Muslims calmed down, though from time to time the sources inform us of new tensions. For example, once some Muslims told Baba that they wanted to cut the throat of all the crazy Hindu worshippers. Sai answered them saying that *he* was the true *pāgal* responsible for their conduct, and thus, if anybody's throat needed to be cut, they should better cut his.[43]

The Muslims, though a minority in the village, played an important role in Baba's life. More of them came to Shirdi in later years, attracted by the saint's fame. One who visits the village today will notice, side by side with four Hindu *samādhis,*[44] the *dargāh* of Abdul Baba, one of Sai Baba's closest devotees known for his high spiritual attainments.[45] In my opinion, the percentage of Muslim followers of Sai Baba during his lifetime, might be estimated around 10 percent.

The text *Ambrosia in Shirdi* reports the conversion of one of Chandorkar's friends:

> Shri Balasaheb Bhate and Shri Nanasaheb Chandorkar were college friends. Shri Balasaheb Bhate was a sceptic. He first came to Shirdi in 1894.[46] He was a Mamlatdar at Sakuri.[47] A Sant by name Bhau Maharaj came to Bhate. The Sant made Kirtan about Kabir and Kamal.[48] Bhate heard this attentively and patiently.... Afterwards,[49] he came to Shirdi and Baba made him stay for six months on leave. He did not go to duty even after the six months. His Superior (Personal Assistant to the Revenue Commissioner) came to Shirdi, and asked Bhate to rejoin duty. Bhate refused.... From that time, he left his post of Mamlatdar.
>
> Kakasaheb Dikshit,[50] Nanasaheb Chandorkar and Madhavrao Deshpande (Shama) went to Baba, as they were very anxious about Bhate's family after he gave up his job. Baba told him to write an application for a pension. Bhate filled out an application, as he had served for 13 years. By the grace of Baba, he got a pension of Rs. 29 per month without trouble. This shows how a sceptic turned into an ascetic and a staunch devotee of Baba.[51]

Similar cases of conversion to religious life were not infrequent, though Baba seldom encouraged the abandonment of family and social ties.

The text *Ambrosia in Shirdi* recounts the first visit to Shirdi of Ganapat Rao Dattatreya Sahasrabuddhe, better known as Das Ganu Maharaj: "Shri Das Ganu first came to Shirdi in 1896[52] and took darshan of Baba on frequent instigation of Nanasaheb Chandorkar. He was not a man to believe in another's words. He will test everything and believe himself."[53]

Das Ganu was born in Akolner, Ahmednagar district, in 1868.

He was a police constable, and when he first came to Shirdi, he came as the "orderly" of Chandorkar. Besides his ambition of becoming a subinspector, he was a skilled composer of village dramas and *lāvaṇī* poetry.[54] A learned man, Das Ganu was especially good at *kīrtans*. He had a fine metallic voice and was a very able performer.

Sai Baba gave a definite spiritual orientation to Das Ganu's life. The latter wrote commentaries on religious texts, such as Jñāndev's *Amritānubhava,*[55] Narada's *Bhaktisūtra,*[56] and so forth. He also wrote devotional works celebrating the lives of famous Marathi saints, including Sai Baba (see the *Bhaktalīlāmrita* and the *Shri Sainath Stavanamanjari*).[57] Often compared to Mahipati because of his diction and his expert handling of the *ovī* verse, he wrote a total of about two hundred thousand *ovīs*.[58] In 1903 he gave up his job in the police department and became one of Sai's closest *bhaktas*.[59]

Another episode sees Baba concerned with granting offspring to Mhalsapati:

> Mhalsapati's main work was to be with Baba, and he never failed to be with and sleep with Baba. But on one occasion..., about 1896, Baba himself said: "Arre Bhagat, listen to my fakiri words, which are always true. You are coming and sleeping here and not with your wife. But you have got only daughters (the only son he had must have died before 1896). Daughters are like tamarind fruit but a son is like a mango fruit. You go and take bed in your house, and you will then get a son." In spite of Baba's pressure, Mhalsapati declined to go home as he did not want his family (samsara) to increase. But his friend, Kasiram Simpi, compelled him and took him home and left him there. Thereafter he took his bed in his house. He started it on the Janmashtami of 1896, and on the next Janmashtami (1897) a son was born to him. Baba's words are ever true and never false. But, having got a son, he resumed his old vow of not developing samsara and ever afterwards slept only near Baba, in the Mosque, and at the chavadi.[60]

Another text anticipates the birth of a male son to Mhalsapati by seven years:

> Baba asked him to sleep in his own house. A son was born to him by Baba's grace on the Gokulashtami day of 1890, named Martanda Mhalsapati, who is now 94 years of age.[61] Baba performed marriage of this Martanda Mhalsapati in the year

1910. He was doing puja work at the Khandoba temple in place of his father.[62]

Sai Baba's will that Mhalsapati should go home and beget a son curiously conflicts with the latter's desire of not entangling himself in *saṃsāra.*

The son's name Martanda (literally "sprung from a seemingly lifeless egg"), designating in Vedic sources the sun or the sun god, is indicative of Mhalsapati's devotion to Khandoba. The *Mallāri Māhātmya,* narrates the story of Martand Bhairav, that is, Shiva/Khandoba, and his exploit of defeating the demon Malla and his army. Martand Bhairav's appearance, in accordance with his Vedic origin, is like that of the sun. His clothing is golden and flaming, his teeth like flashing rubies.[63]

Baba was very fond of Martanda, granting him many favors. At Mhalsapati's death in 1922, Martanda took his father's place as the *pujārī* of the Khandoba temple. When I interviewed him in October 1985, he was still living in his father's house.[64]

In the above story, Sai Baba compares female progeny with tamarind fruit and male progeny with mango fruit. The opposition between the sour tamarind and the sweet mango is evident, implying the higher value of male offspring.

The *puli* tree (*Tamarindus indica*), is a favorite of the Muslims. One of the chief Ahmednagar pregnancy rites is the drinking of its acidulous juice.[65] In Kerala, the branches of the tree are considered to be the abode of female ethereal goddesses, whereas its trunk and lower stems and roots are reserved for evil spirits.[66]

The mango tree (*Mangifera indica*), is valued for its sweet fruit and pleasant shade. Generally, it is never cut down, the belief being that the act of cutting it down may spell disaster. Its fruit is symbolic of male progeny, and for this reason it occupies a prominent place among *prasād* objects.[67]

The first festival performed in Baba's honor was the *urūs.* Of Arabic derivation, *urūs* or *urs* (literally, "marriage with God") is the most important festival at a *dargāh,* commemorating the anniversary of the death of a *pīr.* Here, however, it bears the generic sense of saint celebration[68] and, significantly, Baba had it coincide with the Hindu festival of *Rāmanavamī.*

The *Shri Sai Satcharita* reports:

> Mr. Gopalrao Gund, a Circle Inspector at Kopergaon, was a great devotee of Baba. He had no issue. With Sai Baba's blessings, a son was born to him. In the joy he felt regarding the

> event, an idea of celebrating a fair or "Urus" occurred to him in the year 1897, and he placed it for consideration before other Shirdi devotees, viz. Tatya Patil, Dada Kote Patil and Madhavrao Deshpande. They all approved of the idea and got Sai Baba's permission and blessings.... The day for the Urus was fixed on the Rama-Navami day after consultation with Sai Baba. It seems He had some end in view in doing this, viz. the unification of the two fairs or festivals...and the unification of the two communities, the Hindus and the Mahomedans. As future events showed, this end or object was achieved.[69]

Again, Baba is said to grant male offspring to a childless couple. *Rāmanavamī* was, for many years, the only Hindu festival that Baba showed interest in celebrating. As previously noted, the name of Rama was certainly dear to him, and it may have to do with his identification with Kabir, though the latter didn't have in mind Vishnu's seventh *avatāra* when extolling Rama's name.

The fact that an *urs* was held in Baba's honor confirms his roots in Sufi religiosity as well as the importance of the Islamic component among his devotees. That the Hindus accepted the proposal of celebrating the *urs,* and that both the latter and the *Rāmanavamī* festival could be celebrated side by side, shows the high degree of tolerance achieved between the two communities.

The *Shri Sai Satcharita* adds that, during the festival, water was scarce and brackish. Sai Baba turned it sweet by throwing flowers into a well. Temporary shops had to be constructed and wrestling bouts were organized. Flags were taken in procession through the village and fixed at the two corners of the mosque.[70] Moreover:

> There was another procession started in this fair. This idea of "Sandal" procession originated with one Mr. Amir Shakkar Dalal, a Mahomedan Bhakta of Korahla. This procession is held in honor of great Moslem saints. Sandal, i.e., Chandan paste and scrapings are put in the thali (flat dishes), and these are carried with incense burning before them in procession, to the accompaniment of band and music through the village and, after returning to the masjid, the contents of the dishes are thrown on the "Nimbar" (niche) and walls of the masjid.... This work was managed by Mr. Amir Shakkar for the first three years, and thereafter by his wife. So, on that very day, the procession of the "Flags" by the Hindus and that of "Sandal" by the Moslems went on side by side and are still going on without any hitch.[71]

Perin S. Bharucha, however, reports that this "Sandal" procession was started on *Rāmanavamī* day five years later, that is, in 1902.[72]

Apparently, Tatya Kote Patil looked after all external affairs, while the internal management of the festival was left to one Radhakrishna Mai, a female devotee of Baba. Feeding the poor was an important aspect of the fair, which Baba particularly cared for. The *Shri Sai Satcharita* reports that in the first years of the festival's celebration, about five to seven thousand people came to Shirdi.[73]

Thus, Sai Baba's ideal of mutual tolerance between Hindus and Muslims was made operative. The *faqīr* never encouraged the notion of the homologous nature of the two religions, that is, the idea that Hinduism and Islam are the same, though he underlined the basic ethical values that all religions share: truth, love, peace, justice, nonviolence, and so forth. Contrary to a generic syncretistic approach, he urged his followers to achieve a deeper understanding of *their own* faith. This, in his view, would lead to the discovery of the ultimate identity and oneness of all paths in the final mystical experience (*waḥdat al-wujūd, advaita*). For this reason he opposed the idea of conversion from one religion to another. In the *Charters and Sayings*, we read: "Bade Baba (Fakir Baba) brought with him a recent Hindu convert to Islam to the mosque. Sai Baba, slapping that convert on the cheek: 'Ah! you have changed your father!'"[74]

The biography by A. E. Bharadwaja reports Baba's appearance as Dattatreya in the year 1900: "Binnevala, a close relation of Nanasaheb Chandorkar, was a worshipper of Lord Datta. He saw Sai Baba in about 1900, but only to please Nanasaheb. When he entered the Dwarakamayi, Sai Baba appeared to him as Lord Datta."[75]

This kind of *camatkār* is frequently attested in all hagiographic literature. Baba is said to have identified himself with Maruti, Satyanarayana, Ganapati, Narasimha, Khandoba, and so forth.[76] He is also reported having identified himself with *maulānās*, as well as with a Muslim saint of the Moghul period.[77]

Such practice calls to mind the analogous claims made by the Bengali ecstatic Gadadhara Chatterji (1836–86), better known as Shri Ramakrishna. His identifications came in progressive stages, as Romain Rolland describes: "He became the person of Rama by stages, through the people who served Rama, beginning with the humblest, Hanuman. Then in reward, as he himself believed, Sita appeared to him."[78]

After having experimented with the beliefs and practices of different religious traditions (Hinduism, Islam, Christianity), he claimed that each path led finally to the same ineffable goal.[79]

Finally, sources inform us about Baba's habit of sleeping on a precarious wooden plank hung from the ceiling:

> Mr. Nanasaheb Dengle[80] brought for Sai Baba a wooden plank about 4 cubits in length and only a span in breadth for sleeping upon.[81] Instead of keeping the plank on the floor and then sleeping on it, Baba tied it like a swing to the rafters of the Masjid with old shreds or rags and commenced to sleep upon it. The rags were so thin and worn out that it was a problem how they could bear or support the weight of the plank itself, let alone the weight of Baba. But somehow or other—it was Baba's sheer Leela that the worn out rags did sustain the plank, with the weight of Baba on it. On the four corners of this plank, Baba lighted panatis (earthen lamps), one at each corner, and kept them burning the whole night. It was a sight for the gods to see Baba sitting or sleeping on this plank! It was a wonder to all how Baba got up and down off the plank. Out of curiosity, many observers kept a watch over the process of mounting and dismounting, but none succeeded. As crowds began to increase to detect this astonishing feat, Baba one day broke the plank into pieces and threw it away.[82] Baba had all the eight Siddhis (powers) at His command. He never practiced nor craved for them. They came to Him naturally as a result of His perfection.[83]

Narasimhaswami thinks that Baba's breaking the plank may have occured about 1898.[84] In the *Charters and Sayings* he reports that H. S. Dikshit, soon after this, decided to offer Sai a cot to lie upon. This, however, does not tally with the 1898 date, since Narasimhaswami places Dikshit's first arrival in Shirdi eleven years later, that is, in 1909.[85]

Sai Baba told Dikshit:

> Baba: No. Am I to lie on a cot, leaving Mhalsapati on the floor? Far better would it be that I should be on the floor and that he should sleep higher.
>
> Dikshit: I will give two planks; one for you, one for Mhalsa.
>
> Baba: He will not sleep on a plank. He will sleep only on the ground. Sleeping on the plank is no joke. Who will sleep keeping eyes open, all awake like me? Only such a person can lie on the plank. When I lie down on the ground, I ask Mhalsapati to sit by me and keep his palm on my chest. So, you see

Sai Baba's cāvaḍī

> that a plank will be of no use to him. I lie down making mental Namasmarana. So, I say to Mhalsapati: "Feel it by placing your hand on my heart. If you catch me napping, wake me up." Such was and is my order to him.[86]

Narasimhaswami thinks that, prior to 1898, Mhalsa's and Tatya Kote's habit of sleeping near Baba was customary only at the *cāvaḍī*. After Baba's breaking of the plank, they began sleeping near him at both the *cāvaḍī* and the mosque. Thus, there would appear to be a conflict with what the *Shri Sai Satcharita* states,[87] unless we are willing to interpret its references to a time after 1898. It could also be supposed that Baba made use of the plank for just a short period, and that before and after it he slept at both the *cāvaḍī* and the *masjid* together with his closest *bhaktas*.

Sai's assertion of practicing a mental form of *nāmasmaraṇa*, avoiding sleep, is of particular interest. Such use indeed constituted the central focus of his spiritual practice. He often advised his disciples to engage in it, and we may recall how it was apparently only after Hari, moved by his *nāmasmaraṇa*, revealed himself, that Sai started administering the *udī*.

Once again, Sai Baba is presented as a miracle worker. We

know that the power of becoming extremely light is one of the eight traditional *siddhis* and that Patañjali's *Yogasūtra* mentions, in *sūtra* 42 of its *Vibhūti pāda,* the power of levitation. Apart from any speculation, however, Baba's feat of the plank finds a striking parallel in a story concerning the Marathi saint of Kanhangad Nityananda (d. 1961), future preceptor of the *Svāmin* Muktananda (1908–82), who met him in 1947. I bring the chapter to a close by quoting this episode:

> As is the custom with many Hindus, the narrator of this incident invited the thin, dark sadhu home to stay for the night, as he was impressed by the bearing of the young man. Given a room, the sadhu asked him for a string. Wondering at this strange request, the host decided to sleep in the same room. When he returned, he was surprised to see the young man carefully attaching the string to swing between two walls. The host was even more surprised a few minutes later, when the young sadhu climbed up on the string, stretched out, and went to sleep! He was apparently totally comfortable, as he turned this way and that, a picture of complete rest and tranquility.
>
> Remembering similar incidents in the life of Sai Baba of Shirdi, the devotee lay there, lost in the sheer wonder of it.[88]

Notes

1. Popularly known as Nanasaheb.

2. V. B. Kher argues that Chandorkar first met Sai Baba in 1891, whereas Das Ganu met Sai Baba a year later, that is, in 1892. See Kamath and Kher, *Sai Baba,* 8.

3. On Narayan Govind Chandorkar, see Narasimhaswami, *Life of Sai Baba,* 2:43–121. Baba once said that they had been intimate with each other for the last four births; see Narasimhaswami, *Charters and Sayings,* 211.

4. Shyama's son, Uddhao, was still alive in 1985 and was one of my most valuable informants.

5. See Narasimhaswami, *Life of Sai Baba,* 2:13–14.

6. Literally, "an auspicious or beneficent elder"; an expression designating influential people.

7. Narasimhaswami, *Life of Sai Baba,* 2:18.

8. Ramalingaswami, *Ambrosia in Shirdi* (Shirdi: Shri Sai Baba Sansthan, 1984), 171–72. V. B. Kher reports that Shri Sai Sharan Anand first met Sai Baba on December 11, 1910; see Kamath and Kher, *Sai Baba*, 9.

9. M. E. Burnouf, "Sur les trente-deux signes caractéristiques d'un grand homme," in *Le Lotus de la Bonne Loi (Traduit du Sanscrit): Accompagné d'un commentaire et de vingt et un mémoires relatifs au buddhisme* (1852; reprint, Paris: Adrien Maisonneuve, 1989), 569. My translation from the French.

10. Deriving from Urdu, the correct transliteration of this proper name is Jauhar Ali.

11. Kamath and Kher, *Sai Baba*, 8.

12. Name of a terrifying form of Shiva, embodiment of his wrath. On Virabhadra, see David M. Knipe, "Night of the Growing Dead: A Cult of Vīrabhadra in Coastal Andhra," in Hiltebeitel, *Criminal Gods*, 123–56.

13. The term derives from *īd* (festival). An *īdgāh* is an open place, were a wall is constructed on a raised platform on the western outskirts of a village. Here, the ritual prayer (*namāz*) is performed. The Muslim year has two canonical festivals, namely the *īd al-aḍḥā* or "sacrificial festival," celebrated on the tenth *Dhu'l-Hidjdja*, and the *īd al-fiṭr* "festival of breaking the fast," on the first *Shawwāl*. In India, the *īd al-aḍḥā* is called *bakra īd*.

14. Sai Baba seems to have stayed in Rahata for no longer than a two-month period; see Narasimhaswami, *Life of Sai Baba*, 1:27.

15. Narasimhaswami reports: "Baba did humble *seva* to this Guru, carrying water pots,...lighting up fire, doing hard physical work which others would complain of." See ibid.

16. According to Narasimhaswami's account, Javhar Ali accepted only on condition that both he and Baba might be fed and supported by the people of Shirdi; see ibid.

17. Gunaji, *Shri Sai Satcharita*, 28–29.

18. See Narasimhaswami, *Life of Sai Baba*, 1:26–28.

19. At the time, Sai Baba was staying in Rahata with Javhar Ali. V. B. Kher notes that Shankarrao Raghunath Deshpande, also called Nanasaheb Nimonkar (*ināmdār* of Nimon), also met Sai Baba for the first time in 1890 at the Maruti temple in Rahata.

20. Contraction of the term *sāhūkār* (moneylender, private banker, or rich man).

21. Narasimhaswami, *Charters and Sayings*, 251–52.

22. See ibid., 109–11, 183.

23. The *Īsha Upanishad,* comprising only eighteen verses, is the shortest of the main thirteen Upanishads. It belongs to the white *Yajurveda* collection and constitutes the fortieth and last chapter of the *Vajasaneyi Saṃhitā*. Probably the oldest of the Upanishads in verse, it closes with a prayer of the dying to Pushan, that is, to the sun (as in *Bṛhad. Up.* 5.15), wishing for the vision of universal unity.

24. In the first verse of the *Īsha Upanishad,* M. K. Gandhi saw one of the highest exhortations to universal brotherhood.

25. Narasimhaswami, *Charters and Sayings,* 24–26.

26. An interesting comparison between Ramana Maharshi and Sai Baba's teachings is offered by A. Osborne, *Incredible Sai Baba,* 81–93.

27. Narasimhaswami, *Charters and Sayings,* 265.

28. On such issues, see the following chapter.

29. Narasimhaswami, *Life of Sai Baba,* 3:173.

30. Possession.

31. Narasimhaswami, *Life of Sai Baba,* 3:173n.

32. Bharadwaja, *Sai Baba,* 16.

33. Still, as noted, in the years 1911–12 G. S. Khaparde reported having seen Baba skipping and dancing. G. G. Narke also added that Baba would do so in his mother's presence; Narasimhaswami, *Life of Sai Baba,* 1:20n.

34. See Kamath and Kher, *Sai Baba,* 8.

35. Narasimhaswami, *Life of Sai Baba,* 1:22. See also Gunaji, *Shri Sai Satcharita,* 27–28.

36. See Abu'l-Hasan Qadiri, *Sukh Anjan,* quoted in Eaton, *Sufis of Bijapur,* 277.

37. The *qāzi* is a Muslim judge, appointed by the government to enforce Islamic Law.

38. Most certainly the same person which the *Shri Sai Satcharita* described wrestling with Baba; see Gunaji, *Shri Sai Satcharita,* 26.

39. According to another version, Baba said: "Come in and put sandal paste on my forehead, hands, chest and everywhere"; Narasimhaswami, *Charters and Sayings,* 258–59.

40. This passage corroborates the idea that Sai Baba was a strongly built man.

41. Narasimhaswami, *Life of Sai Baba,* 1:25–26.

42. Mhalsapati, whose family had been goldsmiths *(sonār)* for generations, indeed figures as Sai Baba's closest devotee in these early years. For a biographical sketch on this important figure, see Narasimhaswami, *Life of Sai Baba,* 2:1–42.

43. See Narasimhaswami, *Charters and Sayings,* 222.

44. These graves belong to Nanavalli Baba, V. P. Iyer, Kumbar Baba, and Tatya Kote Patil. The first three are under one roof by the side of the tomb of Abdul Baba.

45. An annual festival (*urs*) commemorating the death date of Abdul Baba was held by his son Abdul Pattan. On the important figure of Abdul Baba see Narasimhaswami, *Life of Sai Baba,* 3:171–77.

46. He probably came to Shirdi following Chandorkar's advice.

47. A *māmlātdār* is a *tālukā* revenue officer. Sakuri is a hamlet a few miles from Shirdi.

48. Kamal was Kabir's son. On the relationship between the two in Marathi hagiography, see the sixth chapter in Mahipati's *Bhaktavijaya,* trans. by Abbott and Godbole, *Stories of Indian Saints,* 92–108.

49. Possibly, several years later.

50. Hari Sitaram Dikshit (1864–1926), better known as Kakasaheb, was one of Baba's closest devotees and an influential lawyer and politician. Apparently, he met Sai for the first time only in 1909; Narasimhaswami, *Life of Sai Baba,* 2:157. Thus, Bhate's radical conversion probably took place after 1909.

51. Ramalingaswami, *Ambrosia in Shirdi,* 83–84.

52. Narasimhaswami, however, places Das Ganu's first arrival between 1890 and 1892. As previously noted, V. B. Kher argues that Das Ganu first met Sai Baba in 1892; see Kamath and Kher, *Sai Baba,* 8.

53. Ramalingaswami, *Ambrosia in Shirdi,* 121.

54. The *lāvaṇī,* together with the *povāḍā,* forms what might be called bardic poetry. The subject of a *lāvaṇī* is generally love, describing the pangs of separation or the joys of union in male-female relationships. A special kind of *lāvaṇī* is that of *Kalagī-turā,* suggesting two opposite religious views, *kalagī* representing *Śakti* or *Prakriti* and *turā* representing Shiva or *Purusha.* When it came to argument, each group strove to establish its own creed and the result was the *Bhedika lāvaṇī,* borrowed from the mystical literature of the saint-poets. Public contests between the two groups were frequent in the eighteenth and nineteenth centuries and often

ended in vulgar verbal bouts. On the *lāvaṇī*, see S. G. Tulpule, *Classical Marāṭhī Literature*, 437–42.

55. For a presentation of this work and its author, see chapter 9. Sources report that Das Ganu's inspiration for writing his commentaries was often due to the words he heard Baba say at the mosque.

56. A medieval Vaiṣṇava work, probably composed after Ramanuja's time (1017–1137). In eighty-four aphorisms, the sage Nārada explains the essence of the devotional approach to the divine. Liberation is said to be attained through grace (*kṛpā*) alone.

57. The most important, together with the *Bhaktalīlāmrita*, is the *Santakathāmrita*. Also worth mentioning is the *Shree Gajanan Vijay*, consisting of twenty-one chapters and of 3,668 *ovīs*, celebrating the life of the Shegaon saint Gajanan Maharaj (d. 1910), about whom more will be said later.

58. The word *ovī* comes from the verb *ovaṇẽ*, "to wreathe." The *ovī* meter, which was recitable and singable in its original form, consists of either six or eight syllables, the quantity as a rule being that of a long syllable: each one is similar to a *tāla-mātrā* or drum-beat unit. The origin of the *ovī* is to be found in folk-songs, as indicated by the famous line: *mahārāṣṭreṣu yoṣidbhiḥ ovī geyā tu kaṇḍane* (In Maharashtra the *ovī* is sung while pounding [the corn]).

59. On Das Ganu Maharaj, see Narasimhaswami, *Life of Sai Baba*, 2:122–54.

60. See ibid. 9–10.

61. This report was made in 1984. The opinions regarding Martanda's age, however, differ. In 1985, Martanda himself told me he was 108 years old (not 95), whereas Shyama Deshpande's son told me he was 92. The number 108 is important symbolically, representing an ideal of completeness and perfection.

62. Ramalingaswami, *Ambrosia in Shirdi*, 52.

63. On the *Mallāri Māhātmya* and Martand Bhairav, see John M. Stanley, "The Capitulation of Maṇi: A Conversion Myth in the Cult of Khaṇḍobā," in Hiltebeitel, *Criminal Gods*, 271–98.

64. Mhalsapati's *samādhi* was built in his own house. Therein one can also see some of the things given him by the saint: Baba's *kafnī*, Baba's stick (*daṇḍa*), Baba's *udī*, three silver rupees which were blessed by the *faqīr*, and one pair of Baba's *pādukās*.

65. See Crooke, *Religion and Folklore*, 412.

66. See P. Thankappan Nair, "Tree-Symbol Worship among the Nairs of Kerala," in Sankar Sen Gupta, ed. *Tree Symbol Worship in India: A New*

Survey of a Pattern of Folk-Religion (Calcutta: Indian Publications, 1965), 95.

67. See K. D. Upadhyaya, "Indian Botanical Folklore," in Gupta, *Tree Symbol Worship,* 10.

68. Unless we want to argue that the *urs* celebrated a local Sufi saint, particularly dear to Sai Baba.

69. Gunaji, *Shri Sai Satcharita,* 32.

70. Ibid. Placing flags at temples is a typically Hindu custom.

71. Ibid., 33.

72. See Bharucha, *Sai Baba,* 9.

73. For more details, Gunaji, *Shri Sai Satcharita,* 33–36.

74. Narasimhaswami, *Charters and Sayings,* 263.

75. Bharadwaja, *Sai Baba,* 36.

76. Ibid., 37–38.

77. See Narasimhaswami, *Charters and Sayings,* 13; also Bharadwaja, *Sai Baba,* 44.

78. Romain Rolland, *The Life of Ramakrishna* (Calcutta: Advaita Ashram, 1960), 37.

79. On Shri Ramakrishna, see Advaita Ashram, *Life of Sri Ramakrishna* (Calcutta, Advaita Ashram, 1948). Also, M (Mahendra Nath Gupta), *The Gospel of Sri Ramakrishna,* trans. Swami Nikhilananda (New York: Ramakrishna-Vivekananda Center, 1942).

80. In the *Shri Sai Satcharita,* he figures as the first devotee to have been blessed with offspring by Baba; see Gunaji, *Shri Sai Satcharita,* 27.

81. Approximately corresponding to 6. 6 feet in length and 9 inches in breadth. Narasimhaswami, however, has it differently: "It was only 5 feet long and about 15 inches broad, and lamps were loosely placed on it"; see *Charters and Sayings,* 115.

82. Narasimhaswami reports: "The wonder was how it could support him, and another wonder was how Baba could swing himself up into it (it was hung up 6 or 7 feet high) and jump down from it, without upsetting the lamps and snapping the threads. Das Ganu and others went to see the wonder and Baba in anger or disgust, broke the plank to pieces." See ibid., 115–16.

83. Gunaji, *Shri Sai Satcharita,* 57–58.

84. Narasimhaswami, *Life of Sai Baba,* 2:9n.

85. Ibid., 157.

86. Narasimhaswami, *Charters and Sayings,* 116.

87. See Gunaji, *Shri Sai Satcharita,* 48–49.

88. M. U. Hatengdi and Swami Chetanananda, *Nitya Sutras: The Revelations of Nityananda from the Chidakash Gita* (Cambridge, Mass.: Rudra Press, 1985), 120. For a brief sketch of Nityananda's life, see the article "Sri Nityananda" of J. Govindappa, in R. Sarath Babu ed., *Dattatreya: Glory of the Divine in Man* (Ongole, 1981). See also M. U. Hatengdi, *Nityananda: The Divine Presence* (Cambridge, Mass.: Rudra Press, 1984) and S. M. Bhatkhande, *Nityasūtrāṇi: A Bouquet of Celestial Songs of the Cidākāśa* (Bombay: Nityananda Institute of Culture, 1986).

6

Shirdi Becomes a Modern Pandharpur (1900–1910)

The sources report many episodes set during the last eighteen years of Sai Baba's life. I shall therefore condense my exposition to the few which best illuminate Baba's personality and teachings as well as the growing devotional cult surrounding him.

Ramalingaswami reports:

> Sri Vasudev Janardhan was a census clerk in 1901. Shri Nanasaheb Chandorkar was the census Superintendent. He compelled Vasudev to go over to Shirdi.... One day, at about 8 A.M., Vasudev, Nanasaheb Chandorkar and about 18 or 20 others went to Shirdi for Baba's darshan. Among them, Vasudev was the youngest one. At that time, Baba was smoking chillim (tobacco). As Vasudev was not a smoker, he felt nothing, but others were eager to get a puff from Baba. But Baba gave the chillim to Vasudev. He hesitated to smoke the chillim. Nanasaheb Chandorkar whispered to him to smoke it, saying that something nice would happen to him. Afterwards, he puffed the chillim thrice.... Baba did not give the chillim to others. After this incident, Vasudev got all the promotions he desired and retired from service with sufficient pension. He said that whatever he did in Baba's name, Baba fulfilled it.[1]

Again, Chandorkar is depicted as a missionary of sorts, leading people to Shirdi. He certainly was one of the most ardent propagators of Baba's fame in the region.

Baba is said to offer the *cilīm* to the only nonsmoker in the group, that is, young Vasudev. Sharing the pipe of a holy man, considered an honor and a token of intimacy and communion, is traditionally believed to carry a special blessing or reward due to one's good conduct.

For the year 1903, P. S. Bharucha reports the following:

> Sapatnekar was a lawyer, practising in Akalkot, in Sholapur district. In his student days, one of the boys in his class had been a young man named Shevde. Some time before the qualifying exams, a group of boys including Sapatnekar and Shevde gathered together to test each other's knowledge. It was discovered that, of the group, Shevde was the least prepared. All the boys teased Shevde about the impossibility of his succeeding, but Shevde, totally unruffled by the jokes, assured his friends that he was not worried because Sai Baba had promised him success. Sapatnekar..., drew him aside and asked about "this fellow, Sai Baba" in whose words he had such great confidence.
>
> "He is a fakir who lives in a mosque in Shirdi," Shevde explained. "He is a great saint. Besides, he is unique. Unless you have accumulated a great store of merit in your earlier lives, you can't even meet him. I believe in him because whatever he's told me has always come true. He has assured me that I will pass the exam and so I am confident that I will." Sapatnekar laughed at Shevde.[2]

Of course, the story goes that the boy passed the examination. Shevde identified Baba as a Muslim, that is, a *faqīr* living in a mosque and stressed the omniscience of Sai, a point insisted upon by all sources. This young man was presumably the son of a couple devoted to Baba living in the Ahmednagar area. Sai Baba seems to have assured school promotion on other occasions as well.[3]

We now examine four stories which see Nanasaheb Chandorkar as the recipient of Baba's grace. In the first three, Baba's wonderful powers help Chandorkar out of his difficulties. The fourth is a detailed account of Sai Baba's interpretation of *Bhagavadgītā* 4.34. All episodes are reported in Narasimhaswami's biography.

The first story runs as follows:

> Harischandra hill, forty miles away from Shirdi, was a noted hill with a Devi's shrine at the top. But the long stretch of barren rock between that temple and the bottom of the hill was one vast treeless, wild, rocky waste, where there was neither water to drink nor any shelter to hide in. Over that hill, Nana was climbing on a hot, summer day, and, after he had gone some distance, the heat of the sun and the toil of the journey told upon him. He felt very thirsty and asked the Sheristadar friend by his side for water. The latter replied that there was

none.... Nana felt the fatigue of climbing greatly, and said he could climb no longer. The Sheristadar asked him to come down. But Nana was unable to do that either, and quietly sat on a huge slab exclaiming: "If Baba were here, he would surely give me water to slake my thirst." The Sheristadar...remarked that such observations about "ifs" were useless. He added: "Baba is not here. What is the good of thinking what would happen if he were here?..."

Meanwhile at Shirdi, Sai Baba spoke out immediately in the presence of some devotees: "Hallo, Nana is very thirsty. Should we not give him a handful of water?..." But the persons around him, who had not the benefit of such vision, were wondering why Baba should talk of Nana's thirst.... People round about Baba could not make it out. Nor did Baba care to explain.

A little time after Nana made his exclamation about Baba, a Bhil, a hill tribesman, was seen coming down the hill towards the party.... Chandorkar accosted him saying: "Hallo! I am thirsty; can I get some water to drink?" People wondered that this Brahmin Deputy Collector should accost a Bhil, who is considered an untouchable or a low-caste man, and ask him for water.... He answered: "What! You ask for water?! Under the very rock on which you are seated, there is water!" So saying, the Bhil moved away and disappeared from view. Nana's subordinates and friends...immediately set about lifting up the slab...and lo and behold! There was just a palmful of water under that rock, attractive and cool.... Nana drank that water, his thirst was gone, and he was able to march higher up and complete his pilgrimage.

After the hill ascent and the darshan of the goddess at the temple,...some days later, Nana had occasion to go to Shirdi. As he stepped into Baba's Dwarakamayi the very first words that Baba uttered to him, before anybody could inform him about Nana's experience on the hill, were these: "Nana, you were thirsty; I gave you water. Did you drink?" Nana's eyes opened with joyous wonder.[4]

This well known story emphasizes Baba's *antarajñāna*. Indeed, his habit of uttering strange and apparently nonsensical words was often interpreted by devotees as referring to a situation that was taking place elsewhere. Once this "contact" was established Baba could intervene, altering the situation to the devotee's benefit. In the episode just given, a devotee might recognize either Baba in disguise, or an unaware agent of his will in the providential arrival of the Bhil. Detecting a water pool already in existence or appositely "created" by Baba, he might interpret the situation as Baba's *saṃkalpa* to augment Nana's faith in his omniscience.

Many kinds of interpretations, in other words, become possible. The awareness of such a peculiar hermeneutic situation is important, since it is part and parcel of the *bhaktas'* mentality and of the atmosphere generally surrounding a holy man. Baba, as usual, gave no explanation relative to his utterances and "miraculous performance."

The second episode runs as follows:

> In Padmalaya[5] forest, there is a Ganapati temple. It is ten miles away from the nearest railway station and the access to it is through ten miles of forest.... Nana's arrival at the railway station was in the evening, very near dusk. But he would not be thwarted. He determined to push along with his companions to the temple, come what may. In the absence of any conveyance, Nana...dared the risk and trouble of walking ten miles to reach the Ganapati temple. So he trudged on. But when he was about half way or more..., it was already 9 P.M. and the pujari of the temple would usually lock it up by 9 or 10 P.M. and retire to his cottage at some distance for his night's rest. So, Nana doubted whether he would get into the temple at all. Further, after having walked wearily six or seven miles, he felt the pangs of hunger. Naturally, he remembered Baba. He prayed: "Baba, I am not asking for much. I am not overgreedy. I will be quite satisfied if, at the end of this journey, I can get one cup of tea to quench my thirst...." It was nearly 11 P.M. when they reached the temple. Instead of the temple being closed..., the pujari was on the watch, and on seeing persons at a great distance...coming, he shouted: "Is Nana coming?" It would be highly impertinent on the part of any priest to call a Deputy Collector by his pet name, as though he was his chum. But here there was no feeling of resentment, but one of gratification.... They approached and said: "Yes. How do you know that Nana is coming?" Then the priest said: "I had an ethereal message from Sri Sai Baba in which he said: My Nana is coming weary, thirsty, and hungry. Keep for him one cup of tea." The priest said: "Here is the tea ready for you all." He then gave Nana his cup.[6]

In this story, as in the previous one, Chandorkar is presented as a pious man undertaking a pilgrimage: a devotional practice extremely popular among the Hindu masses, believed to procure innumerable merits (*puṇya*).[7]

Again, Baba's compassion and *antarajñāna* is celebrated. In both episodes, bodily needs, that is thirst and hunger, are what determine Baba's intervention.

The third episode occured in the year 1904:

> Nana was deeply concerned about the fate, health, and life of his daughter Minatai. About 1904 or so, Nana Chandorkar was Deputy Collector at Jamner (then unconnected by train with Jalgaon). He was at Jamner with his daughter, whose pregnancy was in a very advanced state. Unexpectedly the delivery, being her first, proved troublesome and risky. The pains were prolonged for many long hours, and the poor young lady suffered torture.... Nana knew that Baba was aware of everything, and that there was no necessity to send a telegram or letter to him.... Being a very orthodox and pious Brahmin, he started a Kashtanivarana Homa[8] with the help of his Sastri.... All the while, Baba was fully aware of what was going on at Jamner. At evening time, he called Ramgir Bua, a Gosavi, whom he used to call Babugir. Babugir was about to leave Shirdi. Baba commissioned him to go to Jamner, in order to deliver to Nana Chandorkar a packet of udhi and a set of papers containing Bhishma's aratis for the puja of Baba, modelled on the Pandharpur aratis.... Baba simply told him: "Babugir, go. Everything will be provided." Accordingly, the Gosavi started. He got off the train at Jalgaon and was in a quandary. Railway officials were troubling visitors coming by train from infected areas, with a view to enforce quarantine rules, and there was no method by which he could escape them and go to Jamner. Suddenly he found a liveried peon bawling out: "Who is Babugir of Shirdi?" Then this Bua said: "I am Ramgir Bua whom Baba calls Babugir, and I am from Shirdi." Then that peon said that he had been sent by his "master" with a tonga and a horse to take him to Jamner. He gave him a meal also. Babugir fancied that Baba had sent word or wired to Chandorkar, and thus provided conveyance and meal for him.
>
> The distance of 30 miles was soon covered by the tonga, and when very near Nana's quarters, the carriage stopped. The peon told Bua: "There is the master's house; you better go."
>
> Babugir got down for a natural purpose, and when he turned back and looked, there was no peon, no horse, no car-

riage, nothing at all.... But right in front of him was the Deputy Collector's house. So he went there and found Nana Chandorkar and his wife waiting. They had heard the rumble of a horse and carriage and were anxiously waiting. Babugir handed over to Nana the udhi saying: "This is Baba's udhi sent to you for your daughter's sake." At once the udhi was applied to Minatai, and thereafter it was no longer Minatai who was crying but her new born child, for she had easy delivery.

The arati paper also was handed over to Nana for his approval, so that it might be used for Baba's puja at Shirdi.

When Bua thanked the Deputy Collector for his timely sending of the cart and food, Nana was taken aback. He said he was not aware of anybody coming from Shirdi and so had not sent anything. Then both Bua and the Deputy Collector understood what Baba meant when he said: "Go, Babugir, everything will be provided." It was Baba's extraordinary powers that provided the carriage, the horse, the liveried peon and the meal, without Chandorkar knowing anything about them.[9]

This miraculous story is one of the most popular among Hindu devotees. Of great interest to us, though marginal to the narrative's context, is the sending of *ārtī* songs to Chandorkar, modelled on those in use at Pandharpur. These *ārtīs* were intended for individual worship only. That Nana's approval was needed shows the importance of this wealthy devotee in the development of Sai Baba's cult. By 1905, a detailed liturgy scheme had been elaborated.

The fact that Sai wanted Nana to examine the *ārtī* papers shows his decision of conceding to the will of the Hindu majority. In 1908, Baba's congregational worship would be officially inaugurated.

We now present Baba's exegesis of a verse of the *Bhagavadgītā*. This fragment of his technical *upadeśa* is the only one that has come down to us:

One day when Nana was massaging Baba's feet, he was mumbling something to himself. Baba asked him what it was. Nana said that it was a Sanskrit verse.

Baba: What verse?

Nana: A Gita verse.

Baba: Recite it audibly.

Then Nana gave out Bhagavad Gita, Chapter IV, verse 34, dealing with Sishya and Guru relationship....[10]

Baba asked Nana whether he knew the meaning of the verse and, if so, to give it. Nana gave the general purport, but Baba ordered him to give a word for word translation with strict reference to number, gender, case, tense, mood, and other parts of grammar. Nana wondered how the intricacies of Sanskrit grammar could be understood by Baba who showed no trace of linguistic, literary or any other education. Anyhow, he went on giving the word for word meaning. Then Baba began a cross-examination of the severest sort.

Baba: Well, what does "Tad" refer to?

Nana: Jnana.

Baba: Which Jnana?

Nana: Jnana referred to in the previous verse.

Baba: What does "Pranipata" mean?

Nana: It means prostration or bowing down.

Baba: What does "Pata" mean?

Nana: The same.

Then Baba asked: "If 'Pranipata' and 'Pata' mean the same thing, would the author (Vyasa) have used two extra needless syllables?"

Similarly, about "Pariprasna," Nana said: "'Pariprasna' means questioning, and 'Prasna' also means the same." When asked whether the author was again needlessly adding two syllables, Nana could not explain the difference.

Similarly about Seva. Nana said that it was merely service like massaging, which he was doing.

Baba: Nothing else?

Nana: Nothing else so far as I can see.

In that way, Baba questioned him, word after word and phrase after phrase, puzzling him also with the important question as to why Krishna, a Jnani, should send Arjuna to other Jnanis instead of giving him Jnana himself.

Again, Baba asked: "Is not Arjuna a soul of the nature of Chaitanya i.e. knowledge? Then, when this was answered in the affirmative, he asked: How can knowledge be given to that which is already knowledge?"

Chandorkar was simply dumbstruck.

After putting several other questions like this, Baba finally asked: "By a difference in syllabification, can you add one extra syllable (without damaging the meter or verse)?"

"Yes," answered Nana. "We can say 'Upadekshyanti te (a)jnanam.'"[11] Then, Nana added: "What! This reading of the Guru giving Ajnanam is not in Shankara Bhashya."

Baba said: "That does not matter, if that makes a better meaning."

Nana could not understand how the Guru's giving Ajnana could make a better meaning. Then Nana Chandorkar was thoroughly humbled. He felt that he was before a giant who knew Sanskrit, who knew the Upanishads, and who knew everything.

He then asked Baba himself to explain, and Baba's answers to his own questions revealed a wealth of knowledge of Upanishadic material and a cleverness in twisting the words into a new meaning. So far as the word "Jnanam" is concerned, Baba quoted the Upanishads and said: "Is not Jnana that which is beyond Mind and Speech (quoting Yatovacho Nivartante)?[12] Is not Jnana, Avang Manasa Gocharam, i.e., beyond Vak and Manas?"[13]

Nana had to say: "Yes."

Then Baba said: "Therefore, what the Guru says through his mouth is not Jnana, and what is not Jnana is Ajnana."

Thoroughly humiliated, Nana wondered what it all led to.

Baba, however, explained: "Just as one thorn removes another, the Guru's teaching, which is verbal, begins as Ajnana and removes the Ajnana of the Sishya which is but a cover over the Sishya's knowledge, and the result is Jnana. Therefore, what the Guru teaches is primarily Ajnana, which tends to result in Jnana. Jnana is not created, but is always there, unuttered. The uttered word, like an optician's instrument, simply removes the cataract from the eye of the pupil who, thereafter, sees and recognises himself in a state of pure knowledge."

Thus Baba went on explaining the whole stanza and insisted upon the Sishya's duties. Baba said: "Seva is not any ordinary massage. You must surrender Tan, Man, and Dhan; body, mind and possessions.[14] You must not feel that you are rendering service to the master. Your body already surrendered is the master's property, and you must feel: No merit is in me. I am merely making the body, which is yours, serve you. That is Seva."

> Pariprasna and pranipata were similarly explained to show how thorough must be the spirit of surrender and the spirit of earnestness.
>
> "Pranipata must be Sashtanga dandavat, i.e. like a stick falling down.[15] You must feel that you are nothing. You are only a zero. The Guru is everything, and, therefore, thorough humility is involved in pranipata. Pariprasna means an earnest questioning and repeated questioning, i.e., questioning carried on to the point of getting full and complete enlightenment impressed upon you. This is pariprasna. It is not merely asking questions with a view to tripping up the master and catching him at some mistake, or simply asking for the fun of it."[16]

Arthur Osborne reports that Sai Baba explained one by one all of the eighteen chapters of the *Gītā* to Nanasaheb: "Sai Baba then told Nana to bring the Bhagavad Gita and read a chapter to him each day and Baba would expound it. He did so—but no record was kept."[17]

We have no reason to doubt the trustworthiness of this dialogue, which may go back to Chandorkar's first years at Shirdi.[18]

Sai Baba's knowledge of Sanskrit took his devotees by surprise, confirming that his Hindu background was not inferior to his overall Muslim identity. Baba's analysis of the *Gītā* verse is lucid and precise, never abstract, gradually leading his pupil to total comprehension. His style of argumentation shows great authority, closely resembling that of a *paṇḍit*.

Particularly ingenious is his reading of *jñāna* as its opposite, that is, ignorance, with the negative particle *a* preceding the noun. This change offers him the opportunity to consider the intrinsic weaknesses and ambiguities of language[19] (the guru communicates *ajñāna*), and, at the same time, to underline the all-important guiding function of the teacher in the unveiling of the *ātman*. Thus, paradoxically, ignorance dispels ignorance just as a nail drives away another nail.[20]

Sai Baba utilizes here a nondualistic reading, probably inherited from a Hindu *ācārya* (Venkusha?). Indeed, the familiarity he exhibits in the treatment of classical themes of Shankara's Kevalādvaitavedānta must be underlined. Which texts Baba could have had in mind in formulating his exegesis, however, is hard to say.[21]

Also of interest are his observations on the radicality of surrender (*sāṣṭāṅga daṇḍavat*) and on the burning zeal which must animate a *śiṣya* in posing questions to the guru.

Arthur Osborne, commenting on this episode, aptly states: "Even this teaching...is enough to show that when Sai Baba did talk theory it was the purest Advaita, the doctrine of Nonduality, that is the very essence of spiritual teaching."[22]

Narasimhaswami's biography reports some episodes concerning the devotee Das Ganu Maharaj:

> Baba told him to attend to his kirtans. Das Ganu was specially good at kirtans.... He would hold an audience of 2,000 people spell-bound in rapt attention listening to him sing for six or eight hours, and, as he never asked for even one pie and made no collections, his kirtans were popular.... He would place Baba's picture next to him, and even though his katha was about Tukaram or Namdev or Jnandev, yet he would always refer to Sai Baba as the living Sant or Satpurusha.... As soon as his kirtans ended, people started in numbers to go to Shirdi and see Sai Baba. These numbers included high officials of good and great position, as also the poor. Thus, he has been the means of sending some tens of thousands of people to Baba.[23]

After he left the police in 1903, Das Ganu was directed to intensify his *sādhanā*: "That is why Baba asked Das Ganu to study the *Vishnu Sahasranama*[24] and retreat from the crowds of the Dvarkamayi. He told him to go to an isolated temple like the Vitthala temple in the village, and there go on with his frequent recitals or repetitions of Sahasranama. Baba's advice in this matter was not confined to Das Ganu. He gave similar advice to Shama...."[25]

The importance of *nāmasmaraṇa* is once again stressed. Baba's indication of the Vitthala temple was not arbitrary, since the god worshipped at Jejuri was Das Ganu's *iṣṭadevatā*. A teaching that Baba gave our *kīrtankār* bears special interest. After having narrated how Sai inspired Das Ganu to write a Marathi commentary on Jñāndev's *Amritānubhava,* Narasimhaswami reports:

> Next Das Ganu was anxious to render even a Sanskrit Upanishad, namely, Ishavasya Upanishad,[26] into Marathi. This famous Upanishad consists of only 18 verses.... Having many difficulties...Das Ganu Maharaj went to Baba. Baba said: "What difficulty is there in this? You better go, as usual, to Kaka Dixit's bungalow in Ville Parle, and there that Malkarni (cooly girl), will give you the meaning."

> People would laugh at a great pandit like Das Ganu getting the interpretation of an Upanishad from a cooly girl. But all the same Das Ganu went to Kaka's bungalow. He slept there. When he woke up in the morning, he heard a girl singing songs in great joy. She was praising some orange coloured silk sari, wondering at its fineness and the beauty of its borders, and the floral embroidery on it.
>
> Then, he just peeped to see who the singer was. The singer had no sari. She wore a rag which was not silk, nor orange coloured, had no borders and no embroidery. He pitied the girl and got a friend to give her a sari—a small cheap sari.
>
> She wore it just one day, and went about enjoying it. The very following day, she cast it aside, again wore her tatters and again began to sing joyously the song about the orange coloured sari and its beauty.
>
> Then Das Ganu understood the Upanishad. He found out that the girl's happiness lay not in the external sari which she had thrown away (see *tena tyaktena,* which means: that being thrown away), but within herself.
>
> And the Ishavasya Upanishad says the same: "All this world," says the first verse, "is covered by the Maya of Isvara. So enjoy bliss, not by having the externals, but by rejecting the externals (*tena tyaktena*)."
>
> *Tena tyaktena* might mean being content with what God gives you. The girl was happy because she was contented. Thus, Baba taught the Isha Upanishad to Das Ganu through a cooly girl. Baba's ways of teaching were...peculiar and different in the case of different individuals.[27]

This episode, mentioning H. S. Dikshit (who first arrived in Shirdi in 1909), seems to have taken place about 1909, 1910 or later. The story is symptomatic of Baba's unusual and "mediated" ways of delivering his *upadeśa.*

Das Ganu is confronted with a concrete situation, which, at first sight, appears unrelated to his exegetic difficulties. The unfolding of the story is ironical: the unattached conduct of an uneducated girl reveals to Das Ganu, a *paṇḍit,*[28] the hidden meaning of the first verse of the *Īsha Upanishad.*

R. E. Hume renders the verse thusly:

> By the Lord (*Īśā*) enveloped must this all be,
> Whatever moving thing there is in the moving world.
> With this renounced, thou mayest enjoy.
> Covet not the wealth of anyone at all.[29]

As is well known, M. K. Gandhi saw in this stanza one of the highest exhortations towards universal brotherhood.

True wealth and joy lie within man. Thus, one must accept whatever comes one's way in a spirit of equanimity (*upekṣā*). Freedom, or *mukti*, is paradoxically found in renunciation, in cultivating nonattachment (*vairāgya*): perfect joy or *ānanda* is then "dis-covered." Renunciation, in other words, is not the negation of something positive; it is quite the opposite, that is, the abandonment of what, being ultimately unreal, is not worthy of our attention.

In actual theistically oriented religious praxis, it signifies the discarding of all the obstacles that prevent God from filling our pure emptiness.[30]

According to Narasimhaswami, after Das Ganu heard the girl sing of the orange sari, he was able to complete his translation and exegesis of the *Īsha Upanishad.*

The *Shri Sai Satcharita* reports another popular story concerning Das Ganu:

> The Hindus think that a bath in the holy Tirth of Prayag, where the Ganga and Yamuna meet, is very meritorious, and thousands of pilgrims go there at periodic times to have the sacred bath.
>
> Once, Das Ganu thought that he should go to Prayag for a bath, and came to Baba to get His permission for doing so. Baba replied to him: "It is not necessary to go so far. Our Prayag is here, believe me."
>
> Then, wonder of wonders! When Das Ganu placed his head on Baba's feet, out flowed streams of Ganga and Yamuna water from the toes of Baba! Seeing this miracle, Das Ganu was overwhelmed with feelings of love and adoration, and was full of tears. Inwardly, he felt inspired and his speech burst forth into a song in praise of Baba and his Leelas.[31]

Narasimhaswami reports that Das Ganu wanted to bathe in the Godāvarī, since he considered that river as his Ganges.[32] Be that as it may, this episode is found in all sources, though no dating is given for it. It may be observed that the flowing of water from the guru's feet is a common theme in hagiographic literature.

Apparently, Das Ganu had several extraordinary experiences with Baba. Most of them, as in this case, concern Sai's identification with the various *devatās* of the Hindu pantheon. In particular, Das Ganu celebrated Sai Baba's oneness with Vitthala, his *iṣṭadevatā*, not only in many of his *kīrtans*, but also in the *ārtī:*

> *Shirdi Mājhe Pandharpura Sai Baba Rama Vāra,*
> *Śuddha Bhakti Chandrabhāga Bhāva Puṇḍalīka Jāga.*
> *Yāho Yāho Āvaghe Jāna Kāra Bābāsi Vandāna,*
> *Gāṇu Mhāne Baba Sayi Dhāmva Pāva Mājhe Āyī.*

Narasimhaswami renders the stanza thusly:

> Shirdi is my Pandharpur, and the God worshipped there is Sai Baba. The holy river Chandrabhaga found at Pandharpur is represented at Shirdi by pure devotion, and the holiest spot in that river, i.e., the Pundalika temple, in Shirdi is represented by intense concentration. All you people, come up, come up, and do reverence to Sai Baba. Das Ganu says: "Oh Sai Baba, mother mine, run up and caress me, catching me in your arms."[33]

It should be noted that during the years 1904 and 1905, due to extremely rare rainfalls, the *tālukā* of Kopergaon, together with those of Sangamner, Karjat, Parner, and Nevasa, suffered a severe famine crisis.[34]

I next come to the presentation of a few dated episodes:

> Mrs. Ramabai Kanitkar resided in Yeola from 1905. Some persons called on her to visit Shirdi. But she postponed her visit.... Once she camped with her husband at Kopergaon, and then they came to Rahata. Finally, they made Shirdi their permanent camping place.
>
> They stayed in Baba's chavadi and went to Baba's darshan. She thought that, if Baba gave her darshan of beloved Akalkot Svamiji, her faith in Baba would be confirmed. Baba, however, gave darshan as Akalkot Svamiji to her son and daughter-in-law, but not to her.
>
> When she later knew this..., she was nevertheless satisfied, believing that Baba and Akalkot Svamiji were one and the same.[35]

Sai Baba's identification with the *Svāmin* of Akalkot (d. 1878) is recurrent in the sources:

> Bhai Krishnaji was originally a devotee of Akalkot Maharaj. He had come to Shirdi at the installation of the Padukas in Saka 1834, on his way to Akalkot.[36]
>
> He wanted to go to Akalkot after taking the darshan of Baba. He asked Baba's permission for that. Baba said: "Oh,

> what is there in Akalkot? Why do you go there? The incumbent Maharaj of that place is here, myself."
>
> Hearing this, Bhai did not go to Akalkot. He came to Shirdi off and on after the installation of the Padukas.[37]

As previously noted, many devotees of Sai Baba considered him to be the spiritual successor of Akalkot Maharaj and thus an *avatāra* of Dattatreya. In fact, many are the similarities between the two holy men: their eccentric behavior, their baffling utterances, their miracles (*camatkārs*) of identification with various gods, their love of animals, and so on.[38] Apparently, the *Svāmin* of Akalkot, just before dying, directed some of his devotees to Shirdi.

Another episode reported by Ramalingaswami relates the following story:

> In 1906, Rao Bahadur Chintaman Vinayak Vaidya, a friend of Shri Nanasaheb Chandorkar, went to Shirdi for Baba's darshan. After the Congress session of 1906 in Calcutta was over,...he was on his way back to Shirdi.
>
> At the same time, after finishing Christmas vacation with Baba, Nanasaheb Chandorkar requested Baba to give him permission to leave. Baba told him he could leave the next day, after meals. The next day...Baba said: "Where are you going? Your stout young friend is coming to Shirdi."
>
> At that time...Vinayak Vaidya arrived at Shirdi and went to Baba for darshan. There he saw Nanasaheb Chandorkar. All were astonished....
>
> At that time, Baba told Nanasaheb Chandorkar the following story:
>
> "There was a guava[39] fruit grove with best fruits. All ate about 20 or 25 each. On the next day, I spoiled the grove."
>
> This meant that Baba turned the domestic life of his devotees into spiritual life.[40]

The fact that a member of the Congress Party, a friend of Chandorkar, went to Shirdi to see Baba, confirms the latter's growing popularity.

Sai Baba's cryptic story is another example of his fondness for allegorical speech. An interpretation may be the following: Sai's custom is to satisfy the desires of his devotees, to the point of producing in them a kind of indigestion for worldly things. Once they have thus "evolved," he starts them along the spiritual path. Within such a perspective, Sai Baba, like Dattatreya, could claim to be the giver of both *bhukti,* that is, worldly enjoyments, and *mukti,* that is, freedom from rebirth.

Rao Bahadur S. B. Dhumal (b. 1873), another important *bhakta* of Sai, relates the following:

> I was first devoted to Shri Gajanan Maharaj. I went to Shri Sai Baba in 1907. I was greatly impressed with his extraordinary personality.
>
> I took Srimant Gopal Rao Buty to Shri Sai Baba, i.e., the man who built the Dagadi vada, at present Baba's Samadhi Mandir.
>
> Once, Baba told me: "At every step of yours, I am taking care of you. If I did not, what would become of you, God knows."
>
> Dhumal continued: I was living with my wife...in Nasik. When plague broke out and dead rats were found in the house, I wrote to Baba for directions. After receiving Baba's reply, I moved to a bungalow at Nasik. But the same night, a dead rat was found near the bed of my brother's son at the bungalow. Again, I wrote to Baba for directions. The reply was in the negative, i.e., to remain there.
>
> Later, dead rats were found in the servant's quarters, in the houses, in the neighbourhood, and lastly in the well from which we draw water for drinking, cooking, etc.
>
> At this, I wrote at once to Baba for permission to leave, and meanwhile I packed up all our things and carted them off to the house. I was just trying to lock the door, when a letter from Shirdi was delivered to me.
>
> Baba's reply was: "Why should we give up (change) our residence?"
>
> I obeyed His advice and immediately went back to the infected bungalow and lived therein. As for water, I avoided the well water, getting water from the Godavari.
>
> Even though there were fourteen or fifteen deaths every day due to the plague, we were safe by the grace of Baba.[41]

The point of the story is Dhumal's faith in Baba and his heroic act of obedience: an example of perfect surrender to the guru's will. The letters sent to Dhumal were certainly not written by the *faqīr,* who never wrote a single phrase. Presumably, Sai Baba dictated the words to one of his *bhaktas.*

Plague epidemics occurred periodically in these years. A particularly devastating one first made its appearance in Bombay, in

1896. From there, it spread over the whole Deccan and the South Mahratta country. Up to the date of the Census of 1901, 330 thousand deaths were recorded, though some estimate that the actual mortality level may have been double that amount.[42] Of the three forms in which the disease occurs, that is, the pneumonic, septicemic, and bubonic, the first, acting through the lungs, is the most deadly and easily communicable. Lack of hygienic habits and endemic poverty offered a fertile ground for the virus.

The story reported by Dhumal offers a vivid picture of the precarious living conditions of even important centers such as Nasik.

Shirdi came to be often threatened by plague and cholera, thus requiring Baba to perform magic rituals in order to prevent these evil forces from crossing the boundaries of the village.

Gopalrao Buti, whom Dhumal first brought to Shirdi, was a very rich man from Nagpur. The sources call him "a millionaire." He became an ardent *bhakta* of Sai Baba, and in the last years of the latter's life, he built a large *vāḍā*, soon known as *Būtī vāḍā*, which was originally meant as a visitors' resting place.[43] After Sai's death the *vāḍā* was chosen as the place for Baba's *samādhi*. The building was adapted for its new function and is now the *samādhi-mandir*.

S. B. Dhumal[44] was a devoteee of Gajanan Maharaj (d. 1910), a Śaiva ascetic and miracle worker living in the town of Shegaon, located in the Khamgaon *tālukā* of Buldana district, Berar.[45]

There seems to have been a connection between the saint of Shegaon and Sai Baba. Shri Balaji Pilaji Gurav, an old devotee of Baba, told me that Gajanan visited Shirdi more than once. Also, it is reported that Gajanan directed several people to Sai. Devotees of Baba such as Das Ganu were at the same time devoted to Gajanan. Indeed, many people had the opportunity of visiting and frequenting both saints. The day Gajanan passed away at Shegaon, Sai Baba, at Shirdi, is said to have exclaimed, "My Gajanan is gone."[46]

Gajanan Maharaj, who first appeared in Shegaon on February 23, 1878, is still very popular, particularly in the Vidarbha region of Maharashtra. It is reported that the saint, whom local people recognized as an *avadhūta,* came to be addressed as "Gajanan" because he used to constantly chant the words "*Gaṇ gaṇ gaṇāt bote*" or "*Gaṇāṅgunā gaṇāt hote.*"[47]

I had the opportunity of visiting Gajanan's *āśram* at Shegaon on my way to Shirdi. The place is quite large, charming, and well kept. Many devotees come in pilgrimage to Gajanan Maharaj's *samādhi*. In the small shops near the *āśram,* one can find pictures of Gajanan Maharaj and Sai Baba side by side. Such a spiritual link also seems to be at work in the life of the living woman saint

Sati Godavari Mataji (b. 1914), who succeeded Upasani Maharaj at the Sakuri *āśram* upon the latter's death in 1941. She was born in Shegaon, and her parents were both devotees of Gajanan.[48] Mani Sahukar observes: "On the Guru Purnima of July 1928, Shri Upasani Baba removed from his neck a rudraksha[49] rosary which originally belonged to Shri Sai Baba and put it around Mother's (i.e., Sati Godavari's) neck. This was a supreme gesture of initiation which confirmed Mother's status once and for all."[50]

Bharadwaja's biography reports another interesting episode:

> In 1908, during the holy Chaturmasya (rainy four months), Chandrabai Borkar was at Kopergaon. One day, a fakir asked her for garlic chutney and roti. She said that she did not prepare it during the holy months, and the fakir left.
>
> Later, when she visited Shirdi, Sai said: "You've not given me garlic chutney and roti. Why have you come here?" She replied: "I've come to offer it!" Baba then said to the others: "She has been my sister for the last seven births!"[51]

Again, Sai Baba identifies himself with an anonymous *faqīr*. The comment that Mrs. Chandrabai had been his sister for the last seven births might indicate that she had been his disciple in previous lives. Baba most often referred to his women devotees as either "mother" or "sister" to emphasize his intimate love for them, thus avoiding any possible sexual overtones.

The request of garlic in our story is provocatory, and highlights an aspect of Baba's "unorthodox" personality. Garlic, in fact, is viewed by Hindus as an "impure" substance bearing a *tāmasic* quality and is thus potentially polluting, especially if eaten during a sacred *Caturmāsya*.

Sai Baba did not follow any *brāhmaṇic* code of food purity, and sometimes ridiculed his devotees for doing so. He was always against formal rigorism, caring only for the intentions which prompt the heart. For instance, Sai once forced the orthodox Das Ganu to eat an onion dish, another *tāmasic* food, so as to free him from prejudice.[52]

On an *Ekādaśī* day, it is reported that Baba forced one Kusa Bhav to eat onions. Before doing so, Sai asked him to explain the meaning of *Ekādaśī*. Then, Baba ate the onions first, so as to set an example for Kusa Bhav, who finally agreed to eat them. Sai, to have some fun, told the visitors present at the mosque:

> B.—Look at this Bamniya (corrupt and contemptuous form of the word Brahmin). He eats onion on Ekadasi.

Kusa—Baba ate it and thus I ate it.

B.—No. I ate Kanda i.e. sweet potato. See.

Baba then vomited out sweet potato.

Kusa Bhav, seeing the miracle, voraciously swallowed the sweet potato as Prasad. Baba beat him and said:

"Rogue. Why do you eat the vomit?"

But Kusa did not mind the blows. Baba's heart melted.

B.—(Placing his palm on Kusa's head) I bless you. Think of me and hold forth your palms. You will have my prasad.

Kusa Bhav now holds up his empty palms and warm udhi (Baba's Prasad) falls into them.[53]

Baba discouraged extreme asceticism and fasting. He himself never fasted and sometimes forced some of his devotees to follow his example.[54] He instructed them to eat in moderation, avoiding all extremes. Once, he said: "Do not get over-ascetic by giving up all food, play and exercise. Rather, regulate your meals, rest, etc."[55]

Baba himself ate little. Moreover, he never asked his vegetarian devotees to eat nonvegetarian food, though sometimes he enjoyed testing them. In this context, he once ordered Dada Kelkar, an orthodox Hindu, to go to the market and buy meat.[56] According to A. Osborne, Sai Baba himself was a vegetarian.[57]

The first phase in the expansion of Baba's cult coincides chronologically with the story of Chandorkar's pregnant daughter, Minatai, already cited.[58] The *ārtīs* were intended for individual use only, and Baba did not oppose them: "K. G. Bhishma, a good Kirtankar and a great adherent of Vitthala worship at Pandharpur, drew up the ritual for Sai Baba worship on practically the same lines as the Pandharpur worship, and he brought a set of artis, i.e., ritualistic verses for use by individuals at Shirdi, and these were sent by Baba to Nanasaheb Chandorkar at Jamner, and were approved of by him."[59]

The second phase marks the passage from an individual form of worship to a communal one, beginning in 1908. Such a development required the presence of a *pujārī* to perform the morning, noon, and evening *ārtīs*. Narasimhaswami writes: "For this purpose, Hari Vinayak Sathe, a Settlement officer, who in 1905 was blessed by Baba with the promise of a son in case he married..., sent up one Mega Shyam to Shirdi, so that he might officiate as the pujari and carry on congregational worship."[60]

This Megha (d. 1912) is described as a rustic *brāhmaṇ,* quite dull and ignorant. Being a staunch Śaiva, and having heard that Baba was a Muslim, he didn't want to participate in his worship. When Baba saw him coming to Shirdi for the first time, he apparently exclaimed: "Why does that fool of a Saheb (H. V. Sathe) send this idiot to me?"[61]

Thus saying, Baba sent him away. Megha then went to the sacred site of Tryambakeshvar,[62] and worshipped there for about a year. While there, however, he fell ill, suffering from severe pains in the abdomen.

During that time, he repented of having thought badly of Baba and, thinking that his sickness was due to his ill behavior, came back to Shirdi. There he quickly recovered, and in 1909 the daily congregational worship of Baba began.

The sources inform us that Megha convinced himself that Sai was indeed Shiva, that is, the same as the god honored at Tryambak. Thus, he offered Baba water taken from the Godāvarī together with *bilva* leaves.

Megha died at Shirdi in 1912. Narasimhaswami reports: "Baba's appreciation was shown by his coming to the corpse and placing his hands over it saying: 'This was a true devotee of mine.' Baba bore the expenses of the funeral dinner, and Kaka Saheb Dikshit carried out his order."[63]

From 1909 onward, Baba's cult was gradually enriched, becoming more and more ostentatious. Ramakrishna Ayi, a young widow, was one of the enthusiastic devotees responsible for this development. Baba, in the minds of his Hindu *bhaktas,* had to be honored as a true *mahārāja,* as people now called him.

Thus the use of fans, clubs, silver umbrellas, and other paraphernalia were introduced in his worship. Decorations were also placed around the mosque and the *cāvaḍī.* A palanquin with regal ornaments and a horse were soon acquired by devotees and used during processions to and from the *masjid.*

Sai Baba remained largely indifferent to this exhuberant ritualism and pomp, although he seemed to be more annoyed than pleased about it. One day, when the news of the theft of some silver ornaments from the palanquin was reported to him, he exclaimed: "I say, why was not the whole palanquin stolen?"[64]

Baba nonetheless accepted these new developments, imposed upon him by the enthusiasm of his Hindu *bhaktas.* He maintained a detached spirit, asking his Muslim followers to cultivate an attitude of tolerance and to avoid violence. His appeal was generally respected, and rare were the moments of friction between the two communities.

Such an easy acceptance of Baba's worship on the Muslim side, however, is hard to believe. The absence of any violent eruptions in the last ten years of Baba's life may be explained by the absolute predominance of the Hindu element. By that time, large crowds of Hindu *bhaktas* poured into Shirdi daily. Indeed, around 1909, the Muslim community formed a slim minority of perhaps 10 percent.

Although aging by then, Baba maintained his simple life-style, begging his food, and wearing his old white *kafnī*. Ironically, Hindus honored their *mahārāja* with a regal cult, similar to the one offered to the god Vitthala at Pandharpur, while Sai Baba continued repeating: *faqīr aval padsha*, that is, "the poor is the true emperor."[65]

The evening procession from the *masjid* to the *cāvaḍī*, began on December 10, 1909. The touching scene is recalled in this vivid fashion:

> A little before it was time for Baba to start for the Chavadi, the devotees gathered in the front-yard of the mosque and sang bhajans. With the small chariot (ceremonial procession

The evening pālkhī procession leaves the masjid.

car) behind them, the tulasi stand (the oscimum sanctum) to the right, Baba before them, the devotees gathered in the middle spot.

The young and the old played on various musical instruments like the drum, cymbals, chiplis, etc. as they sang. Some stood at the gates of the masjid, getting torches ready for the night procession. Some decorated the palanquin. Others stood, holding long ornamental staves, now and then loudly hailing: "Sadguru Sainath Maharaj Ki Jai."

Rows of oil lamps burned bright on the walls of the masjid. The mosque and its premises were decorated with garlands, leaves, flowers, and coloured papers. Outside stood the well-bedecked horse, Shyama Karna[66] (Muslim devotees called it Shamsuddin).

A little before the moment of Baba's departure, Tatya, along with several other devotees, came to Baba and told him to get ready for the procession to the Chavadi.... Baba sat in wait. Sai lovingly addressed Tatya as "mama" or uncle. Indeed, cordial and intimate was their relationship. At last, when Tatya came again and helped him to stand up, Baba took his small staff (satka), clay smoking-pipe and tobacco in hand, put a small piece of cloth on his shoulder and got ready to start for the Chavadi. Tatya placed a shawl with golden embroidery over his shoulders. Baba then took a step forward, adjusted the fuel in the dhuni with his right foot, put out the oil lamp with his right hand and started from the mosque.

At once the devotees played on drums and pipes in the most majestic manner. Fire crackers were exploded and missiles fired into the air, which left a beautiful display of colours in the sky. The devotees started moving on while chanting Baba's holy name to the accompaniment of rapturous music. Some of the devotees even danced in ecstasy. Some of them carried flags and standards.

The moment Baba got down the steps of the mosque, all the devotees loudly proclaimed his name with one voice. They stood in two rows on either side of Baba's path. Some of them fanned him with chamaris (tufts of chamar tails), while others spread a cloth along his path.

As devotees held his arms, Baba slowly walked over the cloth. Tatya held Baba's left hand and Mhalsapati held the right. Bapusaheb Jog usually held the ceremonial umbrella over his head. The well caparisoned horse walked ahead of him. Behind him followed the devotees, attendants and the band of

> musicians. The chanting of the divine name of Hari was interspersed with loud proclamations of Baba's name. In this manner, the procession reached the turning at the mosque.
>
> Sai Baba used to stand there, facing the mosque. His form had an unearthly halo around it. His face looked radiant like the rising sun. As he gazed intently towards the north, it looked as though he was inviting some invisible forces mentally. As the musicians played on the instruments, Baba used to wave his right arm up and down several times. Kaka Saheb took a red powder called gulal and, mixing it with flowers, sprinkled them on Baba. The devotees seemed to drink in his heavenly appearance with their eyes.
>
> Late Sri Hemadpanth, who witnessed the scene, remarks: "Words fail to describe the scene and the splendour of this occasion."[67]

V. B. Kher reports that Sai Baba's *shej ārtī* (night *ārtī*), celebrated on alternate days, commenced on February 10, 1910.

An important innovation in Baba's habits began in 1908, coinciding with the inauguration of congregational worship: his use of requesting *dakṣiṇā*.

Narasimhaswami thus explains the new development:

> Specially wanted in a Maharaja's durbar are valuable presents in cash...to offer to various people visiting the durbar.... Pandits, acrobats, dancing girls, wrestlers, kirtankars, musicians, etc. who flocked to real durbars, visited Shirdi Sai Maharaja's durbar also. Sai Baba, therefore, arranged for funds to pay them all. Moreover, Baba wished to shower his favor on those who particularly depended upon him, i.e., Tatya Patel, Lakshmi Bai, Bade Baba, Ramachandra Patel, etc.
>
> ...Some people he would ask for Rs. 5, some for Rs. 25, and some others for Rs. 250. Almost every one that he asked would pay. Baba knew the minds and state of the purse of all, and could get exactly what he wanted. He would not ask for funds, except when he was going to recompense the donor, or if the visitor had already been blessed by God...and was thus bound to pay. He also asked to those whom God pointed out to him.
>
> Many sent "vowed sums" of their own accord. For example, one paid Rs. 6,000. Therefore, Baba easily succeeded in getting varying sums as dakshinas in the course of each day, that totalled up in the evening sometimes to Rs. 300, and sometimes to thousands of Rupees.

> The total income came to a Provincial Governor's income, on which the authorities tried to levy income-tax. But Baba himself retained nothing at all, as every evening he would dispose of the day's accumulations.[68]

Every evening, he redistributed the accumulated money, sometimes large sums, among the people, especially to the poor and the needy. To some, Baba offered a fixed amount daily. Narasimhaswami observed: "Due to the large crowds who offered naivedyas of eatables to Baba, it was possible for 200 beggars to be fed everyday by Baba's bounty and doles."[69]

The *faqīr* thus acted as an egalitarian and an economic leveller of sort. Sai Baba's request for *dakṣiṇā,* though reflecting humanitarian concerns, surprised and scandalized many. Indeed, asking for money and dealing with percentages does not conform with the traditional image of the *saṃnyāsin.* Reflecting such uneasiness, all sources show a degree of embarassment in treating the subject.

Money is viewed by ascetics as closely related to vice, corruption, and impurity. Such a traditional view is well represented by Ramakrishna's attitude: he had a horror of money to such an extent, that he found it repulsive even to touch.[70]

Sai Baba, however, did not fear any contamination. Never caring about cultural barriers and religious taboos, he freely used the *dakṣiṇā* as a means of expressing tangible solidarity.

Baba's requests for *dakṣiṇā* were motivated by various reasons. The main ones can be identified from an examination of the sources:

1. Request for *dakṣiṇā* as Allah's will.
2. Request for *dakṣiṇā* to convey a spiritual teaching by utilizing the symbolism of the number of rupees asked for.
3. Request for *dakṣiṇā* as a pledge, that is, as prophecy of a corresponding future gain, which would compensate the donor.
4. Request for *dakṣiṇā* leading to a condition of indigence of the donor.
5. Request for *dakṣiṇā* to acknowledge a mental desire of a devotee.

Baba almost always promised a higher reward to those who offered *dakṣiṇā*. Once, for instance, he pointed out, "If I take one rupee of dakshina from anyone, I have to return it to him tenfold. I never take anything gratis."[71]

Many people, in fact, voluntarily offered *dakṣiṇā,* praying that he would accept their offerings.

On this issue Upasani Maharaj, in a speech he held on July 24, 1924, observed:

> In order to elevate you to the state of God, if you are not offering anything on your own, some of the Satpurushas demand of you various things—or money in lieu. Sai Baba, Yashavantarao Maharaja, Swami of Akalkot and others used to demand money and other things from the persons who went to them; they used to accept anything.... To take false things and give back real things has always been done by the Satpurushas from time immemorial.[72]

On some occasions, however, Baba took *dakṣiṇā* from someone without giving or promising him any reward. The reasons for such behavior, were the following:

1. The person was in debt with somebody else, or even with a god (such as vows unfullfilled, etc.).
2. The person had acquired money dishonestly in the past.

Thus, Baba would require *dakṣiṇā* in order to settle these karmic debts and restore a balance. For example, in an episode entitled "Dakshina to deprive a man of money which he should not have taken or kept," we read:

> S. B. Dhumal was directed to file a criminal appeal on behalf of a servant of Baba. He filed the appeal, and by Baba's chamatkar, a judgement of acquittal was immediately pronounced, as soon as he presented the appeal. He was given Rs. 300 by the appellants, and when he came with the money to Shirdi, Baba said:
>
> B.—Bhav, will you give me dakshina?
>
> S. B. D.—Yes, Baba.
>
> In this way, Baba repeatedly collected dakshina up to Rs. 300, and did not ask for anything more.[73]

Again in the *Charters and Sayings,* we read:

> Two Brahmins came to Baba.
>
> B.—Shama, ask Rs. 15 of that man (pointing to him).
>
> That man gave the Rs. 15 readily and Baba received it and kept it. The other, unasked, paid Rs. 35. Baba counted it and returned it to the donor.
>
> Shama—Deva, what is this discrimination? I have never seen anything like this. You ask for a smaller sum and receive it. A larger sum is voluntarily paid and you return it.
>
> B.—Shama, you are a child and you understand nothing. I do nothing. I receive nothing. Dattatreya called for his own. He has called for Rs. 15, his due.... So that money has been received.... But this Rs. 35 is not ours, and so it has been returned. At first the man was poor and he made a vow that he would pay his first month's salary to Datta, which proved to be Rs. 15. But he forgot the vow, as time went on. His salary went on increasing.... Then his Karma drove him here, and so I asked him to give me my Rs. 15 under the name Dakshina.[74]

The constant request for *dakṣiṇā* to the point of the visitor being left penniless occured rarely. It usually signified a call to renounce the world (*saṃnyāsa*).

Frequent, on the other hand, was the request for *dakṣiṇā* as a means of conveying *upadeśa*. Through the symbolic meaning attributed to the number of the rupees, Sai came up each time with a specific teaching. In such cases, the amounts he requested were small.

One rupee, i. e., the number one, often stood for the *jīva* or even *Brahman*.

Number two usually emphasized the necessity of cultivating the twin virtues of *niṣṭhā* (faith) and *saburī* (patience).

Number four often indicated the ego complex, that is, *manas, buddhi, citta,* and *ahaṃkāra,* and the need to surrender it at the feet of the guru.

Number five symbolized the senses, that is, the *indriyas*.

Number six refered to the *ṣaḍripus* or six internal enemies: lust (*kāma*), anger (*krodha*), greed (*lobha*), delusion or error (*moha*), pride (*mada*), jealousy (*matsara*).

Number nine stood for the nine steps of the *bhakti-mārga,* that is, the *navavidha bhakti*.

Baba indulged in such numerical symbolism not only when requesting *dakṣiṇā*, but also when redistributing the money among the people. He went on doing so till he breathed his last.

The *Charters and Sayings* reports the following stories:

> Baba asked R. B. Purandhare: Give me Rs. 2 dakshina.
>
> R. B. P.—Baba, why do you constantly ask me for Rs. 2, when you know that I am a poor clerk?
>
> B.—It is not these coins that I want. I want Nishta (faith) and Saburi (patient endurance). Give me these.
>
> R. B. P.—I have given you these. Please, help me to achieve them.[75]
>
> Baba asked B. V. Dev: Bhau, give me dakshina. (B. V. Dev gave one guinea.)
>
> B.—Give me more.
>
> Baba, after getting four, said: Though four were given by you, Baba has got only one.
>
> Dev—Baba, I have given four.
>
> B.—Yes, but I have only one. You will know.

The interpretation is that though the devotee surrenders his fourfold Antahkarana (of Manas, Buddhi, Citta, and Ahaṃkāra), Baba receives only the Jiva…[76]

> Baba said to G. G. Narke: Give me Rs. 15 dakshina.
>
> G. G. N.—Baba, you know I have not got a pie. Why do you often ask me for Rs. 15?
>
> B.—I know you have no money. But you are reading Yoga Vasishta. Get me Rs. 15 dakshina from that.
>
> Getting dakshina here means deriving lessons from Yoga Vasishta, and lodging them in the heart, where Baba resides.[77]

Many similar examples are found in all sources.

When a devotee offered *dakṣiṇā* of his own accord, Baba didn't always accept it. Often, the refusal was attributed to the donor's moral unworthiness. For instance, we read:

> A man living with a mistress and suffering from venereal complaints came to Baba and said: Baba, take this Rs. 500.

Baba (angrily): I want none of your money. You are keeping someone in your house, aren't you? Give it to her.

The man was mortified at this exposure and went away.[78]

Baba would sometimes return the *dakṣiṇā* to the donor, so as to rid that person of the thought that Sai might have asked the money out of personal interest.[79]

In general, devotees considered it an honor and actually a grace, both to offer the *dakṣiṇā* to Baba as well as to receive it from him in the evenings, when he redistributed the money at the mosque.

The remarks of the devotee B. V. Dev of Thana are worth reporting as a final comment:

> Baba did not ask Dakshina from all.... He sometimes accepted it, and at other times refused it. He asked it from certain devotees only.
>
> ...He asked for small or big amounts from devotees according to their wish, devotion and convenience. He asked it even from women and children.... Baba never got angry with those...who did not give it.
>
> If any Dakshina was sent through some friend who forgot to hand over the same to Baba, He reminded him somehow of it and made him pay.
>
> On some occasions, Baba used to return some sum from the amount tendered as Dakshina, and ask the donor to guard it or keep it in his shrine for worship. This procedure benefited the donor or devotee immensely.[80]
>
> ...From some He demanded Dakshina three or four times a day.[81]

Narasimhaswami, in narrating the various illnesses which Mhalsapati's relatives suffered from, observed:

> After 1908,...many doctors visited Shirdi. Meanwhile, Baba told Mhalsapati: "Let the sick people stay in bed," and walking round his Mosque with a short stick, he used threatening words, saying: "Come, whatever may be your power, let us see! I shall show you what I can do with my chot stick,[82] if you come out and face me." This was Baba's treatment of the disease.
>
> However, amongst the numerous visitors, there were doctors who gave medicines to Mhalsapati, to be given to his sick family. Mhalsapati consulted Baba regarding the medicines,

> but Baba dissuaded him from administering them.... In the end, all got well without medicine.[83]

Again, we see Baba "scolding" the disease, personified as a sly and invisible enemy. Baba's "fight" and "victory" over the evil forces, would then magically produce the cure.

The sources report only one case in which Sai was unable to effect a healing. One night Baba was practicing mental *nāmasmaraṇa* inside the *masjid* in order to save the wife of one Nigoj Patil, who had plague. He was, however, disturbed by a crowd of people who wanted to take his *darśan*, and as a consequence the woman died.

> Baba sat up, and hurled foul curses, and told Mhalsapati: "Arre Bhagat, you are a man with family! And don't you know what is taking place at Nigoj's house? This disturbance has caused a failure in my efforts. That Patil's wife is dead. Let that go. What has happened is for the best."
>
> In his anger, Baba threw away Mhalsapati's cloth, telling him that he should not allow disturbance like that during Baba's holy work of contemplation and prayer.[84]

When Sai Baba could not or did not want to intervene, he would simply say, "That *Faqīr* does not want," or "The *Faqīr* does not permit."

Most of the times, however, he would intercede on behalf of his *bhaktas* saying, "That *Faqīr* is good," or "*Allāh acchā karegā*" (Allah will do good). He asked his followers to turn their praise not to him, but rather to Allah, God, or *Brahman*.

Even though many doctors came to the village, Baba never attributed much importance to their official methods of treatment. Apart from administering *udī*, Sai operated cures through unorthodox means. Thus, he would sometimes recommend the eating of some specific food, for instance, walnuts or almonds. P. S. Bharucha's biography reports, "Sai Baba saved the Nagpur millionaire Bapusaheb Buty from death by cholera by recommending to him a mixture of almonds, walnuts and pista boiled in sugared milk, ordinarily a course of action certain to lead to a fatal aggravation of the disease."[85]

Other times, he would recommend the performance of some simple act or ritual. Once, for example, Baba assured that ague would be cured if the sick person would feed a black dog with yoghurt and rice near the Lakshmi temple.[86]

P. S. Bharucha reports a curious story apropos of Baba's unorthodox ways of effecting healings:

> In 1909, Bhimaji Patil, a friend of Nanasaheb Chandorkar, contracted tuberculosis. When every then known remedy had failed, Bhimaji wrote to Nanasaheb about his plight. Nanasaheb's response, predictably, was to suggest a trip to Shirdi. Bhimaji was taken to Shirdi, carried to the Dwarkamai and placed before Sai Baba. The latter declined to be of help. Bhimaji's suffering, he explained, was on account of evil karma in a previous birth. When Bhimaji heard this, he cried out in despair and begged for help. This appeal did not go unheeded.
>
> "Stay then, and put all your anxieties aside," Baba told him. "Your pain will be ended." From the moment this promise was made, Bhimaji stopped coughing blood.
>
> During his stay in Shirdi, Bhimaji had two dreams. In the first dream, Bhimaji saw himself as a boy being subjected to a painful flogging for not reciting poetry before his class teacher. In the second dream, an unidentified individual rolled a large stone up and down his chest, causing him to feel severe pain. What is to be noted is that after the physical distress suffered by Bhimaji in these two dreams, he was completely cured of tuberculosis.[87]

This story shows that even negative karma can be overcome through the power of prayer and Baba's *kṛpā*. Bhimaji's painful dream experiences represent Sai's intervention, which, so to speak, "undoes" the negative effects of karma in a benign way.

In other cases, Baba is said to have taken upon himself the sickness of devotees who otherwise could have not borne the pain. Thus, when in 1911 B. G. Khaparde was ill with plague, Sai is said to have "transferred" the sickness to himself: Baba's body was then covered with bubos.[88]

Arthur Osborne's biography reports another interesting story:

> I first heard of Sai Baba in 1909 and went to see him. I went with no worldly motives, though I was poor and an orphan. I was always desirous of associating with sadhus, and felt drawn to him because I had heard that he was a saint. He appeared to me in a dream and summoned me to Shirdi.... I stayed there for thirteen days.... I did not ask him about anything, but he told my mother that he had been connected with me for seven centuries and would never forget me however far away I was, and would not eat a morsel of food without me.

> With Baba's permission, I...returned to our home at Dadar. On arrival there my wife got an attack of cholera and the doctor gave her up as hopeless.
>
> Then I saw Sai Baba standing beside the little temple opposite my house, and he told me to give her the udhi that I had brought back from Shirdi. I did so and...soon she was all right.[89]

Apart from the miraculous function attributed to Baba's *udī*, this is one of the rare instances in which a person is said to have visited Baba out of pure spiritual interest. Most people, in fact, went to Shirdi because of poor health or problems of the most various sorts. Sai evidently appreciated the man's purity of heart and praised him in talking with his mother, assuring his constant help and presence.

Once, Baba sadly stated:

> My master told me to give bounteously to all that ask. No one listens to me or my wisdom. My treasury is open. No one brings carts to take from it. I say dig, but none will take any pains. I said dig out the treasure and cart it away. Be the real and true sons of the mother, and fully stock your shop. What is to become of us, i.e., this bodily life? Earth will return to the earth, and the air (breath) will return to the air. This opportunity will not return.[90]

Another incident offers a similar message:

> Baba was washing pots and placing them mouth downwards.
>
> Kopergaon Station Master, who had no faith in Baba, asked: "What is all this?"
>
> Baba: "Every pot coming to me comes with mouth downwards, i.e., in an unreceptive fashion."[91]

Narasimhaswami describes Sai Baba's magnetic charisma:

> When Bala Saheb Bhate visited Baba in 1909...the very look of Baba pierced and transfixed him. He sat for half an hour, then for one hour, and when reminded by those near him that it was time to move away, had not the slightest inclination to move.... It was with difficulty that he was pulled away from Baba. Here is a case of what we might term fascination.
>
> ...On the fifth day of his stay, Baba put a gerua cloth (kashaya cloth) over his shoulders, and after that his change of heart was complete.... There was no teaching here. There was only the inner influence changing his heart.[92]

Bhate seems to have been almost hypnotized by Baba's glance and presence. Certainly, much time during meetings with Baba was passed in silence, and a non verbal kind of communication took place.

Among the episodes mentioned by the sources for the year 1909, a few are of particular significance: a case of ubiquity and clairvoyance,[93] another case of ubiquity cum healing,[94] and a teaching after which Baba consented to the desire of Chandorkar and his Hindu devotees, who wanted to offer him *pūjā* on *Gurupūrṇimā* day.[95] From that day onwards, the festival of *Gurupūrṇimā*, dedicated to Baba, was celebrated with great solemnity as one of the three most important festivals of the year.[96] V. B. Kher also reports that Bade Baba (also known as Faqir Baba), whom Sai Baba would have instructed for twelve years before coming to Shirdi, came to stay in the village in 1909.[97]

I now come to an examination of the year 1910.

In an article of *Shri Sai Leela*[98] dated 1932, B. V. Dev gave the following account of how Shirdi looked in 1910, when he first came to the village:

> At that time the village had about 400 houses big and small, two wells, a Marathi school up to the seventh standard as well as a Marathi Mission School, two panmalas,[99] two orchards, one flower garden, nine temples, two masjids, one dharamshala, one sugar mill, one flour mill, and one water mill.... The total population was 2,568, the Hindus being divided into the following castes: Brahmins, Marwadis, Marathas, Dhangars (shepherds), Malis (growers of fruits and vegetables), Sonars (goldsmiths), Sutars (carpenters), Lohars (blacksmiths), Kumbhars (potters), Parits (washermen), Mahars, Mangs, Chamars (leather workers and tanners), Kolis, Bhils (scheduled tribes), Guravs and Vadars.[100]

This valuable information suggests that Shirdi was by that time a self-sufficient and resourceful village, with diversified economic activity—quite a different place from the one Sai must have found when he first settled down! Still, in 1936, Mrs. T. S. Tarkhad reported: "In those days Shirdi was a neglected hamlet without any lighting, sweeping or other conveniences of civilization. It has had some improvements since. But when I was there, the streets and passages were all dark and unlit at night. On the outskirts of the village there was a thick growth of prickly Babul trees."[101]

Arthur Osborne reports:

> It was some time in 1910. Suddenly one morning Sai Baba burst out: "What is the scoundrel coming to see me for? What have I got? I'm just a naked fakir with human organs, like anyone else."
>
> It was one of those outbursts when no one knew what he was referring to. A little later, however, a couple of official carriages drew up with their escort outside the mosque. The wife of the district Revenue Commissioner,[102] an English lady, had long hoped for a child and now thought she would try the wonder-working fakir, whom all the Indians were talking about. She was accompanied by her husband.... They looked round uneasily.... The Assistant Commissioner, who had accompanied them...bade a devotee to ask Sai Baba to finish his morning routine quickly as the sahibs wished to speak to him.
>
> The devotee was aghast.... He declared outright that it was impossible. If they had any business with Sai Baba they would have to wait his pleasure.
>
> It was half an hour before he was free and came that way. The lady stepped up to him and, bowing, said politely: "We wish to have a little talk with you, Maharaj."
>
> However, such politeness was not enough for Sai Baba. It was not the heartfelt devotion he required. He said roughly: "You must wait half an hour; I have to go and beg."
>
> ...It was not half an hour but only ten minutes later when he returned. Again, the lady bowed and repeated her request. "Wait an hour longer," he replied.
>
> The officers of government had not the time. Nor were they disposed to be made fools of in this way by a mere fakir. They got into their carriages and rode away, and the lady remained childless.[103]

The foreigners' pride and lack of patience is here foreseen, tested, and punished. Baba's flights of anger, in fact, were often related to the arrival in Shirdi of seemingly "unworthy" individuals.

An enigmatic episode is presented in Bharadwaja's biography:

> ...In 1910, the brother of one Balakrishna developed breathing trouble during the practice of yoga, and left his home. Balakrishna started in search of him. On the way, a friend detained him at Kopergaon and sent him to Shirdi.
>
> On seeing him, Baba said: "Go to Khandoba!" Balakrishna went and found that his brother was staying there on Baba's order and that he was cured of his illness!

> When the former returned to the masjid, Baba stared at him and said in Hindi: "Lo, there was a tree. Two persons went up. One came down, the other went up!"[104]

Once again, we are told of Baba's clairvoyant and healing powers. Often, as in this case, he sent spiritually inclined persons to reside in seclusion at one of the nearby temples, initiating them to the practices of either *dhyāna* or *nāmasmaraṇa*.

Interesting are the enigmatic words which Sai addresses to Balakrishna. The source reports that those same words in Hindi had been spoken to Balakrishna by an anonymous *sādhu* at Tapovana, where he had gone on a pilgrimage. Sai Baba, repeating those same words, demonstrated his *antarajñāna*. But what do these words mean? Sai does not explain. Bharadwaja thinks that such an allegorical statement may imply that Baba had met Balakrishna much earlier, that is, he posits an identity between Sai Baba and the *sādhu* Balakrishna encountered at Tapovana. Such a conclusion, however, is not very convincing. Baba's words are intentionally cryptic, leaving space for an array of possible interpretations. I suggest the following: climbing the tree symbolically represents the spiritual path, at the top of which is *jñāna*, the "fruit (*phala*) of wisdom." Balakrishna's brother "went up," that is, elevated himself along the path, practicing intense *sādhanā*, while Balakrishna "went down," that is, lost interest in spiritual life, and was thus unable to understand his brother's behavior.

Bharadwaja's biography reports another interesting story:

> In 1910, one Lakshmichand saw in a dream an old bearded man surrounded by his devotees, and later identified him as Baba from a picture in his friend's house. The same evening, when his friend invited him to accompany him to Shirdi, he at once borrowed Rs. 15 from his cousin and started. Along the way, the two pilgrims did bhajan for sometime and, when they met with some Moslems of Shirdi, they enquired about Baba.
>
> When they reached the masjid, Baba said of Lakshmichand: "What a cunning fellow! He does bhajan on the way and yet enquires from others about me. Why ask others? We must see for ourselves. See whether your dream has come true or not. But why borrow money for this trip?"[105]

Baba's call to base one's convictions on direct experience, and not on hearsay, was often stressed. Baba encouraged people to examine him, even test him if necessary, avoiding blind faith.

A well-known *camatkār* of Baba is attested to in all sources:

> On the holy Divali[106] in 1910, Baba, who was adding fuel to the dhuni, suddenly thrust his arm into it, and it was at once scalded. Immediately, Shyama dragged him away by the waist and asked why he did so. Baba smiled and said: "The wife of a blacksmith at a far away village is working the bellows. When her ailing husband called her, she turned round hastily. The infant in her lap slipped into the furnace. I've thrust my hand in and saved it. I don't mind my hand but I'm glad the child is safe."[107]

The *Shri Sai Satcharita* offers further details:

> On hearing the news of Baba's hand being burnt from Madhavrao Deshpande, Mr. Nanasaheb Chandorkar, accompanied by the famous doctor Paramanand of Bombay...rushed to Shirdi and requested Baba to allow Dr. Paramanand to examine the arm and dress the wound caused by the burn. This was refused. Ever since the burn, the arm was dressed by the leper devotee, Bhagoji Shinde. His treatment consisted in massaging the burnt part with ghee and then placing a leaf over it and bandaging it tightly with Pattis.[108]
>
> Baba...said that Allah was his doctor, and did not allow his arm to be examined.... Bhagoji was allowed to treat the hand daily. After some days the arm healed and all were happy.... Every morning, Bhagoji went through his programme of loosening the Pattis, massaging the arm with ghee and tightly bandaging it again. This went on till Sai Baba's samadhi. Sai Baba, a perfect Siddha as He was, did not really want this treatment, but out of love to his devotee, He allowed the Upasana, i.e., service of Bhagoji, to go on uninterrupted all along.[109]

Baba's refusal to have a doctor examine him is noteworthy: Allah, he claimed, is the only true Doctor.

Bhagoji Shinde, however, got permission to dress his burns. A leper, and thus socially discriminated against, he was highly esteemed by Baba. Sai enjoyed his company and always had him nearby. Significantly, Sai Baba gave Bhagoji the honor of holding the ceremonial umbrella (*chattrā*) during ritual processions.[110]

The sources relate how the blacksmith, together with his wife and child, later came to Shirdi and thanked Baba for his miraculous intervention.

Sai Baba seems to have behaved similarly on other occasions

as well. For instance, once it was reported that his robe and head-dress started exuding water, dripping profusely. Three days later, a telegram arrived at Shirdi, sent by a captain, who told of having been shipwrecked during the Russo-Japanese war and of having intensely prayed Baba to rescue him. Sai appeared on the scene and saved the man's life. Thus, the devotee wanted to thank Baba for furnishing timely aid.

The people at Shirdi, by comparing dates, came to the conclusion that Baba's intervention was contemporaneous with the dripping of his robe.[111]

G. G. Narke, Professor of Geology and Chemistry at the College of Engineering in Pune, first met Sai in 1913. With regard to Baba's extraordinary feats, he remarked:

> To one deeply observing him, the startling fact came into greater and greater prominence that Baba was living and operating in other worlds besides this world, and in an invisible body.... Baba frequently spoke of his travels with an invisible body over great distances of space (and time). Sitting near his fire in the morning with several devotees, he would say to what distant place he had been overnight and what he had done there. Those who had slept beside him all night at the mosque or rest-house knew that his physical body had remained at Shirdi the whole night. But his statements were literally true and were sometimes verified and proved true.[112]

Two episodes in which Baba is reported dealing with natural phenomena, bear particular interest. The *Shri Sai Satcharita* narrates:

> Once, at evening time, there was a terrible storm at Shirdi. The sky was overcast with thick black clouds. The wind began to blow forcibly...and the rain began to descend in torrents. In a short time the whole place was flooded. All the creatures, i.e., birds, beasts, and men got terribly frightened and they all flocked in the masjid for shelter.... They all prayed to Baba...to intercede and quell the storm.
>
> Baba was much moved. He came out and, standing at the edge of the masjid, addressed the storm in a loud and thunderous voice: "Stop, stop your fury and be calm." In a few minutes the rains subsided, the winds ceased to blow and the storm came to a stop. The moon rose in the sky and the people then went home well-pleased.

On another occasion, at noon the fire in the Dhuni began to burn brightly, its flames were seen to be reaching the rafters above. The people who were sitting in the masjid did not know what to do. They dared not ask Baba to pour water or do anything to quench the flames.

But Baba soon realized what was happening. He took up His satka (short stick) and dashed it against a pillar in front, saying: "Get down. Be calm." At each stroke of the satka, the flames began to lower and slow down and in a few minutes the Dhuni became calm and normal.[113]

Here, Sai Baba imposed his will by his power of authority, virtually "scolding" the elements. An ascetic's staff is believed to have magical powers.[114] Sai's inseparable short stick, as a true *daṇḍa*, symbolized his sovereignty and was a means of protection against evil forces.[115]

Many episodes are attested to in the sources for the year 1910. It is appropriate to note the main ones: a case revealing Sai's omniscience that sees the involvement of Chandorkar,[116] Baba's intervention in order to satisfy H. S. Dikshit's aspirations,[117] a case of *camatkār*, in which Baba gives vision of himself as the *Svāmin* of Akalkot to R. V. Patankar,[118] and, lastly, an episode that describes Sai helping M. Phasle to start a pilgrimage to Benares.[119]

In 1909, thanks to the intervention of Madhavrao Deshpande (d. 1940), Hari Sitaram Dikshit (1864–1926) arrived for the first time at Shirdi. Dikshit, a well-known lawyer, was a member of the moderate wing of the Congress party, led by Shri Pherosesha Mehta of Bombay.[120]

During his stays at Shirdi, Dikshit kept a diary describing his daily experiences with Baba. An English rendering of this Marathi memo was published in 1933 by Rao Bahadur M. V. Pradhan in his book *Shri Sai Baba of Shirdi*.

In December 1910, with Baba's consent, Dikshit started building a new visitors' lodge, i.e., a new *vāḍā*. The only *vāḍā* present at the time was that which H. V. Sathe had built in 1905–6, known as *Sathe vāḍā*.[121] Dikshit's *vāḍā* was ultimated in April 1911[122] and is still existent, though it is not used for guest lodging anymore.

In 1910, the celebrated Govind Raghunath Dabholkar (d. 1929), whom Sai Baba used to playfully call "Hemadpant,"[123] author of the Marathi *Shri Sai Satcharita*, arrived for the first time at Shirdi.[124] He was convinced by H. S. Dikshit, who described Sai Baba's greatness in a letter to him.

The episode that gave Dabholkar (Hemadpant) the idea of

writing a book on Baba's life took place during one of his first visits to Shirdi:

> One morning, some time soon after the year 1910, while I was in Shirdi, I went to see Sai Baba at his mosque. On reaching there, I was surprised to find him making preparations for grinding an extraordinary quantity of wheat. After arranging a gunnysack on the floor, he placed a hand-operated flour mill on it and, rolling up the sleeves of his robe, he started grinding the wheat. I wondered about this, as I knew that Baba owned nothing, stored nothing and lived on alms. Others who had come to see him wondered about this too, but nobody had the temerity to ask any questions.
>
> As the news spread through the village, more and more men and women collected at the mosque to find out what was going on. Four of the women in the watching crowd forced their way through and, pushing Baba to one side, grabbed the handle of the flour mill. Baba was enraged by this officiousness but, as the women raised their voices in devotional songs, their love and regard for him became so evident that Baba forgot his anger and smiled.
>
> As the women worked, they too wondered what Baba intended doing with such an enormous quantity of flour.... They concluded that Baba, being the kind of man he was, would probably distribute the flour between the four of them.... When their work was done, they divided the flour into four portions, and each of them started to take away what she considered her share.
>
> "Ladies, have you gone mad!" Baba shouted. "Whose property are you looting? Your fathers'? Have I borrowed any wheat from you? What gives you the right to take this flour away?"
>
> "Now listen to me," he continued in a calmer tone, as the women stood dumbfounded before him. "Take this flour and sprinkle it along the village boundaries."
>
> The four women, who were feeling thoroughly embarassed by this time, whispered amongst themselves for a few moments, and then set out in different directions to carry out Baba's instructions.
>
> Since I was witness to this incident, I was naturally curious as to what it signified, and I questioned several people in Shirdi about it. I was told that there was a cholera epidemic in the village, and this was Baba's antidote to it! It was not

the grains of wheat which had been put through the mill but cholera itself which had been crushed by Sai Baba, and cast out from the village of Shirdi.[125]

The grindstone (together with the hearth, the broom, the pestle and mortar, and the water pot) is one of the five destructive domestic implements known as *pañcsunā*. It is one of the five "slaughterhouses" mentioned in Manu's law.[126]

There is a story of saint Ramdas weeping when he found a woman grinding grain, telling her she was destroying life. A story is reported of Kabir weeping at the sound of a grinding mill in Mahipati's *Bhaktavijaya*, in which Kabir compares life to the condition of grain fallen between the millstones of this earthly existence (*saṃsāra*).[127]

Baba's act of grinding grain, symbolically representing the cholera epidemic, is intended to magically destroy the *śakti* of the grain, that is, of cholera.

The devotional songs sung by the four women while grinding, call to mind the Sufi folk poetry of *chakkī-nāma*, so called because it was sung while at the grindstone (*chakkī*). Devotion to God and one's teacher are the typical themes of *chakkī-nāmas*. The Marathi poems that the village women of Maharashtra sing while grinding are indeed functionally identical with this kind of Sufi folk poetry.[128]

Sai Baba's instructions to spread the grain along the village boundaries, in order to prevent cholera from entering Shirdi, responds to the logic of creating a magic circle, which the evil deity of cholera, Mari, will find impossible to cross. As W. Crooke observed: "Among the jungle tribes and menial castes in the plains, such a circle is very commonly drawn round a house or village to ward off cholera and other epidemic diseases. The demon which brings the disease cannot cross this line, formed of milk and spirits."[129]

R. E. Enthoven reports another interesting procedure that also contemplates the drawing of a magic circle:

> The following remedy is resorted to throughout the Presidency for checking the disease of cholera: a small cart of Mango wood is made and worshipped. Five jars, filled with ghee, milk, liquor, cow's urine and water, and a small goat are placed in the cart. The cart is moved from the village temple of Maruti and taken out of the village through the main gate, and thence round the village from left to right. As it moves, five-twisted raw cotton thread is passed along, and the contents of the five jars in the cart are poured out in a small

stream on the ground. When the cart completes the round, that is, comes back to the village gate from which it started, the goat in the cart is buried alive. The cart is then taken beyond the village boundary and there left, it being thought that the disease is left with the cart.... On the day in which this ceremony is performed nobody...is allowed to leave the village, neither are outsiders admitted to it.[130]

It seems appropriate to close this chapter by quoting "Hemadpant"'s puzzled reaction: "I began to ask myself what earthly connection could exist between the grinding of wheat and the eradication of an epidemic of cholera. There was, of course, none. The whole thing was inexplicable. That was when I first thought of writing about Sai Baba's life and his many miracles."[131]

Notes

1. Ramalingaswami, *Ambrosia in Shirdi,* 118–19.

2. Bharucha, *Sai Baba,* 40–41.

3. Cf. Narasimhaswami, *Charters and Sayings,* 157–58.

4. Narasimhaswami, *Life of Sai Baba,* 2:48–52.

5. Literally, the house or residence of the lotus flowers.

6. Narasimhaswami, *Life of Sai Baba,* 2:55–56.

7. On pilgrimage, see S. M. Bhardwaj, *Hindu Places of Pilgrimage in India* (Berkeley and Los Angeles: University of California Press, 1973). See also A. Bharati, "Pilgrimage in the Indian Tradition," *History of Religions,* 3, no. 1 (1963), 135–67.

8. Literally, a sacrifice for the warding off of evil or pain (*kaṣṭa*).

9. Narasimhaswami, *Life of Sai Baba,* 2:62–64.

10. The verse runs as follows: *tad viddhi praṇipātena paripraśnena sevayā / upadekṣyanti te jñānaṃ jñāninas tattva darśinaḥ.* Franklin Edgerton renders it thus: "Learn to know this by obeisance (to those who can teach it), by questioning (them), by serving (them); They will teach thee knowledge, those who have knowledge, who see the truth." F. Edgerton, trans., *The Bhagavadgītā* (New York: Harper & Row, 1964), 26.

11. Here, we have the addition of what is technically known as *virāma.* Thus, knowledge (*jñāna*) is turned in its very opposite, that is, ignorance (*ajñāna*).

12. See *Taittirīya Upanishad,* 2.4.1: *yato vāco nivartante aprāpya manasā saha / ānandam brahmaṇo vidvān na bibheti kadācana.* Which means: "*Brahman* cannot be realized through words and thoughts. Only he who has experienced the bliss of *Brahman* fears no more."

13. Beyond word or speech (*vāc*) and mind (*manas*). The expression *avāṅg manasā gocaram,* appears as the last portion of a verse in the *anuṣṭubh* meter.

14. The giving up of "*tan, man,* and *dhan*" is a common expression, signifying that all identifications and attachments of the ego must fall.

15. *Sāṣṭāṅga daṇḍavat* (also known as *sāṣṭāṅga praṇāma*) means "falling on the ground as a stick, with the eight limbs of one's body touching the ground." It designates perfect surrender (*śaraṇāgati*).

16. Narasimhaswami, *Life of Sai Baba,* 2:88–91.

17. Osborne, *Incredible Sai Baba,* 13–14.

18. See Bharucha, *Sai Baba,* 87.

19. Such reading calls to mind Martin Heidegger's interpretation of the term *hermeneutics* as derived from Hermes, the Greek god of commerce, invention, cunning, and theft; see *Unterwegs zur Sprache,* Pfullingen, 1959.

20. This is analogous to the well-known Sanskrit maxim *astram astreṇa śāmyati* (a weapon is silenced by a weapon).

21. With reference to the gnoseology advocated by Baba, a comparison with the *advaita* text *Ātmabodha,* attributed to Shankara, may prove useful. Concerning the texts Baba was familiar with and recommended reading, see chapter 9.

22. Osborne, *Incredible Sai Baba,* 14.

23. Narasimhaswami, *Life of Sai Baba,* 2:128.

24. The text of the thousand names or attributes of Vishnu. Originally, a portion of the *Anushāsana-parvan* (2.6936–7078) of the *Mahābhārata.*

25. Narasimhaswami, *Life of Sai Baba,* 2:139–40.

26. The *Īsha Upanishad* is sometimes called *Īshavasya,* from its first two words.

27. Narasimhaswami, *Life of Sai Baba,* 2:129–31.

28. He was considered such by the local villagers.

29. R. E. Hume, *The Thirteen Principal Upanishads* (Oxford Univer-

sity Press, 1949), 362. The Sanskrit verse runs as follows: *om īśā vāsyamidam sarvam yatkiṅca jagatyām jagat / tena tyaktena bhunjithā mā gṛdhāh kasyasviddhanam.*

30. On these lines, see Raimundo Panikkar's commentary on the *Īsha Upanishad* in *Spiritualità Indù* (Brescia, 1975), 182–85.

31. Gunaji, *Shri Sai Satcharita,* 19.

32. See Narasimhaswami, *Life of Sai Baba,* 2:132.

33. See ibid., 151.

34. See Bapat, *Economic Development,* 149.

35. Ramalingaswami, *Ambrosia in Shirdi,* 120–21.

36. "Saka 1834" corresponds to 1912 C.E. The *śaka* era begins 78 C.E. For more details, see L. Renou and J. Filliozat, "Notions de Chronologie," Appendix 3 in *L'Inde Classique* (Paris: Imprimerie National, 1953), 720–38. The installation and worship of Sai Baba's *pādukās,* is indicative of his assimilation to an *avatāra* of Dattatreya.

37. Gunaji, *Shri Sai Satcharita,* 26.

38. See Joshi, *Origin and Development,* 136–42.

39. The yellow skinned fruit of a tropical tree, used for jellies and preserves. The Marathi term for it is *perū.*

40. Ramalingaswami, *Ambrosia in Shirdi,* 132.

41. Ibid., 127.

42. On plague in India, see Crooke, *Things Indian,* 373–76.

43. The term *vāḍā* usually refers to a big house owned by a *pāṭīl* or a rich landlord. Iravati Karve describes it thus:

> The structural unit of the house is a rectangular block of four walls.... Sometimes the blocks, which are rooms, are so placed that they make a hollow square with a sun-court in the middle.... In a tightly packed village or a town such a house offers a haven of peace and privacy. The old *vāḍās* had very small and very high windows, really holes in the walls. The whole house was therefore directed to the sun-court in the middle and lived in a world of its own. (I. Karve, *Maharashtra State Gazetteer, Maharashtra: Land and its People* [Bombay, 1968], 138)

44. For a presentation of the main facts of S. B. Dhumal's life, in relation to Sai Baba, see Narasimhaswami, *Life of Sai Baba,* 3:85–98.

45. Shegaon had a population of 15,057 in 1901. The town is an

important center of the cotton trade, and has many presses and ginning factories. The municipality was constituted in 1881. For more information, see *The Imperial Gazetteer of India,* vol. 22, 267–68. On Gajanan Maharaj, see K. R. Kulkarni, *The Saint of Shegaon: A Book of Poems on the Life of Shri Gajanan Maharaj* (Nagpur, 1969); also Das Ganu, *Shree Gajanan Vijay,* translated into English and adapted by N. B. Patil (Shegaon: Shree Gajanan Maharaj Sansthan, 1980).

46. Some Shirdi people at once wrote to Shegaon to inquire about Gajanan Maharaj, and the reply came that he passed away on the day when Baba spoke of his death; see Narasimhaswami, *Charters and Sayings,* 178.

47. See Kulkarni, *Saint of Shegaon,* 2, 151. These words are in praise of the lord of the *gaṇas*, that is, Ganesha or Gajanan.

48. On Sati Godavari Mataji, see M. Sahukar, *Sweetness and Light: An Exposition of Sati Godavari Mataji's Philosophy and Way of Life* (Bombay: Bharatiya Vidya Bhavan, 1966); also see S. N. Tipnis, *Life of Shri Godavari Mataji* (Jabalpur: Aryan Press, 1983). Useful as a brief summary of Mataji's life and teachings is D. P. Sham Rao, *Five Contemporary Gurus in the Shirdi (Sai Baba) Tradition* (Bangalore: Christian Institute for the Study of Religion and Society, 1972), 19–27.

49. Literally, "Rudra-eyed," the berries of *Elaeocarpus ganitrus,* which are used as rosary beads among Śaiva ascetics.

50. Sahukar, *Sweetness and Light,* 17.

51. Bharadwaja, *Sai Baba,* 42.

52. See Narasimhaswami, *Charters and Sayings,* 112.

53. Ibid., 113.

54. See ibid., 109–11.

55. Ibid., 109.

56. Bharucha, *Sai Baba,* 10–11.

57. Osborne, *Incredible Sai Baba,* 50.

58. See Narasimhaswami, *Life of Sai Baba,* 2:62–64.

59. Narasimhaswami, *Life of Sai Baba,* 1:37–38.

60. Ibid., 38.

61. Ibid.

62. Tryambakeshvar is situated in the small village of Tryambak, which is about eighteen miles by road from Nasik. It is an important reli-

gious center for two main reasons: it is one of the twelve privileged abodes (*pīṭhas*) of Shiva in the form of *jyotirliṅga* (the other ones are: Somnath, Mallikarjun, Ujjain, Omkareshvar, Kedarnath, Bhimashankar, Benares, Vaidyanath, Nageshvar, Rameshvar, and Ghushmeshvar), and it stands at the source of the sacred Godāvarī River, often called Gaṅgā by Maharashtrians. On the holy site of Tryambakeshvar and its attached mythology, see Mate, *Temples and Legends*, 140–61.

63. Narasimhaswami, *Life of Sai Baba*, 3:105.

64. Ibid., 1:42.

65. Ibid., 43.

66. Literally, "black ear." Bay, but with a black ear, this horse had been offered to Baba by a breeder as a token of gratitude. The horse was called Shyamsundar by the Hindus.

67. Bharadwaja, *Sai Baba*, 244–46.

68. Narasimhaswami, *Life of Sai Baba*, 1:40–41.

69. Ibid., 41.

70. Ramakrishna constantly warned his followers from the dangers of *kāminī* and *kāñcana*, "women" and "gold." By these two terms, he intended the dangers of lust and greed, viewed as the main forces that enslave people to *saṃsāra*.

71. Narasimhaswami, *Charters and Sayings*, 149.

72. Godamasuta, ed., *The Talks of Sadguru Upasani-Baba Maharaja* (1957; reprint, Nagpur: Shri Upasani Kanyakumari Sthan, 1978), vol. 1, pt. A, 194.

73. Narasimhaswami, *Charters and Sayings*, 93.

74. Ibid., 100–1.

75. Ibid., 95.

76. Ibid., 94–95.

77. Ibid., 95.

78. Ibid., 89.

79. See ibid., 265.

80. According to devotees, Baba could "charge" an object with sacred potency. By touching an offering (even "impure" metallic coins!), he automatically sanctified it.

81. Gunaji, *Shri Sai Satcharita,* 82–83.

82. The noun *cot* literally means "blow," "stroke." Baba's stick (*satka*) can strike and blow away the disease, so to speak.

83. Narasimhaswami, *Life of Sai Baba,* 2:16.

84. Ibid., 14.

85. Bharucha, *Sai Baba,* 63.

86. Ibid. See also Narasimhaswami, *Charters and Sayings,* 167.

87. Bharucha, *Sai Baba,* 62–63.

88. Narasimhaswami, *Charters and Sayings,* 165.

89. Osborne, *Incredible Sai Baba,* 26–27.

90. Narasimhaswami, *Charters and Sayings,* 7.

91. Ibid., 38.

92. Narasimhaswami, *Life of Sai Baba,* 4:34–35.

93. Bharadwaja, *Sai Baba,* 32–33.

94. Osborne, *Incredible Sai Baba,* 66–67.

95. Ramalingaswami, *Ambrosia in Shirdi,* 134–36. *Gurupūrṇimā* falls on the full moon of the month of Āṣāḍh (June–July). On this day, sacred to the memory of the mythical sage Vyasa, disciples worship their teacher. On *Gurupūrṇimā* festival, see Swami Sivananda, *Hindu Fasts and Festivals* (Shivanandanagar: Yoga-Vedanta Forest Academy Press, 1987), 28–36.

96. Besides *Gurupūrṇimā,* there were the already mentioned *Rāmanavamī* festival and *Daśaharā,* during which, after 1918, devotees have also commemorated Sai Baba's death-anniversary (*mahāsamādhi*). The day of *Daśaharā* (literally, "taking away the 10 sins"), a festival in honor of the Ganges, is also known as *Vijaya Daśamī,* and falls on the 10th day of the bright half of the month of Āśvin. It is especially observed as the day when the *avatāra* Rama gained his victory over the demon Ravana.

97. See Kamath and Kher, *Sai Baba,* 9.

98. The first issue of this monthly Marathi magazine was published in April 1923, and its first editor was Lakshman Ganesh, who is also know as Kakasaheb Mahajani. Publication was suspended between 1944 and 1947. Since 1973, a separate English edition of the magazine has been published.

99. Betel-leaf plantations.

100. Reported in Kamath and Kher, *Sai Baba*, 85.

101. Ibid.

102. His name was Sir George Seymour Curtis.

103. Osborne, *Incredible Sai Baba*, 37–39.

104. Bharadwaja, *Sai Baba*, 21–22.

105. Ibid., 23.

106. *Divālī*, *Dipālī*, or *Dīpāvālī*, literally, "a row of lights," is a festival with illuminations on the day of new moon in the month Āśvin or Kārttika (October–November). There are various alleged origins attributed to this festival. Some hold that they celebrate the marriage of Lakshmi with Vishnu. In Bengal, *Divālī* is dedicated to the worship of Kali. It also commemorates the day on which the triumphant Rama returned to Ayodhya after defeating Ravana. On this day, Krishna is said to have defeated the demon Narakasura. On *Divālī*, see P. K. Gode, "Studies in the History of Hindu Festivals: Some Notes on the History of Divālī Festival (between A.D. 50 and 1945)," *Annals of the Bhandarkar Oriental Research Institute* 26(1946):216–62.

107. Bharadwaja, *Sai Baba*, 71–72.

108. Leaves.

109. Gunaji, *Shri Sai Satcharita*, 42–43.

110. This is confirmed by a photograph (probably taken somewhere around 1912) showing Baba on his evening round, accompanied by Gopalrao Buti and Nanasaheb Nimonkar. Bhagoji, holding the ceremonial umbrella (*chattrā*), is visible in the background.

111. See Bharadwaja, *Sai Baba*, 72.

112. Osborne, *Incredible Sai Baba*, 63–65. On the important figure of G. G. Narke, who married the daughter of the Nagpur millionaire Gopalrao Buti, see Narasimhaswami, *Life of Sai Baba*, 3:111–28.

113. Gunaji, *Shri Sai Satcharita*, 66–67.

114. In *Mahābhārata* (13. 95. 47–48), Shunahsakha burns Yatudhani by striking her on the head with his *tridaṇḍa*. In *Rāmāyaṇa* (1. 54. 28, 1. 55. 13), Vasishtha, by means of his *daṇḍa*, overcame all the weapons of Vishvamitra. The *Kathāsaritsāgara* (18. 5. 5–16) tells the story of a Kāpālika ascetic who brought a dead woman back to life with his *daṇḍa*. The magic power left him when the woman's husband got hold of the staff and threw it away.

115. A *saṃnyāsin*, irrespective of his caste, carries a bamboo staff.

Bamboo is associated with Indra's bolt (*vajra*), the divine weapon that destroyed the evil powers and gave birth to the universe. On the material and symbolic relevance of the staff (*daṇḍa*), see P. Olivelle, *Renunciation in Hinduism: A Medieval Debate*, Publications of the De Nobili Research Library (Vienna, 1986), vol. 1, *The Debate and the Advaita Argument*, 35–54. See also A. Glucklich, "The Royal Scepter (Daṇḍa) as Legal Punishment and Sacred Symbol," in *History of Religions*, November 1988, vol. 28, no. 2, 97–122.

116. Gunaji, *Shri Sai Satcharita*, 44.

117. Ramalingaswami, *Ambrosia in Shirdi*, 104.

118. Ibid., 115–17.

119. Ibid., 138–41.

120. For more information on this important figure, see Narasimhaswami, *Life of Sai Baba*, 2:155–211.

121. See Narasimhaswami, *Life of Sai Baba*, 3:99. V. B. Kher, however, reports that the *Sathe vāḍā* was erected two years later, that is, in 1908; see Kamath and Kher, *Sai Baba*, 8. Details concerning Sathe and the construction of the *vāḍā* were recently offered by Satya Sai Baba. See his speech of September 28, 1990 in *Sanathana Sarathi* 33, no. 11 (Nov. 1990): 291–93.

122. V. B. Kher notes that the foundation of the *Dikshit vāḍā* was laid on February 10, 1910.

123. Hemadpant was the Prime Minister of the Yādava kings *Mahādeva* and Ramachandra (1271–1310). Among other things, he was the composer of the *Chaturvarga Chintāmaṇi*, an encyclopaedic work on the *Dharmaśāstra*. The introduction of the *modī* script, to facilitate a fast writing in Marathi, is ascribed to him. Moreover, the Hemadpanti style of many Yādava temples is said to have been enunciated by Hemadpant; see O. P. Verma, *A Survey of Hemadpanti Temples in Maharashtra* (Nagpur University, 1973).

124. On G. R. Dabholkar, see Narasimhaswami, *Life of Sai Baba*, 2:212–27.

125. Bharucha, *Sai Baba*, 66–68.

126. See Manu 3:68–69.

127. See Abbott and Godbole, *Stories of Indian Saints*, 109–12. On the power of grain and the destructive act of grinding with its evil consequences, see John Abbott, *The Keys of Power: A Study of Indian Ritual and Belief* (Seacaucus, N.J.: University Books, 1974), 392–403, 479–81.

128. On the issue of *chakkī-nāma,* see R. M. Eaton, "Sufi Folk Literature and the Expansion of Indian Islam," *History of Religions* (Nov. 1974): 117–27.

129. W. Crooke, *Natives of Northern India* (London: Archibald Constable and Company, 1907), 259.

130. Enthoven, *Folklore of Bombay,* 260–61.

131. Bharucha, *Sai Baba,* 68.

7

1910 to 1915

The sources present two important episodes that took place around the end of 1910. The first one concerns the precarious conditions of Baba's health. Narasimhaswami reports: "Baba in 1910 said to G. S. Khaparde: "For two years, I have been so ill as to live on mere bread and water. I have string worm. People rush and give me no rest. This will continue till I go back to the place of my origin. I do not mind it, because I care more for my people than for my own life.'"[1]

At that time, according to the *Shri Sai Satcharita*, Baba was more than seventy years old. Sai lamented serious intestinal troubles. As already noted, he suffered from asthma at least from about 1886,[2] and these crises worsened in the last years of his life.

Sai Baba's touching words, evidencing his love towards his *bhaktas* to the point of sacrificing his life for their sakes, indicate how the increasing flux of devotees and visitors weakened and tired him more and more.

Ganesh S. Khaparde (1854–1938), an important collaborator of the nationalist leader Bal Gangadhar Tilak (1856–1920), was much devoted to Sai Baba. The historian Stanley A. Wolpert gives the following political portrait of Khaparde:

> Tilak's leading supporter at the Madras Congress in 1898 was the highly successful pleader of Berar, Ganesh S. Khaparde, whose close personal association with the Lokamanya[3] stemmed from their cotrusteeship of Babamaharaj Pandit's estate. For the remainder of Tilak's life, Khaparde continued to serve as one of his most trusted lieutenants, and a mainstay of his party. Because of his singular personal influence in the Central Provinces, Khaparde was popularly known as the Navab of Berar, and in 1897 had acted as chairman of the Amraoti Congress Reception Committee.[4]

The repressive activity of the government, which had already brought about the imprisonment of Tilak and other nationalist leaders, was particularly strong around 1910. This dangerous situation drove Khaparde to seek refuge at Shirdi on December 5, 1910.

The daily diary kept by Khaparde during the 1911–12 period represents a valuable source of information regarding Baba's activities and teachings.[5]

The second episode reports an *upadeśa* of Baba regarding the necessity of the guru's guidance. Only through the teacher's help can the *śiṣya* succeed in such a dangerous world. Dabholkar narrates:

> On the first day of my arrival in Shirdi, there was a discussion between me and Balasaheb Bhate regarding the necessity of a Guru. I contended:
>
> "Why should we lose our freedom and submit to others? When we do our duty, why is a Guru necessary? One must try his best and save himself. What can the Guru do for a man who does nothing but sleep indolently?"
>
> Thus I pleaded Free Will, while Mr. Bhate took up the other side, viz. Destiny, and said:
>
> "Whatever is bound to happen must happen; even great men have failed. Man proposes but God disposes.... Brush aside your cleverness; pride or egoism won't help you."
>
> This discussion, with all its pros and cons, went on for an hour or so, and as usual no decision was arrived at. We had ultimately to stop as we were exhausted. The net result was that I lost peace of mind....
>
> Then, when we went to the masjid with others, Baba asked Kakasaheb Dikshit the following:
>
> "What was going on in the (Sathe's) Wada? What was the discussion about?" and staring at me Baba further added: "What did this Hemadpant say?"[6]
>
> Hearing these words, I was much surprised. The masjid was at a considerable distance from Sathe's Wada....
>
> ...Next day...Kakasaheb went to Baba and asked whether he should leave Shirdi. Baba said yes.
>
> Then someone asked: "Baba, where to go?" Baba said: "High up." Then the man asked: "How is the way?" Baba said:
>
> "There are many ways leading there; there is a way also from here (Shirdi). The way is difficult. There are tigers and wolves in the jungles on the way."
>
> Kakasaheb asked: "But Baba, what if we take a guide with us?"
>
> Baba answered: "Then there is no difficulty. The guide will take you straight to your destination, avoiding wolves, tigers

and ditches etc. on the way. If there be no guide, there is the danger of your getting lost in the jungles or falling into ditches."[7]

Baba makes three main points: (1) The "destination" one must reach, that is, *mukti,* is located "high up"; (2) The ways or *mārgas* leading to it are many, one path originating from Shirdi; and (3) The presence of a guide, that is, a guru, is essential in order to reach the goal safely.

Here, Baba implicitly proposes himself as qualified guru, who knows the way and guides his disciples along a particular path. Such *mārga* may be identified with that of love and devotion, that is, *bhakti,* focal point of his entire *upadeśa.* At its highest point, it is represented by the attitude of serene surrender to the teacher's will, *prapatti,* which Baba constantly recommended.

The path of devotion and surrender is not in contrast to other traditional *mārgas* such as those of knowledge (*jñāna-mārga*) and *yoga* (*yoga-mārga*). These are also present in Baba's teaching, though with minor emphasis, being recommended to a limited number of *sādhakas.*

On the essential role of the guru, Sai Baba once related the well-known account of his meeting with his own teacher, for which no chronological reference is given. Though some authors like A. Osborne identify this anonymous guru with Venkusha, my opinion agrees with that of most commentators, that is, that the nature of the text and certainly its intent are didactic and symbolical, rather than biographical and historical. In other words, I am inclined to view the account as an allegorical one. What might be hypothesised is that Baba, in describing his relationship with this anonymous guru, evoked emotions and feelings of his early years as *sādhaka.*

To quote Baba's narrative as reported by Arthur Osborne:

> Once I was discussing the Puranas and other works we were reading with three friends, and arguing how to attain realization.
>
> One said that we should depend on ourselves and not on a Guru, because the Gita says: "Raise yourself."[8]
>
> The second said that the main thing is to control the mind and keep it free from thoughts and doubts.
>
> The third said that forms are always changing and only the Formless is unchanging, so we must constantly make distinction between the Eternal and the transitory.
>
> The fourth[9] disliked theory. He said: "Let us simply do our

> duty and surrender our whole life and body and speech to a Guru who is all-pervading. Faith in him is all that is needed."
>
> As we roamed through the forest we met a labourer who asked us where we were going in the heat of the day and warned us that we would get lost in the trackless thickets, and for no purpose. He invited us to stay and share his food, but we rejected his offer and advice and walked on. And in fact we did lose our way in that vast, dense forest.[10]
>
> He met us a second time and said that we had got lost through trusting our own skill, and that we needed a guide. Again he invited us to share his food, telling us that such an offer was auspicious and should not be spurned; however we again declined his invitation and continued on our way. Only I felt hungry and went back and accepted a piece of bread from him and drank some water.
>
> Then the Guru appeared[11] and asked what we were arguing about, and I told him all about it. The others left him, showing him no respect, but I bowed down to him reverently.
>
> Then he took me to a well, tied my legs with a rope, and suspended me head downwards from a tree that was growing beside it. My head was about three feet above the water, so that I could not reach it. My Guru left me there and went away, I knew not where. He returned four or five hours later and asked me how I was getting on. I replied that I had passed my time in great bliss. He was delighted with me and embraced me, passing his hand over my head and body. He spoke to me with great love and made me his disciple, whereupon I entirely forgot my mother and father and all my desires.
>
> I loved to gaze on him. I had no eyes except for him. I did not want to go back. I forgot everything but the Guru. My whole life was concentrated in my sight and my sight was on him. He was the object of my meditation. In silence I bowed down.[12]

Here we have a typical example of Sai Baba's metaphoric speech, with its allusive force. The importance of the guru's role could have not been expressed more forcibly.

A. Osborne offers an interesting interpretation of the symbolical elements present in the story:

> The forest is the jungle of the mind in which the quest for Truth takes place, and the four friends are four modes of approach.

> The labourer is the Guru and the food he offers is his Grace. "The Guru appeared" means that after the youth has accepted the food, he discovers that the giver is the divine Guru. Therefore he bows reverently; that is, accepts his authority.
>
> Tying his head downwards over a well is overturning the ego, binding it and holding it within sight of the cool waters of Peace....[13] The absorption in the Guru is the sadhana or Path followed, and the final "In silence I bowed down" is the extinction of the ego in Realization.[14]

The human guru appears indeed as a god (*deva*). Surrendering to him spontaneously leads to the enlightenment experience, to the unveiling of what truly is. No special efforts and studies are involved.

Baba would sometimes give this advice to a devotee: "Stay with me and keep quiet. I will do the rest."[15]

The simple presence or vision (*darśan*) of the teacher is thus sufficient to convey liberation.

In relation to this theme, the *Charters and Sayings* reports another important story:

> Radha Bai Deshmukin came to Baba for Upadesh, got none and resolved upon satyagraha.[16] She started fasting, which should only end with either death or Upadesh from Baba, whichever occurred first. After three days of her fruitless fast I[17] interceded with Baba on her behalf and requested him to utter some divine name in her presence. Baba sent for her and addressed her thus:
>
> Mother, why do you think of dying and torture yourself? Take pity on me, your child. I am a beggar. Look here, my guru was a great saint and highly merciful. I fatigued myself in trying to serve him and yet he did not utter any mantra in my ear. Instead, he first shaved me clean and then begged of me two pice. What he wanted was not metallic coins—he did not care even for gold, but only Nishta and Saburi, that is, faith and courageous patience. I gave these to him at once and he was pleased.
>
> Mother, Saburi is courage, do not discard it. It ferries you across to the distant goal. It gives manliness to men, eradicates sin and dejection and overcomes all fear.
>
> For 12 years I waited on my Guru, who is peerless and loving. How can I describe his love for me? When he was Dhyanasta (in love-trance) I sat and gazed at him; and we

> were both filled with Bliss.[18] I cared not to turn my eye upon anything else. Night and day I gazed upon his face with an ardour of love that banished hunger and thirst. The Guru's absence, even for a second, made me restless. I meditated upon nothing but the Guru and had no goal or object other than the Guru. Unceasingly fixed upon him was my mind. Wonderful indeed was the art of my Guru! I wanted nothing but the Guru and he wanted nothing but my love. Apparently actionless, he never neglected me but always protected me by his glance.
>
> That Guru—I tell thee true, sitting as I do in this Masjid—never blew any mantra into my ear; nor do I blow any into yours. Go thou and do likewise.
>
> If you make me the sole object of your thoughts and aims, you will attain Paramartha, the supreme goal. Look at me with undivided attention; so will I look at you. This is the only truth, my Guru taught me. The four sadhanas[19] and the six shastras[20] are not necessary. With entire confidence, trust your Guru. That is enough.
>
> Shama: The lady bowed, accepted the advice and gave up her satyagraha.[21]

Narasimhaswami thinks that here above Sai may be referring to his Hindu guru Venkusha. This is possible although, as noted previously, some of the elements of the story, such as the number 12, may be symbolical.[22]

Baba asks for *niṣṭhā* and *saburī* from the lady, nothing else. He exhorts her to follow a *sādhanā* of total surrender, as he did with his own guru, and to meditate on nothing other than the guru, that is, himself. Sai Baba insists on the point that if perfect surrender is achieved, then no particular *sādhanās, śāstras* or mantras are necessary. Sai always refused the traditional mode of *upadeśa,* consisting of an initiation through mantra.[23] What counts is a heart full of love and devotion for the guru, perfect hierophany of God.

What is particularly striking in the text is the intense emotion animating Baba's reevocation, revealing the heart of a great mystic.

A text in which Sai approves of the practice of *japa,* and tacitly allows the repetition of his name deserves attention:

> A devotee was staying at the house of Ayi, a woman devotee permanently resident at Shirdi, to whom Sai Baba often sent visitors. The devotee said: "We agreed that japa (invocation) was the best course for us. The important question was what

> name we should use for it." Ayi said that many used a name such as Vittal or Rama but so far as she was concerned, Sai was her God and that name was enough for her. I said that what was good for her was good for me too and that I also would take the name of Sai. So we sat facing each other and repeating the name together for about an hour. Later in the day Sai Baba sent for me and asked me what I had been doing that morning.
>
> "Japa," I replied.
>
> "Of what name?" he asked.
>
> "Of my God."
>
> "Who is your God?" he asked next.
>
> I simply replied: "You know," and he smiled and said: "That's right."
>
> Thus japa of his name was expressly approved by him."[24]

Baba's silent approval of the repetition of his name is significant, since he seldom authorized it publicly. Perhaps, his reserve was motivated by the necessity of maintaining peace between the Hindu and Muslim communities.

Narasimhaswami reports:

> A district magistrate before whom S. B. Dhumal (Pleader of Nasik) appeared in a criminal appeal, and whose mind Baba influenced so as to make him give a verdict in favour of a Sai devotee, overriding all forms, conventions, and procedure asked: "What does Baba teach?"
>
> This was about 1911, when no books on Baba had been written. Even pamphlets were hardly available.... Dhumal's answer was:
>
> "His teaching would be suited to the individual approaching him and the district magistrate must himself go to Sai Baba to learn his teaching."
>
> But the magistrate was not sufficiently serious to approach Baba and get his teaching.[25]

Dhumal's reply to the magistrate underlines an important point: Baba's teachings were adapted according to the situation and needs of each person. It was an individualized, never generic *upadeśa*.

The information that in 1911 no book had yet been written on Baba's life is important. The opening chapters of the *Shri Sai Satcharita* by G. R. Dabholkar, the first work to be published, appeared only in 1917.[26]

Several healing acts are related to the year 1911: a cure from leg palsy and one from plague-fever,[27] the healing of a lame man,[28] the cure from bubonic plague of G. S. Khaparde's son, Balvant. In this latter case, Baba apparently took the illness upon himself.[29]

The *Charters and Sayings* next reports:

> One Shinde of Harda had seven daughters, but no sons. In 1903, he went to Gangapur and prayed for a son to Dattatreya and said that if he got a son in 12 months, he would bring the child to Gangapur for Darshan. He got a son in 12 months, but did not take the child to Gangapur. In November 1911, he came to Baba at Shirdi.
>
> B.—"What! Have you got puffed up? Where was there any male progeny in your destiny? I tore this body (pointing to Sai's body) and gave you one."[30]

During the same year, there was an episode in which Baba is said to have appeared in a dream to one Y. J. Galvankar, asking him to keep chaste and honest.[31]

Another episode worth mentioning is one in which Baba reprimands his *bhaktas* for their lack of hospitality:

> B. V. Vaidya in 1911 went with his family to Shirdi and at 1 A.M. alighted at Sathe Wada. He took light tiffin (pharal) and went to bed.[32] In the morning, Baba angrily told the people at the Wada: "My children arrived. None looked after them, and you made them upas[33] i.e. eat pharal."
>
> With these words Baba drove away the Bhaktas from the Mosque.[34]

On June 27, 1911, at the age of forty-one, Kashinath Govinda Upasani Maharaj arrived at Shirdi. He was to become Sai Baba's most highly developed *śiṣya*.

A learned *brāhmaṇ gṛhastha,* trained in traditional Indian medicine *(āyurveda),* he had been inclined from youth towards asceticism and spiritual life. He had just married for the third time, his two previous wives having both died.[35]

He was led to Shirdi by the insistence of a yogin of Rahuri, to whom he had gone in quest of a cure for a respiratory disease. Upasani planned only a short stay, not being too interested in a holy man who, from the name, he had identified as a Muslim.

Though Upasani left Shirdi on the twenty-ninth, Sai Baba succeeded in having him come back. Upasani returned to the village on July 6, and was soon conquered by Baba's charisma. Sai asked him to remain at Shirdi and "to do nothing."[36] In Baba's parlance, this meant to put oneself in an attitude of total receptivity. Thus, he asked Upasani to passively "allow his grace to fill him," so to speak. For this reason, Baba instructed Upasani to retreat in solitude to the isolated Khandoba temple.

In October 1911, an interesting episode took place: Upasani, not "recognizing" Baba first in a dog and the next day in a *śūdra,* did not offer them food. He went to Baba at the mosque to offer the same food as *naivedya,* but Sai refused it, saying he had already come to him in the form of dog and *śūdra.* These circumstances had a strong impact on Upasani.[37]

Baba said he had precise obligations towards Upasani due to *rīṇānubandha* and that four years of intense *sādhanā* would be necessary for him to attain full realization.

During the first period of his stay at Shirdi, Upasani feared that his respiratory disfunction would trouble him. Sai Baba assured him, saying, "*Ye Jaga Maran Ko Nai, Taran Ko Hai!,*" which means "This Shirdi is no place for death, but a place for crossing death!"[38]

Yet, in the last days of December 1911 or perhaps January 1st, 1912, Upasani confided to his elder brother, Balakrishna Shastri, "I do not understand what this Sai Baba is doing to me. It is totally unintelligible."[39]

I shall in following pages evaluate the progress in Upasani's *sādhanā* year after year, up until 1915.

In bringing to a close the examination of 1911, some excerpts from G. S. Khaparde's diary deserve mention. Due to his political involvement on B. G. Tilak's side, he was in dire straits, having lost a large part of his clientele, and his arrest appeared imminent. He decided to return to Shirdi on December 6 and remained there continuously for ninety-eight days, during which time he kept the aforementioned diary.

Sai Baba, as the diary reports, reassured and protected Khaparde, ordering him to stay in Shirdi and have full faith in him, cultivating *saburī* and an attitude of *prapatti.*

Khaparde was a profoundly religious man and sincerely believed in Sai Baba's saintliness. Acquainted with religious texts, while in Shirdi, he daily lectured on the *Yogavasishtha* and the *Pañcadashī,* together with other learned devotees.[40] These lectures were attended by several people, among whom were Baba's followers Dada Kelkar, Jog, and Upasani Maharaj.

On November 26, Khaparde wrote about Baba's mood after

the morning *kākaḍ ārtī*:[41] "He was rather in an unusual mood and tapped the ground round about him with his baton."[42]

On December 7, he noted:

> We went and sat in the masjid. Then Sayin Maharaj[43] turned to me and said: "This world is funny. All are my subjects. I look upon all equally; but some become thieves. What can I do for them? People who are themselves very near death, desire and contrive the death of others. They offend me a great deal, but I say nothing. I keep quiet. God is very great and has his officers everywhere. They are all-powerful. One must be content with the state in which God keeps him."[44]

The *Charters and Sayings* version of this passage adds these words of Baba: "I am very powerful. I was here eight or ten thousand years ago."[45]

Here, the *faqīr* ponders over the tragedy of human wickedness, which offends and saddens him. Nonetheless, Sai notes that God acts in the world through emissaries, and he himself seems to identify as one of them. Baba's advice to Khaparde on accepting one's fate patiently might be related to the political dangers which afflicted the latter.

On December 20, Khaparde wrote: "Today I pressed Baba's legs. The softness of his limbs is wonderful."[46]

On Christmas Day, he observed: "My son Balvant had a dream last night: he saw Sai in our Elichpur house and offered him food. I thought it was a mere fancy, but today Sai said to him: 'I went to your house yesterday; you fed me but gave no Dakshina. Give me Rs. 25 now!' Balvant paid it."[47]

It seems appropriate to begin an examination of the year 1912 by continuing with excerpts from Khaparde's diary. These, in fact, help illuminate the religious atmosphere surrounding the saint of Shirdi.

On January 1, Khaparde recorded: "Baba narrated the story of a former birth in which he (Baba), Jog, Dada Kelkar, Madhavrao Deshpande, myself and Dikshit lived together in a blind alley with his murshid (guru). He (Sai) has now brought us together again."[48]

Baba's claim of having been a disciple of an Islamic *murshid* in a previous birth, together with some of his *bhaktas*, is noteworthy.

On January 7, Khaparde wrote: "He looked exceedingly pleased and cast yogic glances at me. I passed the whole day in a sort of ecstasy."[49]

On several dates Khaparde noted Baba casting on him or on

others a "yogic glance." These glances, which his followers regarded as being powerful, must have been frequent and much desired, since on some dates he explicitly says that Baba gave *no* yogic glances.

On January 12, he noted: "He was very gracious and repeatedly let me have smoke out of his pipe. It solved many of my doubts and I felt delighted."[50]

On January 17, Khaparde wrote: "The mid-day arti was late. Baba commenced a very good tale: He had a good well. The water in it was sky-blue, and its supply was inexhaustible. Four Motas (bailing buckets) could not empty it, and the fruit grown with the water was very pure and tasty. He did not continue the story beyond this."[51]

Again this offers an example of Baba's allegorical speech. Bharadwaja proposes the following interpretation: "The well is the spiritual heart, the pure water is the chidakash, that is, the spiritual expanse within, the inexhaustible source of bliss. The four buckets are the four purusharthas or objects of man's endeavour, viz. righteousness, wealth, fulfilment of needs and liberation."[52]

The fruit may symbolize the *phala*, that is, enlightenment.

On January 19 the *pujārī* of Baba, Megha Shyam, died.[53] Khaparde offers a touching memory of Megha's death:

> This was a very sad day. I got up very early and after finishing my prayer discovered that it yet wanted an hour or so to day break. So I lay down and was aroused for Kakad Arti by Bapusaheb Jog. Dikshit Kaka told me that Megha had died about 4 A.M. The Kakad Arti was done but Sayin Maharaj did not show his face clear and did not appear to open his eyes. He never threw glances spreading grace. After we returned, arrangements were made for the cremation of Megha's body. Sayin Baba came just as the body was being brought out and loudly lamented his death. His voice was so touching that it brought tears to every eye. He followed the body up to the bend in the main road near the village and then went his usual way. Megha's body was taken under the Bada tree and consigned to flames there. Sayin Baba could be distinctly heard lamenting his death even at that distance, and he was seen waving his hands and swaying as if in Arti to say goodbye. There was a good supply of dry fuel, and flames soon rose very high. Dikshit Kaka, myself, Bapusaheb Jog, Upasani, Dada Kelkar and all were there, and praised the lot of Megha that his body was seen and touched by Sayin Baba on the head, heart, shoulders and feet. . . . I remember how Baba foretold his death three days ago.[54]

This photo, probably taken somewhere around 1912, shows Sai Baba on his evening rounds. To his left is Gopalrao Buti, Nanasaheb Nimonkar stands on his right. The leper Bhagoji Shinde has the honor of holding the ceremonial umbrella (chattrā).

Megha's functions as *pujārī* were assumed by Sakharam Hari (also known as Bapusaheb Jog), a staunch devotee who from that day performed *ārtī* at the *masjid* and *cāvaḍī* till Baba's death. Jog was also entrusted with the duty of reading and explaining the *Jñāneshvarī* and the *Eknāth Bhāgavata* in Sathe's *vāḍā*. He had settled in Shirdi with his wife back in 1909.[55]

On January 20, Khaparde noted: "A Jagirdar[56] came and Baba would not let him approach or worship him. People interceded for him in vain. Appa Kote did his utmost and Sai let the visitor enter the masjid and worship the pillar near the fire-place, but he would not give udi."[57]

On January 22, he wrote: "Lakshmibai Kanjagli attended our Paramamrit class[58] and went to the masjid. Baba called her his mother-in-law and made a joke about her saluting him. Has she been accepted by him as his disciple?"[59]

On January 29, he reported: "I did not get up till 1 P.M. Madhavrao and others tried to awaken me for the arti but I did not respond. They went to the arti. The matter reached Sai and he said that he would awaken me. Somehow, I got up as the arti was being finished and attended the closing portion of it."[60]

On February 7, he wrote: "I found Sai sitting and, in the yard, a man was exhibiting the tricks of his monkey."[61]

On December 14, he noted: "He smiled most benignly. It is worthwhile spending years here to see it even once. I was overjoyed and stood gazing like mad."[62]

Finally, on December 16, 1912: "Today he made passes with his short stick towards East, North, and South. Then he proceeded with hard words as usual.... Immersed in care, he gazed steadily at the East and West and dismissed us all with the usual words: 'Go to the wada...' He was in a pleased mood and danced as he proceeded..."[63]

These excerpts confirm Baba's eccentric and unpredictable personality, his tender and, at the same time, harsh disposition, his love of paradox and symbolism, as well as his passion for unusual and bizarre ritual practices.

In this regard, Das Ganu described a curious ritual performed by Baba. According to the *Charters and Sayings*:

> Baba when alone used to take out coins from his pocket and rub their surface with his fingers (as a result of which all the letters etc. were rubbed out) saying:
>
> "Nanache Nanache (that is, Nana's Nana's), Kakache Kakache, Somyache Somyache, etc."

> By this act, adverse circumstances against these persons were rubbed out. That is what the devotees felt and believed.[64]

Sai Baba thus operated the magical protection of his *bhaktas*: by levigating the coins' surfaces, he symbolically smoothed their lives from possible obstacles or impending disaster.

This episode calls to mind the analogy of the pot and the potter, suggested by Kabir and others: the guru, that is, the potter, removes the faults from his disciples, that is, the pots. He takes away all depressions and protuberances of his "jars," rubbing off and rounding all angularities.

In the year 1912, Bharadwaja's biography signals an episode of Sai's *antarajñāna* that saw S. B. Nachne as protagonist[65] and a second episode in which Baba gave proof of his ubiquity power to a young pilgrim. He also gave proof of knowing the Kaṇṇāda language.[66]

Narasimhaswami reports two episodes of requests for *dakṣiṇā* in 1912.

In the first one, Baba asked Rs. 10 from one S. S. D. Nimonkar. Six months later, the latter got a notice raising his pay by Rs. 10.[67]

In the second one, Baba requested a judge devotee to offer Rs. 40 more than he had already paid. But the man did not have the sum. Baba advised him to go talk with three of his devotees: Shyama Deshpande, H. S. Dikshit, and Nana Chandorkar. They explained to him that the gift Baba really wanted was the surrender of four things, that is, mind, heart, time, and soul. Sai then gave a lesson in humility to Nana.[68]

Related to a *dakṣiṇā* request is another well-known episode that all sources mention: A very rich man came to see Baba, anxious to attain *Brahmajñāna*. He told Sai: "Baba, show me God (Brahman). It is for this reason that I came all this long way. People say that Shirdi Baba reveals Brahman quickly."[69]

The texts describe this man as impatient and stingy, not willing to spend his money on accomodations, transportation, and so forth.

Baba at first spoke about *Brahman*'s nature. Then, he directed someone present at the *masjid* to go look for a loan of Rs. 5 in the village. Though the rich man had Rs. 250 in his pocket, he didn't offer it and kept silent all the time. When, having lost his patience, he again pressed Baba to help him in order to grasp *Brahman*, Sai harshly replied:

"What I have been doing all this while, is to enable you to see God—even as you are now seated. Have you understood nothing? I want five. One must surrender five things to get to Brahman. One must surrender the five senses (indriya), the five Pranas, Manas, Buddhi, and Ahamkar (Mind, Intellect, and Ego), all of which involve Vairagya, that is, detachment. The road to Brahmajnan is hard to tread. All cannot tread it. When it dawns, there will be light. One who feels unattached to things terrestrial and celestial is alone competent to have Brahmajnan."

The man found that Baba had read his strong attachment to Rs. 5, which he considered more important than getting Brahmajnan Upadesha.[70]

Baba rigorously pinpointed how perfect the sentiment of *vairāgya* must be in a disciple treading the arduous path of *Brahmajñāna*. Detachment must be radical: from the terrestrial as well as from the celestial. Celestial aspirations include the pursuit of heavenly realms and *siddhis*.

The year 1912 was a time of difficult challenges for Upasani. We know that he participated in G. S. Khaparde's religious classes from January until March 27 and that on February 6 he composed *ārtī* verses for Baba.

Sai, through the request for *dakṣiṇā* and other means, progressively divested Upasani of all material comforts, placing him in a condition of utter dependence on local people's charity. For example, H. S. Dikshit offered him free meals at his *vāḍā*.

This solution, however, did not last long. The villagers did not show much sympathy for Upasani, a newcomer and a stranger. Many were jealous of him, since Baba gave Upasani much attention and often proclaimed his virtues and spiritual excellence. Upasani himself on June 21, 1924 recalled:

> While in Shirdi I had seen a man in the worst stage of leprosy; he had almost lost his fingers, pus was oozing from them and so on. I used to bathe this man, and wash his clothes; that dirty water, thickened with all that muck, I used to drink. I was in such a state then.... Darshana of a leper and service to him is the simplest method to make one's mind and buddhi pure and to attain the state of Vishnu.[71]

The sources report that Sai Baba would sometimes address him as "pure *Bhagavan*."[72]

The villagers' jealousy was also fed by the fact that Upasani, being far more erudite than most of them, manifested an annoying haughtiness in their eyes. His wierd conduct and aloofness did the rest.

By the month of June or July, Dikshit no longer offered him free meals at the *vāḍā*. Upasani went back to Khandoba's temple, utterly disgusted, and began fasting. He practiced severe *tapas*, refusing solid food for long periods.

On August 15, with Baba's consent and blessings, Upasani and others installed Sai's *pādukās* under the famous *nīm* tree. For the occasion, Upasani composed a *śloka* celebrating the greatness of the *nīm* and Baba's yogic powers: "I bow to Lord Sai Nath, Who by His constant stay at the foot of the Nim tree—which though bitter and unpleasant was yet oozing nectar—made it better than the wish-fulfilling tree."[73]

In November, disconsolate, Upasani told a palmist that his life was miserable and wasted.[74]

Sai Baba, however, continued to reassure him, simply asking him "not to do anything" (*uge muge*), not even to practice *mantra-japa*, which Upasani considered important. Sai told him: "Who asked you to do all this? Keep quiet. Do nothing."[75]

When Upasani expressed his pain and unhappiness to Baba, the latter said: "I am always with you. You need not fear. The more you suffer now, the happier and more excellent will be your future. You are in one scale, and the world is in the other. You are going to be an Avadhuta. Hundreds will rush to take your darshan."[76]

As Upasani himself recalled in a speech he gave on February 7, 1924: "When things became intolerable for me in Shirdi, one day I said to Sai Baba that no more was I able to suffer. At this, he replied that I should suffer all that I could now, as after that, there would be eternal happiness for me, since my state was the highest, without comparison. With these words in mind I began quietly to submit to all the suffering that came my way."[77]

Sai Baba's prophecy came true. In the meantime, Upasani continued his hard *sādhanā* of surrender, facing difficulties with force of character. His third wife died around the end of 1912. Much perturbed, Upasani came to Baba and said, "Here is Rs. 10. Please do something to give Sadgati[78] to my wife." Baba responded, "Keep the money. She (her spirit) has already come to me. What had to be taken from you has already been taken."[79] Sai, consoling Upasani about his wife's death, assured him that his *kṛpā* towards him was already operative.

Next I shall turn to events that are reported to have taken place during 1913.

Arthur Osborne's biography narrates the following episode:

> B. A. Patel was a landowner and revenue officer. His aged father had a stroke. He went to Sai Baba to ask for udhi for him, but Sai Baba said: "I will not give you udhi. Allah Malik hai."
>
> Three days later the father died.
>
> This Patel was very proud of his physical strength. In 1913, when Sai Baba was already old and frail, Patel would often massage his legs and then pick him up bodily and carry him to the fire. One day, soon after his father's death, Patel tried to do this but was utterly unable to move him. Baba laughed at him and Patel records: "He taught me two things, not to be proud of my strength and not to grieve for my father."
>
> Sai Baba said to him: "Why should you grieve? In five months he will return." In five months a son was born to Patel.[80]

The explanation for Baba's refusal to intercede might have been the "unalterable" karma of Patel's father, which had to follow its course. As previously noted, Baba's refusals of "intervention" seem to have been rare. Sai's assurance that the man would be reborn as Patel's son gives us an insight into popular beliefs concerning karmic redistribution.[81]

Patel's intimacy with Baba is noteworthy. The text presents Sai as being by this time "old and frail," almost dependent on the devotee's help to move around. Patel's inability to lift Baba on this occasion may hint at the latter's *siddhi* of increasing one's weight.

The text *Ambrosia in Shirdi* relates a similar instance of intimacy between Tatya Kote Patil[82] and Baba, ascribed to a much earlier date:

> Baba used to wrestle with Ganpat Kote Patil on occasion. Tatya lifted Baba with his one hand. Baba would say: "Leave me, or else I will fall." Then, Tatya would let Baba go, smilingly. Tatya would take away his turban and tie it on Baba's head as a king's turban. He would put his upper cloth on Baba's body and bring a mirror to Baba, so that he could see himself reflected in the mirror.... Afterwards, Baba would remove all these things and hand them over to Tatya.[83]

Tatya was the son of Bayajibai, the woman who first accepted Baba as a holy man and who fed him from the earliest days of his permanence at Shirdi.

Sai Baba was very intimate with her family. Sometimes, as in a game of inverted roles, Sai would prostrate himself at Tatya's feet, exclaiming: "*Jaya deva, jaya deva*" (Hail oh god) producing great puzzlement on the devotee's part.[84] The formal *guru-śiṣya* relationship was infringed and reversed in a playful attitude. I shall return to Baba's peculiar relationship with Tatya Kote when treating Sai's *mahāsamādhi.*

In 1913, Osborne's biography reports that Baba healed the wife of one Abdul Rahim Shamshuddin Rangari of the plague. Sai addressed the husband in Hindustani. He placed his hand on the wife's head saying, *Khudā acchā karegā* (Allah will put it right).[85]

According to Osborne's narration, the man offered *dakṣiṇā* and Baba gave *udī* in return. After a few hours, the woman felt better. The couple then decided to leave Shirdi that very night, without asking for Baba's authorization. Their *tongā,* however, had an accident midway between Shirdi and Kopergaon. Frightened, the two didn't know what to do. About two hours later, a *tongā* said to have been expressly sent there by Baba arrived, and the couple was brought back to Shirdi around 1 A.M. Baba was waiting for them. He said: "You left without permission; that's why you had this trouble."[86] The two admitted their mistake.

Rangari brought his narration to a close saying: "He made us stay near the mosque for the rest of the night while he went in and carried on his usual meditation. In the morning he went out to beg and came back with some bread and vegetables, of which he took a part and gave the rest to us. My wife was able to eat solid food. Then he gave us leave to go.... This was my only visit to Shirdi but it gave me firm faith in Sai Baba."[87]

Besides Baba's act of healing and proof of *antarajñāna,* the account confirms that the *faqīr* spent the night in contemplative practices, comprising vocal as well as silent remembrance of holy names (*dhikr, nāmasmaraṇa*).

Another episode signals how life with Baba stimulated feelings of genuine brotherhood by orthodox Muslims towards the Hindus. Osborne's biography offers the following story of a *paṭhān* Muslim by name Abdullah:

> Someone...told me that there was a great man called Sai Baba at Shirdi, who showered money on fakirs and would send me to Mecca if I wanted; so I went to Shirdi.
>
> As I entered the gate of the mosque Sai Baba was standing there before me. Our eyes met and I felt at once that he was my Guru. I stayed on at Shirdi. He fed me and other fakirs abundantly, and I decided to stay there and lead an easy life. This was in 1913, when I was still quite young and had not begun to take life seriously.
>
> Nevertheless, my stay with Sai Baba brought about a

> marked change in my attitude of mind. When I first came to Shirdi I looked upon Hindus as my enemies, but after I had been about three years with Sai Baba this feeling of animosity passed away and I began to regard them as brothers.[88]

Regarding the issue of tolerance, Baba is reported to have said:

> All Gods are one. There is no difference between a Hindu and a Mohammadan. Mosque and temple are the same. Yet I will respect your (people's) susceptibilities, and not enter the temple (as you object to the entry).
>
> Look at Chokamela's life.[89]

Sai's reference to the exemplary life of the saint-poet Chokhamela is noteworthy. An untouchable Vaiṣṇava *mahār*[90] born in the thirteenth century, he joined the *bhakti* movement centered around Namdev. Most of his songs were in praise of Vitthala. Chokhamela rejected the notion of untouchability and, as E. Zelliot remarks, his radicality consisted in protesting against the idea of pollution. He sang:

> The only impurity is in the five elements.
> There is only one substance in the world.
> Then, who is pure and who is impure?[91]

Sai Baba's statement had a twofold significance; *inter*religious as well as *intra*religious: on one hand, the assertion of Hindu-Muslim tolerance, on the other, the rejection of the Hindu notions of purity and pollution on which religious and caste distinctions are based.

The *faqīr*'s vision of universality seemed to be grounded not only in the belief in the oneness of God, but also on the intuition of the oneness of human nature.

All religions are equally valid in Sai's vision, since each ultimately tends to one and the same goal. Thus, Baba considered the mosque and the temple as typologically equivalent. Nonetheless he avoided offending people's religious sensibilities.

Bharadwaja's biography reports another *camatkār* of Baba, appearing as Vitthala and Rukmini all in one, thus stressing his identity with the Pandharpur deity.[92]

Four of Sai's healing episodes are reported in 1913: curing of a child's fever by appearing in his house and administering *udī*,[93] healing a devotee from pneumonia,[94] restoring sight to a blind person,[95] and curing an asthmatic attack and a fever.[96]

Bharucha's biography narrates Sai Baba's meeting with a desperate couple who had lost their only son. At the end of the conversation, Baba said: "This fellow blames me for his son's death. Why does he come and cry in my mosque? Does he think I go around killing people's children? But never mind about that. What I will do now is bring that very child back to his wife's womb."[97]

Thus saying, Baba placed his hand on the head of the kneeling man and promised that his troubles would come to an end. Before the couple left the village, Sai gave the husband a coconut, instructing him to wrap it in the upper folds of his wife's sari. The woman soon bore a son. In the Deccan, filling a woman's lap with fruits, particularly coconuts, is believed to induce future pregnancy.[98]

The *Charters and Sayings* reports:

> In 1913, one S. B. Mohile brought his daughter to Baba, hoping he might cure her cleft lip. Baba told him:
>
> "I know what you have come for. I can cure her, but it will be of no use. The girl is of a divine sort (Daivi) and consequently her span of life will be very short. Next Magha Shuddha Chathurti,[99] she will expire. If on that day you are not at home and go away to your office, you will not be able to see her alive on your return."
>
> The girl died on that very date when the father was in his office.[100]

Baba's reply is strange indeed. The girl's divine nature might imply her having "burned" all karmic ties, thus having aquired a sort of "angelic" status. As foreseen by Baba, the girl died a few months later.

It is useful to examine some passages describing Baba's compassion, offering a taste of the atmosphere surrounding the saint:

> On the Nama-saptaha[101] of 1913, Baba sat surrounded by a large crowd.
>
> [Baba said,] "Shama, go out. Beyond the wall there is an old man sitting and he has some sugar candy with him. Beg of him some candy for me and bring it."
>
> Shama went out and found an old man, his saliva dripping, stinking pus exuding from a wound on his chest, pestered by flies, and wearing a rag, in one corner of which some sugar candy was tied in a knot. Shama brought him through the crowd to Baba and said: "Here he is."
>
> Baba placed his hand in blessing on the old man's head,

took out a piece of the candy and said: "Take back the rest of the candy" (as prasad).[102]

In a talk with Dabholkar, Baba said:

> By Rinanubandha, you have come to me. Have regard for Rinanubandha. Whoever or whatever creature comes to you, do not drive away but receive with due consideration. Give food to the hungry, water to the thirsty, and clothes to the naked. Then God will be pleased. Do not bark at people. Be not pugnacious. Bear with others' reproach. Speak only gentle words. This is the way to happiness.
>
> Let others and the world turn topsy-turvy but do not mind that. Keep on to your own straight course. The world maintains a wall—the wall of differentiation between oneself and others, between you and me. Destroy this wall.
>
> God is the supreme Lord. Allah Malik. Wondrous, precious and long-enduring are his works. Your object will be fulfilled in due course. We shall both attain bliss by mutual love.[103]

Here is a striking example of Baba's insistence on practicing a virtuous life, full of love and compassion: only in such a holistic perspective can the walls of divisiveness and hatred be overcome.

For the same year, the *Charters and Sayings* reports an enigmatic account:

> In 1913 Baba gave a long personal story of a previous birth of his: We were two brothers. We walked on. On the way my brother went ahead. He was bitten by animals and he died.
>
> Five or six men came up and asked me: "Where is your brother?" I told them the facts and added: "I made a shroud for him." Refusing to believe me they went in search for him, despite my protest, and were eaten up by animals.
>
> A stout lady came next, made the same enquiry and the same search, and shared their fate. I gave her also the shroud.
>
> Then as I went on, six or seven Moslems came with a sheep. They cut it before me and asked me to eat the flesh. I said I was a Brahmin and could not eat it. They then began to force it into my mouth. I said: "I will pray to God and then eat." I covered the flesh with a cloth and then prayed to God. Then the mutton was converted into huge red roses.
>
> They were so big that you could not enclose one rose into your palm. The Moslems went away. Then I walked on.

I was walking on a footpath and was enclosed by a wide expanse of clear water. No path was visible from there. This is God's work.

Baba, turning to Shama: "What is our duty? Behave properly. That is enough. Go to the Wada and read Pothi."[104]

Such an odd and evocative story, comparable to a dream sequence, is clearly symbolical and one out of which many different interpretations might be derived. I shall limit myself to a few basic considerations.

First of all, Baba identifies himself with a vegeterian *brāhmaṇ*. Such characterization, referring to one of his previous births, must have certainly gladdened his Hindu devotees.

According to unfathomable reincarnation processes, Indians believe it perfectly possible for a Hindu to be reborn as a Muslim and vice versa. In fact, hagiographic texts on the lives of Indian saints report such occurrences.

The change of the mutton into "huge red roses" calls once again to mind the legend of Kabir's corpse being converted into flowers. Such a transformation, in Sai Baba's account, might be a ritual of purification.

Lastly, the path that Sai treads, having overcome all difficulties, leads ultimately to a "wide expanse of clear water," that is, to the ocean of *Brahman* in which the individual soul merges itself.

Two short episodes taking place between 1913 and 1914 deserve mention.

In the first one, Baba is said to have intervened to protect his devotee, S. B. Nachne, from having his throat cut by a madman's assault. Sai commented on the episode to one Anna Chinchikar thus: "Anna, if I had delayed an instant, this man would have indeed perished. The mad man had seized his throat with his hands. But I extricated him. What is to be done? If I do not save my own children, who else will?"[105]

In the second episode, one R. K. Dube is said to not have kept his vow of visiting Shirdi. He went to Sasarvada instead, and during the trip he lost a child and his wife fell ill. Then, Baba is said to have appeared in a vision reprimanding Dube for his conduct and to have administered *udī* to his wife, after which she recovered.[106]

Finally, I wish to return to an assessment of Upasani's life in 1913. According to the sources, his hardships did not diminish. In January, his repulsion towards food became intense. Though physically weakened, he was still able to undertake hard manual labor, as, for instance, turning stone rollers on the road.

In April, he was visited by doctor Chidambaram Pillai and, though his heart rate had diminished to forty beats per minute, he was found to be in fairly good condition.

He was always sad, however, and deeply dissatisfied with his life. Remembering those days, in a speech delivered on June 18, 1924, Upasani remarked:

> For days on end—for many a month when I was sitting in a mountain-niche or when I was sitting in the temple at Shirdi, I was without any food or water. My body was reduced to mere skin and bones, but my inner strength had increased. I was doing hard, laborious menial work such as breaking stones, ploughing the fields, drawing water, milling sugar-cane, etc. alone, all by myself. For hours on end I used to do such work without any rest. I was able to walk very fast. This has been seen by many.[107]

So much had pain become part and parcel of his daily life, that he became addicted to it. Upasani, in a speech he gave on February 7, 1924, recalled:

> I used to feel the day devoid of pain as a very tiresome one. I constantly used to try to have pain; pain had become a source of enjoyment for me. While sitting in the Khandoba temple at Shirdi, many a time the scorpions used to sting me, but I had got used to enjoy that pain. I used to hate pleasure. If somebody brought food, I used to throw it away. I felt pleasure in fasting. I did not take any baths for years, as I felt tired of having one. A thick layer of dirt formed over my body. I felt pleasure in lying—in wallowing in dirt and night-soil. Menial labour and hard work in the sun I used to enjoy. I felt pleasure in tasting urine, night-soil, etc. In short, I had become addicted to pain; and even now I like it.[108]

In July his health conditions worsened and, confiding in the Marathi novelist H. N. Apte, he said that his life was bitter, and that he did not expect to live long. The visits which first Balakrishna, his brother, and later his mother paid to him, did not change the situation.

At the same time, his *sādhanā* of surrender went on.

In January 1925, Upasani recalled "the opening of the Brahmarandhra":[109]

> One day while staying in Khandoba temple at Shirdi, I took a pot of water with me and went out to answer nature's call. I went in the fields in the direction of the well. I was walking with my head bent low. I had no thought in my mind, but something was being forced on me—worked on me—from within. Suddenly I felt that something had given way in my head, as if the water from within was sprouting out forcibly in a stream as through a garden-hose, through the center of my head. I alone knew what I felt then; however, no sound as if something had snapped was heard. The inner eye of mine was seeing all this clearly.... It was the Brahmarandhra that had got opened and that inner eye was seeing the whole Brahmanda[110] clearly through that opening.... By the water in the head, here, I mean the inner light. Like a powerful search light, a powerful beam projected itself through my Brahmarandhra.... With the opening of the Brahmarandhra, that is, on the head being broken, that Brahma entered within, or rather the inner and outer Brahma became one.[111]

Moreover:

> Once while in Khandoba temple I was saying: "Oh, I have lost my head." I meant that the head was there, but it had become empty—it contained nothing. What does the new-born child or the child in the mother's womb know? Such must be the state of one's mind.[112]

On July 18th, on the occasion of the *Gurupūrṇimā* celebration, Sai Baba inaugurated Upasani's cult, declaring him to be a guru worthy of worship.[113] Baba sent Chandrabai Borkar to the Khandoba temple so that she could worship Upasani in the same fashion as he was being worshipped at the *masjid*. The woman, in spite of Upasani's remonstrations, celebrated his *pūjā*. Again, Baba's decision appeared incomprehensible to him.

At first, Upasani succeeded in stopping the *pūjā*. After some time, however, it started again with his consent.

Few people participated in his worship at the beginning; many actually opposed it. For instance, Nanavali, a *brāhmaṇ pāgal* ascetic, used to disturb Upasani's *pūjā*, insulting him and even throwing mud at him. Once, he came to the point of tying Upasani with a rope to a pillar, abusing him at length.[114] As Upasani himself recalled: "In Shirdi, during Sai Baba's time, there was a fellow by name Nanavali; he was a man with a very strong prakriti (nature). He troubled me and Sai Baba as well. Once he caught me and pulled me to the Masjid of Sai Baba, took away my clothes leaving me naked, and started behaving like a buffoon."[115]

Sources report that in November Bapusaheb Jog, with Baba's assent, took food to Upasani in order to stop one of his fasts:

> Upasani: Give it to crows and dogs as others do and go away.
>
> Jog: It is for you we have brought the food. Not for the crows.
>
> Upasani: I am not distinct from crows and dogs. Feeding them is feeding me.
>
> Jog: This high philosophy I cannot comprehend. If you will eat it, I will leave it. Else I will take it away.
>
> Upasani: (angrily) Get away, if you do not wish to feed crows and dogs.
>
> Jog: It is to you we have been directed to take this naivedya.
>
> Upasani Maharaj was in an angry mood, in one of his tantrums, and he flung a brickbat at Bapu Saheb, hurting his arm, and making it bleed.
>
> Bapu Saheb asked the villagers present to seize and tie up Upasani Maharaj and carry him to Sri Sai at the mosque. Maharaj was tied with ropes. After some detention at Bapu Saheb's house, Maharaj was carried to Sai. Everything was reported to Sri Sai, who merely ordered Maharaj to be let loose saying: "He is a man of God. Let none trouble him." He also told Maharaj: "You should sit quiet. Go to your temple."[116]

Upasani, however, could not understand Sai Baba's whole attitude towards him. Moreover, not being able to stand the local people any longer, he began planning drastic changes.

Ramalingaswami's text discusses three episodes said to have taken place in 1914: Baba restoring the lost property of one M. R. Tagare, a doctor,[117] Baba accepting the offerings of Sri Sai Sharan Anand,[118] and Baba appearing on a train in order to save one G. D. Kadam from the hands of a gang of Bhils.[119]

The *Charters and Sayings* reports a passage in which Baba shows his appreciation for an elderly woman's devotion:

> In 1914, Ramanavami season, when myriads flocked to Baba, an old woman was shouting:
>
> Hallo, take pity upon me, an old woman! Hallo, Baba, give me your darshan.

Shama went out and elbowed his way back with her into Sai Baba's presence. She melted into tears and held Baba with both her arms round his waist.

B.—Mother! How long have I waited for you! Have you brought anything for me to eat?

Old woman—Here is a piece of stale flat bread and an onion. I started my journey with one flat bread and two onions. But tired by the journey, I sat at a stream in the morning and ate off half the cake with one onion. Here is the remainder. You had better eat it.

B.—(crunching the stale bread and eating it with gusto) How sweet, oh mother, is your bread![120]

In May 1914, in a dialogue between Sai and a woman from Bandra, Tendulkar by name, Baba spoke about his true identity, declaring his omnipresence.

Baba first relieved the woman from a chronic headache by touching her head. He then expressed his approval of her adoration of Ganapati, her family's *iṣṭadevatā*. Baba said he knew her from her childhood. He also said that all the offerings she had made to Ganapati had reached him. He then advised her to keep that Ganapati image, even though it had broken.

Baba [said]: If your child breaks his arm, will you cast it into water? Worship it daily.[121]

Moreover, Baba added:
Mother, I have to go thrice a day to your house.

...A local lady was astonished at this statement as she saw Baba daily at Shirdi, and said:

Baba, what is this strange thing you say?

B: I do not speak falsehood. I am Mahalakshmi. Mother, I come to your house. You give me things to eat, is that not true?

The Bandra lady answered yes.[122]

Baba then, addressing the Shirdi lady, said:

Yes, mother. I go easily to Bhav's house (Bhav's house at Bandra). In the middle, there is a wall. Jumping over it, next comes the railway line, and then Bhav's house (at this point

Baba described the crow's flight from Shirdi to the lady's house at Bandra).

I have to fly across walls and excavations.[123]

The famous episode of Sai Baba's interrogation by a legal officer is of utmost importance. Though no date has been established for the event, I suspect it took place during Baba's last years:

> A person was charged before the Dhulia Magistrate's Court with stealing jewels, etc. The man pleaded that Sai Baba of Shirdi had given him the jewels and cited him as a witness. Summons came.
>
> Constable: Baba, here is a summons for you.
>
> Baba: Take it and throw it into the fire.
>
> Somebody took it and threw it into the fire. The report was sent that Baba was served, and as Baba was absent at the trial a warrant was sent to Shirdi.
>
> Ganpatram, the constable, said to Baba: Baba, they have sent out a warrant. Will you kindly come with me to Dhulia?
>
> Baba, angrily: Throw that piece of paper into—(Baba was cursing and swearing).
>
> The constable was perplexed. Then, as advised by N. G. Chandorkar, a mahajar..., that is, a note was sent to the effect that Baba was worshipped by large numbers as God; that the issue of summons and warrants was improper and undesirable, and that if his evidence was necessary, a commissioner might be sent to take it. Then Nana Joshi, the commissioner, a first class magistrate, came and examined Baba.
>
> Commissioner: What is your name?
>
> Baba: They call me Sai Baba.
>
> Com: Your father's name?
>
> B: Also Sai Baba.
>
> Com: Your Guru's name?
>
> B: Venkusa.
>
> Com: Creed or religion?
>
> B: Kabir.
>
> Com: Caste or race?

B: Parvardigar (that is, God).

Com: Age, please?

B: Lakhs of years.

Com: Will you solemnly affirm that what you are going to say is the truth?

B: Truth.

Com: Do you know the accused, so and so?

B: Yes, I know him and I know everyone.

Com: The man says he is your devotee and that he lived with you. Is that so?

B: Yes. I live with everyone. All are mine.

Com: Did you give him jewels as alleged by him?

B: Yes. I gave him. Who gives what to whom?

Com: If you gave him the jewels, how did you get them and become possessed of them?

B: Everything is mine.

Com: Baba, here is a serious charge of theft. That man says that you delivered the jewels to him.

B: What is all this? What the devil have I to do with all that?

The Commissioner was perplexed. Then it was suggested that the village diaries showing the presence of strangers in the village should be sent for. The diary showed that the accused, a stranger, was not at Shirdi at the time of his alleged receipt from Baba. And it was known that Baba never left the village.

The Commissioner put these facts before Baba and Baba said they were true. That closed the Commission evidence. Baba was not asked to sign or put his mark. Baba does not appear to have signed or put his mark to any paper at any time.[124]

Baba's assertion of belonging to *Parvardigar*'s "race" implicitly supports the belief in his "divine identity," together with the attributes which go with it: omniscience, omnipresence, and omnipotence.

On this important text in which Baba asserts that "Venkusa" was his guru, A. Osborne comments:

Sai Baba was not a name but an epithet.... By giving it as his father's name also, he implied that he was no longer conditioned by human parentage.

Kabir was a great poet-saint...who had both Hindu and Muslim followers; by giving his name, Sai Baba intimated that he also stood above the religions, that is, at their source, and guided his followers on both paths.

'Parvardigar' is a Divine Name;...one who has attained self-realization is above the four castes, in the divine state; this was the implication.

As for the reply about his age, it implies that he was beyond the limitations of time, established in the eternal now of spiritual awareness.[125]

Again on the issue of "what truly is," God, and so forth Chandorkar once questioned Baba on how to recognize such supreme reality. The *Charters and Sayings* reports:

N. G. Chandorkar asked Baba: Who is God? What is He like? Where is He? How are we to see Him?

Baba: I will tell you later on.

Later...

Baba: *Baddhas* (the very worldly)[126] do not know or observe the difference between right and wrong...or what God is. They have no moral tendencies.

Ever immersed in the world (and impure in heart), having no faith in Scriptures or saints, they do not get to God—but go to Hell.

The *Mumukshus,*[127] disgusted with the *baddha* state, begin *vichara* and *viveka* and thirst for the sight of God. They are devoted to God and observe the moral law.

They become *sadhakas,* by adopting *sadhanas* such as the repetition of God's name (*Japa*) and meditation on God (*Dhyana*) in solitude, withdrawing their minds from the objects of the senses. They love to move with saints.

These, when perfect, are called *Siddhas.*[128] At this stage, God becomes the same as man; praise, the same as blame, etc. They have no desires. They are past the notion that the body is their home or their self. They feel their self to be identical with God. 'I am Brahman' is their feeling.

To know God, see how God is viewed by each of these, at each stage. Then ultimately, God is seen as manifested in all forms—moveable and immoveable.

God is everywhere. There is no place from which he is absent. But behold the power of *Maya* that does not allow *Ishvara* to be seen and recognised (in all). I, you and all the world are *Amsa,* that is, parts of the Lord.

Therefore let none hate others. Forget not that God is in every place.

Thereby Love (non-hatred) is there, of itself. When that springs up, everything is achieved.[129]

Sai Baba's Vedāntic terminology and approach are crystal clear, and his presentation of the three fundamental human categories of *baddha, mumukṣu,* and *siddha* is a traditional one. In such a vision, each and everything is a cell, a portion (*aṁśa*) of Ishvara's divine body. When the omnipresence of God is firmly established in one's experience, then *prema* (pure, selfless love) unfolds naturally, crowning the realization of *ātmavidyā.*

The *Charters and Sayings* reports another important text in which, talking with one Abdul Bhai, Sai gave out a complex genealogy of the gods.

Beginning with the *Oṃkāra,* root of all reality, Sai Baba furnished a long list of more than eighty divine potencies, Hindu as well as Muslim. The traditional list of ten *avatāras* is naturally included, and Baba's enumeration ends with the citation of the Kalkin *avatāra.*

What appears most significant is the chaotic blending of Hindu gods, such as Prajapati, Vishnu, Parashuram, and Keshava, with divine forces derived from the Islamic tradition, such as Kadin, Rebak, Kadram, and Nur (the divine light).[130]

Baba, following a traditional scheme, stated that four were the *avatāras* in the *Kṛta-yuga,* three in the *Tretā,* two in the *Dvāpara,* and one there will be in the present *Kali* age.[131]

Then, contradicting himself, he gave the following list of ten *avatāras*: Matsya, Kaccha, Varaha, Narasimha, Vamana, Parashuram, Krishna, Buddha, himself, Kalkin.

Sai Baba here takes the place of Rama. Such an assimilation might be explained by Sai's predilection for this divine figure. Thus, if such an account is true, Baba would have had awareness of himself as an *avatāra.*[132]

Bharadwaja's biography reports Sai's prophetic words to Mrs. Jog: aware of his approaching death, Sai "saw" the site where the future *samādhi-mandir* would be built. "In 1914, the great fakir pointed out a piece of waste land of the village, the dumping ground, to Mrs. Bapusaheb Jog and said: 'It is my site; a big mansion will rise up here and we shall live therein. Big people will look after me.' Mrs. Jog took it as one of the very many inscrutable things he said."[133]

This appears as the earliest testimony in which Baba predicts his imminent death.

Upasani's situation in the year 1914 reached a turning point. On January 14, on the occasion of *Makara Saṃkrānti,*[134] Upasani started taking liquid food daily, interrupting his fast.

On July 25, unable to accept the local villagers' hostility anymore and possibly irritated by Baba's enigmatic behavior, he decided to leave Shirdi. His departure was similar to a flight: Upasani avoided meeting Baba and, during the night, he stealthily departed. In his "escape plan," he was helped by two doctors: the aforementioned Chidambaram Pillai and Ganapat Rao of Shinde.

He visited Shinde, Nagpur, Kharagpur, and several pilgrimage places. Gifted with oratorial capacities, a high moral stature, and *siddhis,*[135] his popularity rapidly increased and he began to be worshipped by more and more people.

We know that he visited Shirdi on at least three later occasions, that is, in 1915, 1916, and 1917, and that he finally settled in Sakuri, a small hamlet a few miles south of Shirdi, in 1917. In the beginning, he lived on the area's cremation grounds, a common practice among Śaiva ascetics.

In time, on that same site, he established an unusual institution: the *Upāsanī Kanyā Kumārī Sthān,* that is, a women's *āśram,* one of the very few in the whole of India, where particular emphasis is placed on the performance of Vedic rituals.[136]

In a speech on August 12, 1924, Upasani paid a significant tribute to Sai Baba:

> For this present state of mine, a huge force is responsible. That force emanated from Shri Sai Baba. When I asked for permission to leave Shirdi,[137] he said: "I will personally conduct you to the place. You do not know the road, and you may have no money to buy the ticket. I myself will buy a ticket for you. I will give you such a pass, that the train you take will lead you to your destination without any halt anywhere."
>
> Subsequently I moved as if on a special train; it hardly ever stopped; it just went on and on. Now I understand what Sai Baba meant by saying that he would give me a special ticket and put me aboard a special train. But about the train and the time and all that, well, how can I say anything?...The force or attraction of my Jiva towards worldly life...was just set back

> and made to revert quickly towards its origin; it is like reversing the train suddenly and despatching it back to its original destination. That is what was done by Sai Baba.... Whatever is happening or will happen here is not my responsibility. Whosoever made me board that train will look to all that. All this has come from him.[138]

Next, Ramalingaswami recounts an experience of a couple visiting Baba for the first time in 1915.

Mrs. Adilakshmiamal thus described the atmosphere around Sai: "I went to Shirdi with my husband and two girls on August 23, 1915, and took darshan of Baba.... We found Baba's darbar very grand. A number of dancing girls danced before him, kathas were performed, acrobatic feats were exhibited. There was always a thrilling crowd at the mosque and the chavadi. We stayed there for a month and a half."[139]

Several of Sai Baba's acts reported as taking place during 1915 I shall simply enumerate: fulfilling one devotee's desire,[140] helping one Tryambak Vishvanath in his return journey to Bombay from Shirdi,[141] advising S. B. Nachne of undertaking thoroughly whatever is begun,[142] curing Dada Kelkar's granddaughter by rubbing the child's eyes with onion,[143] knowing of a sweetmeat offering that Mrs. Tarkhad had sent through Balaram Mankar, who forgot to hand it over to him,[144] curing the fever of Bapusaheb Buti,[145] and finally, saving H. S. Dikshit and S. Moreshvar Phanse from a tiger's attack in the jungle.[146]

Narasimhaswami narrates:

> Doctor C. Pillai, suffering badly from severe guinea-worm,[147] [said] to H. S. Dikshit: Kaka Saheb, this pain is excruciating. Death is preferable. The pain is no doubt for repaying Purva Karma;[148] but go to Baba and ask him to stop the pain now and transfer the working of Purva Karma to ten later births of mine.
>
> H. S. D. went to Baba and conveyed the prayer.
>
> Baba [said]: Tell him not to fear. Why want ten more births? In ten days he can finish all that suffering. Saints exist to give devotees spiritual and temporal welfare, and Pillai wants death instead! Bring him here. Let him not get confused.
>
> The Doctor was brought and Baba gave him his own pillow to lie upon and said: Lean on this. Do not indulge in vain thoughts. Stretch your leg and be at ease. Without actual suffering, Karma cannot be got over. That is true. Karma is the

> cause of joy and sorrow. Therefore, put up with whatever comes to you. Allah Malik. God is the all controller and protector. Think of Him always. He will look after all. Surrender completely to Him. Think always on Him and you will see what He does.
>
> Then N. G. Chandorkar put a bandage over the wound.
>
> Baba—Take it off, Nana is mad. That will kill you. Now a crow will come and peck at the wound. That will make you alright.
>
> Another day, Abdul,...unknowingly put his foot over the wound of Dr. Pillai. The swelling was thus pressed, and the worms were squeezed out. Dr. Pillai first roared with pain.
>
> Pillai (later): Will the crow come and peck me hereafter?
>
> Baba—No, the crow (Abdul) has come. The worms have been thrown out. Go and rest in the Wada.
>
> By applying Udhi and taking in Udhi, without other treatment or medicine, the guinea-worm was cured in ten days.[149]

Ironically, a *brāhmaṇ* doctor is thus cured thanks to the involuntary intervention of a despised Muslim.

Apart from any considerations regarding Sai Baba's bizarre treatment, there are three things that the *faqīr* emphasizes: the function of saints as bestowers of spiritual as well as material benefits, the acknowledgement of karma as that which determines one's destiny, the belief that surrender is the royal path leading to union with God, liberation.

As we know, Abdul remained in Baba's service for nearly thirty years. When he first arrived at Shirdi, around 1890, Baba greeted him with the enigmatic words *Merā kāvā āyā* (My crow has come).[150]

Bharadwaja's biography signals another instance in the year 1915 when Baba admitted his inability to cure an illness, evidently due to karmic reasons:

> In 1915, a rich man of Harda, suffering from tuberculosis, came to Shirdi.
>
> One day his condition grew bad, and Narke was sent to Baba for udi for the patient. Baba just said: "What can it do for him? However, take it as he wants it!"
>
> Shama urged him to interfere with destiny and save the patient. Baba cryptically said: "How can he die? He'll come to life again tomorrow!"
>
> Not catching the hint, the devotees entertained false hopes

> and were disappointed when the man died. Later, Baba appeared in a dream to one of the bereaved kinsman, showed him the diseased lungs of the deceased and said: "I've relieved him of all this suffering."

Bharadwaja comments, "A Sadguru will not interfere with one's destiny unless it is spiritually useful to do so."[151]

On the urgent necessity of *ātmavicāra*, the *Charters and Sayings* notes: "Baba often said: 'Who are we? Night and day think on this.'"[152]

Around 1915, R. A. Tarkhad, managing director of a mill, got into a train compartment at Manmad in the dark, and fought for a seat with a police constable. When he arrived at Shirdi, Baba said: "With whom were you persisting in contest this morning? Bhav (Brother), we should not engage in contest with such people! 'Who are we?' This we must enquire into."[153]

On other occasions he said: "To know me, constantly think 'Who am I?', by Sravana and Manana."[154] He added: "Who are we? What are we? Where am I? Where are you? Where is all the world?"[155] And: "We must see our Self."[156]

In Baba's *advaitic* perspective, knowing oneself is the same as knowing *Brahman*, the Absolute.

The great Vedāntic question *ko'ham*, which the sage of Arunachala, Ramana Maharshi, constantly urged his disciples to meditate upon, is present also in Sai Baba's *upadeśa*.

Again on the necessity of *ātmavicāra*, we read:

> Baba: "Shama. What have the boys come here for?"
>
> Shama: "To take a photograph of you."
>
> Baba: "Tell the boys that no photo should be taken. (To have my real likeness), if the wall is pulled down, that is enough."[157]

The "wall," as Narasimhaswami comments, is the body and the idea that we are our body. Baba's real likeness is *Brahman*.

I shall later come back to Sai's *jñāna-mārga*, a path that, due to its difficulty, appears feasible for only a limited number of *sādhakas*.

Narasimhaswami reports another instance of Baba's alleged power of manifesting himself at different places at the same time:

> Sadu Bhayya (Sadashiv Dundiraj), who was at Harda, on February 15, 1915 was walking with some friends.... Suddenly,

Baba appeared to be coming from the opposite direction. He passed his hand into Sadu Bhayya's and, leaving a toothpick in the latter's hand, disappeared.

...Sadu Bhayya...went to Shirdi and narrated all the facts in Sai Baba's presence.

Sai Baba: "Sadu, go and tell this to Bade Baba." Sadu Bhayya went and narrated it before Bade Baba, Dr. Pillai and others. Bade Baba, very much excited, began to think and came weeping to Baba.

Bade Baba: "What Baba, you have been giving me large sums of money but money only; but to Sadu Bhayya you have given Sakshatkar."

So saying he wept.

Sai Baba: "What is to be done? Each gets what each chooses."

Bade Baba...subsequently lost all fortune and died.[158]

The question of one's identification with the guru is debated in this episode:

> Mr. R. was identifying himself with Baba and in 1915, at Rama Navami, tried to get Baba's approval and sanction for that identification. At Rama Navami, numerous devotees placed new clothes before Baba so that he may touch them and return them.[159] R. brought a very fine Dacca muslin...kept it inside his shirt and then, bowing to Baba, slyly thrust the muslin under Baba's gadi, when no one noticed it.
>
> R. was resolved that if Baba cared for his love, the muslin should be retained and not returned by Baba, as Baba and R. were one. When all clothes were returned, Baba got up.
>
> Baba: "I say, clear off all that lies on the gadi (mattress) and dust it."
>
> The mattress was removed and the muslin packet was revealed.
>
> Baba: (Picking it up and spreading it out) "Hallo! What is this! Muslin! I am not going to return this. This is mine."
>
> Baba then wore it over his body and turning to R. said: "Do I not look nice in this?"
>
> R. was overjoyed to see that Baba recognised that he and R. were one and accepted the present in that spirit.[160]

In another text, Sai narrated a parable with the aim of initiating a devotee along the ninefold path of *bhakti* (*navavidha bhakti*):

Anant Rao Patankar said: "Baba, I have read a good lot of Sastras, etc. but I have no peace of mind. Pray, grant me your blessing."

Baba: "Once a merchant came here. In his presence, a quadruped passed its stomata, that is, nine balls of stool. The merchant, anxious to attain his quest, spread his cloth beneath its tail, gathered all the nine balls and took them away. He got concentration and piece of mind."

Anant Rao, unable to make out this parable, questioned Dada Kelkar: "What does Baba mean?"

Dada Kelkar: "God's grace is the quadruped. The nine balls excreted are the nine forms of Bhakti. You are to be in the position of the merchant. If you follow Nava Vidha Bhakti, you will attain peace."

Again, Anant Rao went to Baba.

Baba: "Have you gathered the nine balls?"

Anant Rao: "For that I must have your grace."

Baba: "God will bless."[161]

This is one more example of Baba's symbolic parlance and, at the same time, of the eccentric and down-to-earth "materiality" of his metaphors.

The popular enumeration of the nine steps of *bhakti* is taken from *Bhāgavata Purāṇa* 7.5.23f.: *śravaṇa* (listening to holy talks), *kīrtana* (singing devotional songs), *smaraṇa* (recollection or mental recitation of a divine name), *pādasevana* (service at the deity's feet or "foot-salutation"), *arcanā* (ritual worship), *vandana* (reverential bowing), *dāsya* (serving or considering oneself the slave of the deity), *sakhya* (friendship), and *ātmanivedana* (self-offering or totally surrendering one's self to the deity).[162]

Ātmanivedana constitutes the summit of *bhakti-mārga*. Sai Baba once remarked, "If you make me the sole object of your thoughts and aims you will gain Paramartha, that is, the supreme Goal."[163]

Moreover: "If one devotes his entire mind to me and rests in me, he need fear nothing for body and soul. If one sees me and me alone and listens to talks about me and is devoted to me alone, he will reach God (Chaitanya).[164] He who worships me as Nitya, Suddha and Buddha comes to me."[165]

An interesting statement of Sai showing his equanimity is reported in the *Charters and Sayings*:

One day during Dassera of 1915, Baba said to H. S. Dikshit: "Kaka, in our Durbar, the good and evil alike come. We should regard them impartially, should we not?"[166] Shortly after saying this, a clerk came to Baba confessing to having stolen money from his master. His senior officer wanted to denounce him to the police, but Baba succeeded in conveniently settling the matter after privately talking with both of them.[167]

In another episode, Sai Baba is seen radically testing the faith of his disciples by asking them to kill an old goat. Here H. S. Dikshit sets an example of full *śraddhā* in the guru:

> Once a goat entered the mosque, old, famished and just about to die.
> Baba (to Bade Baba): "Cut that goat with one stroke."
> Bade Baba (looking at it with pity): "How are we to kill this?"
> So saying, he went away from the mosque.
> Baba: "Shama, you cut it. Bring a knife from Radhakrishna Ayi."
> Ayi sent a knife but, upon learning the purpose, recalled it.
> Shama: "I will go home and bring a knife."
> Shama then went home and stayed there.
> Then Baba to H. S. Dikshit: "You bring a knife and kill it."
> H. S. D. went and brought a knife.
> H. S. D.: "Baba, shall I kill it?"
> Baba: "Yes."
> H. S. D. lifted up the knife and held it up in hesitation.
> Baba: "What are you thinking of? Strike."
> Dikshit obeyed and was bringing the knife down.
> Baba: "Stop! Let the creature remain. I will kill it myself but not at the mosque."
> Then Baba carried the creature a few yards away, after which it fell dead.[168]

In closing this chapter, it is important to note that Baba's health was deteriorating rapidly. Narasimhaswami reports:

> In 1915 Baba was seriously ill. He had asthma and hard breathing. R. B. Purandhare, without knowing of this illness went to Shirdi, saw Baba breathing hard, and cried.
> Baba: "Why do you cry?"
> R. B. P.: "I cannot endure the sight of this state of yours."
> Baba: "Do not fear. In two or four days, I will be alright. Allah has given me this illness and he will make me alright

> within that period. You need not cry. I was remembering you the last two or three days and told Kaka (H. S. Dikshit) to write you to come."[169]

By this time, Sai Baba needed the help of his disciples in order to move around, especially during his rounds of begging. Even though old and frail, Baba never relaxed his rigid life-style of *faqīr,* implicitly setting an example of humility to his followers.

Finally, on December 1915, the sources report the arrival in Shirdi of twenty-one-year-old Mervan Sheriar Irani from Pune (1894–1969); he was later to become famous as Meher Baba.[170]

Allen Y. Cohen, in his well-written biography on the Parsi holy man, reports Mervan's reminiscences:

> Later on (April 1915) I also began to go for long distances on foot or by vehicle.... Finally (December 1915), I felt impelled to call on Sai Baba, the Perfect Master among Masters....[171] Despite the crowds I intuitively prostrated myself before him on the road.[172] When I arose, Sai Baba looked straight at me and exclaimed: "Parvardigar" (God-Almighty-Sustainer).
>
> I then felt drawn to walk to the nearby temple of Khandoba in which Maharaj (Shri Upasani Maharaj) was staying in seclusion. He had been living under Sai Baba's direct guidance for over three years....[173] When I came near enough to him, Maharaj greeted me, so to speak, with a stone which he threw at me with great force. It struck me on my forehead exactly where Babajan had kissed me,[174] hitting with such force that it drew blood. The mark of that injury is still on my forehead. But that blow from Maharaj was the stroke of *dnyan* (divine knowledge).[175]
>
> Mervan then spent several years in the company of those still revered Masters and was given their close attention. He became more and more normally conscious of the ordinary world, while simultaneously experiencing the bliss of realization and the intense suffering connected with the consciousness of the world of illusion.[176]

Mervan is said to have reached full enlightenment at Sakuri, under Upasani's guidance, in the period between July and December 1921.

At that time, as Meher Baba recalled, Upasani greeted him with folded hands, declaring: "Mervan, you are the Avatar and I salute you."[177]

Later in life, Meher Baba said the following about Sai Baba, whom he often addressed as "grandfather":

> Sai Baba had exceptionally lustrous eyes and a wonderful personality. He was fond of smoking chilam (an earthen pipe) and used to cough and spit freely in the presence of his visitors. He always asked point-blank for money of all those who visited him. In some cases he would ask the same person for money again and again, until the visitor was stripped clean, with no money left even for his return journey.[178] However Sai Baba would keep no money for himself and used to give it away.
>
> Bhajans and quavvalis were often sung before him by Hindus and Moslems, who revered him alike. But you will never be able to understand thoroughly how great Sai Baba was. He was the very personification of perfection. If you knew him as I know him you would call him the master of creation.[179]
>
> During his lifetime there were few who really loved him, and there were many who could not understand how one who constantly grabbed money from visitors could be a saint! But now you find Sai mandirs (temples), Sai match-boxes, Sai "this" and Sai "that," mostly made by the same worldly minded people who mocked Sai Baba during his lifetime.
>
> ...Upasani Maharaj was the only one there who knew who Sai Baba really was. Maharaj himself was so great that if his grace were to descend on a particle of dust, it would be transformed into God.[180]

Meher Baba's "*avatāric* career" is a fascinating chapter in the recent history of Indian guru phenomena.

In January 1925, he established a permanent *āśram* at Arangaon, shortly after renamed Meherabad.

He travelled extensively in India and also in the West, where he arrived for the first time in 1931. His fame rapidly increased, and many "Meher Baba Centers" were established in Europe, Australia, and the United States. Myrtle Beach, in South Carolina, was and still is their main headquarters in the United States.

Meher Baba's "lovers," as Western devotees call themselves, were a conspicuous group, particularly in the sixties and early seventies.[181] Since Meher's death in 1969, the movement's power of attraction has gradually decreased. To the present day, however, many Meher Baba Centers are still active.

Among the special features of Meher Baba's life and teachings are the following:

1. His long period of silence starting on July 10, 1925 (from 1927 to 1954 he stopped writing, using an alphabet board to convey messages, and from 1954 until his death he communicated only through gestures)
2. His work with the so-called *masts,* that is, the God-intoxicated
3. Most important of all, his messianic role as the ultimate *avatāra,* who promised to usher humanity into a golden age based on love and universal brotherhood.[182]

Notes

1. Narasimhaswami, *Charters and Sayings,* 222.

2. See chapter 4 relative to Baba's "death" and "resurrection."

3. Literally, "revered by the people," the inseparable surname of Tilak. With reference to the ideology attached to the word, see R. I. Cashman, *The Myth of the Lokamanya: Tilak and Mass Politics in Maharashtra* (Berkeley and Los Angeles: University of California Press, 1975).

4. S. A. Wolpert, *Tilak and Gokhale: Revolution and Reform in the Making of Modern India* (reprint, New Delhi: Oxford University Press, 1989), 126–27.

5. On G. S. Khaparde, see Narasimhaswami, *Life of Sai Baba,* 2:298–335. The monthly *Shri Sai Leela* has recently published his Shirdi diary.

6. This was the first time that Baba referred to Dabholkar by the pseudonym Hemadpant.

7. Gunaji, *Shri Sai Satcharita,* 8–9.

8. Compare *Bhagavadgītā* 6.5: *Uddhared ātmanā 'tmānaṃ nā 'tmānam avasādayet / ātmai 'va hy ātmano bandhur ātmai 'va ripur ātmanaḥ //* Following F. Edgerton's translation, it reads: One should lift up the self by the self, and should not let the self down; for the self is the self's only friend, and the self is the self's only enemy. See Edgerton, *The Bhagavadgītā,* 32.

9. This is Sai Baba himself.

10. On the forest, usually *vana* or *araṇya* in Marathi, see the insightful article of A. Feldhaus, "The Image of the Forest in the Māhātmyas of the Rivers of the Deccan," in H. Bakker, *History of Sacred Places,* 90–102.

11. The "labourer," in other words, reveals his true identity.

12. Osborne, *Incredible Sai Baba,* 3–5.

13. Being caught in a well is a common symbolic theme. Compare *Mahābhārata* 12.244.

14. Osborne, *Incredible Sai Baba,* 5–6.

15. Ibid., 89.

16. Literally, "truth-seizing," one holding on truth (*satya*). Here it is used as a synonym for fasting.

17. Madhavrao Deshpande, according to the text.

18. These words call to mind *Svāmin* Muktananda's way of talking about his guru Nityananda.

19. The four traditional *mārgas,* that is, the paths of action (karma), devotion (*bhakti*), discipline (*yoga*), and knowledge (*jñāna*).

20. The six traditional *darśanas,* that is, Sāṃkhya, Yoga, Vaiśeṣika, Nyāya, Mīmāṁsā, and Vedānta.

21. Narasimhaswami, *Charters and Sayings,* 43–44.

22. As already noted, however, Baba's reference to having spent twelve years with Venkusha, is reported more than once; compare Narasimhaswami, *Charters and Sayings,* 61.

23. On the function and significance of mantras, see the collection of articles in H. P. Alper, ed., *Mantra* (Albany, N.Y.: State University of New York Press, 1989).

24. Osborne, *Incredible Sai Baba,* 87–88.

25. Narasimhaswami, *Life of Sai Baba,* 4:24–25.

26. At Baba's death in 1918, Dabholkar had completed only a few chapters. He finished his work in 1929, the year in which he died. See Narasimhaswami, *Life of Sai Baba,* 2:218.

27. See Bharadwaja, *Sai Baba,* 25.

28. See Ramalingaswami, *Ambrosia in Shirdi,* 144–45.

29. See Narasimhaswami, *Charters and Sayings,* 165.

30. Ibid., 171.

31. See Osborne, *Incredible Sai Baba,* 25.

32. A *pharāl* is a snack, especially when referring to one permitted during a fast.

33. Literally, without food, "fast."

34. Narasimhaswami, *Charters and Sayings,* 225.

35. At the age of thirteen, that is, in 1883, Upasani was first married to a girl of eight who died in 1885. That same year he was married again, to a girl who died a year later.

36. Narasimhaswami, *Life of Sai Baba,* 2:237.

37. B. V. Narasimhaswami and S. Subbarao, *Sage of Sakuri: Life Story of Shree Upasani Maharaj,* 4th ed. (Sakuri: Shri Upasani Kanya Kumari Sthan, 1966), 45–47.

38. Narasimhaswami, *Life of Sai Baba,* 2:249.

39. Ibid., 248.

40. For a presentation of these texts, see chapter 9.

41. It started around 5 A.M. It is called after the lamp used in the *ārtī* which consists of a *kākaḍā,* that is of a course wick of cloth. This rite of the awakening of the god is certainly of great antiquity, since Namdev mentions it in one of his *abhaṅgas.*

42. Bharadwaja, *Sai Baba,* 56.

43. To stress the fact that the term Sai must be nasalized when pronounced, Khaparde wrote *Sayin.*

44. Bharadwaja, *Sai Baba,* 61–62.

45. Narasimhaswami, *Charters and Sayings,* 260.

46. Bharadwaja, *Sai Baba,* 61.

47. Ibid., 58.

48. Ibid.

49. Ibid., 56.

50. Ibid., 58.

51. Ibid., 58–59.

52. Ibid., 59.

53. See Gunaji, *Shri Sai Satcharita,* 156.

54. Quoted in Kamath and Kher, *Sai Baba,* 288.

55. On Jog, uncle of the famous *Vārakarī* Vishnubua Jog of Pune, see Gunaji, *Shri Sai Satcharita,* 239–40. See also Kamath and Kher, *Sai Baba,* 257–58.

56. A holder of landed property given as a reward by the government.

57. Bharadwaja, *Sai Baba,* 59.

58. The "class" refers to the series of lectures that Khaparde and others gave on various religious texts. The *Paramamrit* is the *Pañcadashī.*

59. Bharadwaja, *Sai Baba,* 59.

60. Ibid.

61. Ibid.

62. Ibid., 56.

63. Ibid.

64. Narasimhaswami, *Charters and Sayings,* 267.

65. Bharadwaja, *Sai Baba,* 32.

66. Ibid., 43.

67. See Narasimhaswami, *Charters and Sayings,* 92.

68. Ibid., 96–98.

69. Ibid., 39.

70. Ibid., 40–41.

71. Godamasuta, *Talks,* 1:178.

72. See Narasimhaswami, *Life of Sai Baba,* 2:251.

73. The verse runs as follows:

> *Sadā nimbarvṛkṣasya mūlādhivāsāt*
> *sudhāsrāviṇaṃ tiktamapyapriyaṃ tam*
> *taruṃ kalpavṛkṣādhikaṃ sādhayantam*
> *namāmīśvaraṃ sadguruṃ sāīnātham*

On the installation of Sai Baba's *pādukās* under the *nīm* tree, see Gunaji, *Shri Sai Satcharita,* 24–26.

74. See Narasimhaswami, *Life of Sai Baba,* 2:249.

75. Ibid., 251.

76. Ibid., 254.

77. Godamasuta, *Talks,* 1:112–13.

78. Good or happy state, delivery from *saṃsāra.*

79. Narasimhaswami, *Charters and Sayings,* 142.

80. Osborne, *Incredible Sai Baba,* 40–41.

81. Baba's statement might also be interpreted symbolically, meaning that a new carnal attachment would soon be born.

82. The sources write either Patil or Patel.

83. Ramalingaswami, *Ambrosia in Shirdi,* 136–37.

84. Ibid., 137. Tatya would then respond by saluting him with the words *Salam Alekum.*

85. See Osborne, *Incredible Sai Baba,* 46.

86. Ibid., 47.

87. Ibid.

88. Ibid., 51–52.

89. Narasimhaswami, *Charters and Sayings,* 262.

90. The most numerous among the untouchable castes of Maharashtra. Their hereditary work is to remove the dead cattle from the village, sweep the streets, run errands for the village officers, and keep a watch on the village properties. On *mahārs,* see I. Karve, *Maharashtra State Gazetteer, Maharashtra: Land and its People* (Bombay, 1968), 32.

91. Sakhare, Nanamaharaj, ed., *Śrī sakal sant gāthā,* 2d ed. (Pune, 1967), vol 1, *abhaṅga* 84. On Chokamela, see E. Zelliot, "Four Radical Saints," in M. Israel and N. K. Wagle, *Religion and Society in Maharashtra* (Toronto: University of Toronto, Centre for South Asian Studies, 1987), 134–38. For a presentation of the saint's life in Marathi hagiography, see Abbott and Godbole, *Stories of Indian Saints,* 377–84.

92. See Bharadwaja, *Sai Baba,* 35.

93. See Osborne, *Incredible Sai Baba,* 32–33.

94. See Ramalingaswami, *Ambrosia in Shirdi,* 96–98.

95. Ibid., 107.

96. Ibid., 166–67.

97. Bharucha, *Sai Baba,* 43–44.

98. See Sharif, *Islam in India,* 20.

99. The fourth day in the bright lunar half of the month of Māgha (January–February).

100. Narasimhaswami, *Charters and Sayings,* 131.

101. The repetition of a holy name, which is carried on for full seven days.

102. Narasimhaswami, *Charters and Sayings,* 215–16.

103. Ibid., 45–46.

104. Ibid., 208. A *pothī* is a loose-leaf volume. It refers to one of the sacred texts that were daily read at the *vāḍā*. The practice, called *pothī lavaṇẽ* (to conduct public reading of a religious work), is common all over India.

105. Narasimhaswami, *Charters and Sayings,* 254–55.

106. Ibid., 259.

107. Godamasuta, *Talks,* 1:170.

108. Ibid., 111.

109. Literally, "Brahmā's crevice." A suture or aperture in the crown of the head, through which the soul is said to escape at death.

110. Literally, "Brahmā's egg," that is, the universe.

111. Godamasuta, *Talks,* 1:599–600.

112. Ibid., 601.

113. Narasimhaswami, in another part of his biography, says the day was July 15, not July 18; see *Life of Sai Baba,* 2:341.

114. Narasimhaswami and Subbarao, *Sage of Sakuri,* 84–85.

115. Godamasuta, *Talks,* 1:449.

116. Narasimhaswami and Subbarao, *Sage of Sakuri,* 84.

117. Ramalingaswami, *Ambrosia in Shirdi,* 77.

118. Ibid., 111–12.

119. Ibid., 146–47.

120. Narasimhaswami, *Charters and Sayings,* 215.

121. Ibid., 56.

122. Ibid., 14.

123. Ibid.

124. Ibid., 255–57.

125. Osborne, *Incredible Sai Baba,* 20–21.

126. The past passive participle *baddha* (bound, fastened, imprisoned, caught) is derived from root *bandh.* Here, it refers to those people who are totally caught up in worldly life.

127. Desiderative form of root *muc* meaning to loose, release, liberate. *Mumukṣu* literally means: "one eager to be free" (from mundane existence), that is, striving after liberation (*mukti*).

128. Past passive participle derived from root *sidh* (to attain, to succeed, to be accomplished or fulfilled). *Siddha* thus means the accomplished or perfected one who has attained the highest object.

129. Narasimhaswami, *Charters and Sayings,* 26–27.

130. See ibid., 48–50.

131. The *Kṛta–yuga* or *Satya-yuga,* the golden or perfect age, lasts 4,800 divine years, the *Tretā-yuga* 3,600, the *Dvāpara-yuga* 2,400, and the *Kali-yuga* 1,200 (each divine year amounts to 360 human years). Thus, a complete cycle, called *mahāyuga,* lasts 12,000 divine years. One thousand *mahāyugas,* in turn, correspond to one day in the life of Brahmā, that is, one *kalpa.* Today, according to this traditional Indian chronology, we live at the beginning of a *Kali-yuga* (which, having started in 3,102 B.C.E. with Krishna's death, will last for about 427,000 years more), and we find ourselves about half-way through our present *kalpa,* known as the *Varāha-kalpa,* that is, "the *kalpa* of the boar." The *Varāha-kalpa* is the first *kalpa* of the second half of a life of Brahmā, whose length is 100 years of Brahmā.

132. Narasimhaswami, *Charters and Sayings,* 51.

133. Bharadwaja, *Sai Baba,* 104.

134. One of the few solar festivals of the Hindu calendar, it marks the day on which the sun begins to move northwards, ushering in the new year. The newly harvested corn is cooked for the first time, and joyous festivities mark the celebration in every home. On *Makara Saṃkrānti,* see Swami Sivananda, *Hindu Fasts and Festivals,* 44–49.

135. For instance, when operated on for colics and piles due to his sudden resumption of solid food, the doctors were amazed at his insensibility to pain. See Narasimhaswami and Subbarao, *Sage of Sakuri,* 86–87.

136. On Upasani Maharaj's life and future developments, see Narasimhaswami and Subbarao, *Sage of Sakuri.* See also Shepherd, *Gurus Rediscovered,* 81–142. For a presentation of Upasani's *upadeśa* "in his own words," see Godamasuta, *Talks,* vols. 1–4.

137. Upasani is here referring to his first visit to Baba; see Narasimhaswami and Subbarao, *Sage of Sakuri,* 38–39.

138. Godamasuta, *Talks,* 1:401–2.

139. Ramalingaswami, *Ambrosia in Shirdi,* 143–44.

140. See ibid., 124–25.

141. See ibid., 141–42.

142. See Bharadwaja, *Sai Baba,* 52.

143. See Osborne, *Incredible Sai Baba,* 29–30.

144. See Bharadwaja, *Sai Baba,* 50.

145. See Ramalingaswami, *Ambrosia in Shirdi,* 91–92.

146. See ibid., 170–71.

147. A parasitic worm (*Filaria medinensis*) inhabiting the subcutaneous cellular tissue of humans, frequently in the leg, varying from six inches to twelve feet in length. It is found in some parts of western India. See H. Yule and A. C. Burnell, *Hobson-Jobson: A Glossary of Colloquial Anglo-Indian Words and Phrases, and of Kindred Terms, Etymological, Historical, Geographical, and Discursive,* (reprint, Delhi: Rupa, 1989), 401–2.

148. Karma accumulated in previous births.

149. Narasimhaswami, *Charters and Sayings,* 168–69.

150. See Narasimhaswami, *Life of Sai Baba,* 3:171.

151. Bharadwaja, *Sai Baba,* 77.

152. Narasimhaswami, *Charters and Sayings,* 24.

153. Ibid., 24–25.

154. Ibid., 18.

155. Ibid.

156. Ibid.

157. Ibid., 275.

158. Ibid., 87–88.

159. Through *sparśa* (a holy person's touch), objects are believed to be sanctified.

160. Narasimhaswami, *Charters and Sayings,* 253–54.

161. Ibid., 23.

162. For a comparison with the Śaiva tradition, see *Shiva Purāṇa, Rudra Saṃhitā,* chapter 23.

163. Narasimhaswami, *Charters and Sayings,* 3.

164. *Caitanya,* from *cetanā,* literally means "consciousness." It refers to the Universal Soul or Spirit, that is, *Brahman.*

165. Narasimhaswami, *Charters and Sayings,* 4. *Nitya, śuddha,* and *buddha* might be respectively translated as: "the eternal," "the pure," "the awakened."

166. Ibid., 247.

167. See ibid., 248.

168. Ibid., 271–72.

169. Ibid., 213–14.

170. It was only in 1922 that Mervan adopted the name Meher, the same of the month in which he was born, according to the Zoroastrian calendar. The term *meher* is interpreted by devotees to mean "the compassionate one."

171. Cf. the popular theory of the *Nāth-pañcāyatan,* that is, the existence of five perfect masters, invisibly communicating among themselves and operating the "spiritual hierarchy." On this issue, see, for instance, Gunaji, *Shri Sai Satcharita,* xxiiif.

172. Sai Baba was returning to the mosque from the latrines at the *Leṇḍī,* accompanied by musical instruments. With regard to Baba's stay at the *Leṇḍī,* Mervan observed: "When Sai Baba wanted to move his bowels, people would take him in procession with a band and pipes. He was worthy of all that. He might stay there for an hour, and procession and band would return with him to his seat" (Charles B. Purdom, *The God-Man: The Life, Journeys and Work of Meher Baba with an Interpretation of his Silence and Spiritual Teaching* [London: George Allen & Unwin, 1964], 254). Mervan added some startling comments on Baba's going to the *Leṇḍī*: "There (at the latrine) he would spend an hour, during which time he would bring under his surveillance all the stars. This was routine, and easily done—for at the time he created the universe he had given infinite thought and care to all eventualities and possibilities. Now there was only a touch here and there required to keep it all going smoothly" (F. Brabazon, *The Silent Word: Being Some Chapters of the Life and Time of Avatar Meher Baba* [Bombay: Meher Baba Foundation, 1978], 18).

173. At the time, Upasani had come back to Shirdi for a short stay.

174. This kiss, which brought about an inner change, occured in May 1913. A Sufi woman from Baluchistan, Babajan was always found under a

nīm tree in the center of Pune. Mervan passed by Babajan on his bicycle route home from school. While still attending classes, he spent more and more time with her. His conversion to religious life was due to his encounter with this remarkable Sufi. For some information on Babajan, see Jean Adriel, *Avatar: The Life Story of the Perfect Master Meher Baba; A Narrative of Spiritual Experience* (Santa Barbara, Calif.: J. F. Rowny Press, 1947), 36–41; Brabazon, *Silent word,* 15–17. Also Paul Brunton, *A Search in Secret India* (David Mc Cay, 1934; London: Rider, 1970), chap. 4.

175. The episode calls to mind the similar stroke which young Ramakrishna received from the *saṃnyāsin* Totapuri:

> I (Ramakrishna) tried on several occasions to concentrate my mind on the truth of Advaita Vedanta; but each time the form of the Mother intervened. I said to Totapuri in despair: "It's no good. I will never be able to lift my spirit to the unconditioned state and find myself face to face with the Atman!" He replied severely: "What do you mean you can't? You must!" Looking about him, he found a shard of glass. He took it and stuck the point between my eyes, saying: "Concentrate your mind on that point." Then I began to meditate with all my might, and soon the gracious form of the Divine Mother appeared. I used my discrimination as a sword and clove Her in two. The last barrier vanished and my spirit immediately precipitated itself beyond the plane of the conditioned. I lost myself in samadhi. (Rolland, *The Life of Ramakrishna,* 54–55)

176. A. Y. Cohen, ed., *The Mastery of Consciousness* (Middlesex: Eel Pie Publishing, 1977), 8.

177. Ibid., 9. In commenting on his spiritual development, Meher Baba later observed: "Babajan made me *feel* what I am, Sai Baba made me *know* who I am, and Maharaj gave me God's *powers* which had always been mine." See Brabazon, *Silent Word,* 33.

178. See the *dakṣiṇā* experience of a Parsi devotee of Sai Baba, Gustadji Nusservanji Hansotia, who later came under the influence of Upasani and Meher Baba; Brabazon, *Silent Word,* 40–43.

179. Curiously enough, one day Meher Baba said that it was Sai Baba who "controlled" World War I, though he seemed to be doing nothing, sitting in an out-of-the-way place, Shirdi, unknown to the world at large. See Purdom, *Perfect Master,* 108.

180. Meher Baba, *Listen Humanity,* narrated and edited by D. E. Stevens (Sufism Reoriented, 1957; New York: Harper Colophon, 1967), 63–64.

181. Among Meher Baba's followers one finds Peter Townshend, the English leader of the rock group "The Who." Their famous rock opera *Tommy,* issued in 1969, was dedicated to *Avatar* Meher Baba, and some texts of the songs clearly indicate the guru's influence.

182. For a presentation of Meher Baba's life, see the following works: Naoshervan Anzar, *The Beloved: The Life and Work of Meher Baba* (North Myrtle Beach, S.C.: Sheriar Press, 1974); Tom Hopkinson and Dorothy Hopkinson, *Much Silence: Meher Baba: His Life and Work* (New York: Dodd, Mead, 1974). On Meher Baba's work with the *masts,* see the excellent account of William Donkin, *The Wayfarers: An Account of the Work of Meher Baba with the God-intoxicated, and also with Advanced Souls, Sadhus, and the Poor* (San Francisco: Sufism Reoriented, 1969). On Meher Baba's teachings, see Meher Baba, *Discourses* (San Francisco: Sufism Reoriented, 1967); Meher Baba, *God Speaks* (New York; Dodd, Mead, 1973); and C. B. Purdom, *God to Man and Man to God: The Discourses of Meher Baba* (North Myrtle Beach, S.C.: Sheriar Press, 1975).

8

His Last Three Years

In 1916, Sai Baba consented to G. R. Dabholkar's desire to write his biography. "Hemadpant" advanced his request through Shyama, who often acted as intermediary, obtaining Sai's blessings as well as some methodological advice on how to proceed in his research. Narasimhaswami reports:

> So, Madhavrao Deshpande (Shyama) was requested to tell Baba, and he told Baba thus:
>
> "This Anna Saheb wishes to write your life. Don't say that you are a poor begging fakir, and that there is no necessity to write your life. If you agree and help him, he will write or, rather, your feet (i.e., Grace) will accomplish the work. Without your consent and blessings nothing can be done successfully."

Baba was moved, and blessed Anna Saheb Dabholkar by giving him udhi and placing his Asirvada hand upon Dabholkar's head.

> Baba [said]: "Let him make a collection of stories and experiences, keeping notes and memos. I will help him. He is only an outward instrument. I shall write my life myself, and satisfy the wishes of my devotees.
>
> "He should get rid of his ego. Place (or surrender) it at my feet. He who acts like this in life, him I will help most. What of my life's stories?...When his ego will be completely annihilated, and there will be no trace left of it, I myself shall enter into him and write my life. Hearing my stories and teachings will create faith in the devotees' hearts, and they will easily get self-realization and bliss.
>
> "But let there be no insistence on establishing one's own view, and no attempt to refute other opinions of any sort."
>
> So spoke Baba. Then Dabholkar made the promise that he would be in that mood and would surrender. His close intimacy with Dikshit, Chandorkar, and other devotees enabled him to collect plenty of material.

> This permission was given in 1916, and when Baba passed away, Dabholkar had only written two or three chapters. Most of the work was written after 1918. He wrote 51 or 52 chapters, and passed away in 1929. Meanwhile his chapters were published in the *Sai Lila Masik,* which was started under his and Dikshit's supervision.[1]

Thus was the *Shri Sai Satcharita* composed. This text is revered as *the* holy book by all of Sai Baba's devotees, who believe it to contain his "spirit," the essence of his teachings.

An *upadeśa* concerned with the "inexorability of destiny" was thus recounted:

> In 1916, a halva-maker usually supplying halva[2] for Baba's Arati, died of plague.
>
> Baba to G. G. Narke: "Go to the halvayi's shop and bring naivedya."
>
> G. G. Narke went to the place and asked Mrs. H.: "Baba wants naivedya."
>
> Mrs. H.: "Look.... My husband's plague-stricken corpse is there. The Halva is in the almirah.[3] Take it if you please."
>
> G. G. Narke took it, trembling for himself and for others who were going to take naivedya, with the possibility of catching plague. He placed the Halva before Baba.
>
> Baba: "You think you will live if you are away from Shirdi and that you will die if you stay at Shirdi. That is not so. Whoever is destined to be struck will be struck. Whoever is to die will die. Whoever is to be caressed will be caressed."
>
> The Halva was given as naivedya and none caught plague from it.[4]

Similarly, when H. S. Dikshit asked Baba's permission to kill a poisonous snake, the latter answered: "No. We should never kill it. Because it will never kill us unless it is ordered by God to kill us. If God has so ordered, we cannot avoid it."[5]

Narasimhaswami refers to three healing acts operated by Baba. In the first one he saved Shyama, who had been bitten by a snake, by shouting at the poison agent the words *Brāhmiṇvār māt āv, hāt māge, hāt māge,* "Do not get up, Brahmin, get down, get down."[6] In the second case, Sai is said to have cured the grandfather of one Vitthalrao Y. Deshpande from total blindness after asking four rupees as *dakṣiṇā* from the old man.[7] Lastly, to a blind woman of Bassein who ardently desired to have Baba's *darśan* with her own eyes, Sai granted temporary eyesight.[8]

The *Charters and Sayings* reports:

> In 1916, Bhadrapad, Das Ganu was keen on going to Pandharpur, but N. G. Chandorkar took him to Shirdi and made him perform kirtans and wanted to detain him there, even till Asvin, evidently with Baba's assent.
>
> Das Ganu then thought within himself, without saying so: "How is he (Baba) a guru, who blocks my way to God (at Pandharpur)?"
>
> Baba to Das Ganu: "Go to Pandharpur."
>
> So Das Ganu went to Pandharpur for Asvin, as Vitthala of Pandhari alone was God to him and not Baba. Later, he returned to Shirdi.[9]

This episode demonstrates how Das Ganu, though highly revering Baba, could not identify him *tout court* with his *iṣṭadevatā*. This, however, was precisely the realization that Baba wanted to impart to Das Ganu, that is, that Sai and all deities are verily "one and the same."

Bharadwaja's biography describes an episode in which Baba gave vision of himself as Rama:

> In 1916, a Madrasi family of devotional singers belonging to the Kabirpanth was on a pilgrimage to Varanasi. On the way, they heard of Baba's generous rewards to devotional singers and visited him. Except for the man's wife, who was very devoted to Sri Rama, they all sang in expectation of gifts of money. At the noon arti, Baba graced her with the darshan of Sri Rama in his own person. With tears of joy she clapped and sang ecstatically.[10]

This episode confirms the comments on the *darbār*'s generosity and renown.

Sai Baba believed in the existence of evil deities and spirits and once explained how, by the action of grinding wheat and pouring flour along the village boudaries, he prevented the evil godlings of cholera, plague, and so forth, from trespassing and "eating" humans:

> In May 1916, a lady devotee from Bombay came to Baba for darshan. At that time, Baba and two other women, Janabai and Lakshmibai, were grinding wheat flour in the grinding stone.

She asked Baba if she could also grind the wheat. Baba told her that she would feel fatigued in grinding.... She replied that she would grind as much as she possibly could. Baba then asked Lakshmibai to leave the grinding stone to her. She began to grind the wheat.

She questioned Baba why the wheat was to be ground. Baba replied that by doing so he would save devotees at times. She also questioned why Baba was going to the stream side and throwing the wheat flour. Baba said that at times "Akkabai"[11] (Mari Ayi, Mariamma,[12] cholera and smallpox, etc.) wanted to enter the village, and he prevented her on the other side of the stream, not allowing her in the village.[13] He said: "That is why I have to feed her and why I throw flour at her." She again asked Baba whether "Jari"[14] and "Mari" (Durdevathas)[15] really exist. Baba replied: "Durdevathas exist, but they won't do us any harm...."

She then told him that when she was in Naigaom in Bombay a figure of an evil spirit used to come from the well side, enter her house, go to a room upstairs, and disappear.

Baba told her that he knew him, saying that he used to be the owner of her house, and later became an evil spirit. He also added that he used to disappear only in the room where she delivered.

She asked Baba how he was able to know all these facts. Baba replied that he knew her from her childhood and added that, in time, she had forgotten him.

He said: "I will call my children even if they are one thousand miles away. My care will always be alike towards all. All men; good, bad, rowdies, are coming to me. I have to look after all of them."[16]

The *Charters and Sayings* narrates another startling episode, one in which Baba is said to have protected a boy from an attack by the terrible cholera goddess:

In May or June 1917, a Bombay lady and her younger son sat before Baba at noon Arati.

Baba: "You must come here exactly at 2 P.M."

Boy: "Yes."

Accordingly the boy was there at 2 P.M. at the Dvaraka Mayi.

Baba: "Boy, come here. Sit at my feet on this mat. Be massaging my feet and do not let go my feet till I tell you."

> Accordingly the boy went on massaging. At 3 P.M. a terrible female figure appeared, with wild dishevelled hair, begrimed face and head and a protruding long tongue shot out. Moving like a dog, she jumped over the compound wall. Coming near the boy she said:
>
> "I want this person."
>
> Baba: "I will not give him."
>
> She: "This exactly is the person I want."
>
> She then approached the boy and pulled him. Baba got up enraged and holding the boy with one hand, kicked her on the breast. She roared and ran away.
>
> Baba: "Boy, are you not watching? Do you know the woman that came? Hallo! That woman was wanting you to be given up. But how could I give you up? I refused."
>
> Boy: "When this was going on, I sat benumbed like a statue. I saw everything, but my body was inert or stonelike."
>
> Baba declared that the female form was the goddess Cholera. And the very next morning, Baba permitted the boy and his mother to go back to Bombay. Cholera then began to rage in Shirdi.[17]

A similar episode, or perhaps the same in a somewhat different version, is reported by Ramalingaswami:

> In 1917, during the month of Vaishak, a doctor, his wife, and his son came to Shirdi for Baba's darshan.
>
> The doctor thought that Baba's throwing of flour on the outskirts of the village in order to stop evil spirits from entering in it was unwarranted.
>
> Baba asked him to come at 3 P.M. The doctor, his wife, and his son came back at 3. Baba asked them to massage his legs. The doctor and his son massaged Baba's legs.
>
> Then an ugly lady with her hair untied came, caught hold of his son, and wanted to snap him away. Baba gave her a blow with his satka. She ran away crying, leaving the doctor's son.
>
> Baba told the doctor that she had come there to eat his son because she had not got her food. Also, because the doctor thought that Baba's throwing flour to her for food was unnecessary. "But I drove her away," said Sai Baba.
>
> Baba then gave them permission to leave on the next day.[18]

The function of flour as food (*anna*), that is, sacrificial libation for the hungry angry godling, is once again presented. The horrible female figure is the personification of Mari, the cholera goddess. Her appearance in human form is not uncommon, according to regional beliefs and folklore.

Baba was also believed to perform exorcisms on persons possessed by ghosts or evil spirits (*bhūt bādhā*):

> Sri Narasing Maharaj was a great saint of Nasik. Hansraj of Sakuri, who had no children even years after his marriage, once visited him.
>
> The saint said that Hansraj's body was possessed by a spirit which was killing his children and advised him to go to Sai Baba, who would give him two slaps and exorcize the spirit.
>
> Accordingly, Hansraj visited Shirdi in 1916. Baba slapped him twice and said: "Evil spirit, get away!" Later, Hansraj was blessed with offspring.[19]

As John M. Stanley observes, active belief in *bhūt bādhā* and black magic (*karṇī*) is still very strong in present day Maharashtra.[20]

Sai Baba is said to have foreseen the date of his approaching death:

> In 1916, Vijaya Dasami day (October), Baba was in a rage. He tore off all his clothes and threw them into the fire (dhuni) before him and stood there stark naked. Baba, with red eyes, shouted: "Fellows, decide for yourselves now if I am Moslem or Hindu."[21]
>
> After two hours of this rage, Bhagoji Shinde, his leper companion, tied a langoti on him and said: "Why all this? Today is the festival of Simolangan." Baba (striking the ground with his baton): "This is *my* Simolangan (my going beyond the boundary of life)."[22]
>
> People could not understand his meaning then, but it was on the Vijaya Dasami day (2 years later, that is, 1918) that Baba crossed over the boundary of life.
>
> In 1916, before Vijaya Dasami, Baba had been seriously ill and the rumour got around that he was about to die. The devotees conducted a sapta[23] at Shirdi with mass feeding for the recovery of his health. Thereafter he recovered.[24]

The following episodes are ascribed to the year 1917.

On one occasion, Baba spoke of the previous lives of a devotee:

> Rao Saheb Yesvant Rao J. Galvankar went to Baba in 1917.

Baba, placing his palm over his head (thereby putting him into ecstasy) said: "This is a person who has had integrity and purity in his previous births. I therefore placed him in his present mother's womb and he still retains those qualities."[25]

A. Osborne quotes the following words of Galvankar:

> When...he put his hand over my head...this had a strange effect on me. I forgot myself and my surroundings and fell into a state of ecstasy. I learned afterwards that while I was in that state Sai Baba was telling those present that I was characterized by integrity and purity. He described to them various forms and conditions that I had passed through in previous lives and said that he had placed me in my mother's womb in this birth and I had still retained my integrity and purity.[26]

Baba's followers frequently attested to his ability to induce states of ecstasy through mere touch. Indeed, to devotees Sai Baba's physical presence, gaze, and gestures, had a purifying force.

One Narayan Ashram, a *saṃnyāsin* of Vai, noted how Baba had different ways of touching people's heads: "Sometimes he barely seemed to touch. Sometimes he seemed to press out something from the head. Sometimes he made passes without touching the head. Each of these had its own peculiar effect."[27]

Baba is said to have performed numerous healing acts during 1917. I shall mention three: curing one Gajanan Narvekar from fever by taking the illness upon himself,[28] causing the fits of Dabholkar's pregnant daughter to cease,[29] and supplying the *udī* that Shri Talvalkar used to save a dying patient's life.[30]

On May 19, 1917, the Maharashtrian political leader, Bal Gangadhar Tilak, paid a visit to Sai Baba. G. S. Khaparde, Tilak's lieutenant, gave the following report in his diary:

> I got up early in the morning, but so many people gathered that I could not pray. There was a movement to keep us here[31] and not let us go till after noon, and Kelkar appeared to throw his weight on the side of the movement, but most unaccountably I felt angry and insisted upon starting. So, after a Pansupari[32] in the house of Mr. Sant, a leading pleader of Sangamner, we started about 8:30 a.m.
>
> We reached Shirdi about 10 a. m., after a tire puncture on the way. We put up in Dikshit's Wada. Bapu Saheb Buti, Narayan Rao Pandi, and the establishment of Buti were there.

> My old friends, Madhavrao Deshpande, Balsahib Bhate, Bapusaheb Jog, and others gathered.
>
> We went to the Musjid and paid our respects to Sayin Maharaj. I never saw him so pleased before. He asked for Dakshina as usual and we all paid. Looking at Lokamanya he said: "People are bad, keep yourself to yourself." I made my bow and he took some rupees from me. Kelkar and Paregonkar also paid.
>
> Madhavrao Deshpande asked permission for us to proceed to Yeola. Sayin Sahib said: "Why do you want to go in the heat to die on the way. Have your food here and then go in the cool of the afternoon. Shama, feed these people."
>
> So we stayed, had our food with Madhavrao Deshpande, laid down for a few minutes and then again went to the Musjid and found Sayin Maharaj lying down as if sleeping.[33]
>
> People gave Lokamanya a Pansupari in the Chavadi there, and we returned to the Musjid again. Sayin Maharaj was sitting up and gave us udi and permission to go, so we started by motor.[34]

Tilak's presence in the Ahmednagar district was surely motivated by political interests. He came to Shirdi probably yielding to his lieutenant's insistence. Or perhaps, the curiosity of meeting the *faqīr* whom so many people marveled about contributed to his decision of visiting Baba.

Moreover Tilak, though "using" religion for his political goals, as in his campaigns all over Maharashtra for the popularization of Ganesha's cult,[35] was a very religious man indeed. His celebrated commentary on the *Bhagavadgītā*, that is, the *Gītā Rahasya* ("The Secret Meaning of the *Gītā*") constituted his magnum opus. Here, in keeping with his robust patriotism and activistic views, he stressed disinterested action (*naiśkarmya*) as being the central teaching of the *Gītā* rather than quietism, renunciation, or devotion.[36]

It may well be that Tilak, in visiting Shirdi, was especially interested in verifying the tolerant atmosphere between Hindus and Muslims that was attributed to Baba's influence.

Khaparde reported that Baba was extremely pleased by meeting the party. His advice to Tilak to beware of people and keep on guard was certainly justified. Unfortunately, Tilak's own impressions regarding his short visit have not come down to us.

Bharucha's biography describes how Haribhau Karnik of Dahanu, desiring to offer Baba one more rupee *dakṣiṇā* and not succeeding in his intent, finally agreed to offer it to a Kala Rama temple priest at Nasik who insistently asked for it, saying, "Give me my one rupee."[37]

Bharucha concludes, "The incident convinced Karnik that Sai Baba had known about his last minute wish, and this was his way of obtaining the rupee he had wanted to give him."[38]

The *Shri Sai Satcharita* relates:

> Mr. Sathe...came to Shirdi in 1917. Seeing Baba's form...his mind lost its restlessness and became calm and composed. He thought that it was the accumulation of merits in his former births that brought him to the holy feet of Baba.
>
> He was a man of strong will. He at once started to make a parayana (study) of Gurucharitra. When the reading was finished in the saptaha (seven days), Baba gave him a vision.... It was to this effect: Baba, with Gurucharitra in His hand, was explaining its contents to Mr. Sathe, who was sitting in front and listening carefully. When he woke up, Sathe remembered the dream and felt very happy.
>
> ...Next day he informed Kakasaheb Dikshit of this vision and requested him to consult Sai Baba regarding its meaning or significance—whether one saptaha (week's) reading was sufficient or whether he should continue.
>
> Kakasaheb Dikshit, when he got a suitable opportunity, asked Baba: "Deva (Oh God) [*sic*], what did you suggest to Mr. Sathe by this vision? Whether he should stop or continue the saptaha? He is a simple devotee, his desire should be fulfilled and the vision explained to him, and he should be blessed."
>
> Then Baba replied: "He should make one more saptaha of the book. If the work be studied carefully, the devotee will become pure and will be benefited, the Lord will be pleased and will rescue him from the bondage of mundane existence."[39]

Sai Baba often asked his more educated devotees to read sacred texts as part of their *sādhanā*. Sometimes, he advised the reading of particular *adhyāyas* or *sūtras* dealing with specific issues.

Among the texts he most often recommended to his Hindu *bhaktas* were the following: *Jñāneshvarī*, *Bhagavadgītā*, *Pañcadashī*, *Eknāth Bhāgavata*, *Adhyātma Rāmāyaṇa*, and, naturally, the *Gurucharitra*.[40] On the other hand, Baba warned his followers of the dangers of intellectualism, emphasizing the uselessness of erudition per se.

To return to the *Shri Sai Satcharita* narration:

At that time, Hemadpant was present. He was washing Baba's legs. When he heard Baba's words he thought as follows:

"What! Mr. Sathe read for a week only and got a reward; and I am reading it for forty years with no result! His seven days' stay here becomes fruitful while my seven years' stay (1910–1917) goes for nothing. Like a chatak bird[41] I am ever waiting for the Merciful Cloud (Baba) to pour its nectar on me and bless me with His instructions."

No sooner did this thought cross his mind than Baba knew it.... Baba asked Hemadpant to get up, go to Shama (Madhavrao Deshpande), get from him Rs. 15 as Dakshina, sit and chitchat with him for a while, and then return.

...Hemadpant immediately left the Masjid and went to Shama's house...

Hemadpant: "I have come with a message from Baba. He has asked me to come back with Rs. 15 as Dakshina from you, also to sit with you for a while and have a pleasant chitchat, and then return to the Masjid with you."

Shama (with surprise): "I have no money to give. Take my 15 Namaskars (bows) in lieu of rupees as Dakshina to Baba."

Hemadpant: "All right, your Namaskars are accepted. Now let us have some chitchat. Tell me some stories and Leelas of Baba which will destroy our sins."

Shama: "Then sit here for a while. Wonderful is the sport (Leela) of this God (Baba). You know it already. I am a village rustic while you are an enlightened citizen. You have seen some more Leelas since coming here. How should I describe them to you?...

"The Leela of this God (Baba) is inscrutable; there is no end to His Leelas. Who can see them? He plays or sports with His Leelas, still He is outside of (unaffected by) them. What do we rustics know? Why does not Baba Himself tell stories? Why does He send learned men like you to fools like me? His ways are inconceivable. I can only say that they are not human."

With this preface, Shama added:

"I now remember a story which I shall relate to you. I know it personally. As a devotee is resolute and determined, so is Baba's immediate response. Sometimes Baba puts the devotees to severe test and then gives them Upadesh (instructions)."

As soon as Hemadpant heard the word "Upadesh," a flash of lightning crossed his mind. He at once remembered the story of Mr. Sathe's Gurucharitra reading, and thought that

Baba might have sent him to Shama in order to give peace to his restless mind.

However, he curbed this feeling and began to listen to Shama's stories. They all showed how kind and affectionate Baba was to His devotees. Hemadpant began to feel a sort of joy while hearing them.[42]

In particular, Shyama told him the story of Radhabai Deshmukh wanting Baba to whisper a mantra in her ear. (This episode was discussed in the previous chapter.) In listening to the account, Hemadpant understood how Baba, as with Mrs. Deshmukh, refused to give him any particular instruction, asking him to cultivate an attitude of complete surrender instead.

This is a good example of Baba's indirect approach, for he once again adopts Madhavrao Deshpande (also called Shyama) as his intermediary. Indeed, these "triangulations" were not infrequent. The narrative offers an insight into the thoughts and feelings dominating the devotees' minds: they appear to be in constant interior dialogue with their guru.

The *Charters and Sayings* reports a conversation of Sai with a mother and son in which Baba first denies his divine identity and later gives a vision of himself as a four-armed god. Sai asked the son for eight rupees. Since the boy didn't have them, he directed him to Jog. The latter was reading from the *Dhruvacarita*[43] and, commenting on it, told the boy: "Saints, though not God, have some powers derived from Him."[44]

The boy came back to Baba quite angry and told him how there were persons who said that he was merely a man and not God. Then Baba said: "Then what is the untruth in that? Hallo! What am I? A petty fakir! I am not God. How great is God! No one can compare with him."[45]

Here the *faqīr* adheres to the basic tenet of Islam concerning God's radical transcendence and unknowability. Soon after having said this, however, he is reported to have given a vision of himself as a four-armed Hindu god, thus confirming the boy's faith in his divinity!

The story is a good example of Sufi as well as Hindu mysticism, elucidating a paradoxical *coincidentia oppositorum*, that is, the transcendence and at the same time immanence of the divine: God, in other words, is both everywhere and nowhere.

Several other stories are attested to in the year 1917. In these accounts Baba's acts include: giving proof of his all-knowing nature,[46] showing mercy towards a dog,[47] freeing one D. V. Sambare from the vice of drink,[48] and appearing in a dream to Dabholkar, fulfilling his desire.[49]

Baba often reiterated the necessity of cultivating *ātmavicāra,* to free oneself from the vicious circle of *avidyā-karma-saṃsāra.* The *Charters and Sayings* reports:

> In October 1917, Baba spoke to a Bombay lady.
>
> Baba: "Mother, what do you want? Ask for it."
>
> Lady: "Let me be free from the wheel of births and deaths."
>
> Baba (laughing): "Is this all you want? What! Have you come to die?"
>
> Lady (shocked): "Baba, I do not at all understand you."
>
> Baba: "Think who you are."
>
> Lady: "I do not understand."
>
> Baba (pointing to her husband): "He will tell you."
>
> Then the lady went with her husband to her lodgings and asked him what Baba meant.
>
> Husband: "Baba's words are mysterious. I cannot be sure I have made out his meaning. Probably he means something like this: the Jiva goes on reincarnating any number of times till it gets Sakshatkar, that is, sees or realizes God. Baba is God. But people seeing him do not get full faith..., that is, do not feel him to be God, and hence they do not get Mukti.
>
> "One must learn from the Shastras that essentially Jiva and Shiva are one. You think yourself to be a Jiva, don't you?"
>
> Lady: "Yes."
>
> Husband: "Baba and the Shastras want you to regard yourself as Shiva or God."
>
> Lady: "No, no. I am a petty sinner, a Jiva and not the great God Shiva."
>
> Husband: "No doubt that is your feeling. But Baba means that by constantly regarding yourself as God, your deeply ingrained belief that you are only a finite Jiva will be removed. If this process is continued through numerous births, and strengthened and helped by contact with saints, it will give you the firm belief that you are Brahman. That must be Baba's meaning."
>
> The pair again returned to Dvaraka Mayi.
>
> Baba: "Mother, I have listened (from here) to all that your husband told you. Keep that in mind."[50]

Once again, we are offered testimony of Baba's *antarajñāna* and of his use of an intermediary for expressing his *upadeśa*.

Sai's ironic reply to the woman's request is noteworthy. Baba laughs at the lady's naiveté in not realizing the radicality of her own desire. Getting off the wheel of *saṃsāra* implies dying to one's own individuality; truly a "blowing out" of one's limited self.

The lady's husband, a Śaiva, expounds the Upanishadic teaching of the identity *ātman-Brahman*: the woman must stop thinking of herself in terms of *nāma-rūpa,* that is, body-mind finitude. Such a belief, although thoroughly "human," is counterproductive to spiritual progress, weakening the *śiṣya* and breeding only *avidyā*. What is required is the acquisition of a heroic (*vīrya*) attitude, that is, a *sādhanā* of recognition of her own *ātmic* reality. She will then succeed in unveiling her true, eternal nature which is pure joy (*ānanda*).

Such a traditional teaching, far from discouraging an attitude of reverence and humility in the pupil, has, to the Hindu eye, the merit of constantly reminding oneself of one's glorious essence and of the necessity of striving valiantly so as to live up to that divine inheritance. It is a call to devote one's whole life to the *dis*-covery of ultimate freedom (*mokṣa*).

Ramalingaswami offers some important information about Baba's last years:

> When the Almighty Shri Sai Baba was in flesh and blood, there were other Sai Babas. One Sai Baba was in Kopergaon, called Kopergaon Sai Baba. One Sai Baba was in Bandra, called Bandra Sai Baba. One Sai Baba was in Nagpur called Nagpur Sai Baba. They were all telling their devotees that they were Shri Sai Baba, thereby making their own ends meet. Even knowing all their acts and affairs, Baba tolerated and allowed them to go on in their own way, as he pretty well knew the ins and outs of their actions. Gradually, all Sai Babas vanished without leaving trace.[51]

What strikes a chord is the fact that these other Sai Babas appeared while Sai Baba of Shirdi was still living. There was even a Sai Baba at Nagpur, the "second capital of Maharashtra," proving the reknown of the Shirdi *faqīr*. Perhaps, since Sai never spoke of a successor to his *gādī* or of any *guru-paramparā*, these figures hoped to take his place at the time of his death.[52]

Finally we come to 1918, Baba's last year.

In one short passage Baba is reported saying:

> The Shadripus (lust, anger, greed, delusion, pride and jealousy) are all delusive. They make the unreal appear as real. If a rich man wears a gold ornament, the poor man gets jealous, and thinks he must have one. This is Lobha (greed).
>
> All are like this. So one must conquer the six enemies. If they are conquered, waves of passion will not arise. Else they will enslave you. If they are subordinated and reason made the commandant, then the delusive pleasures and pains will no longer hold sway over you.[53]

On another occasion, Baba added:

> Yet you can (and must) use the inner enemies within limits. Besides Kama (sexual desire) towards the wife, have Krodha (anger) against unrighteousness, Lobha (greed) for Hari Nama, that is, uttering God's name, Moha (fondness) for Mukti (salvation), Matsar (hatred) for evil action. But have no Mada (pride).[54]

Only *mada* is said to have no beneficial application whatsoever. The *ṣaḍripus* are generally viewed as being interrelated and "hierarchically" ordered: thus *kāma*, or lust, figures as "enemy number one" and, if not controlled, is believed to favor the emergence of *krodha* and so on.

The *Charters and Sayings* reports a dialogue between Baba, Mrs. Tarkhad, and her son:

> [Baba:] "Mother, nowadays I am much pestered. Some want wealth, some women, some sons. Hallo! What I have, none wants. I wait and wait; and one day I will suddenly disappear. I am quite disgusted."
>
> Mrs. T.: "Baba, why do you say so? Then, what is to become of us?"
>
> Baba: "Why are you anxious? Is not God taking thought for your welfare? I am very much pleased when my children come to me, and then I take my two morsels of food with gusto and put on more flesh."
>
> Son: "We come to you to ask just what you have got. You know that?"
>
> Baba: "Yes. You will get it."

Son: "Yes, we are quite sure of it. But when?"

Baba: "Very soon."

Son: "Baba,...how many more births I will have to take before getting it?"

Baba: "Three more lives will be sufficient."

Son: "But Baba, will you not always be with us?"

Baba: "Hallo! During how many births have I already been with you! We shall meet again and again. I have to take care of my children night and day, and give an account of every pie to God."[55]

Another quote of Sai's:

(In 1918) People have gotten bad and give trouble. They are pestering me for money. Moreover, they have become shameless. Now, I am disgusted.[56]

Moreover:

The times are degenerating. People mostly think ill and talk ill of others. But I do not retaliate, I do not care to listen to such talk.

People become more and more sceptical; they look more at the evil side of things.

Fakirs also are seldom dispassionate.

It is hard to find a good fakir.[57]

Thus, in his last months Sai Baba sadly pondered over man's tragic condition of ignorance. Everyone asked for material benefits and petty things. Few were interested in his precious treasure, that is, the priceless pearl of *mokṣa* and the path leading to it. The waste of such a unique occasion is aptly expressed in the famous poem *Vivekacūḍāmaṇi,* which tradition attributes to Shankara: "Three things are, indeed, hard to attain and due only to divine grace: the human condition, the desire for liberation, and the association with an eminent sage."[58]

Baba's pining reflections are striking for their bitter realism.

His solitary sadness, however, does not prevent him from being favorably inclined towards Mrs. Tarkhad and her son. His assurance "we shall meet again and again" is especially noteworthy, implying that he would incarnate again as he already had in the past. Baba seems to have made a similar promise to other devotees as well, for instance to M. B. Rege and H. S. Dikshit.[59]

The belief in a series of *avatāras* of Sai Baba developed because of this and other alleged assertions of the saint. As Narasimhaswami observed: "He mentioned numerous births of his own in the past, and said that he would be born again.... He said that as long as any pupil of his was still undeveloped, he would be born again and again with him until he took him to God. Being reborn again and again to see to the safety and success of people's lives, Baba's existence is far from being a life of sorrow. It is a series of Avatars."[60]

I shall return to this issue shortly, when examining the situation that developed at Baba's death.

Bharadwaja's biography reports another of Baba's *camatkārs*: "In February 1918, one Bapuji Sastri had brought Ganges water to Shirdi and did abhishek to Baba's feet and then sought his permission to visit Sajjangad for Dasanavami. Baba said: 'I am here, and I am there also.' Later, Bapuji went to Sajjangad. At 5 a. m., on the day of holy Dasanavami, Baba physically appeared before Bapuji."[61]

Some final episodes deal with Sai Baba's death:

> Uddhavesa Bua was writing a letter to Baba every Ekadasi day, that is, once every 15 days. He visited Baba some months before Baba passed away.
>
> Baba: "Well, go. You need not be coming here every fifteen days. I am always with you and will ever be. Tell all people there (that is, convey my best wishes to all)."
>
> This was really bidding farewell. Uddhavesa did not however understand it, but somehow, owing to forgetfulness, he did not send his Ekadasi letter thereafter. Obviously Baba's reference to the 15 days' visit was a reference to these letters.[62]
>
> ...Early in October 1918,...Madhav Phasle lifted the brick and carelessly allowed it to fall, whereby it broke into two. Baba, seeing the broken pieces, expressed his grief and said: "My fakir's wife left me with Venkusha at Selu. I stayed with him 12 years, and left Selu. This brick (which Baba always lovingly used to support his arm or head) is my Guru's gift, my life companion. It is not the brick that is broken now, but my Karma (prarabdha) it is that has snapped. I cannot survive the breaking of the brick."[63]

Baba viewed the breaking of the brick, here represented as Venkusha's *guru-dīkṣā,* as ominous. This is confirmed by Mhalsapati's testimony:

> Baba asked: "Who broke the brick?" Mhalsapati mentioned that Madhav Phasle had broken it. Then Baba got very angry with Madhav, and placed his hands on his own head and felt extremely sad. Baba said: "*Sobat tutali*" i.e. the companion is broken.
>
> Next day, Kaka (H. S. Dikshit) came and said there was no need to deplore the breaking, as he would join the pieces with silver joints. Baba said: "Even if you join them with gold, what would be the use? This brick is my *Sobatya* (companion, evidently from his Selu days) and its breakage betokens evil."
>
> From that time onwards Baba was dispirited. At least Mhalsapati thought so.[64]

The *Charters and Sayings* reports the occasion which led to the construction of the *samādhi-mandir*:

> One night both Shama and Bapu Saheb Buti dreamt that Baba wanted the latter to build a vada and a temple. H. S. Dikshit went to Baba to verify this with Shama.
>
> Shama: "Deva, what mysterious wonders are you working?"
>
> Baba (shutting his ears): "I am in my own place and say nothing to anyone."
>
> Then Baba was asked for permission to build and he gave it.
>
> Later,[65] Buti wanted to instal Murlidhar's image[66] in the central hall, without having a special garbha-griha.[67] When Baba's consent was asked, he said:
>
> Baba: "After the temple is built, we shall reside there."
>
> When Baba was unwell and fast approaching his end, he said to Bayaji[68] and others: "I am going. Place me in the (Buti) vada. Brahmins will reside near me."[69]

Baba's permission for the building of the *vāḍā,* which was to house a *mandir,* was given some years before 1918. The site chosen for it was behind the plot of land on which Baba had tended a garden during his early years (*Leṇḍī*). The construction of the whole edifice was completed just a few months before the saint's death.

Sai Baba's words "we shall reside there" were not understood by Buti. The fact that he wanted to be buried there became apparent only when Baba was on his deathbed, when he asked the devotees present to "place him in the *vāḍā.*" The comment ascribed to

Baba, "*Brahmins* will reside near me," that is, near his tomb or *samādhi,* would indicate his awareness of the future presence of *brāhmaṇ* temple priests. Naturally, the Hindu community read these facts as a confirmation of Baba's Hindu identity.

Concerning Baba's death, Bharadwaja's biography and Ramalingaswami's work report a local belief according to which Sai sacrificed his life in order to save that of his friend Tatya Kote Patil, who was also very ill at the time. In other words, Baba would have died in lieu of Tatya. What follows is the moving testimony of Baba's last meeting with Tatya:

> As the terrible day neared, Tatya fell ill and was bedridden. He could not go to Dvarakamai, though Baba was also down with fever. Their condition grew worse with the passage of days. Buti was afraid that if Baba passed away, his vada would not be consecrated by the touch of his feet.
>
> One day Baba summoned Tatya to the mosque for lunch. As Tatya could not walk, he was carried thither by a fellow devotee. The master gave him a little rice boiled in milk, which he ate with great difficulty.
>
> Then, himself ailing, Baba applied udi to the forehead of his beloved devotee and said: "Tatya, at first I got two cradles for both of us, but now I've changed my mind. I don't want to take you now. I'm going alone. Go home!"[70]

Thus, Baba's followers believe that he spared Tatya's life. The latter recovered from his illness soon after.[71] Baba's love for him and his family, particularly his mother Bayajibai, was well known to all.

Till he breathed his last, Sai Baba indulged in allegorical speech: with gruesome irony, reminding us of the tragedy of the *saṃsāric* cycle, the "cradles" he referred to were, in reality, tombs.

Baba's condition continued to worsen rapidly as he also suffered from severe asthmatic attacks.

During his last days, the *Charters and Sayings* reports: "Baba [said,] 'Go on reading Rama Vijaya[72] here so that Mrityunjaya[73] may be pleased thereby.' That was done."[74]

Sai Baba's request to keep reading this devotional text, most certainly aloud, is significant: such an uninterrupted recitation to stimulate remembrance of God in the mind of the dying is common practice. In India it is popularly believed that dying with one's mind fixed on God will lead to salvation. Being *Daśaharā* time, the choice of the *Rāma Vijaya* text was most appropriate.

From left to right, the Shirdi villagers Martanda Mhalsapati, Lakshmibai Shinde, Appaji Lakshman Ratnaparkhi, Balaji Pilaji Gurav, and Bayaji Kote Patil.

Narasimhaswami further narrates:

Baba had told Uddhavesa Bua some months back not to be 'paying his fortnightly visits' and bade him final farewell. At Dasara time, Baba was unwell for a number of days, as was also Tatya Patel. In the earlier part, he went and begged food in the accustomed places supporting his body on some others. During the last two or three days, he was not able to go out.

On the 15th of October, 1918 i.e. Dasara day, after Arati was over, Baba said:

"You, Kaka (H. S. Dikshit), Buti, etc. go for your meal."[75]

They soon left. Baba sat upon his bed, reclined on Bayajibai's lap and said:

"I am going. Carry me to the Vada. All Brahmins will be living near me." He then breathed his last.

Nana Nimonkar poured water into his mouth, but the water came out. It was about 3 p.m. The day was no doubt Vijaya dasami, but Ekadasi had begun at that time.

In anticipation of his passing away, Sai had given gifts (dana) in the morning of that dasami. He sat up and paid from his pocket first Rs. 5 and then Rs. 4 to Lakshmibai Shinde who was daily preparing and giving him food and daily receiving Rs. 4 from him.

A few days before Baba passed away, he sent Rs. 200 for the feeding of fakirs and the chanting of prayers with drum beating, at a holy place.

> He sent word to another Moslem saint in these terms:
> "The light that Allah lit, he is taking away."[76] That saint received the intimation with tears.[77]
> Rama Vijaya had been read during the 14 days of Baba's illness and on the 9th, 10th, 11th day of Dasara, within Baba's hearing, as he had said that "Mrityunjaya would be pleased thereby."[78]

According to the *Shri Sai Satcharita* the day Baba died was a Tuesday, around 2:30 P.M.[79] This date was confirmed to me by the elderly villagers I interviewed in Shirdi.

The *Shri Sai Satcharita* informs us that Baba was not alone at the *masjid,* though he had sent away most of his devotees with the excuse that they had to go take their meal. At least six persons remained there, assisting him until the end: two women, that is, Lakshmibai Shinde and Bayajibai, and four men, that is, Bhagoji Shinde, Lakshman Bala Shimpi, Nanasaheb Nimonkar, and Shyama Deshpande, who was sitting on the steps of the mosque.[80]

Just before he died, Baba gave Lakshmibai a total of Rs. 9, which the *Shri Sai Satcharita* interprets symbolically as referring to the nine characteristics of a good disciple mentioned in *Bhāgavata Purāṇa* 11.10.6.[81] These "holy coins" have been kept in a family shrine by Lakshmibai's relatives. Pilgrims who go to Shirdi can visit Lakshmibai's old house and have *darśan* of Baba's unusual *prasād*.[82]

That Sai Baba had maintained his vow of leading a *"faqīri* life" was proven by the fact that, when he died and the Government took possession of his cash, it amounted to only 16 rupees.[83]

Up to the very last minute Sai Baba appeared lucid, and his passing, which occurred when he was reclining on old Bayajibai's lap, was a serene one: "Bhagoji noticed that His breathing had stopped and he told that to Nanasaheb Nimonkar who was sitting below. Nanasaheb brought some water and poured it into Baba's mouth. It came out. Then he cried out loudly: 'Oh, Deva.' Baba seemed just to open His eyes and say 'Ah' in a low tone. But it soon became evident that Baba had left His body for good."[84]

The *Shri Sai Satcharita* gives a vivid account of the profound grief that immediately swept through the village: "The news of Baba's passing away spread like wild fire in the village of Shirdi and all people, men, women, and children ran to the Masjid and began to mourn that loss in various ways. Some cried out loudly, some wallowed in the streets, and some fell down senseless. Tears ran down from the eyes of all and every one was smitten with sorrow."[85]

The news of Baba's death rapidly spread to the neighboring areas.

Devotees were confronted with a major problem: though both Hindus and Muslims agreed on the necessity of giving Baba a burial,[86] there were different opinions concerning where and how. A dispute soon arose.

The Muslims wanted to bury Baba on an open land, perhaps the same spot that Baba, thirty-two years previously, had indicated to Mhalsapati.[87] The Hindus wanted to bury him inside Buti's *vāḍā* as Sai Baba himself, they argued, had expressely wished. Twenty-four hours had not yet elapsed since Baba's death, but already this dispute had grown hot and divisive.

Finally, it was decided that a *māmlātdār* from Kopergaon, that is, the *tālukā* revenue officer, should be called in to Shirdi for settling the matter. The *māmlātdār* came and decided to have all the devotees and villagers vote: naturally the plebiscite was largely favorable to the Hindu majority.[88]

Thus it was decided that Sai Baba should be buried within the Hindu temple, that is, the *vāḍā* built by Buti. Such a decision had crucial importance, since it brought to completion the process of Hinduization of the saint.

Bappa Baba, an old devotee of Shirdi, witness to the events, told me:

> Soon after Baba had dropped the body, many disputes arose in Shirdi between the Muslim and Hindu communities. The Hindu and Muslim groups each claimed Baba's body, by saying that Baba really had been one of them. The Hindus said: "Baba was Hindu, therefore his body should be given to us." The Muslims said: "Baba was a Muslim," and so forth.
>
> While this argument raged on, Mr. Sitaram Dikshit sent a telegram to the district collector of Nagar.[89]
>
> For three days, Baba's body was kept on a plank inside the cāvaḍī.[90] Then the district collector arrived, and he decided the issue.

Bappa Baba added:

> He [the collector] inspected Baba's body and, seeing that Baba wore a langoṭī and other garbs in the Hindu style, came to the conclusion that Baba couldn't be a Muslim; he could only be a Hindu. The langoṭī is a Hindu underdress; emblematic of his belonging to Hinduism.
>
> After these things, the body was given to the Hindus for the celebration of the funeral rites.

Moreover, the elderly man particularly noted how Baba's manner of departing from this world was that of a *brāhmaṇ* Hindu saint: sending away his devotees (an act signifying compassion) and dying in full awareness and serenity. The expression used by Bappa Baba was: *Hindu paddhatī brāhmaṇe,* "according to the *brāhmaṇ* Hindu custom."

Baba's wearing a *langoṭī,* however, does not necessarily prove his Hindu identity: the *Shri Sai Satcharita* recalls how Baba had already adopted a *langoṭī* after being defeated in his wrestling bout with Mohidden Tamboli![91] The *langoṭī* is a common item of clothing among all Indians, Hindu and Muslim, and it is known to be worn by Sufis as well.[92]

Moreover, Sai Baba's display of compassion and lucidity at the moment of death is not an exclusive prerogative of Hindu *brāhmaṇs*: such a "heroic" and detached attitude is common among all kinds of ascetics.

Be that as it may, once Sai Baba's Hindu identity was established, polemics and disputes gradually waned.

Uddhao Madhavrao Deshpande, Shyama's son, was present at Baba's funeral rites:

> At that time, about seven thousand people assembled here in Shirdi. They were all agitated and weeping, and there was intense commotion all over the place. Solemn ceremonies were held with great pomp. There was a long procession and everyone lamented and wept. It was then that Baba's body was placed in the Būṭī vāḍā, which became the present samādhi-mandir. From that time on, it has always been kept there.

Bappa Baba added some interesting details concerning the burial of Sai:

> Camphor was placed in the tomb, as well as other essences. Sprinklings were also done. Then the body was laid about one and a half metres beneath the earth.... Baba had been dressed in white. He was not naked.... Flowers, garland, incenses, and various scents were placed on him. Then the samādhi was closed. These things I have seen with my own eyes.

The process of Sai Baba's Hinduization was thus completed. Devotees decided that sites that had been particularly sanctified by Baba's physical presence, such as the mosque, the *cāvaḍī,* the *dhunī,* and so on needed to be preserved. Soon, a Sai Baba organization, that is, a Sansthan, was created, and the village gradually became transformed into a pilgrimage site.

Starting in the forties, visitors by the hundreds began pouring into Shirdi on festival days. A major factor in the growth of Baba's fame can be ascribed to the success obtained by Narasimhaswami's publications, which presented Sai Baba as a great miracle worker.

The escalation in Baba's fame has continued up to the present day, making Shirdi virtually one of the most popular *tīrthas* of modern India.

Before closing this exposition of Sai Baba's life, it is important to consider some of the assurances that he is said to have pronounced regarding his omnipresence, even after death. Narasimhaswami reports:

> I shall be active and vigorous from the tomb also.
>
> Even after my Mahasamadhi, I shall be with you, the moment you think of me, at any place.
>
> As soon as a devotee calls unto me with love, I will appear. I require no train to travel.[93]
>
> My tomb will speak and move with those who make me their refuge.[94]
>
> They do not talk of saints as dying. They take Samadhi.[95]

This explains why devotees have such firm faith in Sai Baba's omnipresence and omnipotence: today, as when he was incarnated in Shirdi, he continues to protect and foster the well-being of his beloved *bhaktas*.

Some followers reported having had dream experiences soon after Baba's death.

On October 16, Sai Baba is said to have appeared in a dream to Lakshman, the village astrologer (*jośī*).[96] He was the maternal uncle of Shyama and an orthodox *brāhmaṇ* who daily worshipped Sai and the village deities. In this dream Baba told him: "Get up soon; Bapusaheb Jog thinks that I am dead and so he won't come; you do the worship and the kakad (morning) Arati."[97]

On that same day, Baba is said to have also appeared in a dream to Das Ganu, who at the time was in Pandharpur: "The masjid has collapsed; all the oil-men and grocers of Shirdi have teased me a lot; so I left the place. I therefore came to inform you here; go there quickly and cover me with 'Bhakkal'[98] flowers."[99]

A similar vision is reported to have been experienced by one Kaka Mahajani:

> On November 13, 1918, Baba appeared to devotee Kaka Mahajani in his dream and said: "Why, are you still sleeping? Wake up and worship me. Today is the thirtieth day after my Mahasamadhi!"
>
> Kaka woke up and found it so. He at once arranged the celebration and invited Kaka Saheb Dikshit, Pradhan and Dabholkar for dinner. They all sang Baba's bhajans the whole day.[100]

These claims of dreams and visions served the function of strengthening faith in Baba's omnipresence: after all, Sai Baba himself had repeatedly stated his *Brahman* nature.

Bharadwaja's biography reports another visionary experience:

> Sadashiv of Harda was very dejected after Sai's Mahasamadhi in 1918. One night Sai appeared in his dream and said: "Now I am at Saikheda. Come for darshan."
>
> At that time, saint Shri Dhunivala Dada was living there. Sadashiv went for his darshan and saw Sai seated in the place of Shri Dada. Henceforth, he looked upon the latter as the living form of Sai.[101]

This alleged *camatkār*, through which Baba identified himself with a local saint, brings one to reflect upon the delicate issue of Sai Baba's "successive incarnations."

As we know, Baba did not explicitly nominate any heirs or successors: there was no *dīkṣā* or any mechanism of *guru-paramparā*.[102]

Some hoped that Upasani Maharaj would succeed to Sai's seat. After all, Sai Baba himself had praised his spiritual excellence, defining him "pure *Bhagavan*."[103] This, however, did not occur, although most of Upasani's followers at Sakuri viewed and still view the latter as Sai Baba's natural heir.[104]

Moreover, Sai never manifested any desire in promoting a religious institution, that is, an *āśram*, and gave no indications of how things should be managed after his death.

He only assured his followers that he would be with them always. Most of the times these assurances were quite generic. At other times, he apparently confided to some of his *bhaktas* that he would incarnate again and again, as he had done in the past.

Precisely such utterances have drawn attention to the possibility of a future incarnation of Sai Baba, about which all sources speak, though with comprehensible reluctance.

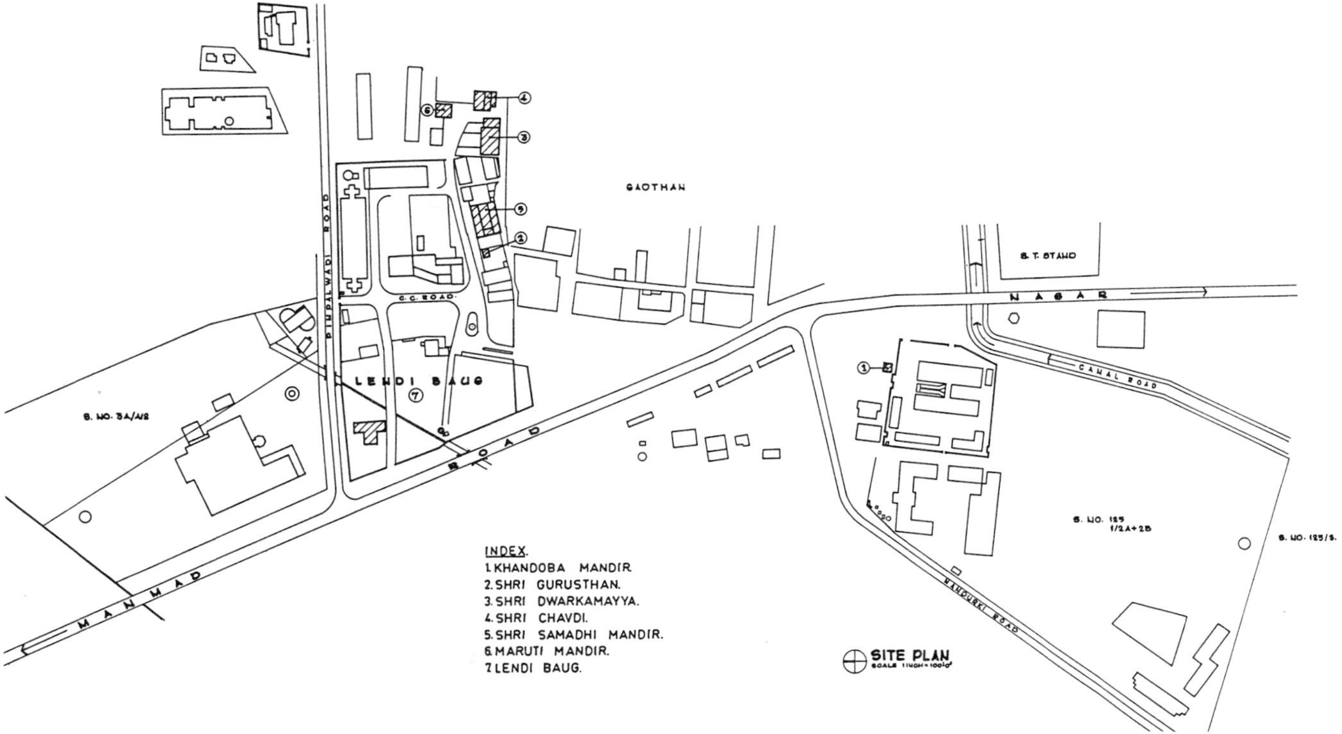

Present site plan of the village of Shirdi.

The *Shri Sai Satcharita* reports:

> (After Sai's death) Some people started remembering the words of Sai Baba. Somebody said that Maharaj (Sai Baba) told his devotees that, in time to come, he would appear as a lad of eight years.
>
> These are the words of a saint and hence nobody should have doubt about them; because in the Krishna Avatar, Chakrapani[105] (Lord Vishnu) performed this very deed. Krishna appeared before Devaki in the prison as a lad of eight years; he had a bright complexion and wielded weapons in his four arms. In that incarnation He (Lord Krishna) lightened the burden of the earth.
>
> This incarnation (Sai Baba) was for the uplift of his devotees. Then what is the reason for doubt?
>
> The ways of saints are really inscrutable. This contact of Sai Baba with his devotees is not only for one generation; but it was there for the last seventy-two generations. Generating such ties of love, it appears that Maharaj (Sai Baba) has gone for a tour and the devotees have a firm belief that He will return soon.[106]

Narasimhaswami states that H. S. Dikshit was the devotee to whom Baba said he would reappear as a boy of eight: "Kaka Dikshit...seems to have said: 'Baba said that he would appear suddenly as a boy of eight and show himself, that is, his powers and nature.'"[107]

The Sansthan has always advised devotees to place their faith in the Shirdi saint alone. This, of course, is in the interest of the organization and of Shirdi's prestige as a pilgrimage place. Indeed, words such as those which Baba was said to have spoken in Das Ganu's dream, that is, "the *masjid* has collapsed; all the oil-men and grocers of Shirdi have teased me alot, so I left the place," would certainly not favor Shirdi's image!

The idea of a possible future incarnation of Sai, however, soon brought various claims by persons declaring themselves to be *avatāras* of Baba.

Narasimhaswami reports on two of these cases: that of a boy of Karur and that of a girl of Bangalore. The *Svāmin* visited these youngsters personally and concluded that they were impostors purely interested in fame and money. As a matter of fact, they were soon identified as frauds and disappeared from public view.[108] That Narasimhaswami took the pains to meet these youngsters attests to his fascination with the *avatāra* theory.

The presence of such claims in southern India just a few years after Sai Baba's death is not unduly surprising. Shirdi Baba's fame, particularly as a wonder worker, had spread quickly. Narasimhaswami's books proved extremely influential in propagating Sai Baba's renown: even in the forties, photographs of the *faqīr* were not difficult to obtain.

In more recent years, Narayana Baba of Hyderabad has claimed that Shirdi Baba has not yet been reborn: his spirit is still moving around, doing good to humanity. Concerning this mystic, Mayah Balse reports:

> He says the disembodied soul of his dead guru (that is, Sai Baba) talks to him. He sits before a framed photograph of the Sai Baba of Shirdi and looks at it for enlightenment.... With the help of his guru's spirit, he is even able to materialize rings, lockets, and vibhuti from thin air. When asked how he produces these things he declares that the spirit of his departed guru gives them in his hands, so that when he opens his fists the object is there.[109]

A claim of being an *avatāra* of Sai Baba was made by one Basheer Baba (1942–80?) of Hyderabad. A doctor, he underwent a major crisis in his youth: "Fed up with the mounting fret and fever of his life, he ran away into Dattatreya Hills in a desperate mood to end his life. There he saw the effulgent figure of Sri Sai Baba, who by 'sparsa diksha'[110] imparted a spiritual aura on the boy. Thus he became a disciple of Sri Sai Baba."[111]

He subsequently claimed that he was Prahlada, the son of Hiranyakashipu,[112] then Kabir, and, next, Sai Baba of Shirdi.[113]

The site of his *āśram* at Ram Sai Nagar was one and a half miles from Duvvuru village, in the Cuddapah district of Andhra Pradesh.

In a conversation with the Shirdi Sansthan on October 19, 1985, I was told that Basheer Baba, together with some of his followers, used to come to Shirdi every year on pilgrimage. One Shivner Swami told me that Basheer Baba had acquired some powers (*siddhis*), which, however, he lost due to his greed for wealth. After Basheer's death, his movement seems to have dissolved.

The case of the living Hindu saint of Puttaparthi, Satya Sai Baba, is different. Born of a *kṣatriya* family as Satyanarayana Raju on November 23, 1926,[114] he is presently venerated by millions of people in India as well as abroad as an *avatāra* of Shirdi Baba. Agehananda Bharati in 1989 estimated that Satya Sai's devotees number as many as ten million.[115] Bharati observed that "his espousal of a Muslim (Shirdi Sai Baba) as his metempsychotic forbear has no positive or dysfunctional effect whatever upon his status with high caste Hindus, or with anyone else."[116]

Teacher of a *bhakti* form of Vedānta and a promotor of social services through the creation of hospitals and schools, Satya Sai Baba enjoys fame that is due especially to his alleged miraculous and healing powers and to his personal charisma.[117]

Of course the most obvious difference between the two saints is that Satya Sai, like Upasani, never had any Muslim connections, though the former's identification with Dattatreya might represent an opening in that direction.[118]

This notwithstanding, on May 23, 1940, at the age of thirteen, Satyanarayana suddenly announced to his startled family that he was "Sai Baba." Samuel H. Sandweiss, in his book *Sai Baba: The Holy Man and the Psychiatrist* reports:

> In May 1940, Satya's father saw a crowd gathering around his son. He appeared to be manifesting candy and fruit out of thin air, and many people were falling to the ground, calling him an incarnation of God. Confused and frustrated by his son's strange behavior and now by this display of sleight-of-hand or, worse, black magic, Satya's father picked up a stick and approached threateningly. "Who are you...who are you?" he demanded angrily. In a calm but firm voice, the boy announced: "I am Sai Baba."
>
> Naturally, it was difficult for many in the village to accept this boy.... Then a couple of months later, on Thursday—Guru Day in India—a group of questioning villagers approached him, pleading: "Show us a sign!"
>
> With a quick and unexpected gesture, Satya threw a bunch of jasmine flowers onto the floor. There, it is reported, they clearly spelled out—in Telugu script, the language of the village—"Sai Baba."[119]

Apparently, nobody in that remote hamlet had ever heard that name before. By furnishing various "proofs" of his identity through his *antarajñāna* and miraculous activity, he has, over the years, convinced many devotees of Shirdi Baba of the validity of his claim.[120]

Satya Sai Baba has announced that he will die at the age of ninety-six, and that eight years after his death, that is, in 2028 or 2029, he will be reborn as *Prema* Sai in the Mandya district of the state of Karnataka.[121]

In a speech he delivered on October 23, 1961, Satya Sai Baba declared that what Shirdi Baba had actually told Dikshit, was that he would reappear again as a boy *in* eight years (i.e., in 1926), not *of* eight years:

> When this Mahashakti decided to leave the previous body in 1918, Kaka Saheb Dikshit was told that in 8 years time this will take birth again.
>
> Abdul Baba was also informed that in 7 years this will appear in Madras State.
>
> Three months after the Samadhi, appearing before a house at Kirkee, the declaration was made in answer to a query that the body had passed away: "The body has gone, but I will appear again."
>
> It was also said 6 months after the Samadhi, when there was an appearance at Dvarakamayi with familiar tin can. Word was sent to Das Ganu and Mhalsapati.
>
> The statement made to Kaka Saheb was that the manifestation would take place after 8 years, not "as an eight-year-old body." It was recorded so, because Kaka Saheb relied on his memory and wrote it down only much later.[122]

Narasimhaswami, by dedicating a chapter of his biography to the description of Sai's numerous *līlās* in southern India, and particularly in Andhra, has given involuntary support to Satya Sai Baba's claim.[123]

Whatever the value of these various claims, what appears significant is the persistence and topicality of the *avatāra* theory, which will certainly reappear vigorously at the time of Satya Sai Baba's death.

It should be noted that the majority of Shirdi Sai Baba's *bhaktas* have not shifted their devotion to the present Satya Sai. Many of them ignore him or are critical of him: when I was doing research at Shirdi, people preferred to avoid the issue altogether.

Nevertheless, it can be said that an atmosphere of general respect reigns nowadays between the two groups.[124]

In conclusion, what Charles S. J. White has appropriately termed "the Sai Baba movement,"[125] initiating with Shirdi Sai, may indeed be classified as one of the major religious phenomena of neo-Hinduism.

Notes

1. Narasimhaswami, *Life of Sai Baba,* 2:218–19.

2. A sweet prepared with flour and sugar, which is then fried in *ghī.*

3. A cupboard.

4. Narasimhaswami, *Charters and Sayings,* 245–46.

5. Ibid., 118.

6. Narasimhaswami, *Life of Sai Baba,* 4:170.

7. Narasimhaswami, *Charters and Sayings,* 143–44.

8. Ibid., 144.

9. Ibid., 36.

10. Bharadwaja, *Sai Baba,* 36.

11. Literally, the "elder-sister (*ākkā*) lady (*bāī*)." A feminine spirit of disease, Akkabai's worship is particularly attested to in northern India.

12. The proper names Mari, Mari Ayi, Mariamma all designate the fearful Devī bringing smallpox, cholera, or plague. She is often represented as a fire surrounded by snakes.

13. Baba's drawing of magic lines and circles, acting as barriers, has close analogy with the drawing of mystical diagrams such as the *yantra,* which is often made with flour.

14. Literally, "the old woman," that is, the witch.

15. The evil godlings, feminine entities who are all manifestations of the untamed and destructive power of the goddess (Devī).

16. Ramalingaswami, *Ambrosia in Shirdi,* 100–2.

17. Narasimhaswami, *Charters and Sayings,* 133–34.

18. Ramalingaswami, *Ambrosia in Shirdi,* 166.

19. Bharadwaja, *Sai Baba,* 39.

20. See Stanley, *Gods, Ghosts, and Possession,* 33.

21. People could thus verify if he was circumcised, as according to Islamic law. No reliable testimony exists on this matter.

22. *Sīmollanghān,* which literally means "crossing the border" (*sīmā*), coincides with *Vijaya Daśamī* day. From the time of Shivaji (1630–80), it

was viewed as the auspicious day on which to invade a neighboring state. Baba's reference to *sīmollanghān* is, of course, symbolical, meaning the day of his death, that is, of his "trespassing" life's boundaries.

23. It usually refers to a seven-day period of uninterrupted reading of a holy text or of the repetition of divine names.

24. Narasimhaswami, *Charters and Sayings,* 135.

25. Ibid., 199.

26. Osborne, *Incredible Sai Baba,* 25.

27. Narasimhaswami, *Life of Sai Baba,* 4:35. On Sri Narayan Ashram, see ibid., 3:128–32.

28. See Ramalingaswami, *Ambrosia in Shirdi,* 155–56.

29. See ibid., 92–93.

30. See ibid., 154–55.

31. Khaparde, together with Tilak and others, was at Sangamner, a locale about thirty-five miles southwest of Shirdi. The nationalist leader was presumably touring the district on a political campaign.

32. Literally, "leaf-*supārī* nut." This is a roll of betel leaf with *areca* nut, cloves, and lime, also known as *viḍā*. Usually chewed after a meal, it is believed to be a digestive and a mouth purifier. It is often distributed after a *kīrtana* or any public assembly.

33. The expression "as if" might indicate that Baba was not sleeping but rather found himself absorbed in some kind of meditation.

34. *Shri Sai Leela* (Feb. 1986), 13. (Official organ of Shri Sai Baba Sansthan of Shirdi.) Uddhao Madhavrao Deshpande, however, told me that Baba advised the party to avoid passing through Yeola, which they did.

35. On this issue, see R. Cashman, "The Political Recruit of God Gaṇapati," *Indian Economic and Social History Review* 7, no. 3 (Sept. 1970): 347–73.

36. Cf. B. G. Tilak, *Śrī Bhagavad Gītā Rahasya or Karma-Yoga Śāstra,* translated into English by A. S. Sukhankar (Pune, 1980). For an analysis of Tilak's *Gītā Rahasya,* see D. Mackenzie Brown, "The Philosophy of Bāḷ Gaṅgādhar Ṭiḷak: Karma vs. Jñāna in the Gītā Rahasya," *Journal of Asian Studies* 17, no. 2 (Feb. 1958): 197–206. Tilak wrote his commentary while in jail.

37. Bharucha, *Sai Baba,* 57.

38. Ibid.

39. Gunaji, *Shri Sai Satcharita,* 94–95.

40. For a presentation of these texts see chapter 9.

41. The sparrow.

42. Gunaji, *Shri Sai Satcharita,* 95–97.

43. Literally, "the story of the fixed or immovable one," perhaps with reference to the polar star personified as the son of Uttanapada and grandson of Manu.

44. Narasimhaswami, *Charters and Sayings,* 119.

45. Ibid.

46. Ibid., 178, 244–45. Also, Gunaji, *Shri Sai Satcharita,* 185.

47. Narasimhaswami, *Charters and Sayings,* 118.

48. Ramalingaswami, *Ambrosia in Shirdi,* 158.

49. Gunaji, *Shri Sai Satcharita,* 222–24.

50. Narasimhaswami, *Charters and Sayings,* 25–26.

51. Ramalingaswami, *Ambrosia in Shirdi,* 174.

52. Similarly, we know of the existence of one pseudo Satya Sai Baba, claiming to be the living saint of Puttaparthi. This impostor was met in Benares in Spring 1991 by two friends of mine, who also had the opportunity of taking a photo of him. It is quite possible that other pseudo Satya Sai Babas may be operating across the Indian subcontinent.

53. Narasimhaswami, *Charters and Sayings,* 21.

54. Ibid., 127.

55. Ibid., 16–17.

56. Ibid., 52.

57. Ibid.

58. *Vivekacūḍāmaṇi,* 3: *Durlabhaṃ trayamevaitaddevānugrahahetukam / manuṣyatvaṃ mumukṣutvaṃ mahāpuruṣasaṃśrayaḥ //*; my translation.

59. See Narasimhaswami, *Life of Sai Baba,* 2:348. On Rege, retired Judge of the Indore High Court, see ibid., 3:68–85.

60. Ibid., 4:64.

61. Bharadwaja, *Sai Baba,* 31.

62. Narasimhaswami, *Charters and Sayings,* 270.

63. Ibid., 61.

64. Narasimhaswami, *Life of Sai Baba,* 2:20.

65. The year was almost certainly 1918.

66. Literally, "the bearer of the flute," that is, Krishna. As he is said to have done with the *gopīs,* he is believed to enchant the minds of all through the charming melody of his flute (*muraḷī*).

67. The "womb chamber," that is, the most internal sanctuary of a temple, often situated at the very center of it, where the most sacred image or symbol of the deity is venerated. On temple construction, see G. Michell, *The Hindu Temple: An Introduction to Its Meaning and Forms* (Chicago: University of Chicago Press, 1988).

68. Bayajibai Patil, the mother of Tatya Kote Patil.

69. Narasimhaswami, *Charters and Sayings,* 137–38.

70. Bharadwaja, *Sai Baba,* 111.

71. See also Narasimhaswami, *Life of Sai Baba,* 1:237: "It is even said that in 1918, when Baba said that Tatya would die, Tatya was saved. Some people believe that Baba gave up his own life in order to save Tatya's life."

72. This text celebrating Rama's life story, written in 1703, is a popular work of the famous poet Shridhara. As S. G. Tulpule observes: "The sight of an assemblage of commoners including farmers and their families listening in rapt attention to some loud recitation of his work, the Rāmavijaya or the Harivijaya, is not uncommon in rural Mahārāṣṭra, even today." Tulpule, *Classical Marāṭhī Literature,* 408.

73. Literally, "the victorious over death," an epithet often attributed to Shiva. As M. Chakravarti remarks: "Śiva is symbolized both as the god of death, *Mahākāla,* playing the dance of destruction, and also as the vanquisher of death, *Mṛtyuñjaya*"; M. Chakravarti, *The Concept of Rudra-Śiva Through the Ages* (New Delhi: Motilal Banarsidass, 1986), 45. The name could also possibly refer to the historical Mrityuñjaya (1575–1650), also known as Muntojī. He came from a royal Muslim family of the Bahāmanī dynasty of Bedar, and was under the influence of the Kādrī branch of the Sufis. Under the influence of Sahajānanda of Kalyāṇī, who initiated him into the *Ānanda saṃpradāya,* he converted to Hinduism. S. G. Tulpule remarks: "It was really a very bold and abnormal conversion to Hinduism and the Muslims continued to call him Shāh Mutabjī Kādrī, and after his death transformed his shrine at Nārāyaṇapūr into the *dargāh* of Murtajī Kādrī which is still known by that name. Mṛtyuñjaya was the author of a number of works relating to *Advaita* philosophy." Tulpule, *Classical*

Marāṭhī Literature, 363–64. Mrityuñjaya's background offers one more example of the eclectic nature of Maharashtrian spirituality.

74. Narasimhaswami, *Charters and Sayings,* 70.

75. After noon *ārtī,* Baba would usually ask his devotees to leave the *masjid* and go to the Dikshit's *vāḍā* for their meal.

76. *Navdin, navtarik: Allāh meyane āpnā dhuniā lagāyā, merjī Allākī. Navdin navtarik* means ninth day of the ninth month, which corresponds to the date on which Baba passed away. See Narasimhaswami, *Life of Sai Baba,* 3:166.

77. This is said to have happened four months before Sai Baba's death. The holy man, as Narasimhaswami reports, is to be identified with Banne Mea or Banemiyan Baba, a Sufi who lived in the city of Aurangabad. Apparently, Sai Baba, following the Islamic practice, had also asked Bade Baba's son, Kasim, to go see the *faqīr* Shamsuddin Mea at Aurangabad. He told Kasim: "Give him this Rs. 250. Let him do Moulu, Qavvali, and Nyas." See ibid., 164. *Moulu* is the singing of songs in praise of God, *qavvālī* is the singing about saints, and *nyās* is preparing food and distributing it to people. On Banemiyan, see also Shepherd, *Gurus Rediscovered,* 29.

78. Narasimhaswami, *Charters and Sayings,* 136–37.

79. See Gunaji, *Shri Sai Satcharita,* 230.

80. Ibid., 235.

81. Ibid., 233–34.

82. A picture of Lakshmibai proudly displaying the coins may be found in Osborne, *Incredible Sai Baba,* plate 3, between pages 54 and 55. While in Shirdi, I was also given permission to photograph the coins.

83. Narasimhaswami, *Life of Sai Baba,* 3:205.

84. Gunaji, *Shri Sai Satcharita,* 236. Local people told me that Baba, just before dying, was given betel leaves to chew on.

85. Ibid.

86. Hindus never cremate ascetics or renunciants, since they are believed to be already perfectly purified and free from *saṃsāra.*

87. Compare Baba's seventy-two-hours' *samādhi;* Gunaji, *Shri Sai Satcharita,* 238.

88. The *Shri Sai Satcharita* reports: "The proposal to use the Vada secured double the number of votes" (ibid., 237).

89. Nagar stands for Ahmednagar. The *Shri Sai Satcharita* reports that, after the voting, H. S. Dikshit wanted to refer the matter to the district collector of Ahmednagar and have his opinion (ibid.). According to Bappa Baba, the collector came to Shirdi three days after Baba's death.

90. According to Baba's followers, this wooden plank was sanctified by coming in contact with him. It is still kept inside the *cāvaḍī*.

91. See Gunaji, *Shri Sai Satcharita,* 26.

92. See Sharif, *Islam in India,* 285.

93. Narasimhaswami, *Charters and Sayings,* 7.

94. Ibid.

95. Ibid., 129.

96. On astrology in India, see Crooke, *Things Indian,* 36–40. See also Judy F. Pugh, "Astrology and Fate: The Hindu and Muslim Experiences," in C. F. Keyes and E. V. Daniel, *Karma: An Anthropological Enquiry* (Berkeley and Los Angeles: University of California Press, 1983), 131–46.

97. Gunaji, *Shri Sai Satcharita,* 237.

98. The term stands most probably for *bakūḷ,* the fragrant flower of the *Mimusops elengi* tree.

99. Bharadwaja, *Sai Baba,* 122.

100. Ibid., 149.

101. Ibid., 45.

102. This point is much emphasized by the organization of the Shirdi Sansthan. One can find leaflets and signs on the walls saying: "Baba has no heirs nor successors."

103. See Narasimhaswami, *Life of Sai Baba,* 2:251.

104. On this controversial issue, see Narasimhaswami, ibid., 2:339f., who argues against viewing Upasani as Sai's successor, and Shepherd, *Gurus Rediscovered,* 118, who, on the contrary, supports such view.

105. Literally, "discus handed."

106. Gunaji, *Shri Sai Satcharita,* 236.

107. Narasimhaswami, *Life of Sai Baba,* 2:348.

108. Ibid., 347.

109. Mayah Balse, "The Supernatural in the Age of Science," in S. P.

Ruhela and D. Robinson, *Sai Baba and His Message* (Delhi: Vikas, 1982), 133–34.

110. Literally, "initiation through contact or touch."

111. Mayah Balse, *Mystics and Men of Miracles in India* (New Delhi: Orient Paperbacks, 1978), 62.

112. Literally, "having a golden cushion or clothing (*kaśipu*)." Name of a Daitya king noted for his impiety. When his pious son Prahlada praised Vishnu, that god appeared out of a pillar in the form of Narasimha, the fourth *avatāra,* half man and half lion, and tore Hiranyakashipu to pieces.

113. See Balse, *Supernatural,* 133.

114. On November 24, 1926, Arvinda Ackroyd Ghose (1872–1950), better known as Shri Aurobindo (the famous Vedāntic guru-philosopher who resided in Pondicherry), experienced the so-called "day of the siddhi," that is, the "descent of divine consciousness on the physical plane," which represented the acme of his spiritual life. From that date, he remained silent, absorbed in meditation and in the writing of his "evolutionistic" teachings. Interestingly, devotees of Satya Sai Baba relate Shri Aurobindo's extraordinary experience to the birth, that is, "the *avatāric* descent" of their master.

115. See A. Bharati, "Religious Revival in Modern Times," in F. Robinson, *The Cambridge Encyclopedia of India, Pakistan, Bangladesh, Sri Lanka* (Cambridge: Cambridge University Press, 1989), 348.

116. A. Bharati, *Hindu Views and Ways and the Hindu-Muslim Interface: An Anthropological Assessment* (Santa Barbara, Calif.: Ross-Erikson, 1982), 87–88.

117. For an introduction to Satya Sai Baba's religious persona, see D. A. Swallow, *Ashes and Powers,* 123–58. On Satya Sai Baba's miracles, see E. Haraldsson, *Modern Miracles: An Investigative Report on Psychic Phenomena Associated with Sathya Sai Baba* (New York: Fawcett Columbine, 1988).

118. A. Bharati notes, for instance, the symbiosis of a Datta shrine with the Sufi saint Baba Qalandar Shah in the Chikmagalur district of Mysore: "The *mahant* of the temple is a Muslim with the title *bābā* or *pīr*.... The *prasād* given by the *mahant* consists of all the items Hindu *prasāds* in the area do (pieces of plantain, sugar, coconut, and milk on a plantain leaf), and it is received and consumed by Hindus of all castes including Brahmins. Hindu visitors outnumber Muslims by about three to one. This, to my knowledge, is the only place, at least in the highly orthopractical South, where Brahmins accept a food prestation from a Muslim" (Bharati, *Hindu Views,* 78–79).

119. Samuel H. Sandweiss, *Sai Baba: The Holy Man and the Psychiatrist* (San Diego, Calif.: Birth Day Publishing Company, 1975), 95. Divination through the scattering of flowers, a common practice in southern India, has complex symbolic meanings attached to it.

120. Compare, for instance, the case of H. S. Dikshit's nephew and that of the wife of the *rāja* of Chincholi. Mr. Savant, head of the Shirdi Sansthan for years, subsequently became an ardent devotee of Satya Sai; see Satya Sai Baba, *Sathya Sai Speaks,* 4:105. On this interesting issue, see the hagiographic booklet of A. D. Bharvani and V. Malhotra, *Shirdi Sai and Sathya Sai Are One and the Same* (Bombay: Sai Sahitya Samithi, 1983). For a presentation of Satya Sai Baba's life and his connection with Shirdi Sai Baba, see N. Kasturi, *Sathyam Shivam Sundaram: The Life of Bhagavan Sai Sathya Sai Baba,* 4 vols. (Prasanthi Nilayam: Sri Sathya Sai Books and Publications, 1981).

121. The first public announcement of his future incarnation as *Prema* Sai was made on July 6, 1963, day of *Gurupūrṇimā*. Satya Sai related the Sai Baba *avatāric* lineage to Shiva's mythology, that is, to a boon Shiva and Shakti would have granted to *ṛṣi* Bharadwaja, due to the latter's piousness in the preparation of a sacrifice (*yag*) taught to him by Indra. "After the Yaga was over, They (Shiva and Shakti) were so pleased that they conferred even more boons on the sage. Shiva said that they would take Human Form and be born in the Bharadwaja lineage or Gothra thrice: Shiva alone as Shirdi Sai Baba, Shiva and Shakti together at Puttaparthi as Sathya Sai Baba, and Shakti alone as Prema Sai later" (Satya Sai Baba, *Sathya Sai Speaks,* 3:23–24). For an excellent analysis of this claim and of the Bharadwaja myth, see D. A. Swallow, *Ashes and Powers,* 136–45.

122. Satya Sai Baba, *Sathya Sai Speaks,* 2:111.

123. See his chapter "Baba's Recent Lilas in South and Their Purpose," in Narasimhaswami, *Life of Sai Baba,* 4:175–84.

124. For instance, it is significant that Mani Sahukar, in the third edition of her book in 1983, added a final chapter on Satya Sai Baba, presenting him in favorable terms.

125. See White, *Sai Baba Movement,* 863–78.

Part 2

THE TEACHINGS

9

The Path of Love

In order to elucidate Sai Baba's teachings more clearly it is important to understand the "spiritual horizon" from which he derived inspiration. Thus, it is useful to explore the religious texts mentioned by the sources as being ones he advised his followers to read.

With the Muslim minority, Baba, of course, recommended readings from the Koran, and he apparently also quoted verses from it. Some of his Muslim devotees habitually read the holy book aloud in his presence at the *masjid.*

Unfortunately, however, no record has been kept regarding Sai's comments on Koranic passages. Nor do we know of any other Islamic or Sufi text that he ever talked about or recommended to his Muslim devotees. Possible explanations for such a lack of information are twofold: the minority status of the Muslim community surrounding Baba and the fact that the sources written by Hindus omit the Islamic elements for sectarian reasons or through ignorance of Sai Baba's relations with his Muslim devotees.

Nonetheless, V. B. Kher reports:

> From Abdul Baba's unpublished works in Urdu, it is clear that Sai Baba had a profound knowledge of Islam; Sira (the life of the prophet Mohammad), Sunna (his code of conduct), Hadith (traditions), the Fakah, Shariat, and the Tarikat.... He was...at ease with all the Muslim religious works and traditions, including the writings of Sufi shaikhs or orders like Kadariya, Chistiya, Suhrawardiya and Nakshabandhi.[1]

Narasimhaswami, however, states that when the *maulānā* Javhar Ali, in the early years, asked Sai whether he knew the Koran and the *sharī'at,* the latter replied he had no knowledge of them.[2]

The sources inform us of numerous Hindu texts which Sai Baba either talked about or recommended reading; therefore I shall offer a brief presentation of them: the *Bhagavadgītā,* the *Īsha Upanishad,* the *Purāṇas* in general and the *Bhāgavata Purāṇa* in particular, the *Yogavasishtha,* the *Adhyātma Rāmāyaṇa,* the *Pañcadashī,* the

Vishnusahasranāma, the *Jñāneshvarī*, the *Amritānubhava*, the *Eknāth Bhāgavata*, the *Dāsabodha*, and the *Gurucharitra*.

Sai Baba was familiar with these texts, perhaps even knowing some of them by heart. We know for sure that these texts had large circulation in Shirdi and that many of Sai's *bhaktas* studied them daily.

The *Bhagavadgītā*, the celebrated "Gospel of India," is certainly the most illustrious example of a philosophical-devotional poem within Hindu orthodoxy, and, at the same time, represents the summit of epic literature.

Sources report that Baba discussed the whole text of the *Gītā* for the benefit of Nanasaheb Chandorkar. Unfortunately, only Sai's exegesis of chapter 4, verse 34 has come down to us.[3] As mentioned earlier, Baba's interpretation of that verse showed typical traits of *advaita-vedānta* philosophy in the way he discussed the relationship between knowledge and ignorance, and of the *bhakti* approach in his recommendation of total surrender to the guru. I have also hypothesized how he might have utilized a nondualist Śaiva text, such as the *Ātmabodha*, in his hermeneutics.

Moreover, his mention of a verse from the *Taittirīya Upanishad* when discussing the nature of *jñāna*, is noteworthy: it seems plausible to assume Sai Baba's knowledge of Upanishadic texts, at least of the major ones. Such an assumption is strengthened by the help Sai Baba is said to have given to Das Ganu in his exegesis of the *Īsha Upanishad*.[4]

Baba also appears to have assimilated various themes derived from Purāṇic literature. Not only did he once describe himself "as a young lad discussing the Puranas and other works,"[5] but we know that he often recommended the reading of *Purāṇas* to his Hindu devotees, particularly of the *Bhāgavata Purāṇa*.

The *Purāṇas*, taken collectively, might be viewed as an immense, popular encyclopedia of post-Vedic Hinduism: religious, philosophical, historical, biographical, social, and political treatises, all in one.

The canon comprises eighteen major *Purāṇas* or *Mahāpurāṇas*, distinguished from the so-called minor ones, or *Upapurāṇas*. The contents of Purāṇic collections serve the function of supplements to the Vedas by illustrating the characteristics of the past ages of the world and then of the present corrupt age. With reference to the latter, a whole series of myths and legends is presented: vows, ritual practices, religious and social obligations, as well as spiritual paths leading to salvation.

Indeed, Purāṇic collections are repositories of tradition, that is, *smṛti* (literally, "that which is remembered"). Thus, it is not possible to identify the whole corpus of the *Purāṇas* as the expression of one philosophical system or of any particular school of thought: it is common heritage of all Hindus.

As a vehicle intended for the religious instruction of the masses, the *Purāṇas* attempt a conciliation of the three traditional *mārgas* leading to *mokṣa*, that is, of *jñāna*, *yoga*, and *bhakti*, as well as of the six *darśanas*, that is, the classic philosophical systems. However, in all *Purāṇas*, the *bhakti* element figures predominantly.

The *Bhāgavata Purāṇa*, together with the *Vishnu Purāṇa*, undoubtedly represents the most important document of Vaiṣṇava *bhakti*. Presumably written in the tenth or eleventh century, it bears an *advaita-vedānta* metaphysical perspective, proclaiming the ultimate reality to be an eternal nondual consciousness. The *Bhāgavata Purāṇa* recognizes both the *nirguṇa* and *saguṇa* aspects of the Absolute, called *Brahman*, *Paramātman*, or *Bhagavat*.

One might recognize the most interesting aspect of the *Bhāgavata Purāṇa* philosophy in its doctrine of *līlā*, to which is linked the theme of the *avatāravāda*. The story of Lord Krishna's life constitutes the most vital part of this *Purāṇa*.

The *Bhāgavata Purāṇa*, which profoundly influenced the philosophical systems of Rāmānuja and Madhva (considered to be the major inspirers of the great Maharashtrian *bhakti* movement, beginning with Jñāndev), stands as one of the most important texts of Vaiṣṇava mysticism for all Marathi saints and for common people as well.[6]

The *Yogavasishtha* and the *Adhyātma Rāmāyaṇa* were two other texts that Baba seemingly encouraged reading.

The *Yogavasishtha*, a popular and influential work outside of Shankara's orthodox tradition, occupies the first place among the so-called philosophical *Rāmāyaṇas*. Though tradition ascribes it to Valmiki, the author is unknown and the date of its composition is generally estimated as being between the ninth century and the twelth century.

Basically, the *Yogavasishtha* is a Vedāntic devotional text, describing experiences and cognitions acquired during meditation. It is in the form of a dialogue between Rama and the Vedic sage Vasishtha and revolves around the doctrine of salvation, said to be reached only through a completely new vision, a radical transformation of one's conceptions. In contrast with other systems, which demand the preliminary acceptance of metaphysical dogmas, the *Yogavasishtha* encourages an autonomous search for truth, which is to be realized through unmediated experience and intuition (*anubhūti*).

The path of yoga is identified as the practical way leading to ultimate truth, that is, to the realization of the world for what it is: pure illusion. Such a path is also called the path of mental liberation *(cetya-muktatā)*.

The text also treats the theme of *jīvanmukta* in some detail, describing the liberated living saint as one who, though unattached to anything whatsoever, observes all formal worldly duties.[7]

The *Adhyātma Rāmāyaṇa* was apparently composed around the end of the fifteenth century. This work, held in great esteem by all of Rama's devotees, aims not only at completing the *Rāmāyaṇa* epic, but also at interpreting it in a new way, conciliating Shankara's Kevalādvaitavedānta with faith in Rama's salvific grace.

The spiritual aspirant is expected to constantly concentrate on Rama through the repetition of his name, mantras, ritual acts, and so forth. *Bhakti*, with its nine "limbs" (*navāṅgāni*), is strongly encouraged in the *Adhyātma Rāmāyaṇa,* since through devotion grow *prema*, "pure love," and *anubhava*, "the direct experience of God."

This same attempt at a synthesis between *advaita-vedānta* and Vaiṣṇava *bhakti* is found in Ramananda, traditionally claimed to have been Kabir's teacher. Though there is no proof of any historical relationship between the *Adhyātma Rāmāyaṇa* and the movement originated by Ramananda, the internal evidence, that is, the contents of the work, supports this hypothesis.[8]

The *Pañcadashī* (so named because it consists of fifteen chapters, *pañcadasha prakaraṇa*), ascribed to Vidyaranya, is perhaps the greatest among the post-Shankara *advaita* treatises. Vidyaranya, whose original name was Madhava, was the famous minister of the *rājas* Harihara and Bukka, founders of Vijayanagar, the last autochthonous monarchy in Indian history. Brother of the Vedic commentator Sayana and conqueror of Goa, Madhava apparently retired to ascetic life around 1368, at which time he assumed the name of Vidyaranya. He was head of the Sṛṅgeri *maṭha* from 1377 to 1386 and author of numerous important works, most notably of the *Sarvadarshanasaṃgraha*, a compendium of all philosophical views.

The *Pañcadashī,* composed by Vidyaranya in old age, has always been an extremely popular text illustrating his interpretation of Shankara's philosophy.[9]

The *Vishnusahasranāmastotra* (The Hymn of the Thousand Names of Vishnu), figures in *Mahābhārata* 13.2.6936f. It is a devotional text particularly recommended for the practice of *japa* and *nāmasmaraṇa*. This work was almost certainly commented upon by Shankara himself, who interpreted it according to *advaita* principles.[10] Sai Baba seems to have often recommended the recitation of the *Vishnusahasranāma* as a powerful inspirer of *bhakti*. I shall return shortly to consideration of the importance of *nāmasmaraṇa* in Baba's teachings.

Two of the most important classics of Marathi mysticism are the *Jñāneshvarī* and the *Amritānubhava* of the great Jñāndev. It is reported that Sai recommended the reading of the *Jñāneshvarī* and also, through his *upadeśa*, inspired Das Ganu to write a commentary on the *Amritānubhava*.[11]

The *Jñāneshvarī*, or *Bhāvārthadīpikā* (The Lamp of Simple Explanation), is a vast poetical work of about nine thousand verses in the *ovī* meter. According to tradition it was composed in 1290 as an explanation of the *Bhagavadgītā*. As S. G. Tulpule observes, "It is not a commentary in the strict Sanskritic sense of the term, but a rather popular interpretation of the Bhagavadgītā presenting its teaching in an extremely poetical manner."[12]

It follows along general lines the principles of Vaiṣṇava *bhakti* salvific doctrine, though it is distinguished for its *advaita* character and its dependence upon Shankara. The theme of devotion towards the guru is one of Jñāndev's principal concerns, together with classical themes such as the importance of *japa* and *nāmasmaraṇa*, the description of mystical love and the descent of grace, the ecstatic and visionary experiences, and so on.

Jñāndev states that God may be realized through the path of *bhakti* alone: he envisions no contradiction between *advaita-vedānta* philosophy and *bhakti-mārga*. He significantly declares: "In Advaita, there is still Bhakti. This is a matter of experience, and not of words."[13]

If the *Jñāneshvarī* is a composite work, intertwining mystical experience with philosophical monistic speculations, the *Amritānubhava* (The Intuitive Comprehension of Immortality) is a versified philosophical work of *advaita-śaiva* inspiration. Its theme is the essential unity of the individual soul with the supreme soul, Shiva.

The influence upon Jñāndev of Śaiva circles, and of the philosophy of Vasugupta's *Shivasūtras*, seems undeniable: technical terms such as *piṇḍa, pāda, śakti*, and so forth are frequently employed by him.

Jñāndev's *advaita-bhakti* orientation or fundamental tenet of "unitive devotion" clearly emerges,[14] along with insightful analyses of the relationship between ignorance, knowledge, and language, calling to mind Baba's interpretation of the *Gītā* verse previously reported.

At this point, it is appropriate to take a brief look at the life of Jñāndev, founder of the *Vārakarī saṃpradāya* of the Marathi saint-poets.

According to some scholars he was born at Alandi, Pune district, while according to others he came from Apegava, Aurangabad district. The year of his birth was either 1271 or 1275. The only source for a life account of Jñāndev is Namdev's biography written in three parts: "Ādi," "Tīrthāvaḷī," and "Samādhi."[15] S. G. Tulpule says of Jñāndev's life:

> All that we know about him for certain is that along with his two brothers, Nivṛtti and Sopāna, and his sister Muktā, he was the offspring of an ascetic turned householder; that consequently they became outcasts and had to go to Paiṭhaṇ, then the centre of learning, to obtain a certificate of purity (*śuddhipatra*) from the learned Brahmins of that place; that on securing it they all went to Nevāsẽ where Jñāndev wrote his monumental work, Jñāneśvarī; that he entered into a spiritual comradeship with Nāmdev, the great devotee of Viṭṭhala from Paṇḍharpūr; that together they undertook a pilgrimage to the holy places of the North; and finally, that on their return from the pilgrimage he passed away at Āḷandī, while in the state of meditation, or entered "live *samādhi*," in 1296.[16]

According to tradition, Jñāndev's father, Vitthalpant, belonged to the Nāthas, and Jñāndev was initiated into it by his elder brother Nivṛtti, who was himself a disciple of Gahininatha, the fourth in the Nātha lineage of western India.

Thus, we find in Jñāndev a fusion of two main currents of religious life: the yoga of the Nāthas with its Śaivite background, and the monistic Vaiṣṇava *bhakti* of the *Bhāgavatas,* through Namdev's influence. This blending contributed to the molding of his eclectic *advaita-bhakti* form of spirituality.

Jñāndev, besides producing his two major works already mentioned, is author of the *Chāṅgadeva-pāsaṣṭī,* a poem of sixty-five quatrains addressed to the yogin Changadeva, and of the *Gāthā,* a collection of his devotional lyrics (*abhaṅgas*).[17]

Adopting the terminology of the great Marathi scholar R. D. Ranade, after the "philosophical mysticism" of Jñāndev and the "democratic mysticism" of his contemporary Namdev, we meet with the "synthetic mysticism" of Eknath, who lived between 1533 and 1599.

Eknath was another major figure of the *Vārakarī sampra-*

dāya and the author of the celebrated *Eknāth Bhāgavata,* a work known to Sai Baba.

A *brāhmaṇ* born in 1533 at Paithan, Eknath lost his parents during infancy and was brought up by his grandfather, who was the son of Bhanudas (1448–1513), a prominent figure in the history of the Vitthala cult at Pandharpur.

Influenced by the Vaiṣṇava *bhakti* of Pandharpur through his grandfather, Eknath was initiated to religious life by his guru Janardana, a devotee of Dattatreya, who represented a blend of Vedanta *cum* Sufism. As S. G. Tulpule writes: "Ekanātha...stands on the confluence of three different currents, namely those of Datta, Viṭṭhala and the Ṣūfis, all merging in his mystical writings. Ekanātha was a devout *gurubhakta* so much so that he entwined his own name with that of his *guru* and wrote, without exception, under the joint pen-name of Ekā-Janārdana meaning the Ekā of Janārdana."[18]

Eknath was a prolific writer. His works include the *Bhāvārtha Rāmāyaṇa* and his *abhaṅgas* and *bhāruḍas* (short poems similar to folk songs, but with a double meaning, one secular and the other spiritual).

The *Eknāth Bhāgavata,* certainly his magnum opus, is a Marathi commentary on the eleventh *skanda* of the *Bhāgavata Purāṇa.* Begun at Paithan in 1570 and completed in Benares in 1573, it is a voluminous work, containing more than eighteen thousand *ovīs.*

In the *Bhāgavata,* Eknath displays his great skill as a *bhakti* poet, through his ability to create mystical imageries of divine love: the nine traditional "limbs" of *bhakti* (*navāṅgāni*) are explained through examples of great saints of the past. He delves particularly into the uplifting value of *kīrtana* (singing God's glories). Similarly, remembrance of the sacred name (*nāmasmaraṇa*) and loving absorption (*dhyāna*) are indicated as sublime devotional practices.

Eknath distinguishes between two forms of *bhakti*: as an end in itself and as a means. The highest form of devotion is attainable only by a very few: then, every distinction between the two forms of *bhakti* is vanquished.

Eknath observes how the purified mind of the *bhakta* who has surrendered himself to God intuitively realizes the supreme Self, thanks to the guru's loving grace (*kṛpā*): the highest form of devotion is thus dedicating all thoughts and actions to one's teacher or to God, rendering perfectly selfless service (*parama-sevā*).

Evident in Eknath is his dependence upon Shankara and the Vedāntic monism of Jñāndev. He produced a reliable edition of the

Jñāneshvarī that is free of interpolations and still regarded as the standard text.

Perhaps the major achievement of Eknath's *Bhāgavata* was the popularization of Vedānta philosophy to an extent unknown before him. Written in a clear Marathi style, it reached even the poorest social strata and was received with great enthusiasm by all. As R. D. Ranade observes, "With Jñāndev, philosophy had reigned in the clouds; with Ekanātha, it came down upon earth and dwelt among men."[19]

The *Dāsabodha* is the celebrated work of the *deśastha brāhmaṇ* Narayana, better known by his religious name of Ramdas (1608–81). It is not clear whether Sai Baba explicitly recommended reading this text, but it certainly circulated widely at Shirdi, and G. S. Khaparde often mentioned it in his diary.

Illustrious exponent of the Marathi saint-poets, Narayana was born on *Rāmanavamī* day in the village of Jamb. At the age of twelve he left that place and went to the village of Takali on the Godāvarī River, near Nasik: here, according to tradition, Rama had stayed with Sita and his brother Lakshmana. Ramdas remained here for full twelve years (1620–32), practicing severe austerities and dedicating his life to the worship of Rama, his *iṣṭadevatā*. At Nasik his name was eventually changed to that of Ramdas, "the slave of Rama," identifying him with the ideal *bhakta*, Hanuman.

From 1632 to 1644, he is said to have travelled on pilgrimage all over northern India (*pādayātrā*), up to Badrinath in the Himalayas.

Back in Maharashtra, Ramdas began the most active and controversial period of his life, corresponding with his social involvement. In 1648 he established Rama's cult at Chaphala, and it was here that he met with the great Maratha prince and nationalist leader Shivaji, who became his disciple either in 1649 or 1672, receiving *dīkṣā* from Ramdas at Shinganavadi.

A spiritual activist, Ramdas not only spread faith in the name of Rama and Vaiṣṇava piety throughout western India but also, with the help of Shivaji, erected innumerable *maṭhas* (at least seventy but more than eight hundred, according to Rāmdāsī tradition) for the restoration of *sanātana dharma* and, specifically, of *Maharashtra dharma*, in opposition to Islamic influence.

His program, differing from the more conservative attitude of the *Vārakarīs*, was to combine an intense religious life with social solidarity and political engagement: Ramdas encouraged a *brāhmaṇic* renaissance centered around the Rama cult within a framework of *advaita-bhakti*. He also acted as a counsellor to the political class.

For ten years, from 1654 to 1664, Ramdas established his main residence in a cave near Mahad, south of Bombay, called "Shivtar Ghal" (Shivtar's gorge): it was here that he started dictating to his disciple Kalyan Swami his magnum opus, the *Dāsabodha* (The Awakening of God's Servants). Divided into twenty sections (*daśak*) each comprising ten chapters (*samāsa*) with a total of 7,752 *ovīs*, all dedicated to Lord Rama, the work represents the compendium of Ramdas's thought.[20]

As S. G. Tulpule notes:

> The Dāsabodha is a peculiar combination of the poet's observation of the ways of the world, his devotional fervour, metaphysical thought, socio-political understanding and mystical experience. It is, in fact, a history of the doings and thoughts of a great thinker-saint, who was also a poet. The chief value of its counsels lies in the practical hints and the inspiration they give to those who aspire for direct Realisation.[21]

Among the salient themes treated in the *Dāsabodha* are the following: the need to find a guru, liberation being unattainable without his guidance; the need to actively perform *nāmasmaraṇa* and *kīrtana*; the need to cultivate *ātmanivedana* (surrender), identified as the fulfillment of *bhakti*.

Thus, also in Ramdas's "active mysticism," Vaiṣṇava *bhakti* and *advaita* philosophy are highlighted, although it is Rama and not Vitthala who constitutes the focus of worship.

Finally I come to a presentation of the *Gurucharitra*, a Marathi work in fifty-one chapters containing more than seven thousand *ovīs* written by Sarasvati Gangadhara around 1538. Tradition divides the text into the following three sections or *kāṇḍas: Jñānakāṇḍa* (chap. 1–24), *Karmakāṇḍa* (chap. 25–37), and *Bhaktikāṇḍa* (chap. 38–51).

Much of the *Gurucharitra* (chap. 11–51) concerns the miraculous life story of Narasimha Sarasvati (c. 1378–1458), mythical founder of Dattatreya's cult. The text also presents the life of Shripad Shrivallabha (c. 1323–53), the first historical figure of the *Datta saṃpradāya*, viewed as the first *avatāra* of Datta.[22]

The Datta cult in Maharashtra seems to have originated as a revivalistic movement, so as to preserve the caste system and the ritual dimensions of Vedic religion.

Although not a great literary composition, the *Gurucharitra* is considered one of Maharashtra's most sacred devotional texts, that is, a "sacred mantra" of sorts. Its author, Sarasvati Gangadhara, was the first to expound the ideal of a *Maharashtra Dharma,* which was later taken up by saint Ramdas.

Regarding the *Gurucharitra,* S. G. Tulpule notes:

> Although the Gurucaritra does not excel as a work of literature, it occupies an important place in the religious life of Maharashtra, even today, and is almost held in awe and read devoutly by the common man in the faith that it is a great healer of ailments, both physical and spiritual. It enjoys the same popularity with the theistic masses as a work like the Jñāneśvarī does among the followers of the cult of Paṇḍharpūr.[23]

This brief survey of the above texts throws sufficient light on Baba's Hindu background: the *advaita-bhakti* elements of the *faqīr*'s *upadeśa* derive from the glorious secular tradition of the Marathi saint-poets and are in total harmony with it.

The overall subordination of the Śaiva element vis-à-vis the Vaiṣṇava one, verily a leitmotif within Marathi *bhakti* cults, poignantly expressed by god Vitthala bearing the *liṅga* on his head at Pandharpur, is also attested to in Sai Baba's life: his mysterious guru Venkusha, his love of Hari and Rama's names, his calling the mosque *Dvārakāmāī,* and other details confirm it.

It now becomes important to focus attention on the most typical expressions of *bhakti* in Baba's *upadeśa.* Before doing so, however, I shall offer a brief, general characterization of the *bhakti-mārga.*

Etymologically, the term *bhakti* is derived from the verbal root *bhaj,* meaning to divide, share with, partake of, both in the transitive sense of having someone participate in something and in the intransitive sense of participating in it. Such a twofold understanding is preserved in the idea of *bhakti* as *mārga*: the *active* participation of the Lord, *Bhagavan* to the devotee, and the *passive* one of the worshipper, that is, the *bhakta* to the deity.

God loves and communicates Himself to the devotee, the latter worships Him and thus participates in His love: the *bhakta* must offer himself completely to the deity. A *bhakti* attitude thus requires a radical submission of man to God as well as a progressive feeling of intimacy: as the religion of love, it may be viewed as the personal path par excellence.

On the relationship of God with his *bhaktas,* Lord Vishnu, in *Bhāgavata Purāṇa* 9.4.63–64, declares: "I (the Lord) am the slave of my servants..., my heart is completely dedicated to them, since I love those who dedicate themselves to me. I do not wish absolute happiness for myself if I cannot share it with my devotees, of whom I am the supreme refuge."[24]

Grace is absolutely central in *bhakti-mārga*: God's blessings and favors are totally free and undeserved.

The first traces of *bhakti* may be found in Vedic hymns, for instance in those dedicated to Varuna and Savitṛ. In the latest Upanishads of the first period, such as the *Shvetāshvatara*,[25] belonging to the black *Yajurveda*, the term *bhakti* appears with the same meaning which will be found in the *Gītā*[26] and later works.[27]

Bhakti finds its great development within Viṣṇuism: the *Vishnu Purāṇa* and *Bhāgavata Purāṇa* are certainly its two most important documents. The thirteenth and sixteenth centuries may be considered *bhakti*'s golden age, although *bhakti* does not rest on scriptures alone but renews itself continuously.

If *bhakti*'s fundamental presupposition is theism, its unfolding lies in *praxis*, that is, a series of devotional acts orienting one's life. *Bhakti* in its true sense is not a purely intellectual feeling, nor is it a mere loving sensation. It is, rather, a force that gradually takes over the whole of a person. For this reason, the *bhakti-mārga* is perceived as a dynamic and progressive movement.

Tradition distinguishes between two types of devotion: the love that is imperfect (*apara*), relative (*saguṇa*), secondary (*gauna*), and interested (*haituka*); and the love that is perfect (*siddha*), supreme (*para*), absolute (*nirguṇa*), and noninterested (*ahaituka*).

In the first type, that is, *aparabhakti* (imperfect devotion), when the *tamo* and *rajo guṇas* predominate, devotion is mixed with sloth, egoism, attachment. Only a *sāttvika*, that is, a person with pure *bhakti*, loves God for His own sake.

It is when the *sattva guṇa* predominates that a devotee can be initiated into the *navāṅgāni*, the nine "limbs" or forms of devotion. The *Bhāgavata Purāṇa* compares it to steps of a staircase at the top of which is the salvific power of pure love (*prema*), coinciding with *ātmanivedana* (perfect surrender). The lover and the Beloved become one inseparable entity.[28] The mind of the *bhakta*, being fixed (*ekānta*) on the Beloved, is then indifferent to all things.

Bhakti may direct itself towards three goals: (1) the Absolute in its *nirguṇa* character (an extremely elitist path, requiring the renunciation of theism); (2) a particular *iṣṭadevatā*; and (3) a guru who is revered as a divine incarnation.

The high degree of compatibility of *bhakti* with other schools of Hindu thought must be remembered. *Bhakti-mārga* is indeed flexible and polimorphous: there exist a wide range of schools of *bhakti* spirituality. As previously noted, India offers examples of rich and intense devotional practices even within the purest *advaitism*.

Sai Baba, besides encouraging his followers to be devoted to their *iṣṭadevatā* or to the attributeless *Brahman*, constantly emphasized devotion to the guru. As Sai noted, without a guide it is difficult to tread the path. There are "tigers" and "bears" along the way. However, if the guru is present, then there are no difficulties.[29]

Baba assured his *bhaktas* that he would bring them to full realization, always protecting them along the path: "If one devotes his entire mind to me and rests in me, he need fear nothing for body and soul. If one sees me and me alone and listens to talks about me and is devoted to me alone, he will reach God (Chaitanya)."[30]

Moreover: "If you make me the sole object of your thoughts and aims, you will gain Paramartha (the supreme goal)."[31]

Paraphrasing *Bhāgavata Purāṇa* 9.4.63–64, discussed above, Baba announced:

"I am the bond slave of my devotee (bhaktaparadina). I love devotion."[32]

Sai Baba insisted on the intensity which should animate *guru-bhakti*. In this regard, it is important to recall Sai's relationship with his own master:

> I sat and gazed at him; and we were both filled with Bliss. I cared not to turn my eye upon anything else. Night and day I pored upon his face with an ardour of love that banished hunger and thirst. The Guru's absence, even for a second, made me restless.[33] I meditated upon nothing but the Guru and had no goal or object other than the Guru. Unceasingly fixed upon him was my mind.... I wanted nothing but the Guru and he wanted nothing but my love."[34]

This bond of love uniting teacher and disciple is regarded by Baba as the key to spiritual progress. Such a view is characteristic of all Indian culture: the importance or, better still, the weight of the guru figure would indeed be difficult to overestimate. The word guru is, with *ācārya*, the most common term designating the teacher, and literally is an adjective meaning heavy (often opposed to *laghu* "light"). In the experience of Hinduism the guru is verily God; the deity "uses" the guru as an instrument or receptacle of his/her grace.[35]

Jñāndev compares the guru to "the sun of absolute reality" and thus calls him *citsūrya*:

> How very wonderful it is that while the celestial sun makes the phenomenal world rise into view, the sun of absolute reality makes the phenomenal world hide its face altogether. He eats up the stars in the shape of both knowledge and ignorance, and brings on illumination to those who seek self-knowledge. At the dawn of the spiritual light, individual souls like birds leave their nests on their spiritual pilgrimage.[36]

What constitutes the relationship between guru and *śiṣya* is faith (*śraddhā* or *niṣṭhā*).[37] The term *śraddhā* is composed of *śrat,* meaning both "truth" (Indian tradition relating it to *satya*) and "heart" (it is semantically related to Latin *cor* and Greek *kardía*), and the verbal root *dhā* (to put, place, set, lay). Thus, *śraddhā* means "putting one's heart or one's trust and confidence in something or someone."

The term *niṣṭhā* (firmness, steadiness, attachment, devotedness) is derived from the verbal root *sthā* and designates profound loyalty. As we have seen, Sai Baba often requested "two coins" from his devotees, that is, the twin virtues of *niṣṭhā* and *saburī* (patience).

The wife of one of my interpreters at Shirdi confided that she believes the couplet of *niṣṭhā-saburī* constitutes the very heart of Baba's *upadeśa*. The coupling of these terms, written along the alleys of Shirdi as well as inside the *samādhi-mandir,* is emblematic of the way in which Baba blended the Vedāntic and Sufi traditions.[38]

With reference to the complete faith a disciple must have in the guru, Sai taught:

> There are innumerable saints in this world, but "our father" (Guru) is the Father (real Guru). Others might say many good things, but we should never forget our Guru's words. In short, love your Guru wholeheartedly, surrender to Him completely and prostrate yourselves before Him reverentially, and then you will see that there is no sea of the mundane existence before you to cross, as there is no darkness before the sun.[39]

On another occasion, Baba is reported saying:

> Stick to your own Guru with unabated faith, whatever the merits of other Gurus and however little the merits of your own.
>
> Pant, we must not give up attachment to our own Guru. Be ever firmly resting in him and in him alone.[40]

Moreover:

> Look to me, and I will look to you. Trust in the Guru fully. That is the only Sadhana. Guru is all the Gods.[41]

> My Guru, after depriving me of everything, asked me for two pice. I gave them to him. He did not want metallic gifts. What he asked for was faith (nistha) and patience, cheerful endurance (saburi).[42]

Notice how in Baba's teachings the path of *bhakti* is never opposed to that of *jñāna*. These two *mārgas* are seen in a relationship of complementarity and interdependence.

The sage of Arunachala, Ramana Maharshi (1879–1950), cogently expressed the fundamental unity of the two paths: "To know God is to love God, therefore the paths of jñāna and bhakti come to the same."[43]

Sai Baba pointed out that the way of *bhakti* is easier than the way of *jñāna*, and is open to all:

> Jnana marga is like Ramphal. Bhakti marga is like Sitaphal (custard apple), easy to deal with and very sweet. The pulp of the Ramphal is inside and difficult to get at. Ramphal should ripen on the tree and be plucked ripe. If it falls down, it is spoiled. So if a Jnani falls, he is ruined. Even for a Jnani there is the danger of a fall, e. g., by a little negligence or carelessness.[44]

I shall now discuss the nine "limbs" of *aparabhakti*, that is, the list of *navāṅgāni* taught by the *Bhāgavata Purāṇa*.

The practice of *śravaṇa*, literally, "audition," constitutes the first "limb." Listening to spiritual discourses or reading holy texts was often recommended by Baba: "Go on daily reading the Pothi (Jnaneshvari), go and sit in the Vada, read something regularly every day and while reading, explain the portion read to all with love and devotion."[45]

At Shirdi, as everywhere in India, *śravaṇa* was a common devotional act. The usual procedure was for devotees to gather at the *vāḍā* and each of them, taking turns, would read passages from holy texts. A discussion would then follow.

Śravaṇa stands at the beginning of the *navāṅgāni* since it is the very root of knowledge: one must first hear or read that which one wants to know. This practice aims at the absorption of the mind into God's glory (*mahimā*) through the consideration of his wonderful deeds. Thus, it is a form of *bhakti* that, purifying the mind, awakens one to spiritual life, starting him/her on the path.

Kīrtana, the second "limb," derives from the verbal root *kīrt* (to narrate), and signifies the singing of God's name while narrating his exploits. This traditional custom was also very popular in Shirdi: Das Ganu, a great *kīrtankār*, would often perform at the village.

The *kīrtana*, as all religious rites, begins with an invocation to the elephant-god Ganesha, the remover of obstacles (*vighnavināśaka*), and ends with the recitation of a Purāṇic story.

Eknath, in his *abhaṅga*[46] *Saguṇacaritrẽ paramapavitrẽ*, sums up the requirements of *kīrtana-bhakti*:

> With great reverence, we should sing the holy deeds of the Blessed, and with all our hearts, utter the Divine Name in the company of saints.
>
> At the height of the kīrtana, we should sway in joy before God.
>
> No talk other than devotion or knowledge should be indulged in, and the way of remembrance should be explained in all enthusiasm.
>
> The only restraint saints impose on the performance of kīrtana is that the form of God is thereby firmly fixed on the mind.
>
> Unitive devotional singing and incessant remembrance, accompanied by the clapping of hands, instantly lead Ekā-Janārdana to salvation.[47]

Closely related to the practice of *kīrtana* is the singing of *bhajans* (devotional hymns): these were sung daily in Baba's presence.

It is known that Sai himself, in his youth, loved to sing. Though this practice is to be referred in the main to his Sufi background, on which I shall shortly comment, Baba's love of music, be it in the form of *kīrtanas, bhajans* or *qavvālīs*, was known to all.

Smaraṇa (remembrance of the divine name) is the third "limb" of the *navāṅgāni*. *Smaraṇa-bhakti* is the heart of devotional life, and saint-poets have always praised it as the means to God-realization: Baba constantly recommended it and practiced it himself throughout his life.

Such an exercise may be vocal or silent, its aim being the concentration (*dhāraṇā*) of all faculties on the name, which is itself the deity, leading in time to pure contemplation (*dhyāna*) and absorption (*samādhi*). As S. G. Tulpule observes:

> Nāmasmaraṇa...is, in a way, the silent prayer of God. Its technique consists in unremitting inward repetition of the divine Name.... The power of this prayer consists not in its contents, but in the Name itself. Saints testify that in this Name resides the power of the presence of God.... Beginning with simple repetition, gradually but inevitably, the Divine power which is hidden in it, is disclosed and takes on the character of a ceaseless uplifting of the heart, which persists through the distractions of the surface life.[48]

Apart from Sai's repetition of his favorite phrase *Allāh Mālik,* we know he also used to recite Vishnu-Krishna's name, that is, Hari: "Baba (to H. S. Dikshit): 'I was always saying Hari, Hari. Hari then appeared to me. I then stopped giving medicine and gave Udhi.'"[49]

This *smaraṇa* exercise is to be ascribed to Baba's early years.

On another occasion, Baba said: "I had heart disease. I kept Vishnusahasranama close to my chest. Hari descended from it. I was cured."[50]

The implication is that Baba practiced the silent repetition of Vishnu's thousand names during the night. Though Sai Baba was heard uttering the sacred name aloud or in a low tone at the *masjid,* he most often practiced a silent *smaraṇa.* The name he most frequently advised his Hindu followers to repeat was that of Rama:

> "Ram Rami Ghya" i.e. repeat the name of Rama.
>
> Always say Raja Ram Rajah Ram. If you do so your life will be fruitful. You will attain peace and infinite good.
>
> What should we say? Sri Ram Jaya Ram Jaya Jaya Ram.
>
> Say Ram Ram. God will bless.[51]
>
> On occasions he allowed the repetition of his own name (Sai):
>
> Simply say "Sai, Sai" with heart overflowing. I care not for show of respect and forms. I rest in such devotees.
>
> Repeat my name. Seek refuge in me. But to know "who I am" have Sravana and Manana.
>
> Those who perpetually repeat my name reach their Goal.[52]

Similar to vocal *smaraṇa* is the practice of *japa,* which Sai Baba also encouraged. Derived from root *jap* (whispering, muttering), *japa* means repeating in a low, murmuring tone passages from scriptures, mantras, or names of a deity.

Concerning the practice of *nāmajapa,* it is worthwhile to quote a passage from a dialogue between a devotee of Sai Baba and Ramana Maharshi.

> Devotee: "My practice has been continuous invocation of the names of God while breathing in, and of the name of Sai Baba while breathing out. Simultaneously with this I see the form of Baba always. Even in Bhagavan[53] I see Baba. The external appearances are also much alike. Bhagavan is thin. Baba was a little stout. Should I continue this method or change it? Something within tells me that if I stick to name and form I shall never get beyond them but I can't understand what further to do if I give them up. Will Bhagavan please enlighten me?"

> Bhagavan: "You may continue with your present method. When the japa becomes continuous all other thoughts cease and one is in one's real nature which is invocation or absorption. We turn our minds outwards to things of the world and are therefore not aware that our real nature is always invocation. When with conscious effort, or invocation, or meditation as we call it, we prevent our minds from thinking of other things, then what remains is our real nature, which is invocation.... There is no difference between God and His name."[54]

Sai Baba would have certainly agreed with Ramana Maharshi: *nāmajapa* must be practiced constantly so as to result uninterrupted, even during sleep. Sai used to force Mhalsapati to stay awake at the mosque during the night, thus "participating" in his mental *nāmasmaraṇa*: "When I lie down on the ground, I ask Mhalsapati to sit by me and keep his palm on my chest.... I lie down making mental Namasmarana. So, I say to Mhalsapati: 'Feel it by placing your hand on my heart. If you catch me napping, wake me up.' Such was and is my order to him."[55]

In this dark age of *Kali, smaraṇa-bhakti* is said to constitute the easiest path towards enlightenment.[56]

The ninth step of the *navāṅgāni,* together with *nāmasmaraṇa,* represents the very core of Baba's *upadeśa.*

Ātmanivedana (presentation or introduction of one's self) is the entrusting or offering of one's whole being to the deity, the crowning point of devotional life leading to *nirguṇa bhakti*. Thus it encompasses the preceeding "limbs" (*pādasevana, arcanā, vandana, dāsya,* and *sakhya*). S. G. Tulpule aptly describes *ātmanivedana*: "It consists in the utter annihilation of the sense of egoism and bodily consciousness, as if cutting off one's own head at the feet of God. It is the silent experience of the unitive life, of which no word can give any account."[57]

The annihilation of mind and ego, that is, what might be called "the nakedness of being," brings about the natural effulgence of the self. In particular, Baba mentions *prapatti* in his instructions on how to attain *mokṣa*:

> Have Sadhana Chatushtaya[58] i.e. nitya-anitya-viveka i.e. inquiry into what is real and what is unreal, vairagya i.e. dispassion, sama i.e. quiet of mind...and mumukshutva i.e. desire for Mukti. Have navavidha bhakti i.e. ninefold devotion, etc. Practice these. Surrender yourself to God (atmanivedana), have prapatti.
>
> Daily take darshan of siddhas i.e. perfect saints. Live a moral life. Then you will be pure even at death. At the time of death, have no desire at all. Concentrate on God i.e. your Ishta Devata. If death comes when your mind merges in the Ishta Devata (God), Mukti (salvation) is attained.[59]

When one's surrender is perfect, then the practices of *japa* or *nāmasmaraṇa* are no longer necessary and can be abandoned. G. G. Narke acutely observed:

> According to the tradition of Sai Baba, the disciple or devotee who comes to the feet of a Guru in complete surrender has, no doubt, to be pure, chaste and upright, but he does not need to continue any active practice of japa or meditation. On the contrary, any such practice or any intellectual process which involves the postulate "I am doing this" is a handicap.... The Guru does not teach, he radiates influence. This influence is poured in and is absorbed with full benefit by the soul which has completely surrendered itself, blotting out the self; but it is obstructed by mental activity, by reliance on one's own exertions and by every kind of self-consciousness and self-assertion.[60]

Sai Baba sometimes recommended his devotees to sit quietly and simply "do nothing," as in the case of Upasani Maharaj. Baba

A rare photo of Sai Baba

told him: "Sit quiet, Uge Muge. I will do the needful. I will take you to the end."[61]

From other devotees Sai required a total oblation of oneself:

Baba to B. V. Dev: "Bhav, give me dakshina."

B. V. Dev gave one guinea.

Baba: "Give me more."

After getting four, Baba said: "Though four were given by you, Baba has got only one."

Dev: "Baba, I have given four."

Baba: "Yes, but I have only one. You will know."

The obvious interpretation is that, though the devotee surrenders his fourfold Antahkarana (of Manas, Buddhi, Ahamkara, Chitta) Baba receives only the Jiva.... So the mind must surrender multiplicity unto the Guru to attain unity.[62]

Moreover:

Baba said to Mrs. Tarkhad: "Give me Rs. 6 dakshina."

Mrs. Tarkhad (to her husband): "We have no money. It is so painful to be asked when we have nothing."

Mr. Tarkhad: "Baba wants only your six inner enemies (lust, anger, etc.) to be surrendered to him."

Baba, again to Mrs. Tarkhad: "Will you give me Rs. 6 ?"

Mrs. Tarkhad: "Baba, I have given them."

Baba: "See that you do not wander off."[63]

Frequently, Sai asked his *bhaktas* to surrender "*tan, man,* and *dhan,*" that is, the attachments of body, mind, and riches.

The theme of surrender constitutes the heart of Baba's *upadeśa,* be it active, involving devotional activities as in the *navavidha* path, or passive, as in the culminating condition of pure *prapatti.*

Recall that Sai, commenting on a verse of the *Gītā,* told Chandorkar how *praṇipāta* (submission) must be *sāṣṭāṅga daṇḍavat,* that is, an offering of one's whole self to the guru, symbolized by the eight limbs of the body touching the ground in the act of *namaskār* (knees, feet, palms, chest, intelligence [*dhī*], forehead, word, sight).

Ātmanivedana is "located" between the active and passive moments of this *itinerarium ad Deum.* While in an initial phase it may be viewed as active, implying an intense effort of the will, in its mature stage, that is, when the ego has been thoroughly silenced, it gives place to a quiescient, passive attitude: *prapatti* then shines forth of itself.

Maturing through these gradual and successive stages, the *bhakta* naturally becomes a *prapanna.* This being the rule, note however that the deity's special grace may grant the *bhakta* sudden enlightenment.

The feminine noun *prapatti* derives from the verbal root *pad* + *pra* (to fall or drop down). The word thus means pious resignation, seeking refuge at the guru's feet. Among the synonyms of *prapatti* is *śaraṇāgati* (to approach one in search of shelter and protection).

Prapatti has been inherited as a technical term from the Rāmānujīya schools, that is, from the immediate successors of Ramanuja, the theoretician of *Viśiṣṭādvaita* Vedānta (the Vedānta School of 'qualified nondualism'). The latter seldom uses the term in his works, and, when he does, he uses *prapatti* almost in the same sense of *bhakti*, or indicating a "refuge" leading to the perfection of *bhakti*.[64]

The concept of *prapatti* was especially developed within the *Teṅgalai* school, headed by Lokacharya Pillai (c. 1300–27). This school taught that the individual soul (*jīva*), realizing its own nothingness, should surrender completely to God, passively waiting for the descent of His grace. Thus, it was also called the "cat school" or *mārjārakiśoranyāya*, in an analogy to the kitten (the devotee) who is impotent and passive and of whom the mother (God) takes complete care.

The *Vaḍagalai* school, headed by the famous master Vedantadeshika (c. 1360), taught that divine grace cannot release a person from his karmic responsibilities, and that the *bhakti* attitude presupposes activity. For this reason, the school became known as the "monkey school" or *mārkaṭakiśoranyāya*, in an analogy to the new born monkey who actively clutches his mother and does not let go.

Prapatti is not subject to any kind of limitation, be it spatial, temporal, or social. Lokacharya Pillai declared that the guru's love for a *bhakta* who has totally surrendered to him may bring divine grace upon the pupil, nothing else being required.

The way leading to *prapatti* may be delineated thus: first, the determination to be faithful (*ānakūlya-saṃkalpa*). The will must be definitely oriented towards Ishvara, that is, all actions, thoughts, and feelings must be dedicated to God. At the same time, there must be a renunciation of all resistance and opposition (*prātikūlyavarjana*), the relinquishing of all ideas of "I" and "mine." At this stage, the devotee, convinced that the Beloved will protect him/her in all situations (*rakṣiṣyatiti viśvāsa*), shows a complete trust in Providence and in the promises of Ishvara.

The next step is *ātmanikṣepa*. This term may be understood as "entrusting oneself to God," that is, an act of submission: the abandonment of one's self in oblation to the deity (*ātmatyāga, ātmahavis*).

There are three *samarpāṇas*, "deliverings," that the *prapanna* must perform. First, the devotee must renounce gains (*lābha*), in the form of merits or consolations, that he/she might derive from virtuous conduct. Secondly, the devotee must give up all feelings of protagonism: this attitude is technically known as "relinquishing the burden" (*bhara*) and signifies the radical silencing of the will. In a way, one could say that the *bhakta* abandons all claims relative to a "heroic" act of surrender. Thirdly, he/she must "deliver" the entire being to Ishvara, that is, abandon all pretenses at being an individual *jīva* bearing specific traits (*svarūpa*). Human initiative can only extend so far.

The last stage is called "poorness of spirit" (*kārpaṇya*) or "nullity" (*akiñcanya*) and constitutes the perfection of *prapatti*. It is characterized by a condition of total vulnerability: the awareness of being wholly impotent, thus accepting all that happens as Ishvara's grace. One then "belongs" to the deity, having renounced all individual rights.

One must be fixed (*ekānta*) on one's Lord or guru, cultivating an attitude of vigilant receptivity, so as to be able to intuit his or her will.[65]

Love and service to the guru banish all other concerns and make one utterly dependent upon him. Baba explained it aptly: "The Guru, mightily pleased with me, drew me near him, passed his palm over my head and body and spoke to me tender words dripping with love, and he put me into his school, where I entirely forgot my father and mother and all attachments and desires."[66]

Moreover: "God is the Actor. We must recognize His independence and our dependence on Him, and see all acts as His. If we do so, we shall be unattached and free from Karmic bondage."[67]

Sai Baba's mostly nonverbal and nontheoretical approach, shows that surrender has little or nothing to do with intellectual discourse. I believe that it is precisely for this reason, and not because of a lack of intellectual articulation, that most of the elderly villagers I interviewed had difficulty in explaining Sai's teachings: as G. G. Narke pointed out, Sai Baba did not teach in a formal sense but rather "radiated an influence."

Śaraṇāgati and *prapatti* have nothing to do with conceptualization, since they are grounded in *experience*: love and devotion cannot be explained theoretically; they must be communicated from heart to heart. Thus, the crucial significance of the guru's vision (*darśan*) and the import of his charismatic influence. A simple gesture, smile, or gaze of Baba's, in the silent atmosphere of *darśan* filled with poignant expectation, would be interpreted by devotees as a divine experience. The guru is here perceived as divine hierophany, that is, the very icon of the deity.

In the Indian context, seeing and touching is truly a kind of knowing. The art historian Stella Kramrisch, observes: "Seeing, according to Indian notions, is a going forth of the sight towards the object. Sight touches it and acquires its form. Touch is the ultimate connection by which the visible yields to being grasped. While the eye touches the object, the vitality that pulsates in it is communicated."[68]

A silent exchange takes place: the saint or the deity "gives *darśan*" (*darśan denā*) and the people "take *darśan*" (*darśan lenā*). The initiative is always that of the divine offering his grace (*kṛpā*), if only the expectant devotee is able to "tune in" with it.

Agehananda Bharati aptly notes, "There is absolutely no parallel to the conception of darśan in any religious act in the West."[69]

The path of *prapatti* appears to be perfectly compatible with a nondualistic approach. Ramana Maharshi poignantly elucidates the correct attitude of surrender:

> Surrender to Him and abide by His will, whether He appears or vanishes; await His pleasure. If you ask Him to do as you please, it is not surrender but command. You cannot have Him obey you and yet think you have surrendered. He knows what is best and when and how. Leave everything entirely to Him. The burden is His.
>
> You have no longer any cares. All your cares are His. That is surrender. That is bhakti.[70]

The theme of surrender is also related to the renunciation of material things, to the choice of poverty (*daridratā*). This is a classical theme within Hinduism: the Lord is the poor man's brother (*dīnabandhu*). I shall, however, reflect on this issue from within the Sufi tradition, since Baba always characterized himself (but also God!) as *faqīr*.

Surrender is particularly evidenced in the story of how Das Ganu succeeded in writing a commentary on the first verse of the *Īsha Upanishad* (see the episode in chapter 6 of the poor girl renouncing her beautiful sari). Raimundo Panikkar offers this insightful comment on that famous verse:

> The path, realization, salvation are all rooted in despoilment, in renunciation, in the abandonment of all obstacles, in letting go of the old skin, in the relinquishing of mere appearances. Detachment is not only the necessary condition for leading a spiritual life, it is also the sufficient condition, since

> in renouncing what we are not, what we truly are will surely appear.... Thus, detachment is not a negative virtue or merely a necessary condition; it is rather the highest achievement, that is, the surrendering of oneself *in* that Being which penetrates and permeates us. Through this detachment (*tena*),... we must resolve to harmonize ourselves with this world filled by God. The attitude must be that of discovering happiness in renunciation, of being joyful in radical spoliation, sustaining ourselves in this way.[71]

Finally, here are Sai's own words on how, by virtue of his *prapatti*, he was able to attain *mokṣa*: "Realization flashed upon me of itself, without effort or study, purely by the Guru's grace. The Guru's grace is our only sadhana. Jnana comes as experience (that is, follows in its wake)."[72]

It is now necessary to evaluate Sai Baba's teachings in the light of Sufi *taṣawwuf* (mysticism).

The classic spiritual path of Sufism (*ṭarīq*), is represented by seven *maqām* or stations. These stations are reached through personal effort, while the effects experienced (*aḥwāl*, literally "state") are said to be the consequence of divine mercy.

Three are the fundamental stages along the *ṭarīq*: that of beginner or novice (*murīd, mubtadi'*), that of the advanced (*sālik*), and that of the perfectly realized soul (*kāmil, wāṣil*, or *muḥaqqiq*).

The seven stations are the following: repentance (*tawba*), fear of God (*wara'*), renunciation or detachment from all worldly possessions, even if legitimate (*zuhd*), poverty (*faqr*), endurance of all adversities, that is, patience (*ṣabr*), confident surrender to God (*tawakkul*), and joyful acceptance of all that happens as God's will (*riḍā*).

This ascending pathway of progressive destruction of the ego is veritably a struggle (*mujāhada*), a spiritual fight (the great *jihād*) that the disciple must valiantly combat under the direction of a competent guide (*murshid*).

From the ninth century, three main theories concerning the crucial issue of divine union were debated by orthodox Islam and Sufism: (1) union as "junction" (*ittiṣāl* or *wiṣāl*), excluding the idea of the identity of the soul with God; (2) union as identification (*ittiḥād*), that is, usually implying a union of natures; (3) union as indwelling (*ḥulūl*), God's spirit dwelling in the purified soul of the mystic.

The doctors of Islam viewed only the *ittiṣāl* kind of *unio mystica* as acceptable: one of the major accusations lodged against the great Sufi mystic al-Hallaj (858–922), was, in fact, his advocacy of *ḥulūl*.

Within Indian Sufism, disputes concerning the distinction of natures, the danger of pantheism, and so forth, were prevalent among the elite only. In popular religion, the exchange and borrowing of customs and ideas between *faqīrs* and Hindu holy men was often pronounced: Sai Baba, in the crosscultural milieu of the Deccan, represents indeed a "heterodox" blending of Sufism *cum* Vedāntic doctrines.

I shall first concern myself with three fundamental stations of the *ṭarīq*, which are eloquently attested to in Sai Baba's life: poverty (*faqr*), patience (*ṣabr*), and surrender (*tawakkul*). Next, I shall discuss two other important features of Baba's religious life: the practice of music and dance (*samā*), and the recollection or repetition of Allah's name (*dhikr*).

The fourth station of the Sufi path is poverty (*faqr*). As we know, Baba always identified himself as a *faqīr*. He did so in a spirit of humility, emphasizing his nullity before Allah: "What am I? A petty fakir! I am not God. How great is God! No one can compare with Him."[73]

Moreover: "What is the scoundrel coming to see me for? What have I got? I'm just a naked fakir with human organs, like any one else."[74]

Sai Baba lived the life of an indigent beggar, with no material comforts whatsoever, until he breathed his last. He was fond of praising the value of poverty: "Poverty is the highest riches and is a thousand times superior to a lord's position. God is the brother of the poor. The fakir is the real emperor. Fakirship does not perish, but an empire is soon lost."[75]

Baba would address God Himself as "*Faqīr*." A. Osborne notes: "It was a peculiar custom of his to refer to God as 'the Fakir', and when refusing a request he would often say: 'The Fakir will not let me do that' or 'I can only do what the Fakir orders me to.'"[76]

Moreover, the human *faqīr* related himself to the Supreme *Faqīr*, declaring: "*Maiṅ Allāh hūṁ*" ("I am Allah").[77]

Faqr is indeed the distinctive mark of the life of a Sufi. It is viewed not solely as a station along the path but rather, in most cases, as a permanent condition.

The *faqīr* is one who finds himself/herself in constant need, both in a material as well as in a spiritual sense. Significantly, the saying "Poverty is my pride" (*al-fakr fakhrī*), ascribed to the Prophet, has always been cited by Sufis as proof that *faqr* was advocated by Muhammad himself.

The torn mat on which so many Sufis are described to sleep, often constituting their only material possession, is indicative in this regard. Baba's own belongings were limited to the bare necessities: his dress, a sack, an alms bowl, and a staff. For many years he slept on the floor of the dilapidated mosque.

A true *faqīr* does not desire anything for himself, neither in this world nor in the next: it is believed that only through nonpossession may he avoid being "possessed" by somebody or something. Here also the highest degree of perfection is surrender, achieved by forgetting one's own condition of indigence. Such a state of pure equanimity is technically called *tark at-tark,* meaning "to leave what has already been left," "to abandon what has already been abandoned."

The general position of Sufism regarding *faqr,* defined in late medieval times, is identical with that of Sai Baba: poverty is superior and preferable to riches, on the condition that it be accompanied by a feeling of fulfillment or contentment (*ṣabr*).

As Khidr, the immortal guide of all Sufis, said to two dervishes, concerning the attainments of the Sufi master Ibrahim ben Adam:

> You two dervishes wonder about Ibrahim. But what have you renounced in order to follow the dervish Path? You gave up the expectations of security and an ordinary life. Ibrahim ben Adam was a mighty king, and threw away the sovereignty of the Sultanate of Balkh to become a Sufi. This is why he is far ahead of you. During your thirty years, you have gained satisfaction through renunciation itself. This has been your payment. He has always abstained from claiming any payment for his sacrifice.[78]

Poverty has often been exalted as the essential virtue of a mystic. Sometimes, *faqr* has even been assimilated with supreme enlightenment, that is, *fanā,* "one's annihilation in God." A popular saying of later Sufism declares: *al-faqr idhā tamma huwa Allāh,* "When poverty becomes perfect, it is God."

Sai Baba, though praising the superiority of *faqīri* life, never encouraged it among his devotees. He applied it in a radical fashion only to himself. On the contrary, he always showed interest in the material side of his followers' lives, often advising them on business and economic matters: Sai constantly endeavoured to alleviate the indigence of his people through gifts, often of a monetary kind, and through his miracles and *antarajñāna.*

In his teachings, Baba insisted on the need for equanimity, inviting his devotees to lead a simple, sober life. He avoided extreme formulations, that is, strict asceticism on one side and worldly indulgence on the other, advocating moderation in all things.

In some few cases, however, we know that he initiated devotees into the renunciant's life: Baba would then symbolically offer them the ochre robe (*kāṣāya*) or the *kafnī*, without any formal ceremony.

Sai Baba viewed *faqr* not so much as an act of material spoliation but rather as the concrete sign of the surrender of one's will to the guru or *pīr*. Everything then belongs to the teacher, that is, to God. This, however, does not automatically imply that all religiously oriented persons should divest themselves of their material well-being: renunciation is first and foremost a mental, internal submission to Allah's will.

The devotee, as the servant, must view himself as the temporary administrator of a "treasure" that has been given to him by his master, that is, God. The *dāsa* (servant) must humbly recognize that all that he has, his very life, is a loan stemming from the grace of the Beloved. Only by cultivating this attitude will he be able to cut off the roots of attachment and offer himself entirely to the teacher, so that the latter may do with him what he thinks best. The disciple lives only for his teacher, seeing him in everything, so that his own will may die out completely: only then shall *tawakkul* and *riḍā*, the Sufi equivalents of *ātmanivedana* and *prapatti*, dawn.

Patience (*ṣabr*) is the fifth station of the *ṭarīq*. Among the characteristics of a *faqīr*, *saburī* is perhaps the most important one: Kabir himself says that it is only by *saburī* that one can attain God.[79]

I have stressed how *saburī* (equivalent to the Arabic term *ṣabr*), coupled with *niṣṭhā*, represents one of the most constant themes in Baba's teachings.

According to the Arabic lexicographers, the root *ṣbr* from which the noun *ṣabr* is derived, means "to restrain or bind." In the Koran, derivations from the root *ṣbr* frequently occur, and indicate the general meaning of patience: Muhammad is warned to be patient like the Apostles of God before him (38.17). A double reward is promised to the patient man (28.54). In 39.17 it is said that the *ṣābirūn* shall receive their reward without measure or limitation. Patience or endurance is also described by the Koran as the virtue that was common to both Job and Jacob: in the Joseph *ṣūra* (12.18) Jacob, on hearing of the death of his son, says: "Now goodly resignation is befitting (*faṣabr^{un} djamīl^{un}*)."

Ṣabūr is included among the traditional ninety-nine names of Allah. It figures as the last one, designating Allah as *al-Ṣabūr, the* Patient One.

Sheikh Tosun Bayrak al-Jerrahi al-Halveti thus comments:

> Allah does not hasten the punishment of the sinful. He sends them their sustenance, protects them from harm, and lets them live in health and prosperity, for He has set a determined time for everything. Everything has to run its course. His patience with sinners is to give them time to be heedful, to realize their wrongs and come to repent. Allah is Merciful; His Mercy is in giving time for repentance and accepting repentance.
>
> Patience is in Allah's divine disposition; therefore, patient men reflect this honored disposition. A patient man is he who refuses things that his flesh and ego desire but that are unacceptable to reason and to religion....
>
> The meaning of Islam is submission: to forego one's appetites, desires and will in favor of the will of Allah. To be able to submit, one has to be patient. In Islam, patience is a sign of faith; abasement and humiliation are sins. Do not confuse humiliation caused by fear and laziness with patience and endurance.[80]

Sufis have traditionally distinguished patient people among three categories: the *mutaṣabbir,* who strives to be patient; the *ṣābir,* who is patient in sorrow and pain; and the *ṣabūr,* who is perfectly patient under all circumstances. As the great Sufi master Muhasibi (781–857) declared, "Ṣabr is to remain unmoved before the arrows of the divine decrees."[81]

Sai Baba intended *saburī* as a virile and heroic attitude: endurance rather than resignation. He told Mrs. Radhabai Deshmukin:

> What the Guru wanted from me were not metallic coins, he did not care even for gold, but only Nistha and Saburi i.e. faith and courageous patience. I gave these to him at once and he was pleased.
>
> Mother, Saburi is *courage,* do not discard it. It ferries you across to the distant goal. It gives manliness to men, eradicates sin and dejection and overcomes all fear.[82]

Sai viewed impatience or restlessness in general as an illness of the spirit, even if motivated by noble ideals:

> Uddhavesa Bua (at his first interview with Baba): "Where is my Moksha Guru? How is he to be got?"
>
> Baba: "Wait for five years and you will know. How can you

gulp down in one gulp an entire loaf of bread? Wait for five years and see."[83]

Niṣṭha and *saburī* are coupled in Baba's teachings because the endurance of adversity is helped by a firm faith in God: the two virtues support and sustain one another. Sai would often admonish his devotees, saying: "Why are you anxious? I take all care of you."[84]

Moreover, paraphrasing Matthew 6.25f., he observed: "People must put full faith in the Lord's providence. They should not worry about food and clothing. Do not waste your life on these. In the abode of my devotees there will be no dearth of food and clothing."[85]

The theme of pain and suffering, putting the disciple's resistance to a hard test, is a very popular one within Sufism: in some cases one's extraordinary endurance is given the status of an ascetic feat.

The concept of *tawakkul* (trust in God) describes the state of mystical abandonment into God's hands. Indeed, to be a Muslim means to surrender to Allah's will and to obey his laws.

Tawakkul is the sixth station along the *ṭarīq* and is perhaps the most important, since the last one (*riḍā*) may be viewed as the crowning of *tawakkul*. The great Islamic theologian Abū Hamīd al-Ghazālī (1058–1111), in the fourth part of his *Ihyā' 'ulūm al-dīn* (The Restoration of the Sciences of Religion), highlights, by a series of ascending comparisons, the psychological state of one who surrenders himself/herself. He distinguishes between three levels of abandonment.

At the first level, the adept relies on God in the same way as a person rightly accused depends on an attorney, in whose qualities he/she has full faith. At this stage the devotee has control over his/her initiative.

The second level presupposes a higher degree of surrender. Ghazālī compares it to the spontaneous but conscious trust a child has in its mother: he/she clutches on to her, calls to her even if she leaves for a moment, cries if he/she needs her. Similarly, the devotee knows that God is everything, thus he/she calls on him and supplicates him unceasingly. Surrender to the divine will extends to all acts of life.

The third level designates the peak of *tawakkul*. Surrender has become so radical that it is compared to the condition of a corpse in the hands of the washerman; indeed a popular image in Sufism.

At this stage, there is no more request or petition on the devotee's part: God does all and his servant enters into a condition of quiet passivity, perfectly emptied, not expecting anything whatsoever, not even that the Beloved take care of him/her.

Ghazālī's text leaves the doors open to the final annihilation of the subject, that is, to the attainment of supreme *fanā*, later elaborated in Sufi works.[86]

There are similarities between the path that, through *bhakti*, leads to *prapatti* in Hinduism and the one that leads to the peak of *tawakkul* in Sufism. Each of them may be viewed as a kind of *preparatio*: divine grace, in its absolute freedom, may then choose to "enter" the mystic and "transmute" him.

Once a person has entered the highest *tawakkul* he or she is naturally brought to the condition of *riḍā*, in which one opens himself/herself to the effects or states (*aḥwāl*) of divine grace. There are different opinions regarding these states: some Sufi masters believe them to be permanent, others to be only temporary.

Abu Nasr as-Sarrāj of Ṭūs (d. 988), one among the principal systematizers of Sufi mystical doctrine, in his work *Kitāb al-Luma' fit-taṣawwuf*, gives a list of ten *aḥwāls*: constant awareness (*murāqaba*), proximity (*qurb*), reciprocal love (*maḥabba*), fear (*khawf*), hope (*rajā*), desire (*shawq*), intimacy (*uns*), tranquillity in peace (*tuma'nīna*), contemplation (*mushāhada*), certainty (*yaqīn*).

Along the *ṭarīq*, the fourth, fifth, and sixth stations, that is, *faqr*, *ṣabr*, and *tawakkul* (which may be viewed together with *zuhd*, "renunciation" and *riḍā*), are the three pillars around which Sai's life and teachings revolved, although he never explicitly mentioned the *aḥwāls*.[87]

Above all, love and compassion stand as the premise, the means and the end of Baba's message. As al-Ḥallāj sings:

> Your place in my heart is all my heart, and in Your place
> there is no space for any created thing.
> My spirit has placed You between my skin and my bones.
> What would I do, then, if I lost You?[88]

Samā (literally, "audition") was a religious practice much enjoyed by Sai Baba. Musical sessions, often accompanied by chants from the Koran and the singing of mystical poetry, were held by the Sufis to induce a mystical experience.

Though a characteristic of early Sufism, the legitimacy of music as an aid to spiritual experience was viewed as problematic in legal and Sufi circles, long before the formation of the orders.

In India, the practice of *samā*, together with the performance of *qavvālīs*, has always been a major feature of the Chishti order:

members of this brotherhood defined their advocacy of *samā* as the pride and adornment of their devotion to inner, and often also to outer, poverty.

The techniques of *samā* are based on the performance of three main movements: dancing, whirling, and jumping, all of which bear precise symbolic meanings. Dance actualizes the cosmic creative energy, the very rhythm of the universe, and is compared to the divine act of creation.

Within Hinduism, the eternal movement of the cosmos is symbolized *par excellence* by Shiva Nataraja's *Tāṇḍava* dance.

As Lilian Silburn observes:

> With one of his many hands, he holds the drum, the sound vibrations of which give rise to the universe as they generate time and space; with another hand, he brandishes the fire of resorption. The movement of the dance conceals his essence, as it whirls about him the flames of the manifestation, while the fire of resorption, sweeping away everything, reveals it. Standing still at the center of this twofold activity, as the seat of all power, he unfolds, with impassibility, the fiercest energies, the most antagonistic movements: emanation and resorption, concealment and grace, retraction and expansion.[89]

The demon-dwarf of chaos and forgetfulness (Apasmarapurusha) lies defeated under Shiva's foot: the dance symbolizes the supreme joy and freedom brought about by enlightenment, arising once the veils of illusion have been pierced.

When Shiva dances above the figure of a child, his movements are light and soft; when he dances with a woman his movements are graceful and lovely. When he dances alone, however, his ascetic mood potently emerges and the deity appears in his violent and destructive aspect.

Nataraja's dance truly illustrates the fundamental conceptions of nondualistic Kashmir Śaivism, Shiva being conscious light (*prakāśa*) and, at the same time, self-awareness (*vimarśa*), the vibration (*spanda*) of divine energy. As the great Abhinavagupta (c. 1100) stated: "Siva, conscious, free, and of transparent essence, is always vibrating, and this supreme energy reaches to the tip of the sense organs; then he is nothing but bliss and like him the entire universe vibrates. In truth, I do not see where transmigration, a mere echo, could find a place."[90]

Within Sufism, the whirling dances of the dervishes are said to symbolize the rotation of a planet on its axis around the sun or the cycles of existence that are included in the divine all-encompassing *Pnevma* (Spirit).

One of the chief effects desired by *samā* practitioners is *tawājud* (a state of mind bordering on ecstasy), which precedes the attainment of *wajd* (ecstasy) and *wujūd* (unity of being).[91]

Sai Baba loved to sing and dance in his early years, at least up until 1890: Persian and Urdu motives, some of them concerning Kabir, could be heard emanating at night from the *takiyā*, where Sai exhibited in the company of Muslim dancers and musicians.

Even in 1913, Baba was strongly affected by music as this dialogue with a follower of a Chishtiyya master proves:

> Baba said to Abdul Rahim Rangari:
>
> "If you had come yesterday, it would have been better."
>
> Abdul: "Why?"
>
> Baba: "There was music. I wept all night. They abused me."
>
> Abdul: "Why did they abuse you?"
>
> Baba: "When I say abused, people do not understand; but you will understand."
>
> Abdul: "One who loves God would weep, laugh, or dance as the songs in praise of God go on."
>
> Baba: "Just so. You are right. Have you your own Guru?"
>
> Abdul: "Yes. Babi Balishah Chishti Nizami."
>
> Baba: "That is why you understand."
>
> (This Chishti Guru was accompanied by music whenever he travelled...)[92]

Sai Baba's love for music and dance is an indication of his possible connection with Chishtiyya circles. Though the practice of *samā* was never recommended by him explicitly, the singing of *bhajans* and *qavvālīs* were common practice at the *masjid*. Evidently, Sai encouraged songs and music as devotional exercises capable of inducing ecstatic states of particular intensity.

As the great poet and mystic Jalāluddīn Rūmī (b. 1207) declared, "The House of Love is made completely of music, of verses and songs."[93]

The practice of *dhikr* was perhaps the most important aspect in Sai Baba's spiritual life. The term *dhikr*, derived from a root meaning "to remember or recollect," is a religious exercise designed to invoke God's presence throughout one's being. It can be performed silently, in a low tone, or aloud.

The Sufis justified the orthodoxy of *dhikr* on the basis of Koranic passages stressing the importance of God's remembrance (see 18.24; 39.22; 43.36; 63.9). What strikes an observer, is the universality of *dhikr* practice within Sufism: most teachers advocate it as the royal path towards the unitive experience of *waḥdat al-wujūd*.

Ghazālī, whose works contributed substantially to the acceptance of Sufism within Islamic orthodoxy, explains the exercise of *dhikr* in his *Ihyā' 'ulūm al-dīn*:

> Having seated himself in solitude, he (the Sufi) does not cease to repeat "God" (Allah) with his mouth; he does this without intermission, keeping the presence of the name in his heart. This he does until he comes to the point of wiping out the image of the word, its letters and their shape from his heart: then the meaning of the word alone remains in the heart, present in him as if in unison, without ever leaving him. It is in the Sufi's power to reach this limit and to make this state endure driving out temptations; it is not in his power, however, to attract the mercy of the Almighty God on himself.[94]

There are two major traditions: that of solitary *dhikr* and that of collective *dhikr*. The first one dates back to the eleventh or twelfth century, as al-Ghazālī's text demonstrates.

Sai Baba, from the days of his arrival at Shirdi, was heard repeating the phrase *Allāh Mālik*, and he practiced a solitary form of *dhikr* all his life.

In principle, the Sufi mystic is given ample freedom in the choice of the formula: the name of Allah or that of the Prophet, a divine attribute or one of the traditional ninety-nine names of Allah of Koranic origin.

Brotherhoods, however, usually impose the choice of one or more fixed formulas on their adepts. The one usually given to novices is the first "member" of the "testimony of faith" (*shahāda*): *lā ilāh illā Allāh*, "There is no other god eccept Allah." Advanced disciples often concentrate solely on the name of Allah. To ones who are even more advanced along the mystical path, formulas praising Allah's ineffability are recommended: *Huwa* (He; the great pronoun of the divine Ipseity), *al-Ḥaqq* (The Real), *al-Ḥayy* (The Living).

Sai Baba took his beloved formula *Allāh Mālik* from the collection of ninety-nine names, though it is not known if he himself chose it. One might suppose he got it from his first tutor, that is, the mysterious *faqīr*.

In the traditional list of the ninety-nine names *al-Malik* figures as the fourth, and *Mālik al-Mulk* as the eighty-fourth.

The term *malik* (pl. *mulūk*), "king," derives from the old semitic root *mlk*, conveying the idea of possession and, by extension, that of rule or government. In the Koran, besides being used for kings of this world, the word *malik* is also applied to Allah: "So is Allah exalted, the King, the Truth" (20.113).

In 3.25, Allah is also the *Mālik al-Mulk*, that is, possessor of royal power or of the kingdom (*mulk*), which He gives to and takes from whom He wills.

With the spread of Islam and the Arabic language into Asia, *malik* became used as the equivalent of the Persian *shāh*, and as a royal title it was particularly favored by medieval dynasties of Turkish origin.

In the course of time, the term *mālik* was integrated into the Marathi language with the meaning of owner, lord, master. Other Marathi terms such as *māl* (goods, material) and *mālkī* (ownership) are also derived from the old semitic root *mlk*.

In his work *al-Maqṣad al-Asnā*, al-Ghazālī thus commented on the name *al-Malik*:

> Al-Malik is the one whose essence and attributes are independent of all existing things, but everything in existence is dependent upon (in need of) Him. To be sure, nothing can exist without Him, whether it be in respect to its essence, its attributes, its existence or its continued existence (baqa). Each and every thing derives its existence from Him or from that which is derived from Him. Everything other than He Himself is subject to Him in respect to both its attributes and essence. But He has no need for anything. This, indeed, is the absolute al-Malik.[95]

Most probably, however, Sai Baba had in mind the name *Mālik al-Mulk*, a name of perfection as well as of essence. As the possessor of the kingdom, this name reveals Allah's function as the universal king, whose will reigns everywhere sovereign. As Ghazālī commented:

> Mālik al-Mulk is the One who carries out His will in His kingdom in the manner He wishes..., bringing into being, destroying, perpetuating and annihilating (as He pleases). (The

> word) al-Mulk here has the meaning of "kingdom," and (the word) al-Malik has the meaning of "the potent one, the one who possesses perfect power." The totality of everything in existence forms a single kingdom, and He is the one who rules and has power over it. The totality of existing things are a single kingdom because they are dependent upon each other; for even if they are numerous in one respect, they still remain a unit in another. An example of this is the body of man. Certainly it is a kingdom for the real nature of man. It consists of different members, but they (all) give the appearance of cooperating in attaining the goal of a single manager, (and thus) the kingdom is one.[96]

Baba often emphasized the infinite greatness and sovereignty of Allah over His whole creation. In fact, Allah is not only king of the visible world, which is subject to corruption (*al-Mulk*), but also of the invisible one, eternal and permanent, in which his absolute regality (*al-Malakūt*) shines forth. Pondering over Allah's unfathomable splendor and power should thus induce humility in man. Sai Baba remarked:

> God is great. He is the Supreme Master. Allah Malik. How great is God! No one can compare with him.
>
> He creates, supports, and destroys. His sport (Lila) is inscrutable.
>
> Let us be content to remain as He makes us, to submit our wills to His. Allah Rakega Vahisa Rahena. Take what comes. Be contented and cheerful. Never worry. Not a leaf moves, but by His consent and will.[97]

When practicing *dhikr*, Sufis are recommended to sit cross-legged, that is, in *tarabbu'u* posture, placing their palms on the knees, with eyes closed or partly closed, sitting in a circle, if engaged in a collective session (*ḥaḍra*), or with one's body oriented towards the *qibla* in the direction of Mecca, if practicing a solitary remembrance. Often, it is also recommended to choose a place with no light, to perfume oneself with benzoin and to wear ritually pure clothing.

Sai Baba practiced *dhikr* in different postures: most often seated in front of his *dhunī* and at the *masjid* or *cāvaḍī* during the night.

Duration of *dhikr*, of course, varies. Time can be measured, for instance, by counting the repetitions of the formula, or not measured at all. Practice is linked to one's breathing rhythms: *dhikr* is harmonized with the acts of inspiration and expiration, which constitute an invaluable aid for concentration. Once the continuity of *dhikr* has been attained, it can be carried on without intermission.

Sai Baba practiced a silent, interiorized form of *dhikr* every day for long periods. He also possibly achieved an uninterrupted rammemoration, as the frequent night watches he undertook suggest.

Sufis distinguish between three types of *dhikr*: that of the tongue, that of the heart, and that of the "ground of the soul" (*sirr*).

The first type, in which the formula is repeated aloud, is especially advised for beginners. The adept must strive to focus attention "onepointedly" on the formula. Two levels are usually distinguished here: that of voluntary recitation, and that of the formula "dripping on the tongue," which signals the highest depth of attainment.

Some scholars have compared the first type of practice to that of *dhāraṇā*, concentration in classical yoga.

In the second type, the Sufi "cancels" every trace of the formula from the tongue, and thus begins to "hear" the repetition internally, localizing it in the heart. At a more advanced stage of practice, this kind of *dhikr* takes place spontaneously, that is, with no special effort of the will. The presence of the formula is identified or related to the pulsations of one's heart. At this point, even mental repetition is said to cease, the words acquiring a sort of independent life in the seat of the heart.

This phase has been classified as absorption, viewed by some as a parallel to *dhyāna*, or meditative state of yoga.

From an examination of the sources, it seems likely that Sai Baba practiced a kind of heart *dhikr*:

> When I go to sleep I often ask Mhalsapati to sit by My side, place his hand on My heart and watch the "chanting of the Lord's name" there, and if he finds Me sleepy, wake Me up. He can't do even this. He himself gets drowsy and begins to nod his head. When I feel his hand heavy as a stone on My heart and cry out "Oh, Bhagat," he moves and opens his eyes. How can he, who can't sit and sleep well on the ground and whose asan (posture) is not steady and who is a slave of sleep, sleep high up on a plank?[98]

The third and highest type of *dhikr*, that of *sirr* (mystery), is defined as a subtle condition, subtler even than spirit. Ghazālī, who viewed the highest attainment as solely due to Allah's mercy, does not mention *sirr*. However, the Sufis of following centuries speak of it. Its distinctive sign is that the subject has abandoned the formula but the formula does not abandon him/her: by this time, *dhikr* has "penetrated" the mystic's being. The Sufi's whole body becomes, to use a poignant image, "a tongue which *dhikrs*" with no words being pronounced, in an effusion of light. The mystic's passivity or abandonment is now total: in such perfect annihilation of the ego, the sudden irruption of divine grace is made possible.

The descriptions of *sirr dhikr* seem interpretable as experiences of perfect oneness or 'isolation'. For this reason, a correlation between this highest form of *dhikr* and the state of "enstasis" or *samādhi* of yoga, is sometimes advanced.

According to Sufi authors, this highest *aḥwāl* is identical with *fanā* (literally, "passing away"), that is, perfect annihilation.

The systematic exposition *Kashf al-Maḥjūb* (Revelation of Concealed Matters) of al-Hujwiri (C.E. 1074), gives a detailed exposition of the concept of *fanā*. Two levels of *fanā* are traditionally distinguished: in the first, the adept "disappears," so to speak, from himself, that is, flees towards his Beloved. Finally, when he is totally annihilated in God, this is the highest attainment, that is, the "*fanā of fanā*." This "*fanā* of *fanā*" would be assimilable, if indeed such comparison is legitimate, to the yogic attainment of undifferentiated *samādhi* or *nirvikalpa samādhi*.

Established in *sirr*, the mystic experiences flashes of light, interpreted as divine light. It is believed that the radiance of such light envelops the *Malakūt* (God's incorruptible Kingdom), from which the sanctity of the *Ālam al-Lāhūt*, the world of the Godhead, shines forth. It is thought that the Sufi who has achieved the state of *sirr* may envision the divine throne as well as all the worlds, to the point of "fusing" himself with the divine essence.

It does not seem unreasonable to relate Sai Baba's repetition of *Allāh Mālik* with the mysticism of light, since in Islam light is viewed as the distinctive sign of Allah's sovereignty. In this regard, Baba's passion for lights should be recalled: not only did he constantly feed his sacred fire (*dhunī*), often gazing at it while practicing the recollection of a divine name, but he also kept earthen lamps burning all night long inside the *masjid*.

Of course, within a Hindu majority context, Sai Baba emphasized the importance not of *dhikr* but of its Hindu counterpart, that is, *nāmasmaraṇa* coupled with *japa*. However, with Muslim followers such as Abdul Baba or Abdul Rahim Rangari, Sai encouraged the repetition of one of Allah's "most beautiful" names.[99]

A brief comparison between Sai Baba's and Kabir's teachings regarding the theme of *bhakti* is illuminating.

Kabir's background as a low-caste weaver makes it presumable that he was more or less illiterate. Indeed, there is no evidence that he ever composed a single work or wrote a single verse. As he himself is supposed to have stated in the *Bījak, sākhī* 187: "Ink or paper, I never touched, nor did I take a pen in my hand. The greatness of the four ages I have described by word of mouth."

Kabir's contempt for the written word and holy scriptures in general is evident: he viewed only the speech communicated from the guru's mouth as reliable and precious. Nevertheless, many volumes of poetry and religious literature have been attributed to Kabir over the course of centuries. As Charlotte Vaudeville remarks, "There is hardly an ethical or spiritual truth in Northern India that has not taken the form of a sākhī ascribed to Kabir."[100]

To him are attributed innumerable *bāṇīs,* that is, terse utterances having the metrical form of either distichs (*dohā*) or of short rhymed lyrics (*padas*). In the *Guru-Granth* of the Sikhs, the *dohās* attributed to Kabir are called *sākhīs* (literally "witnesses").

Besides *dohās* and *padas,* poems called *śabds* and *ramainīs* are found in some collections of Kabir's verses: the *śabds* seem to be another name given to *padas,* while the *ramainīs* are a type of satiric or didactic composition.

Charlotte Vaudeville thus summarizes the issue relative to Kabir's literature:

> There are only a few fairly ancient recensions of Kabīr's verses. They are to be found in four compilations: the Bījak (literally "seed" or "chart" of secret treasures), in its various forms, which is the most sacred book of the Kabīr-panthīs and was certainly compiled in the east, either in Benares or in Chattisgarh; the Ādi-Granth or Guru-Granth of the Sīkhs, compiled towards the end of the sixteenth century; the compilation known as Kabīr-Granthāvalī which represents the tradition of Dādū Dayāl (a sixteenth-century disciple of Kabīr) and of the Dādū-panthīs, and finally the Sarbāngī of the poet Rajjab, who flourished in the middle of the seventeenth century. There are no manuscripts of Kabīr's verses which can be dated earlier than the seventeenth century A.D.[101]

For a parallel with Sai Baba, I shall focus on the following characteristics traditionally attributed to Kabir's persona and teaching: (1) the way he used to define himself, (2) the fundamental importance he gave to the teacher, (3) the path of devotion leading to surrender, (4) the essential role played by the remembrance of the divine name, (5) the use of attributing many different names to God, (6) the prominence of Rama's name, and, finally, (7) the refusal of "tantras" and "mantras" as being deceptions of the power of *māyā*.

Apparently Kabir, like Sai, referred to himself in various ways: God's slave or servant, a devotee of God, *faqīr*, even God himself.

According to the *Granthāvalī*, Kabir said: "I am Hari's humble slave, and I would not let go of His lotus feet for anything the world might offer me."[102]

Moreover: "I am your humble servant, oh Lord, and You are the light which illuminates all of my recesses."[103]

Kabir identifies himself *tout court* as *faqīr*: "I am the faqir who has found his truth: one and the same God created Hindus and Muslims alike, and these, poor fools, fight each other in His name!"[104]

In another place, he says, "I am Your devotee, oh Lord, and I come towards You with the hope in my heart of finding refuge."[105]

In the ecstasy of union with God, Kabir declares:

I am present in all things,
  and all things are present in me:
Apart from me, there has never been anything.
I am the One embracing the three universes,
  and this coming and going is my pastime.
Through births and deaths I take a thousand forms, as
  I please.
I am the attributeless God,
  and I am also the one whom they call Kabir,
  and Kabir is also the One whom I keep in my
  heart![106]

Kabir particularly insisted on the necessity of finding a guru. From the *Ādi Granth, basant* 3, we read:

Can a man without feet ever leap?
Can a man without a mouth burst into laughter?
Without sleep can man repose?
Can one churn milk without a churn?
Can a cow without an udder give milk?
Can one accomplish a long journey without a road?
So the way cannot be found without a true guru,
Kabir saith, and admonisheth all men.[107]

The guru is everything in Kabir's vision, and innumerable are the passages in which he extols his supremacy.

In his *sākhīs* Kabir says: "Infinite is the Guru's kindness, and incalculable the help which he lavishes. Only he knows how to open the disciple's eyes, so that the vision of the Infinite may bless his sight."[108]

From the *Ādi Granth, gauṛī* 20, we read: "Regard your guru as a knife grinder, let him grind your heart; cleansing the heart from all impurity, let him make it bright as a mirror."[109]

Moreover: "Says Kabir: 'Only the knowledge which the Guru grants makes it possible for one to save himself.'"[110]

As Vaudeville notes, the exaltation of the guru as a manifestation of the supreme reality, and the tendency to identify his instruction with the divine word (*śabda*), probably explains the substantial silence Kabir maintained on his human guru.[111] Such a discreet attitude is common among Siddhas and Nātha yogis, and it was also advocated by Sai Baba.

In some allusions to his own guru, Kabir said:

> It was his good fate which helped Kabir to find his Guru, otherwise every hope of salvation would have escaped from his fingers.[112]
>
> The Guru welcomed Kabir in his embrace, and it was as when salt mixes itself with flour. Then there were no more foolish distinctions of caste and creed. What abuse could now upset Kabir?[113]

He then observed:

> When the true Guru granted him his comfort, Kabir finally knew peace and confidence. Now, seated on the river's edge, he looks like an iridescent pearl amidst pebbles.[114]

The *sākhīs* that concern the true teacher end with these words: "When Kabir knew himself, all his doubts vanished. Forever Kabir shall revere the Guru who turned his heart into a pure spring."[115]

In his *padas*, Kabir sang:

> Blessed be that moment, that day, that month in which the
> Guru entered my house.
> Just seeing Him, the veil of māyā fell from my eyes, and
> in hearing His voice even my fear of death vanished.
> At His divine touch, my body emanated dazzling light,
> and all my past actions fell,
> as rotten fruits fall from their branch.

Says Kabir: Meeting with the Sant, I met the Lord
Himself.[116]

Devotion is the foundation on which Kabir based his religious life. He insisted on the notion of surrender, of totally submitting oneself to God (*aslāmā*):

> Thy commands are acceptable to men;
> I consider not their propriety.
> Thou art the river, Thou art the pilot,
> from Thee is salvation.
> O man, embrace the service of God,
> whether He be angry with thee or love thee.
> Thy name, o God, is my support, as a woman
> rejoiceth on beholding her son.
> Saith Kabir, I am the slave of Thy house,
> preserve me or destroy me.[117]

Moreover:

> Without God what succour hath man?
> The love of parents, brethren, sons,
> and wife is all fleeting.
> Construct a raft for the other world;
> what reliance can be placed on wealth?
> What confidence can be reposed in this vessel,
> if it be chinked in the slightest?
> Thou shalt obtain the fruit of all religion and
> good works if you desire to become the dust
> of everybody's feet.[118]

Kabir, like Sai Baba, insisted upon the necessity of practicing God's remembrance, not in a mechanical way but by reminding oneself of God's presence in one's heart, bringing to mind all that the divine name connotes. The divine name constitutes the only safe path leading to realization:

> Devotion to Rāma is the only sure vessel, all others reserve only pains. Says Kabir: "Sing Rāma's glory with your heart, tongue, and actions.[119]

> Kabir has only one fear: that of falling asleep while glorifying Rāma's name. No other harassing thought does Kabir know! Those who linger on things which aren't Rāma, incite the destructive fury of Kāla.[120]

In one of his *padas*, Kabir sang:

> My heart is a wool-winder, and my tongue is a spindle.
>
> The name of Rāma is the fabric of the cloth which I weave on my loom, whose tireless pedal moves the wheel of simple devotion.
>
> My mother-in-law[121] hinders my work, but I know that liberation will be granted to me only at the end of my weaving.
>
> Says Kabir: The loom at which I work is not any ordinary loom: it will procure me a bench at Hari's Feet.[122]

In the *Ādi Granth, rāmkalī* 9, Kabir instructs:

> Remember the Beloved day and night,[123]
> And thou shalt have no regard for men;
> Thou shalt sleep at home in silken bed-clothes,
> And thy heart shall be gladdened by a pleasant couch.
> Ever remember God in thy heart and sing His praises.
> By remembering Him thy troubles shall depart,
> And Māyā affect thee not.
> From the true guru learn how to remember God;
> Remember Him every day and night.
> Standing or sitting, at every expiration and inspiration,
> Waking or sleeping, enjoy the sweets of remembering Him;
> By remembering God thou shalt be united with Him.
> Make the remembrance of God's name thy support;
> By remembering Him no weight of sin shall oppress thee.
> Neither written nor spoken incantations can prevail
> with Him,
> Saith Kabir, who hath no limit.[124]

Kabir, like Sai Baba, used different names, taken from both the Muslim and Hindu traditions, to designate God: the prevalence in both of Vaiṣṇava names, such as those of Rama and Hari, is particularly noteworthy.

Kabir viewed all names as equally valid: "To me Rāma, Rahīm, Karīm, and Keśava are all truth. And the same are Bismil and Viśvambhara."[125]

In one of his *padas*, Kabir sang:

> Oh Lord Niranjana,[126] You are the Invisible and Inaccessible
> One; thus how can I render homage to Thee?
> You have permitted a current of light to run over the earth
> for those whose eyes can perceive it.

You are indeed the True Kṛṣṇa, the Creator of us all,
You are Govinda, and You are Rāma,
You are Allāh, and You are also Khudā,[127]
You are Karīm, Protector of the Cosmos,
You are the One to whom Gorakh is devoted, and You are also the One to whom Śiva renders homage.
Says Kabir, astonished: Undescribable indeed is the Lord![128]

Kabir's predilection for the name of Rama is parallel to Sai Baba's preference for this divine name. The proper name *Rāma* derives from the verbal root *ram* meaning to set at rest, to delight in (most often bearing a sexual connotation), and denotes the charming or pleasing one. In Kabīrian literature, however, *Rāma* does not indicate the hero of the *Rāmāyaṇa* (Ramachandra) or the *avatāra* of Vishnu, nor does it indicate Parashuram or Balaram. It designates that Supreme Being or Reality, wholly transcendent, who, at the same time, dwells in the heart of man (*ātmarāma*). *Rāma* thus designates the *nirguṇa* aspect of the Supreme Being.

In the *Bījak, śabda* 8, Kabir said, "The Creator did not marry Sītā nor did he make a stone bridge across the waters."

Moreover:

> Follow the true Sāhīb (God) who will uphold you in all your trials.
>
> He was not born in Daśaratha's family and did not oppress the king of Laṅkā (Ceylon).
>
> He did not fight with king Bāli nor did he kill Hiraṇyākṣa, throwing him down on the ground.[129]

Thus Kabir sang the supreme majesty of the *nirguṇa* Rama:

To Lord Rāma, to whom millions of luminous stars make a crown,
at whose feet millions of Śivas sit in contemplation from their Kailāsa,
at whose presence myriads of Brahmās recite sacred verses of the Vedas,
to that Sublime King of the three worlds I shall set forth my petition,
since there is no other God who might be esteemed equal to Him.[130]

Only Rāma, sang Kabir, can free man from the terrible clutches of Yama (death).[131]

Moreover:

Gorakhnāth, the Avadhūta, cultivated the vine of Rāma's Name,
that Vine which is formless and shadowless, which does not require water nor manure,
and which reaches the frontiers of the sky![132]

In another *pada*, Kabir sang:

Without Rāma, the sultriness of my body does not find relief, and the easy life I lead stirs up even more those high blazes, as if water vomited fire.

You are the ocean, and I am the fish wriggling in Your salty waters.

If the tide suddenly withdraws, I am left behind, struggling in agony on the sandy beach.

You are the cage, and I am the imprisoned bird.

Show Yourself to me, so that You may bless me!

You are the True Guru, and I am your faithful disciple.

Says Kabir: I have surrendered to Rāma, thus winning my battle.[133]

With Rama's name as his support, Kabir declares that both tantras and mantras are deceptions of *māyā*. This offers another interesting parallel with Sai Baba, who always refused to give out tantras or mantras. G. G. Narke stated, "Sai Baba never gave me any mantra, tantra or upadeśa, and so far as I know he gave them to nobody."[134]

In one of his *padas*, Kabir stated:

There is he who takes on the appearance of a ragged beggar,
and who superbly mantles himself with his own liberality;
There is he who passes his time getting drunk,
and who grows silly on tantras and mantras;
Some try to acquire siddhis,
others observe all sacred fasts,
or go on pilgrimage to sacred places,
but none of these has ever thought of abandoning himself in the arms of devotion.[135]

In another *pada,* Kabir sang:

> Oh my disarmed heart, ask surrender to Hari!
> The day on which you will invoke Him with the voice of the forlorn,
> He shall stretch out His arms.
> I know neither tantra, nor mantra, nor my poor body can boast any beauty.[136]

In the closure of a *pada,* he resolutely declared, "Tantra and Mantra are deceptions of māyā. Rāma alone is the Support of us all!"[137]

These passages taken from Kabīrian literature show a strong affinity with Sai Baba's religious orientation, although their styles could scarcely have been more different! Indeed, Baba's measured and largely inarticulate speech are no match for Kabir's poetic and passionate outbursts. Yet the peculiar syncretistic quality of Kabir's life and teachings appears to have constituted Sai Baba's paradigmatic model. As Sai himself stated in front of a magistrate, his "religion" was Kabir.[138]

Notes

1. Kamath and Kher, *Sai Baba,* 93.

2. See Narasimhaswami, *Life of Sai Baba,* 1:27. For Baba's meeting with Javhara Āli, see chapter 5.

3. See chapter 6.

4. Ibid.

5. See Osborne, *Incredible Sai Baba,* 3.

6. On Purāṇic literature in general as well as on the *Bhāgavata Purāṇa* in particular, see the excellent study of Ludo Rocher, "The Purāṇas," in Jan Gonda, ed., *A History of Indian Literature,* vol. 2, fasc. 3 (Wiesbaden: Otto Harrassowitz, 1986).

7. For a preliminary introduction to the *Yogavasishtha,* see B. L. Atreya, *The Yogavasiṣṭha and its Philosophy* (Benares: The Indian Bookshop, 1939). See also V. L. Sharma Pansikar, The *Yogavasiṣṭha of Valmiki: With the Commentary Vasiṣṭhamahārāmāyaṇatatpāryaprakāśa* (Sanskrit text with Sanskrit commentary and introduction in English), 2 vols. (Reprint, Delhi: Motilal Banarsidass, 1984).

8. A fine edition of the *Adhyātma Rāmāyaṇa* Sanskrit text with Hindi translation has been published by Gita Press, Gorakhpur, 1958.

9. The first English translation of the *Pañcadashī* was by N. Dhol, Calcutta, 1879. For a more recent one, see Swami Svahananda, published by Ramakrishna Math (Madras, 1975).

10. See R. Anantakrishna Sastry, trans., *Viṣṇusahasranāma, with the Bhāṣya of Śrī Śaṁkarācārya* (Madras: Adyar, 1980). Also Shankara Bhagavatpada, *Śrī Viṣṇusahasranāma Stotram,* with English translation of the commentary, Bhavan's Book University, 228 (Bombay, 1978).

11. See chapter 6.

12. Tulpule, *Classical Marāṭhī Literature,* 331.

13. R. D. Ranade, *Mysticism in Maharashtra* (Reprint, Delhi: Motilal Banarsidass, 1982), 136. For an English rendition of the *Jñāneshvarī,* see the translation of V. G. Pradhan, edited by H. M. Lambert, 2 vols. (London: Allen & Unwin, 1967). See also the recent rendering of Swami Kripananda, *Jnaneshwar's Gita: A Rendering of the Jnaneshwari* (Albany, N.Y.: SUNY Press, 1989).

14. The *Amritānubhava* has been critically edited by V. D. Gokhale (Pune, 1967). For a recent English rendering, see S. Abhayananda, *Jnaneshvar: The Life and Works of the Celebrated Thirteenth Century Indian Mystic-Poet* (Naples, Fl.: Atma Books, 1989), 110–218.

15. See T. H. Avate, *Nāmadeva Gāthā* (Pune, 1923), 81. See also R. D. Ranade and S. K. Belvalkar, *History of Indian Philosophy,* vol. 7 (Pune, 1933).

16. Tulpule, *Classical Marāṭhī Literature,* 329–30.

17. There is some controversy relative to the authorship of this last work: some scholars attribute it to another poet of the same name. The theory of two Jñāndevs was first propounded by S. A. Bharade (also known as Bharadvaja) in 1898–99; see *Jñānadeva va Jñāneśvara* (Pune, 1931).

18. Tulpule, *Classical Marāṭhī Literature,* 354.

19. R. D. Ranade, *Mysticism in Maharashtra,* 256. On the *Eknāth Bhāgavata,* see the text published by the Government of Maharashtra, *Śrī Ekanāthī Bhāgavata* (Bombay, 1971).

20. There are two authentic editions of the *Dāsabodha.* The first is based on the undated manuscript of Kalyana edited by S. S. Dev (Dhule, Ś. 1827). The second is based on the manuscript of Dattatreya (Ś. 1606), edited by L. R. Pangarkar (Pune, 1923). The *Dāsabodha* has been partly rendered into English by V. H. Date, *Spiritual Treasure of St. Rāmadāsa* (Delhi, 1975).

21. Tulpule, *Classical Marāṭhī Literature*, 397.

22. On the life and works of Shripad Shrivallabha and Narasimha Sarasvati, R. C. Dhere, *Datta Sampradāyācā Itihāsa*, 2d ed. (Pune, Ś. 1835), 78.

23. Tulpule, *Classical Marāṭhī Literature*, 353. On the *Gurucharitra*, see R. K. Kamat, *Śrī Gurucaritra*, 3d ed. (Bombay, 1966).

24. *ahaṃ bhaktaparādhīno hyasvatantra iva dvija / sādhubhirgrastahṛdayo bhaktairbhaktajanapriyaḥ // nāhamātmānamāśāse madbhaktaiḥ sādhubhirvinā / śriyaṃ cātyaṃtikīṃ brahman teṣāṃ gatirahaṃ parā //*

25. See *Shvetashvātara Up.* 6.23.

26. See chapter 12 on the so-called yoga of devotion.

27. See for instance the *Nārāyaṇīya* section of the *Mahābhārata*, which may be viewed as an exposition of *bhakti* doctrine.

28. See *Nāradabhaktisūtra*, 41.

29. See Narasimhaswami, *Charters and Sayings*, 60.

30. Ibid., 4.

31. Ibid., 3.

32. Ibid.

33. This tormenting desire of the soul for the absent Beloved, known as *viraha*, is a typical theme in Kabir and the *Sant* tradition generally. The Sufi concept of *'ishq* (passion) comes close to this notion of *viraha*.

34. Narasimhaswami, *Charters and Sayings*, 43–44.

35. On the role and function of the guru from Vedic times, see Jan Gonda, *Change and Continuity*, 229–83.

36. *Jñāneshvarī* 16.1f. See R. D. Ranade, *Mysticism in Maharashtra*, 70.

37. On the role of the guru and his relation with the disciple, see the excellent treatment of S. G. Tulpule, *Mysticism in Medieval India* (Wiesbaden: Otto Harrassowitz, 1984), 104–25.

38. I shall shortly examine the concept of *saburī* when dealing with the Sufi's path (*ṭarīq*) and Kabir.

39. Gunaji, *Shri Sai Satcharita*, 244.

40. Narasimhaswami, *Charters and Sayings*, 60.

41. Ibid., 3–4.

42. Ibid., 46.

43. A. Osborne, *The Teachings of Ramana Maharshi* (London: Rider, 1971), 168.

44. Narasimhaswami, *Charters and Sayings,* 23.

45. Gunaji, *Shri Sai Satcharita,* 228.

46. The *abhaṅga* meter is nothing but a prolongation of the original *ovī* meter. The term *abhaṅga* is also explained as the colophon or the signature of the author appearing at the end of a composition. Father Ribeiro defines the *abhaṅga* as "Fin de escritura" in his *Dictionary of Koṅkaṇī*; see A. K. Priyolkar, *Grānthika Marāṭhī bhāṣā āṇi Koṅkaṇī bolī* (Pune, 1966), 92.

47. *Eknāth Gāthā,* no. 1675. Quoted in Tulpule, *Mysticism in Medieval India,* 93–94.

48. Ibid., 133.

49. Narasimhaswami, *Charters and Sayings,* 71.

50. Ibid., 72.

51. For these citations, see ibid., 71.

52. Ibid., 4.

53. A title expressing veneration, attributed to gods as well as holy men. Literally, the term *bhagavan* means "one who is possessed of glory, splendor, or prosperity."

54. Osborne, *Teachings of Ramana Maharshi,* 169–70.

55. Narasimhaswami, *Charters and Sayings,* 116.

56. On the issue of *nāmasmaraṇa,* see Tulpule, *Mysticism in Medieval India,* 127–45. See also the monographic issue on the divine name, with more than seventy articles, of *Kalyana Kalpataru* 5, no. 1(Jan. 1938).

57. Tulpule, *Mysticism in Medieval India,* 99.

58. Literally, "the fourfold practice."

59. Narasimhaswami, *Charters and Sayings,* 28–29.

60. Osborne, *Incredible Sai Baba,* 88.

61. Narasimhaswami, *Charters and Sayings,* 4. On this issue, see also Narasimhaswami, *Life of Sai Baba,* 2:237.

62. Narasimhaswami, *Charters and Sayings,* 94–95.

63. Ibid., 96.

64. Cf. J. A. B. van Buitenen, "Rāmānuja on the Bhagavadgītā," diss. (Utrecht, 1953), 24. See also A. Hohenberger, *Rāmānuja, ein Philosoph indischer Gottesmystik* (Bonn, 1960), 132.

65. For this presentation of the path leading to *prapatti* in *Viśiṣṭādvaita,* I am indebted to Mario Piantelli, "L'autonomia umana e la libertà divina nell'ambito dell'Induismo," in *Peccato e riconciliazione nelle religioni* (Bologna, 1984), 123–27.

66. Narasimhaswami, *Charters and Sayings,* 59.

67. Ibid., 107.

68. S. Kramrisch, *The Hindu Temple* (2 vols. Delhi: Motilal Banarsidass, 1977), 136.

69. A. Bharati, *The Ochre Robe* (New York: Doubleday, 1970), 161. On the theme of *darśan* as "auspicious mutual sight," see Lawrence A. Babb, "Glancing: Visual Interaction in Hinduism," *Journal of Anthropological Research* 37(1981): 387–401. For an erudite introduction to the theme of vision and sight, see J. Gonda, *Eye and Gaze in the Veda* (Amsterdam: North-Holland Publishing Company, 1969).

70. Osborne, *Teachings of Ramana Maharshi,* 167–68.

71. Panikkar, *Spiritualità Indù,* 183–84 (my translation).

72. Narasimhaswami, *Charters and Sayings,* 59–60.

73. Ibid., 119.

74. Osborne, *Incredible Sai Baba,* 37.

75. Narasimhaswami, *Charters and Sayings,* 105.

76. Osborne, *Incredible Sai Baba,* 40.

77. Narasimhaswami, *Charters and Sayings,* 9.

78. Idries Shah, *Wisdom of the Idiots* (London: Octagon Press, 1979), 99–100.

79. Tulpule, *Mysticism in Medieval India,* 74.

80. Tosun Bayrak, comp., *The Most Beautiful Names* (Putney: Threshold Books-Amana Books, 1985), 134–35. On *al-ṣabūr,* see also Ibn Ata Allah, *Traité sur le nom Allāh* (Paris, 1981), 237.

81. Quoted in A. Schimmel, *Mystical Dimensions of Islām* (Chapel Hill: University of North Carolina Press, 1975), 124.

82. Narasimhaswami, *Charters and Sayings,* 43.

83. Ibid., 109.

84. Ibid., 4.

85. Ibid., 105.

86. In the presentation of al-Ghazālī's *tawakkul,* I have followed the exposition given in G. C. Anawati and L. Gardet, *Mistica islamica: Aspetti e tendenze, esperienze e tecnica* (Torino: Società Editrice Internazionale, 1960), 160–66.

87. Sai Baba's teachings may be usefully compared to those of a Naqshabandiyya Indian Sufi: see the interesting book (having the form of a diary) of Irina Tweedie, *The Chasm of Fire* (Shaftesbury, Dorset: Element Books, 1979).

88. M. M. Moreno, *Antologia della mistica Arabo-Persiana* (Bari: Laterza, 1951), 136 (my translation).

89. L. Silburn, *Kuṇḍalinī: The Energy of the Depths: A Comprehensive Study Based on the Scriptures of Nondualistic Kaśmīr Śaivism,* trans. Jacques Gontier (Paris: Les Deux Oceans, 1983; Albany, N.Y.: SUNY Press, 1988), 5.

90. Ibid., 6. On Nataraja, see A. K. Coomaraswamy, *The Dance of Śiva* (Bombay, 1948).

91. On these issues, see Lawrence, *Early Chishti Approach,* 69–93.

92. Narasimhaswami, *Charters and Sayings,* 76–7. On Abdul Rahim Rangari of Thana, see Narasimhaswami, *Life of Sai Baba,* 3:177–79.

93. Quoted in Schimmel, *Mystical Dimensions,* 183.

94. Quoted in Anawati and Gardet, *Mistica islamica,* 197 (my translation).

95. R. C. Stade, *Ninety-nine Names of God in Islam: A Translation of the Major Portion of Al-Ghazālī's Al-Maqṣad Al-Asnā* (Ibadan: Daystar Press, 1970), 18–19.

96. Ibid., 116. On *Malik, Mālik al-Mulk* and the divine names generally, see the excellent work of Daniel Gimaret, *Les Noms divins en Islām: Exégèse lexicographique et théologique* (Paris: Les Editions du Cerf, 1988).

97. Narasimhaswami, *Charters and Sayings,* 106–7.

98. Gunaji, *Shri Sai Satcharita,* 245.

99. On *dhikr,* see Anawati and Gardet, *Mistica islamica,* 195–272; J. Spencer Trimingham, *The Sufi Orders in Islam,* 2d ed. (Oxford: Oxford University Press, 1973), 194–217. Also, Mir Valiuddin, *Contemplative Disciplines in Sufism* (London: East-West Publications, 1980).

100. See Vaudeville, *Kabīr,* 1:53.

101. Ibid., 56.

102. L. P. Mishra, *Mistici Indiani Medievali* (Torino: Unione Tipografico-Editrice Torinese, 1971), 527, *pada* 392. All translations from the Italian are my own.

103. Ibid., 532, *pada* 402.

104. Ibid., 353, *pada* 58.

105. Ibid., 486, *pada* 323.

106. Ibid., 492, *pada* 332.

107. Quoted in M. Hedayetullah, *Kabir: The Apostle of Hindu-Muslim Unity* (New Delhi: Motilal Banarsiḍass, 1977), 239.

108. Mishra, *Mistici Indiani,* 229, *sākhī* 3.

109. Quoted in Hedayetullah, *Kabir,* 238.

110. Mishra, *Mistici Indiani,* 231, *sākhī* 21.

111. See Vaudeville, *Kabīr,* 1:137.

112. Mishra, *Mistici Indiani,* 231, *sākhī* 20.

113. Ibid., 230, *sākhī* 15.

114. Ibid., 232, *sākhī* 30.

115. Ibid., *sākhī* 36.

116. Ibid., 528, *pada* 394.

117. *Ādi Granth, gauṛī* 69. Quoted in Hedayetullah, *Kabir,* 234.

118. *Ādi Granth, sārang* 3. Ibid., 234–35.

119. Mishra, *Mistici Indiani,* 233, *sākhī* 4.

120. Ibid., *sākhī* 6.

121. *Māyā,* that is, the force of illusion that alienates man from God. Kabir often likens *māyā* to a clever beguiler, full of lascivious charm, an evil woman, a witch, who entangles men with her deceit.

122. Mishra, *Mistici Indiani,* 434, *pada* 228.

123. Compare Koran 76, 25.

124. Quoted in Hedayetullah, *Kabir,* 228–29.

125. Mishra, *Mistici Indiani,* 353, *pada* 58. *Rahīm* designates Allah as

the All-Beneficient One, *Karīm* as the Merciful One. *Keśava* is an epithet of Krishna, meaning "the One having long hair." *Bismil* is an abbreviated form of Arabic *Bismillah,* God. *Viśvambhara* is an epithet applied to the Supreme Being of the Hindus, literally, "the All-Bearing, All-Sustaining One."

126. Literally, "the spotless one, the pure." Name of the Supreme Being, which, for Kabir, is the equivalent of Rama: *Rām-Niranjan* is "totally other," that is, transcends all creation and its *guṇas.* On the concept of *Niranjan* in Kabir, see Ch. Vaudeville, *Kabīr Granthāvalī* (*Dohā*) (Pondichéry: Publications de l'Institut Français d'Indologie, 1957), xv–xvi.

127. Another name for Allah.

128. Mishra, *Mistici Indiani,* 488, *pada* 327.

129. Quoted in G. H. Westcott, *Kabir and Kabir Panth,* 2d ed. (Calcutta: Susil Gupta, 1953), 39.

130. Mishra, *Mistici Indiani,* 496, *pada* 340.

131. See ibid., 429, *pada* 217.

132. Ibid., 401, *pada* 163.

133. Ibid., 380–81, *pada* 120.

134. Osborne, *Incredible Sai Baba,* 82–83.

135. Mishra, *Mistici Indiani,* 523, *pada* 385.

136. Ibid., 382, *pada* 122.

137. Ibid., 514, *pada* 368.

138. See Narasimhaswami, *Charters and Sayings,* 256.

10

The Path of Knowledge

Sai Baba's instructions to his Hindu devotees relative to the path of *jñāna* were focused on the issues of *ātmavicāra* and the concepts of *Brahman, saṃsāra,* and *māyā.*

The term *jñāna* derives from the root *jñā* (to know, understand, experience, ascertain) and especially designates the highest knowledge derived from spiritual insight. The underlying principle concerning the notion of correct versus fallacious forms of knowledge is the idea that you become what you know. This is a very archaic notion, connected with the theory of karma. True knowledge or *jñāna* gives one control over the laws of destiny.

Jñāna, moreover, expresses the highest human action, which is an interior sacrifice (*yajña*), that is, the oblation of one's self in the pursuit of truth: only so does *jñāna* acquire its salvific power, not being reducible to mere intellectual cognition. The path of *jñāna* bears a fundamental experiential and "practical" content: what one knows means, in this context, what one does.

Of course, Absolute Reality, the goal of the *jñānin,* does not "come into being," nor does it vary: it is eternally immutable. *Jñāna-mārga* gradually leads to a pure discovery, to the unveiling of what "truly is." To achieve this state, destruction of all obstacles preventing realization must be brought about, that is, *ajñāna* (ignorance) must be dissipated.

The word *Brahman* is most probably derived from the verbal root *brh* (to grow, to become strong or great, to increase). Two basic interpretations have been given of *Brahman*: the earlier Vedic conception has been linked with the idea of a mysterious dynamic power, animating sacred words and rituals. The later Vedāntic conception of *Brahman,* is more abstract: an all-pervading, transcendent principle. Though the three characteristics of the Vedāntic Brahman are being (*sat*), consciousness (*cit*), and bliss (*ānanda*), it is "pure being" that dominates its understanding. It is this latter conception that interests us here. As Bettina Baumer states:

> *Brahman*, the absolute, cosmic, transcendent principle and immanent womb of everything, one of the most pervasive concepts of the Indian tradition, evades every clear definition, though the religious literature is full of attempts to describe the indescribable.... *Brahman* is both being and non-being, fullness and void, it is the totality (*sarvam*) and yet it is not exhausted by any conception of it.[1]

Sai Baba, in presenting the necessary qualifications needed by a *sādhaka* along *jñāna-mārga*, is reported listing the classical ones formulated by Shankara in the introduction to his commentary on the *Brahmasūtras*:

> N. G. Chandorkar: "Baba, again I am asking you for the third time, who is God, what is he like, and where is he?"
>
> Baba: "I have already told you. If you act upon what I have said, you will be equipped with the Sadhana Chatushtaya, that is, the four aids."
>
> N. G. Chandorkar: "What are they?"
>
> Baba: "First is Nitya-Anitya Vastuviveka,...Vairagya,... Sama,...Mumukshutva."[2]

I shall examine these four qualifications following Shankara's order, that is, starting with the last one, *mumukṣutva*.

The term *mumukṣutva* is a desiderative form derived from the verbal root *muc* and literally means "the striving for emancipation," that is, the state of desiring liberation, *mukti*. Without this essential predisposition, no spiritual advancement is possible. The desire for *mukti* is accompanied by an ardent desire to know *Brahman* (*Brahma-jijñāsā*).

The second condition is that of *nitya-anitya-vastu-viveka*, meaning the capacity to discriminate between the temporal and the eternal. The adept must cultivate *viveka* (discrimination) in order to recognize all that is transient and ephemeral, not conducive to liberation, thus becoming unattached to temporary "things."

The third condition is known as *ihāmutra-phala-bhoga-virāga* and corresponds to what Sai Baba synthetically defines as *vairāgya*: renunciation of the pleasures one may derive from the fruits of his/her actions, both in this world and in the next. In his search for the Absolute, the *sādhaka* must cultivate a perfectly non-utilitarian attitude: "what truly is" must be sought for its own sake, not for the reward it may offer!

The fourth indispensable qualification is the acquisition of the six fundamental virtues: *sama* (equanimity, designating mind control), *dama* (sense control), *uparati* (renunciation), *titikṣa* (patience and fortitude), *samādhāna* (concentration), and *śraddhā* (faith). These virtues must be perfected by the adept along the path.

Within *advaitism*, nonetheless, the gratuity of the enlightenment experience is emphasized together with the inadequacy of all human means to acquire it. In short, what is required by these four conditions is conversion, a radical change in one's life orientation.

I shall now discuss Sai Baba's teachings on *jñāna* and subsequently offer a brief panorama of his ideas on God, the world, *saṃsāra*, and *māyā*.

I begin by briefly recalling Baba's insistence on the need for *ātmavicāra* (inquiry into the *ātman*):

> Baba often said: "Who are we? Night and day think on this."[3]

> "Who are we? What are we? Where am I? Where are you? Where is all the world?"[4]

These fundamental queries, verily the primary ones in all religious and philosophical reflections, are formulated in an analogous fashion in one of the minor works attributed to Shankara, the *Aparokshānubhūti*: "Who am I? How has all this come into existence? Who has made this (world)? Of what is it made? This is the way in which the inquiry must be conducted."[5]

A lover of paradoxes, Baba once stated: "He that slays, saves. He that saves, slays."[6]

Self-realization is what slays the ego, saving the individual. What saves, that is, sustains the ego, is what slays, determining spiritual "death."

At other times Baba simply said, "Think of God and kill the ego."[7]

Sai pressed his devotees regarding the urgency of *ātmavicāra*: "To know me, constantly think 'Who am I?', by Shravana and Manana."[8] Likewise: "Who are we? This we must enquire into."[9] Moreover: "We must see our Self."[10]

Ramana Maharshi clearly explained:

> The inquiry: "Who am I ?" really means trying to find the source of the ego or of the "I" thought. You are not to occupy the mind with other thoughts, such as "I am not the body." Seeking

> the source of the "I" serves as a means of getting rid of all other thoughts. You should not allow any scope for other thoughts...but should keep the attention fixed on finding the source of the "I" thought by asking, when any other thought arises, to whom it occurs; and if the answer is "to me," you then resume the thought: "Who is this I and what is its source?"[11]

Of course, it is not easy to control one's mind and maintain one's attention alert at all times. Sai Baba commented on the nature of the mind:

> The mind is turbulent. Effort must be made to make it steady. Just as a fly flies and sits on all objects but turns back when it approaches fire, so the mind longs after sense objects, rejoices in them and merges in them. When it approaches or tries to see Brahman, it turns its face away. When thus the unruly mind does not merge in God (Brahman), samsara, that is, rebirth, is inevitable. Till the mind is conquered, one is reborn. But among births, human birth is most precious.
>
> Therefore do Murti Puja i.e. worship God in form, in his images, to make the mind steady and concentrated. Even the image is God (Parameshvara). Do not reject images. When an image is worshipped with deep devotion, the mind attains concentration, without which there is no steadiness of mind.
>
> Next practice Manana and Dhyana i.e. recollection and meditation, and study spiritual works. Practice what is mentioned in them. Atma Vidya, the science of the Self, is the highest wisdom. If that is mastered, salvation (Mukti) is achieved and Hari (Personal God) is one's slave. The easy steps to get to that wisdom and to Moksha (that is, to real seeing or knowledge of God-Brahman) are these.[12]

Jñāna requires mental strength and ability to focus on a single point. Thus Sai encouraged the worship of images as the easiest way for developing *dhāraṇā* and *ekāgratā*. Baba also related the practice of *dhyāna* to the study of sacred texts (*abhyāsa*): these two must proceed together step by step in order for one to reach the goal of *ātmavidyā*.

Regarding meditation, Sai Baba taught the following to G. R. Dabholkar:

> Our art is unique. Remember this. To get Atmajnan, Dhyana is needed, that is, the Atma-anusthana[13] that pacifies and carries the mind into Samadhi. So give up all desires and dwell

> in your mind upon God in all. If the mind is thus concentrated the Goal is achieved.
>
> For Dhyana, meditate on me either with form or as formless, mere Ananda. If such formless contemplation is hard, then think of my form, just as you see it here. Think of it night and day. With such meditation, the mind dissolves into unity, that is, attains Laya. The difference between subject and object (me and you) and the act of contemplation will be lost. This results in Chaitanya Ghanata,[14] Brahma Samarasata.[15] The Guru's glance is bread and milk for the pupil.[16]

Dhyāna may thus be *rūpa* (with form) or *arūpa* (formless): Sai Baba's encouragement to devotees to adopt his own form as an easy aid to concentration is noteworthy.

After relating how Sai gave sugar candy as *prasād* to Dabholkar, Narasimhaswami's text continues:

> [Sai Baba:] "If you keep this instruction in mind, it will be as sweet as this sugar-candy."
>
> Baba recommended the study or shravana of the Katha followed by Manana, Nidhi Dhyasa, Smarana and Dhyana, all of which lead to Ananda Ghana,[17] realization.[18]

Audition (*śravaṇa*), reflection (*manana*), and profound and repeated meditation (*nididhyāsana*) constitute, according to Vedānta, the three subsequent stages of learning: in Shankara's teaching they represent the continuous line along which the rigorous inquiry into the *ātman* must be carried out. Baba then continued:

> That which is seen is the manifestation of Brahman through Maya and will dissolve again into Brahman. Look into the six Shastras[19] to see if the Atman is one or as many as there are jivas.
>
> The crown of Jnana is the realization of the one Atman, from which everything has issued.[20]

To the question "What am I," raised by one Uddhavesha Bua, Sai Baba replied: "I am you. You are I. There is no difference between you and me. That which constitutes me constitutes you."[21]

On another occasion he is reported saying:

> People differentiate between themselves and others, their properties and others' properties. This is wrong: I am in you and you in me.

> This is the Teli's, that is, oilmonger's wall, that separates you from me (a Teli lived next to the mosque). Pull down this wall, and then we shall see each other clearly face to face.
>
> Saints do not recognize differentiation. To serve me, remove this differentiation. Continue to think in this way and then you will realize it.
>
> Search the Scriptures and see if the Atma is one or many.[22]

This experience of oneness and all-inclusiveness (*ekatva*) reveals the epistemic error inherent in the idea of separation, that is, the illusiveness of the principle of distinction. The *ātman*, constituting the root of everything, in the internal or the external world, is also the very content of all experience. In other words, the *ātman* is the sole real entity, enveloping all forms as well as the formless.

Such a realization radically overturns one's ordinary "distorted" or "veiled" perception of reality. We may recall Baba's identification with ill people and dogs, giving proof of his "physical" oneness with these creatures. These concrete and down to earth demonstrations of the truth of nondualism or *waḥdat al-wujūd*, were more powerful than any purely theoretical discourse.

As Shankara solemnly declares in commenting on *Bṛhadāraṇyaka Upanishad* 2.4.6:[23] "Because everything springs from the Self, is dissolved in It, and remains imbued with It during continuance, it cannot be perceived apart from the Self. Therefore everything is the Self."[24]

On this crucial issue of experiencing a state of unity, a dialogue between Satya Sai Baba and John S. Hislop, one of his devotees, appears illuminating:

> Hislop: "I have the conviction so strong that it is into the marrow of my bones that life is one, and that other beings and myself are one. The Atma is that One and it is fully here at this moment, and I am constantly engaged in sadhana; so the question remains: Why do I not actually experience that unity as none other than myself?"
>
> Satya Sai: "Your conviction of unity is an idea, a thought. It is not experience. For instance, your wife has a chest pain. Do you have the chest pain? If not, where is the unity? The unity of life must be experienced—not idea or thought without experience."
>
> Hislop: "Now! Swami has to talk about experience! If sadhana and conviction do not bring that unity as real experience, then how is one to get it?"

> Satya Sai: "With steady sadhana, no special effort is needed to try and get the experience of One. Just as with ourselves in this car. We need only concern ourselves with the careful driving of the car, and in due course we will arrive at Ananthapur. With correct and steady sadhana, in due course, the actual experience of One will naturally come about."[25]

Shirdi Sai Baba also invited his followers to practice a regular *sādhanā*, without worrying about the result: striving, after all, reinforces dualism and separation, whereas the realization of oneness should occur spontaneously, like the blossoming of a flower or a snake shedding its skin.

The Bombay *advaita* teacher Maruti Kampli, better known as Nisargadatta Maharaj (1897–1981), of the Maratha Navnāth *saṃpradāya,* stated how even an animal might attain *jñāna* if in physical proximity to a guru. A dialogue between Nisargadatta and a devotee makes this point:

> Devotee: "...Consciousness. Can an animal also develop a sense of Reality?"
>
> Maharaj: "Yes. If associated with a jnani, animals can in turn become jnanis, though they will never be able to express it through speech. Such was the case with the cow of Ramana Maharshi or with the horses of Sathya Sai Baba or Shirdi Baba."[26]

We may recall that Shirdi Baba had, in fact, a horse that the Hindus called Shyamsundar and the Muslims, Shamsuddin: this horse was duly honored, and his *samādhi* stands to the present day in the *Leṇḍī* area, venerated by all Baba's devotees as an enlightened soul.

Since the *ātman* pervades everything and is the only reality, even the guru may, in some circumstances, be viewed as superfluous. Sai once observed: "There is no need for a guru. It (the upadesh) is all within you. Try to listen within and follow the direction you get. We must look at ourselves, that is, the monitor, the Guru."[27]

The *ātman* which is within us and constitutes our own very nature (*svarūpa*), is self-effulgent: the indweller (*antarayāmin*) is our true guru, that is, the voice of the conscience. *Brahman* is the authentic identity of man: whosoever embarks on the search for *mokṣa* without realizing this fundamental assumption is similar, to use a poignant example of Ramana Maharshi, to one looking for darkness while holding a lamp: he already possesses what he endeavors to obtain! Liberation or the awareness of the *ātman* is something that must be realized as immediately present, coinciding with one's unborn conscience.[28]

This, of course, does not mean that spiritual exercises are unimportant. In particular, Sai recommended the practice of *dhyāna*. The foremost characteristic of contemplation is immediacy, that is, the disappearance of distance between subject and object. When such an identity or "fusion of horizons" is reached, *dhyāna* becomes not only contentless but also devoid of intentionality. Though the object of contemplation may have been obliterated, this does not imply a state of empty absorption or a nihilistic vacuum: the ineffable experience of nondualism transcends one's being altogether, and mind activity consequently ceases. The process of *dhyāna* is then a loosening of the ego, leading to absolute freedom, perhaps the best translation of the term *mokṣa*.

Adapting his *upadeśa* to the devotee's capacity of comprehension, Baba once taught: "Moksha is not Heaven, Kailas or Vaikunta. It is subtle and not gross. It is the invisible origin of the Universe—pure consciousness, pure being, Shuddha Chaitanya.[29] Being or becoming that, is Moksha. That is immortality and that is the goal of human life. All other aims are worthless."[30]

Rare philosophical utterances are attributed to Sai Baba concerning the nature of *Brahman*, *māyā* and *saṃsāra*. Narasimhaswami reports an interesting conversation between Sai and N. G. Chandorkar:

> N. G. Chandorkar: "Pray, tell us about Shuddha Chaitanya, what it is."
>
> Baba: "That is the origin, the essence, the foundation and the permeator of the entire universe, sentient and insentient, as also the end of it. The source is Shuddha Chaitanya. You cannot exactly describe Chaitanya, but every moment it exists in your existence. There is no place without it but it has no form or name. It resembles air, which has no colour or form to be seen, but whose existence is unquestionable.
>
> "Shuddha Chaitanya is called Brahman. The wise do upasana[31] of it under the name Brahman and are called Brahmavit.[32]
>
> "Vegetable, animal, human, and all other lives are contained within it. It is the original cause of all appearances, percep-

tions and knowledge. It is the one root of the many. It pervades everything. It may be characterized as Sat, reality, Cit, consciousness, Ananda, bliss and Ekatva, unity. All of us are that. We are not distinct from it."

N. G. Chandorkar: "Baba, you say Brahman is bliss, that is, without pain, and that it is unity, that is, without multiplicity. Yet, you say the same Brahman is all or everything in the world, wherein there is not merely multiplicity but also suffering.

"How can bliss appear as pain and suffering? How can the one appear as the many? How can the real appear as the unreal?

"Again, if all of us consider ourselves as Chaitanya or Brahman, there must be many Brahmans (and not one) because we are so many. Further, if all of us are the one and same Brahman, each man must feel the pain and pleasure felt by others; but he does not. Just as our bodies are different, our souls also must be different and not one. Please explain."

Baba: "You are wrong. Just listen. Red, black, white, blue, yellow, etc. are different colours. Add them to water. Is not water still one and the same water, despite the different colours? That you will see by separating the colours from the water. The result will be that you get water in each case.

"Just like that, the Atman or Brahman is one. But the hearts it occupies, are different. It is one and the same Atman that runs through all the hearts. As for pain and pleasure, these are not the functions of Brahman or Atman, but only of the hearts. To make the heart a heart, is the function of the Atman or Brahman.

"I will further explain the matter. Chaitanya appears through three gunas, and is classified further as Paramartika-Satya, Vyavaharika-Satya and Pratibhasika-Satya. Just as one body has three stages; childhood, manhood, and old age, so Satya has these three stages.

"A person in the Paramartik stage (called the sage) sees truth as truth, and acts according to Shastras, that is, without differentiation. One in the Vyavaharik stage (called the good one) tries to follow the Shastras but goes on differentiating at every step, selecting the good and rejecting the evil. One in the Pratibhasik stage (called the ignorant one) does not see the truth either entirely as it is, or merely with the addition of differentiation, but sees it quite inverted, that is, in the way quite opposite to the Vyavaharik person's view. He sees good as evil and evil as good. But Atman or Brahman is common to all these three stages.

"I will give one more illustration. There are the King, the King's deputy, and the King's messenger. You see the common point running through all the three, that is, Kingliness; yet the three are different. It is just like that: Brahman runs through all the three classes, which appear different."

N. G. Chandorkar: "How can you divide regality? It is indivisible."

Baba: "Right. Regality is one and indivisible; but in point of fact we note the division of Regality in the above three and the difference between them. Similarly, Chaitanya (Brahman) is unlimited, but each limited ego partakes of it, that is, to the extent of its capacity, and exhibits it, that is, this Chaitanya or Kingship.

"Take another example, viz. space or akasha. Akasha, though illimitable, is found in a small pot (then called ghatakasha), in a big pot (then called kumbhakasha) and so on. All have akasha in degrees. Just like that Brahman appears in different forms in this world, which is the play of Maya. It is the union of Brahman with Maya that causes Brahmanda,[33] the universe."[34]

Sai Baba's argumentation is thoroughly Vedāntic, both in content and in terminology, with perhaps the exception of the theme of regality and the king, which might betray a Sufi influence.

In particular, Baba focuses on the three modes of apprehending reality. Among the successors of Shankara, it was Dharmarajadhvarindra who classified these three "levels" of reality or truth (*satya*). In descending order, he distinguished between the *pāramārthika* (transcendent truth), *vyāvahārika* (conventional truth), and *prātibhāsika* (illusory truth).

Multiplicity has no reality beyond the forms that it takes. These forms (*rūpa*), with their names (*nāma*), constitute the illusory side of experience, subsisting only through the concealing power (*āvaraṇa*) of *ātman-Brahman*. When enlightenment dawns, multiplicity dissolves and is recognized as mere illusion, that is, *prātibhāsika-satya*, due to a previous state of ignorance: the experience of the *ātman* coincides with *pāramārthika-satya,* the only reality. As long as *mukti* has not been attained, the reality of the world with its daily conventions, that is, *vyāvahārika-satya,* must be acknowledged.

The *ātman* is thus the root cause of all appearances, perceptions, and cognitions: everything, as Baba says, is based and depends upon the *ātman.*

Shankara, in his commentary to *Kaṭha Upanishad* 2.2.15,[35] stated: "Just as (hot) water, fire-brand, etc., owing to their contact with fire, burn according as the fire does, but not independently, similarly, it is verily *tasya bhāsā,* that is, by His effulgence, that *sarvam idaṃ,* that is, all this—the sun, etc. *vibhāti,* that is, shines variously. This being so, it is that Brahman Itself that is effulgent and shines variously."[36]

Such dependence upon *Brahman* is so absolute that it is also defined as *ananyatā* (nonotherness), in the sense that, as Vacaspatimishra notes, it is not a state contrary to difference (*abheda*), but rather it excludes difference (see *Bhāmatī* 2.1.14).[37]

Significantly, Sai Baba declares that, "As for pain and pleasure, these are not the functions of Brahman or Atman."[38] Indeed, from the standpoint of *advaita,* all sensations belong to the sphere of illusion. The implicit call in Baba's long answer, is to find out *who* is suffering or rejoicing, the *ātman* being beyond all opposites.

Ramana Maharshi noted: "All unhappiness is due to the ego. With it comes all your trouble."[39] Furthermore: "The way of eliminating pain is to not continue living. Kill the one who grieves, then who will be left grieving anymore? The ego must die. This is the only way.... When one realizes that all are the one Self, who is there to love or hate?"[40]

Joy and sorrow and all pairs of opposites subsist as long as one identifies himself/herself with body and feelings, mind and desires. Once one is liberated from these, *avidyā* vanishes, and the person becomes established in *Śuddha Caitanya*: the experience of the Self totally transmutes one's life and figures as *the only* "real" experience possible!

Chandorkar next inquired of Baba about the nature of *māyā*:

> N. G. Chandorkar: "Who is this Maya? Who created her? What is she like? You just now said that the root of the whole world is Chaitanya. Then where does Maya come in?"
>
> Baba: "I will describe to you where and how she comes. Maya is the name given to the Shakti or Power of Chaitanya, which

makes Chaitanya appear in different forms. Can you separate Chaitanya from its Shakti? You cannot, just as you cannot separate jaggery from its sweetness and the sun from its brilliance. The separation comes only at the end of Maya (if merger in Brahman is separation). Maya ends when Chaitanya is realized. Chaitanya is endless. Both Chaitanya and Maya are beginningless. Maya and Chaitanya are also named Prakriti and Purusha, which are fully described in the Jnanesvari from which you must get your Atma Jnana.

"Chaitanya is a cave and he who enters into that cave never returns but becomes the cave.

"Maya is Karya and has wonderful qualities. I am such and such a person, you are such and such, etc.—all this is the result of Maya. All these are unreal differences. You see, if you are under Maya, (undifferentiated) Reality does not appear. Maya has two aspects: (1) The Avarana, covering up the consciousness of the soul or Atman, and (2) Vikshepa, producing illusory appearances over that covering. Here is an illustration.

"A cooly dreamt that he became a king. Thereby he forgot his coolyship. That coolyship was covered up (avarana) by Maya, and kingship was produced by Maya over that cover (vikshepa). Similarly, Maya covers up Brahman and produces worldly appearances. In reality, the world does not exist. Only one Real (Sat) exists, but these appearances are taken to be real. That causes the mischief (akalyan). So, kick out Maya and regain Brahman. How? Regard yourself as pure Chaitanya. Water, when relieved of impurity, is pure water. Similarly, remove the impurity of Maya from this world of appearances. Then that appearance becomes reality. This is the upasana of the Real (Sadvastu).[41]

"Think of this always. This is my advice to all. This constant thought of the Sadvastu or Atman is the Adhyatma.[42] You should realize this Atman as yourself and become Mukta, that is, liberated in this life."[43]

Sai Baba's explanation of the nature and function of *māyā* is in perfect harmony with *advaita* tenets. *Māyā* is defined as the *śakti* (energy, potency) of *Caitanya.*

Shankara himself viewed *māyā* as the "seed-potency" (*bīja-śakti*) of *Brahman,* the divine energy through which the Absolute creates, maintains, and dissolves the cosmos.

Sai, after equating *Śuddha Caitanya* and *māyā* with the Sāṃkhyan categories of *Purusha* (pure consciousness) and *Prakriti* (*natura naturans,* materiality) respectively, encouraged Chandorkar in his reading of the *Jñāneshvarī.* In fact, the *Jñāneshvarī,* following the metaphysical lines of the *Bhagavadgītā,* takes the concepts of *Purusha* and *Prakriti,* their nature and relationship, as its fundamental religious horizon.[44]

Baba reminded Chandorkar of *māyā*'s beautiful qualities. *Māyā* is indeed *kārya,* a "product," a "result" of Ishvara's will (*saṃkalpa*) through which the magic play/drama (*līlā*) of creation is enacted. In the Vedāntic metaphysical scheme, Ishvara functions as a fundamental link, a *trait-d'union* between the Impersonal *Brahman* and the world.

The notion of *māyā* in Shankara denotes primarily the mysterious power of *saguṇa Brahman,* that is, of Ishvara in the function of creation and manifestation of the universe. Thus, if *māyā* is unreal (*mithyā*), it is not however to be regarded as negative, nor should one discount or disparage nature for this reason: the problem arises because one identifies himself/herself with *māyā.*

Māyā "presents itself" as *avidyā* (fundamental ignorance) through a triple action: (1) representing the infinite as finite, (2) originating the appearance of nonexisting things perceived as different and apart from ourselves, and (3) making oneself appear as if a limited entity.

After Shankara, these activities of *māyā* were subsumed under two main functions: the veiling of the Absolute (*āvaraṇa*) and the projecting upon It of multiplicity (*vikṣepa*).

In conclusion, the problem of freedom (*mokṣa*) is not to be solved by rejecting or annihilating *māyā* (which is, after all, an impossible task), but rather by "healing" the fundamental epistemological distortion (*avidyā*) which leads one to identify himself/herself with sense objects. If it is true that ignorance (*avidyā*) is fed by attachment/aversion (*rāga-dveṣa*) to the alluring realities of the world (which is *māyā*!), it does not follow that *māyā* is negative in and of itself. The world is a neutral ground. It is the mind that projects its illusions upon it.

Whereas *avidyā* can be eliminated by correcting the way in which a person normally apprehends things (through the practices of *viveka/vicāra* and *śravaṇa, manana, nididhyāsana*), the world (*jagat*) does not disappear once *mokṣa* dawns. The discovery of the truth of nondualism simply reveals the true ephemeral character of *māyā*: it was never binding in and of itself.

Baba's *upadeśa* about the nature of *saṃsāra* and the codes of conduct one should observe in life is demonstrated in this other dialogue with Chandorkar:

> N. G. Chandorkar bowed to Sai Baba and said: "Enough of this Samsara for me. As the Shastras describe it, Samsara is really nissara, that is, worthless. Break its fetters off from me, Baba. What first seems to be joy here is seen to be but sorrow at the end. Fate gives us a nice dance here and there. I cannot discover even a bit of happiness in this Samsara. I am quite disgusted. I do not wish to touch it, Baba, any further."
>
> Baba: "What crazy and delusive talk is yours! There is some truth in it—mixed up with error.
>
> "As long as the body remains, Samsara remains. None escapes it. How can you? Even I am caught up in it.
>
> "Samsara is of various sorts. It is like the surface of the body. Kama (desire), Krodha (anger), etc. and any mixture of these is Samsara. All mental and bodily processes are Samsara. The contact of any two things is Samsara. By going away to a forest you cannot escape Samsara.
>
> "Your present condition has been brought about by yourself. What is the use of irritation at it? This Deha Prarabdha[45] is the result of the Karma done by you in former births. This body was, therefore, born. The Jiva takes birth in the body to work out former Karma. Without suffering the results of Prarabdha Karma, you cannot get rid of it. All persons, all creatures differ in form, etc. Why? Because of the previous Karma of each.
>
> "Differences between species, like differences between individuals, is due to the same cause. See the difference between the rich man's dog lolling on a sofa and the poor man's running about in search of crumbs. That is due to Deha Prarabdha."[46]

On another occasion, Chandorkar asked Baba: "Joys and sorrows of Samsara disturb one so much. Should we not renounce Samsara therefore?" Baba replied:

> Joy and sorrow are mere delusion. Mere appearance of worldly joy is not true happiness. The worldly man is forcibly drawn to it, as he believes it to be true happiness.
>
> According to the Prarabdha of each, one person gets delicacies (panchamrita),[47] one stale crumbs, and one mere bran-gruel. The latter fancies himself unhappy at that, and the for-

mer fancies he lacks nothing. But the result of eating any of these is merely the satisfaction of hunger.

Some cover themselves with laced shawls, others with rags. Both serve only one purpose, covering the body.

This joy and this sorrow are due to *opinion,* which is mere illusion and is ruinous. Whenever any idea of joy or sorrow arises in your mind, resist it. Do not give room to it. It is pure delusion.[48]

Baba's arguments conform to tradition: the law of transmigration (*saṃsāra*) regulates justly and precisely all existences, in conformity with the karma sown by each *jīva* in previous lives. As the *Upadeshasahasrī* so eloquently states: "Actions result in union with the body, such union results in pleasure and pain. From these inevitably descend attraction and repulsion, which result in activity. From activity descends merit and demerit for the ignorant one, and from these a new union with the body: thus, forever, this mundane existence turns like a wheel."[49]

Each and every person is submitted to this law of cause and effect, since nobody can abstain from acting or moving, physically or mentally. Only the achievement of highest knowledge (*jñāna*) may accomplish the miracle of truncating the fatal spiral of *avidyā-karma-saṃsāra*. When the sage is established in the awareness of the *ātman,* the binding force of karma "evaporates" as in a dream, since all attachment has been relinquished once and for all.

Sai Baba warns Chandorkar to avoid attributing any importance or substantiality to the opposite pair (*dvandva*) of joy and sorrow, purely a mental fabrication binding one more and more to the tragic wheel of *saṃsāra*.

From the standpoint of Ultimate Reality, there never was a condition of slavery from which to be freed: one who has "gotten off" the wheel of *avidyā-karma-saṃsāra,* realizes that such a wheel never really existed and that no "jumping off" has taken place, since "there is nothing besides the *ātman*" (*ad Bṛhadāraṇyaka Upanishad* 4.3.21). This experience is conveyed with subtle irony in the *Vivekacūḍāmaṇi*: "Where has this universe gone? Who has taken it away? In what has it sunk? Up till now it was seen by me, and now it is not here anymore! What a great wonder is this!"[50]

These speculations, however, were beyond the grasp of a common man like Chandorkar, who felt the painful weight of *saṃsāra* upon himself.

Sai Baba's teachings contained forthright and practical advice, as this dialogue with one of his *bhaktas* illustrates:

> I will tell you how to conduct yourself in Samsara. The wise should be cheerful and contented with their lot in life, as it is the result of Deha Prarabdha. Do not kick against the pricks.
>
> If wealthy, be humble. Plants bend, when they have fruits. But humility is not to be had towards all. Severity is needed in dealing with the wicked. But towards saints, be humble. Respect them.
>
> Spend money in Dana (charity) and Dharma (piety)—but be not extravagant. The world perishes no doubt, but while it lasts, wealth is a real necessity, as bile is for health. Be not obsessed by the importance of wealth. Do not be entangled in it, or be miserly. Be liberal and munificent—but not lavish or extravagant.
>
> Get on cheerfully with your worldly round of activities but do not forget God. Remember God. "This Samsara is not mine but God's": think thus all the time you are awake. Have consideration for the poor and wretched. Do not persecute and tease them. Inquire always: "Who am I?"[51]

Here is another fine example of Baba's balance and sobriety, a call to moderation and discrimination in all situations of life. Apart from his general exhortations to practice humility, charity, and piety, his advice to consider *saṃsāra* as implicitly divine is noteworthy. If one is able to consider it so, his capacity for detachment (*vairāgya*) will be much increased: *saṃsāra*, as well as *māyā*, may thus be viewed as the all-powerful *śakti* of *Śuddha Caitanya*.

It seems appropriate to bring this overview on *jñāna-mārga* to a close by quoting some comments of Sai Baba on the theme of death. Speaking to the wife of one Appa Kulkarni, who was on his deathbed, Baba said:

> Death and life are manifestations of God's activity. You cannot separate the two. God permeates all. However, in fact, none is born. None dies. See with your inner eye. Then you realize that you are God, and not different from Him.
>
> Like worn-out garments the body is cast away by God. Appa wants to change his dress (kafni) before I do. Let Appa go. Do not stop him. Do not ask for Udhi.
>
> Gain and loss, birth and death, are in the hands of God. But how blindly do these people forget God! Look after life, just so long as it lasts. When death arrives, do not be grieved. The wise ones do not grieve over death; the fools do.
>
> Behold! The five Pranas[52] were lent for use till now. Now

> the owner claims back his own; and they are returned. Air goes back to air, fire to fire. Every one of the five elements thus goes back to its place. The body is made up of earth. See, really they are the same. Therefore its return to the earth is not a thing to bemoan.[53]

Unfortunately, the sources do not offer any information for an examination of Sai Baba's "path of knowledge" in the light of Sufism. Nonetheless Baba's adherence to the Islamic conception of Allah as the one transcendent God to whom all men must submit, should be underlined. To quote a few of Sai's sayings in this regard:

> God is great. He is the Supreme Master. Allah Malik. How great is God! No one can compare with Him.
>
> He creates, supports, and destroys. His sport (Lila) is inscrutable.
>
> Let us be content to remain as He makes us, to submit our wills to His. Allah Rakega Vahisa Rahena.[54]
>
> Once when rain was beating inside the chavadi wherein Baba sat, he was asked to move up onto a higher place where an image of Maruti was kept.
> Baba: "How can we be seated on the same level as God?"[55]
>
> Moreover, he would say:
>
> To God be the praise. I am but the slave of God.[56]
>
> Without God's permission, nothing can be done by me.[57]

Possible affinities between Sai Baba and Kabir deserve consideration. Three elements strike me as being noteworthy: (1) the overall absence of ritualism and exterior religiosity, (2) the refusal of casteism and untouchability, and (3) the reiteration of being but servants and slaves of the one transcendent God.

Kabir's rejection of all religious formalities and rituals, as well as his iconoclasm, are proverbial. He vehemently criticized *brāhmaṇs* for their customs and all forms of superstition and popular piety, to the point of condemning even scriptures as useless: "Tear to pieces and throw your papers to the wind, if you want to give up your doubts! Your salvation is in the arms of Hari."[58]

Though Sai Baba never took such extremist attitudes, some affinities with Kabir may be noted: for instance, at the *masjid* he never respected any of the customary ritual rules. Apart from the rare and extemporaneous recitation of the *namāz* and the care for his *dhunī*, Baba's cultual activity was practically nil: everything was left to improvisation, to the mood of the moment.

Sai Baba's religious life bore an unmistakable *nirguṇa* character: like Kabir, the *faqīr* believed that true worship consisted only in God's silent revelation in the depths of one's soul.

As Kabir said in the *Ādi-Granth, basant* 1:

> Whither shall I go? I am happy at home.
> My heart will not go (with me): my mind has become a cripple.
> One day I did have an inclination to go,
> I ground sandal, took aloes paste and many perfumes
> And I was proceeding to worship God (Brahma) in a temple,
> When my Guru showed me that God is in my heart.
> Wherever I go, I find only water and stones,
> But Thou art equally contained in full in everything.
> The Vedas and the Purāṇas, all have I seen and searched.
> Go ye thither, if God be not here!
> O Satguru, I am a sacrifice unto Thee
> Who hast cut away all my perplexities and errors.
> Rāmānand's Lord is the all-pervading God (ramata Brahma)
> The Guru's śabda cuts away millions of karmas![59]

Another point of similarity is their refusal to accept castes and untouchability. Kabir's rejection was a scornful and polemic one:

> By the touch of others you brāhmaṇs
> consider yourselves polluted.
> Great pride never produces any good.
> How will He, Who is called the vanquisher
> of the proud
> bear with your pride?
> Do not oppress the weak;
> their sighs have great power.
> By the puffs of the bellows
> iron is converted to flames.[60]

In the *Granthāvalī*, *gauṛī* 41, Kabir declares: "If you are a Brāhmaṇ, born from a Brāhmaṇ woman, then why did you not arrive by another orifice? If you are a Muslim, born from a Muslim woman, then why were you not circumcised in the womb? No one is (by nature) low. He is low on whose tongue Rām is not."[61]

Sai Baba expressed his refusal of casteism and untouchability through example, by taking differences of caste into no account: a *vaiśya* or an outcast leper, a *brāhmaṇ* or a Muslim, all were equally dear to him.

Although Baba sometimes declared himself a *brāhmaṇ*,[62] he did so almost certainly to highlight his spiritual excellence and purity, not to posit caste distinctions.[63] Indeed, Sai particularly favored untouchables such as his leper servant Bhagoji Shindhe, one of his closest companions, with whom he partook food and tobacco; this servant was a privileged soul in the eyes of Baba's *bhaktas*.

Regarding Kabir's and Baba's attitude of submission to God, two factors should be noted: their devotional ardor of a *nirguṇa* type and their belief in the "monotheistic principle."

Kabir sang:

> Hari is One, and One only. Who worships Him under false pretences does not know Him.
> He is the very air, He is the very water and the very light which constitute the Universe.
> He filled with the same ash all the urns of the earth.
> He is the One, the True, the Creator.
> He, Our Lord, is that very Brahman who is present in us under various aspects, though māyā, the great deceiver, clouds our minds with her variegated illusions.
> Says Kabir, God's minstrel: I know no more fear, māyā does not dare trouble me.[64]

Moreover:

> Immense, Indefinable, and Omnipresent, the Lord presides in the heart of each,
> though very few are the ones who intuite His Presence!
> ...Says Kabir: I, slave of the Lord, obtained the sweet Juice of His Love, though the Donor I have not yet seen![65]

Finally, one of Kabir's beautiful hymns of submission:

> Let me dedicate to You, O Lord, this *ārtī* of mine, may it help my soul to reach that place where You, Eternal Source of light, abide in solitude.

I will make my senses the flowers of the offering,
I shall intertwine a garland with them and then dedicate it to You, O Niranjana.
I shall kneel down in front of You, laying my forehead at Your Feet, until my soul will be lost in Your immensity.
The Word of the Guru shall be my forerunner, and the Music of Anahada[66] shall lead me where You live, O Revealed Lord.
Says Kabir: I am Your humble servant, Lord, and You are the light which illumines all of my recesses.[67]

Notes

1. Vatsyayan, *Kalātattvakośa,* 1. For a good overview of the concept of *Brahman,* see her whole article, 1–22. Also, see Jan Gonda, *Notes on Brahman* (Utrecht: J. L. Beyers, 1950).

2. Narasimhaswami, *Charters and Sayings,* 29f.

3. Ibid., 24.

4. Ibid., 18.

5. *Aparokshānubhūti* 12: *ko 'haṃ kathamidaṃ jātaṃ ko vai kartā 'sya vidyate / upādānaṃ kimastīha vicāraḥ so 'yamīdṛśaḥ //*

6. Narasimhaswami, *Charters and Sayings,* 51.

7. Ibid., 78.

8. Ibid., 18.

9. Ibid., 24.

10. Ibid., 18.

11. Osborne, *Teachings of Ramana Maharshi,* 115–16.

12. Narasimhaswami, *Charters and Sayings,* 27–28.

13. Literally, "the religious practice (*anuṣṭhāna*) leading to the *ātman.*"

14. Literally, "firmness or solidity of consciousness."

15. Literally, "the equal feelingness of *Brahman.*"

16. Narasimhaswami, *Charters and Sayings,* 44–45.

17. Literally, "(a state) consisting of pure bliss or joy."

18. Narasimhaswami, *Charters and Sayings,* 45.

19. The six orthodox *darśanas* of Indian philosophy, that is, Sāṃkhya, Yoga, Nyāya, Vaiśeṣika, Mīmāṁsā and Vedānta.

20. Narasimhaswami, *Charters and Sayings,* 45.

21. Ibid., 19.

22. Ibid.

23. *brahma taṃ parādādyo'nyatrātmano brahma veda, kṣatraṃ taṃ parādādyo'nyatrātmanaḥ kṣatraṃ veda, lokāsta parāduryo'nyatrātmano lokānveda, devāstaṃ parāduryo'nyatrātmano devānveda, bhūtāni taṃ parāduryo'nyatrātmano bhūtāni veda, sarvaṃ taṃ parādādyo'nyatrātmanaḥ sarvaṃ veda; idaṃ brahma, idaṃ kṣatram, ime lokāḥ, ime devāḥ, imāni bhūtāni, idaṃ sarva yadayamātmā //* Swami Madhavananda renders the verse as follows: "The Brāhmaṇa ousts (slights) one who knows him as different from the Self. The Kṣatriya ousts one who knows him as different from the Self. Worlds oust one who knows them as different from the Self. The gods oust one who knows them as different from the Self. Beings oust one who knows them as different from the Self. All ousts one who knows it as different from the Self. This Brāhmaṇa, this Kṣatriya, these worlds, these gods, these beings, and this all are this Self." Swami Madhavananda, trans., *The Bṛhadāraṇyaka Upaniṣad (with the commentary of Śaṅkarācārya),* 5th ed. (Calcutta: Advaita Ashrama, 1975), 248.

24. Ibid., 249.

25. J. S. Hislop, *Conversations with Bhagavan Sri Sathya Sai Baba,* 4th ed. (Prasanthi Nilayam: Sri Sathya Sai Books and Publications, Bangalore, 1982), 69–70.

26. Nisargadatta Maharaj, *Sois!* (Paris, 1983), 54 (my translation). Nisargadatta met his guru Shri Siddharameshvar Maharaj of the Navnāth *saṃpradāya* around the age of thirty. He was given the mantra *Aham Brahmāsmi* and attained realization after three years of intense *sādhanā.* He often observed how his enlightened state had been the consequence of his placing complete faith in the guru. For an introduction to Nisargadatta Maharaj's teachings, see Maurice Frydman, *I Am That* (Bombay: Chetana, 1973).

27. Narasimhaswami, *Charters and Sayings,* 182.

28. On this issue, see Mario Piantelli, *Śaṅkara e la rinascita del Brāhmaṇesimo* (Fossano: Editrice Esperienze, 1974), 155.

29. Literally, "pure consciousness"; sometimes improperly translated as "pure spirit." The term *cit,* from which *caitanya* is derived, has the

meaning of perception, comprehension, attention, and immediate evidence all in one. As a technical term for consciousness, *caitanya* is found as early as the works of the materialistic schools (Cārvāka), where it is argued that consciousness is generated by the material elements and thus is just a quality of the body, present when the body is present and absent when the body is absent. As they say: "Consciousness is produced by the material elements even as intoxicating liquor is produced by molasses when it undergoes fermentation" (*madaśaktivat caitanyam upajāyate;* see *Sarvadarshanasaṃgraha,* chap. 1). In Kevalādvaitavedānta, *śuddha,* together with *nitya* (eternal), *buddha* (conscious, intelligent), and *mukta* (free, liberated), figures as one of the four essential attributes (*svarūpalakṣaṇa*) of *Brahman.* The *Vedāntasāra* treatise by Sadananda Yogindra (c. 1500), states: "Hence the experience of the learned in the Vedānta is that the inmost self is *spirit alone* (*caitanyam eva*) which reveals these several things and which, in its essential nature, is *eternal, pure, intelligent, free* and true. Such (is the nature of) superposition" (*atastattvadbhāsakaṃ nityaśuddhabuddhamuktasatyasvabhāvaṃ pratyakcaitanyamevātmavastviti vedāntavidanubhavaḥ / evamadhyāropaḥ //*) (Sadananda, *Vedānta-Sāra: A Work on Vedānta Philosophy,* edited and translated by M. Hiriyanna [Pune: Oriental Book Agency, 1929], 54). The compound *śuddha-caitanya,* along with its variants, is frequently found in late Vedāntic literature. To just quote a few examples: *Yogavasishtha* 5.34.16c: "I indeed am pure consciousness" (*śuddhacetana evāham*); *Tejobindu Upanishad* 6.64: "I alone am Hari. Personally, I alone am Sadashiva. I am of the nature of pure consciousness. I am the enjoyer of pure sattva" (*ahameva hariḥ sākṣādahameva sadāśivaḥ / śuddhacaitanyabhāvo 'ham śuddhasattvānubhāvanaḥ //*); *Brahmajñānavalimālā* 5a: "I am the form of pure consciousness" (*śuddhacaitanyarūpo'ham*); *Shivarahasya* 6.10.12: "I am pure consciousness" (*śuddhacaitanyamātro'ham iti*).

30. Narasimhaswami, *Charters and Sayings,* 31.

31. Literally, "homage," "adoration," "worship." In Ramanuja's *Viśiṣṭādvaita, upāsana* consists of five parts: *abhigamana* (approach), *upādāna* (preparation of offering), *ijyā* (oblation), *svādhyāya* (recitation), and *yoga* (devotion).

32. Literally, "knowers of *Brahman*"; see *Upadeshasahasrī* 1.1.6.

33. Literally, "the egg of Brahmā." Brahmā, by breaking open the egg, source of the seed of all creatures, gave rise to the whole process of creation. On the "cosmic egg," see *Vamana Saromāhātmya* 22.17–22, 30–39.

34. Narasimhaswami, *Charters and Sayings,* 31–34.

35. *na tatra sūryo bhāti na candratārakaṃ nemā vidyuto bhānti kuto 'yamagniḥ / tameva bhāntamanubhāti sarvaṃ tasya bhāsā sarvamidaṃ vibhāti //* Swami Gambhirananda renders the verse thus: "There the sun does not shine, neither do the moon and the stars; nor do these flashes of

lightning shine. How can this fire? He shining, all these shine; through his lustre all these are variously illumined"; Swami Gambhirananda, *Eight Upaniṣads (with the commentary of Śaṅkarācārya)*, 4th ed., vol. 1 (Calcutta: Advaita Ashrama, 1977), 198.

36. Ibid.

37. On these issues, see Piantelli, *Śaṅkara e la rinascita del Brāhmaṇesimo*, 139–44.

38. Narasimhaswami, *Charters and Sayings*, 32.

39. Osborne, *Teachings of Ramana Maharshi*, 36.

40. Ibid., 38.

41. *Sadvastu* literally means "the good thing" or "the true object."

42. Literally, "the Supreme Spirit or Soul."

43. Narasimhaswami, *Charters and Sayings*, 34–35.

44. On *Purusha* and *Prakriti* in the *Jñāneshvarī*, see Ranade, *Mysticism in Maharashtra*, 52–54.

45. The present body or form, which is the result of karma done in the past.

46. Narasimhaswami, *Charters and Sayings*, 20.

47. The five kinds of divine food: milk, coagulated or sour milk, butter, honey, and sugar.

48. Narasimhaswami, *Charters and Sayings*, 21.

49. *Upadeshasahasrī* 2.1.3–4: *karmāṇi dehayogārthaṃ dehayoge priyāpriye / dhruve syātāṃ tato rāgo dveṣaścaiva tataḥ kriyāḥ // dharmādharmau tato 'jñasya dehayogastathā punaḥ / evaṃ nityapravṛtto 'yaṃ saṃsāraścakravadbbṛśam //*

50. *Vivekacūḍāmaṇi*, 483: *kva gataṃ kena vā nītaṃ kutra līnamidaṃ jagat / adhunaiva mayā dṛṣṭaṃ nāsti kiṃ mahādbhutam //*

51. Narasimhaswami, *Charters and Sayings*, 22.

52. The five *prāṇas* or "breaths" are: *prāṇa*, or the ascending breath, including both inhalation and exhalation; *apāna*, or the breath associated with the lower half of the trunk; *vyāna*, or the diffuse breath circulating in all limbs; *udāna*, or the "up-breath" held responsible for speech and the ascent of *śakti* in higher states of consciousness; *samāna*, or the breath of the abdominal region, where it is connected with the digestive processes.

53. Narasimhaswami, *Charters and Sayings*, 127–8.

54. Ibid., 106.

55. Ibid., 47.

56. Ibid., 165.

57. Ibid., 17.

58. Mishra, *Mistici Indiani*, 37. On Kabir's and the Kabīrpanthīs' relation with the caste system, see David N. Lorenzen, "Traditions of Non-caste Hinduism: The Kabīr Panth," in *Contributions to Indian Sociology* n.s. 21, no. 2 (1987), 263–83.

59. Quoted from Vaudeville, *Kabīr*, 112.

60. Quoted from B. Sarasvati, "Notes on Kabīr: A Non-literate Intellectual," in S. C. Malik, *Dissent Protest and Reform in Indian Civilization* (Simla: Indian Institute of Advanced Study, 1977), 172.

61. Quoted from Lorenzen, *Traditions of Non-caste Hinduism*, 271.

62. See his saying: "This is a Brahmin, a white Brahmin, a pure Brahmin. This Brahmin will lead lakhs of people to the Subhra marga and take them to the Goal, right up to the end. This is a Brahmin's masjid"; Narasimhaswami, *Charters and Sayings*, 8.

63. See Osborne, *Incredible Sai Baba*, 58.

64. Mishra, *Mistici Indiani*, 352, *pada* 55.

65. Ibid., 404, *pada* 169.

66. Literally, "without limit," that is, the music of Infinity. It represents the ineffable vibration which the yogin experiments once he has awaken his *kuṇḍalinī* energy. On *śabda* and *anahada*, see Vaudeville, *Kabīr Granthāvalī (Dohā)*, xxii–xxiii.

67. Mishra, *Mistici Indiani*, 532, *pada* 402.

11

The Path of Action

This chapter is dedicated to some of Sai Baba's most significant sayings with regard to "orthopraxy" and individual and social ethics, as well as to the function of karma and the way it operates.

As we have seen, Sai Baba encouraged his devotees to lead an active life, engaged in society. His proposed ideal was that of a "lay spirituality." Arthur Osborne underlines the modernity of Sai Baba's position:

> Perhaps the most important consideration is that a path suited to modern times should be invisible, unencumbered by ritual, capable of being followed in the conditions of modern life, in the office or workshop, as well as in the hermitage. There are many sincere aspirants who have to lead a business or professional life with no facilities or time for ritualistic observances.... This has been provided for.... We have seen in the present book how Sai Baba encouraged family life. There were fakirs and sadhus among his followers, but those who were householders when they first came to him remained such.[1]

Baba's activities eloquently show his keen interest in the material and worldly welfare of his followers: miraculous healings, cures of sterility, monetary gifts, arrangement of weddings, help in economic affairs, and so forth.

In particular, Sai's interest in the economic matters of his devotees deserves mention. The sources report advice that Baba gave to people pertaining to job choices, rent prices, the buying or selling of plots of land, and so on. Apparently, by following Baba's suggestions, many people were able to increase their fortunes.

For instance, the *Charters and Sayings* reports:

> Baba was giving regularly Rs. 4 per diem to Bayyaji Appaji Patel for years.
>
> Baba: "Do not lend these sums, nor give them away to others. Do not eat and excrete these."

Baba evidently wanted the money to be invested in land purchases. Accordingly, Bayyaji purchased 84 acres of land which he is still retaining.[2]

Another anecdote reveals:

S. B. Dhumal was offered the Public Prosecutorship at Nasik. He wrote to Shama for Baba's approval.

Baba: "Why should he accept the new? The old is good enough."

S. B. Dhumal rejected the Public Prosecutorship and his income was still good.[3]

Devotees who didn't follow Sai Baba's advice would find themselves in trouble.

Sugarcane was the vogue and everybody was planting the Godavari valley with sugarcane.

Bayyaji: "Baba, shall I plant sugarcane?"

Baba: "Don't."

But the example of others and the hope of large profits from sugarcane made Bayyaji disregard Baba's advice and go in for sugarcane planting. What was the result? First, a loss of Rs. 300 in the money invested, and next the going without the usual supply of dry crops he would have gotten on the land.[4]

Damodar S. Rasane had an offer for speculation in cotton from a broker in Bombay. The broker promised him lakhs of rupees by way of profit. D. S. Rasane wrote to Shama to get Baba's permission. Shama brought the letter to Baba. Before it was read, Baba spoke.

Baba: "Damia wants to reach for the sky. He is not content to keep what God has given him. Damia's mind is confused. Write to him that his present state is not unhappy. His present half loaf is enough. Let him not be bothered about lakhs."

Then Damia went in person, and thinking of starting that speculation and giving Baba a share in the profits, massaged Baba's feet.

Baba, loudly: "Damia, I am not in anything (i.e. I do not wish to get entangled in any samsara, like sharing profits)."

So, that enterprise was given up.

Again Damia had a proposal, when prices of grains were running high, to buy a lot of grain and store it for some months or years and then sell it. Damia went to Baba and said: "Shall I trade in grain?"

Baba: "No, you will be buying at five seers and selling at seven."

But for weeks, the rise in prices was kept up and Baba's prophecy seemed to be wrong; but a month or two later i.e. in Shravan, there was abundant rain on all sides, and the prices suddenly fell and remained low for a long time. The grain storers had a serious loss. Baba saved Damia from that fate.[5]

Though Sai Baba never was involved in any business affairs or speculation himself, his active interest in and advice on these matters were unusual: indeed they do not respond to the traditional image of the ascetic or holy man. This peculiarity of Baba's, that is, of being viewed as a bestower of both spiritual freedom (*mukti*) and temporal welfare (*bhukti*), was perhaps the reason why he was identified as an *avatāra* of Dattatreya, traditionally considered to be the bestower of all boons.

The biographer of Satya Sai Baba, N. Kasturi, confirmed this belief to me in the course of an interview in October 1985:

> Think of this other attribute of Datta: "Sometimes a *yogī*, sometimes a *bhogī*, sometimes a *vairāgī*...." *Bhogī* means a person who bases his life on worldly things. At times he renounces the world as a *yogī*, at other times he binds himself to the world as a *bhogī*. He also appears as a *vairāgī*, that is, as a person having renounced all things. These traits may be found in Shirdi Baba.... People prayed to him in order to attain prosperity, mundane happiness. Even here,[6] there is no barrier or separation...*bhukti* and *mukti*, *yogī* and *bhogī*.... This is something really great.

The *Svāmin* Muktananda (1908–82) of Ganeshpuri, near Bombay, once said about Shirdi Baba:

> Sai Baba of Shirdi was equally great. He appeased his hunger through the alms he received daily. He loved to listen to music very much. At any given moment, he could offer people handfuls of money which he extracted from his empty pockets. He wore a long and straight robe and a band around his head. He was a great Siddha. Sai Baba was adored by all, rich and poor alike. If someone made him a gift, he would always give it away to somebody present there. He had no desire for posses-

> sions. He was supremely compassionate and soothed the pain and sufferings of the poor. His influence is still felt around the world. The crowds which ran up to him had absolute faith in his greatness. When he left the body, he told the people: "Now the stones of my samadhi shall answer you." From that time on, Shirdi has become a magnificent sacred place. There is a constant flux of visitors, who come from near and far. Everything is organized so that a great number of people may sojourn in Shirdi. It has become a great Siddha sanctuary.[7]

Devotees were often anxious to offer Sai money, believing that the *faqīr* would then reward them with special grace. In this regard, Muktananda said:

> All these beings; Sai Baba, Zipruanna, Nityananda Baba were great Siddhas. Food and money heaped up around them, but in their hearts they had no attachment for such things.
>
> Devotees would go visit Sai Baba at Shirdi with their pockets loaded with money, hoping that he would ask for it from them. However, he just asked for small quantities and only from certain people whom he chose.[8]

It was natural that Sai Baba, inviting devotees to lead a religious life *in* the world, placed emphasis upon virtue and the necessity of acting righteously. Indeed, ethics, that is, the principle of *sanātana dharma* (eternal religion) represents the foundation of Indian culture. As Wilhelm Halbfass puts it, *sanātana dharma* characterizes "the 'unshakable, venerable order' and the particular rules and norms of life which have been ever valid and are hallowed by tradition."[9]

Action and its results cannot be avoided: they constitute the motor of life and of *saṃsāric* existence. Karma makes man both the master of his destiny as well as the moulder of his prison. The temporary consequences of an action, as *Muṇḍaka Upanishad* 1.2.12 says, can be only four: (1) production, (2) modification, (3) purification, and (4) acquisition of a limited object.

Sai Baba's aim was to utilize the force of karma as a means of purification (*viśuddhi*) through disinterested and selfless action. Dedicating one's karma to God or the guru, sanctifying it, means that all activities must be performed with concentration, devotion, and detachment.

With reference to ethics, Sai's insistence on adherence to the five basic human values, that is, truth (*satya*), righteousness (*dharma*), peace (*śānti*), love (*prema*), and nonviolence (*ahiṁsā*) cannot be overstressed.

Regarding *satya*, Baba taught: "You should have truth always with you. Then I shall always be with you, wherever you are, and at all times."[10]

To his devotee R. B. Purandhare, Sai gave the following recommendation:

> Baba: "You must always adhere to truth and fulfil all the promises you make. Have faith and patience. Then I will be always with you wherever you are and at all times."
>
> R. B. Purandhare: "Please get that done by me, Baba."
>
> Baba: "Do not battle and quarrel. I feel sick and disgusted, when you quarrel with others."[11]

With reference to *satya* applied to speech, Sai Baba placed accent on three basic moral tenets: (1) Avoid falsehood, (2) Parsimony in speech, (3) Keep one's promises.[12] On the second tenet, Baba said: "If anyone says ten words to you, let us answer with one word, if we reply at all. Do not battle with anyone."[13] Regarding the third, he told a devotee: "Whatever you do, do it thoroughly. Else do not undertake it."[14]

Baba always insisted on the need for *vairāgya* (detachment) and *upekṣā* (equanimity). Only through the cultivation of such virtues can *śānti* be achieved. Baba said to a Rāmadāsī:

> You are reading pothi, Adhyatma Ramayana, unceasingly. Yet your heart is not pure. You repeat Sahasranama and yet your troubles are not gone. You call yourself a Ramadasi. If you are one, you must be indifferent to all objects. You ought not to have Mamata, attachment, but must have Samata, viewing everything with equal eye. You behave like a boy and fight for your book. Books can be had by the ton for money, but not men i.e. friendship.[15]

Scolding one Swami Vijayananda of Madras, Baba said:

> If you are so fond of your mother, why did you assume the garb of a Samnyasin? Kashaya and Mamata (attachment) cannot go together. Go and stay at your quarters. There, you have many thieves, who will carry away everything. Bolt your doors and be on your guard. The inevitable must happen.

> Wealth, kith and kin are all transient, tended with fear. Do Bhagavatha Saptaha thrice with intense meditation. That will quench all vasanas. All illusion will end.[16]

Baba once put H. S. Dikshit's *vairāgya* to test. The latter had offered Sai a trunkful of silver rupees, earned through hard work. Having accepted his gift, Baba proceeded to distribute handfuls of these rupees among the people present at the *masjid*. In a few minutes, not a rupee was left. Though Dikshit witnessed all this, he remained unperturbed.[17]

Sai Baba emphasized the need of developing a compassionate attitude, filled with *prema*: the sharing of food and assistance to the needy were among his most recurrent concerns. On this subject Baba said, "Feed the hungry first. Then feed yourself."[18]

This is also clear in a conversation with Bhimabai, a woman devotee:

> Baba: "Bhimabai, take this leper woman home, and attend to her."
>
> Bhimabai: "Baba, but she is a leper."
>
> Baba: "Never mind. What of that? She is my own sister. Take her home."
>
> Bhimabai then took the leper and attended her for one month, whereafter, the leper died.[19]

On another occasion:

> Baba (to Balaji Patel Nevaskar): "Bala, do not go home; stay and attend this Dagdu Bhav (a Moslem leper)."
>
> Bala obeyed and tended the leper for a month whereafter the leper died.[20]

Nonviolence (*ahiṁsā*) towards men as well as animals was part and parcel of Baba's teachings. For example, when H. V. Sathe was pushing down Nana Vali (who was the aggressor) Baba said to Sathe, "Saheb, do not do so."[21]

In one story, Sai Baba protects a dog from violence:

> In Vaisak 1917, a small dog bitten by a rabid one began to chase big dogs. The villagers, clubs in hand, then chased the small dog. It ran through the streets and finally got into Dvaraka Mayi, stood behind Baba and made him its sanctuary.

> Villagers: "Baba, that dog is mad. Drive it out and we will kill it."
> Baba: "You mad fellows, you get out. You want to persecute and kill a poor creature."
> Thus Baba saved the life of that dog and it proved to not be rabid.[22]

Another story concerning a dog reports:

> One day Mhalsapati hit a bitch full of sores with a stick, and he later went to Baba.
> Baba: "Bhagat, in the village there is a bitch sickly like myself and everyone is hitting her."
> Mhalsapati felt that Baba was rebuking him and so repented for his mistake.[23]

Baba's love of dogs is perhaps linked to the fact that these animals are among the favorites of god Dattatreya. A more obvious reason, however, is that Indian dogs are generally shunned, viewed as unclean and cause of pollution by Hindus and Muslims alike: the eccentric *faqīr* typically identified himself with these most discriminated against creatures.

Concerning *ahiṁsā*, recall this peremptory answer given by Baba to H. S. Dikshit, who had asked if it was all right to kill a poisonous snake: "No. We should never kill it. Because it will never kill us unless it is ordered by God to kill us. If God has so ordered, we cannot avoid it."[24]

Sai Baba heartily recommended *satsaṅga* (the company of the good) as an important aspect of every devotee's *sādhanā*: "Satsanga i.e. moving with the virtuous is good. Dussanga i.e. moving with evil-minded people is evil and must be avoided."[25]

Many sayings are attributed to Baba concerning the six mortal enemies of man, that is, the *ṣaḍripus*: lust, anger, greed, hatred, pride, and envy or jealousy. With reference to lust, Sai once commented tersely, "A person that has not overcome lust cannot see God i.e. attain God-realization."[26]

Sai gave an interesting lesson on lust to N. G. Chandorkar, emphasizing that he should focus upon internal beauty, that is, the God within, rather than be carried away by external appearances:

> Two Moslem ladies wearing veils came to take darshan of Baba at the mosque and N. G. Chandorkar was sitting by him. N. G. Chandorkar tried to get up and go away.

Baba: "You had better remain. If they wish to take darshan, let them come."

The ladies came. The older removed her veil and took darshan. As the younger removed her veil, Nana, smitten with her beauty, thought to himself: "Shall I have one more opportunity to see that angelic face?"; but he said nothing. Baba struck him on the thigh. Then the ladies left.

Baba: "Nana, do you know why I struck you?"

Nana: "How can I hide anything from the omniscience of my guru? But I do not understand how such low thoughts should sway my mind, when I am in your immediate presence."

Baba: "You are a man after all, are you not? The body is full of desires, which spring up as soon as a sense object approaches. But are temples with lovely and well-coloured exteriors scarce in the world? When we go there, is it to admire the exterior or to see the God within? When you are seeing the God in the shrine, do you care for the outside beauty of the building or for that of the image of Paramatma within? Does God remain only in temples? Is he not found in every object in the world as in temples? We are not to bother ourselves about the beauty or ugliness of the exterior, but to concentrate solely on the form taken by God and revealing Him.

"Of course, there is nothing wrong in looking at the exterior, but as one looks at it, he must think how clever and powerful is the God Who produced such a beautiful abode, how He resides therein and how nicely ornamented He is. Nana, if you had directed your thoughts in this way, you would not have had the desire to get one more look at the Moslem beauty's face. Keep this always in mind."[27]

On anger (*krodha*), Baba once said: "If anyone is angry with another, he wounds me to the quick. If any one abuses another, I feel the pain. If any one bravely endures the abuse, I feel highly pleased."[28]

Moreover: "If you avoid rivalries and bickerings, God will protect you. Return not evil for evil. Return good for evil. Other's words cannot harm you."[29]

Sai condemned idleness: "Do not be idle. Work. Utter God's Name, read scriptures."[30]

On one occasion, it is reported that Baba offered a rupee to one Lakshmana, together with a copy of Tilak's *Gītā Rahasya*. By giving this commentary, which emphasizes *karma-yoga* as the most suitable means for liberation, Sai implicitly recognized the validity of Tilak's interpretation.[31]

As to the nature and function of karma, Baba was in perfect accordance with Hindu tradition. He defined the law of karma succinctly: "What you sow, you reap. What you give, you get."[32]

He once assured his *bhaktas* by saying: "If one ever meditates on me, repeats my name, sings my deeds, and is thus transformed into me, one's Karma is destroyed. I stay by his side always."[33]

Baba taught:

> What you can account for, as the result of your present effort, is the result of present Karma. What you cannot trace, is due to your past Karma. Results accrue differently to two persons doing the same acts; that difference may be put down to the difference in their Purva Karma.
>
> Inexplicability of unforeseen and unforeseeable results may disappear in view of Purva Karma. So do not go on exulting or being dejected; nor should you blame others. Recognize the existence of the Moral Law as governing results. Therefore, unswervingly follow the Moral Law. If you do not get the fruits or results of your actions now, they will come in later births. As for the Vasanas, the Moral Law is inexorable and evident. So, by following and observing the Moral Law, you reach your goal—God, the perfection of the Moral Law.[34]

On one occasion, Baba reiterated how rigorous the law of karma is. N. G. Chandorkar and his family had come to visit him. At the time, they were in great sorrow for the passing away of their beloved daughter Minatai, who had died very young,[35] as well as for the previous death of her young husband. They all sat before Baba, glum in sullen silence. Usually, whenever Chandorkar came to visit, Sai would question him and all would be cheerful. Baba broke the ice and told them:

> If you care for child (or son-in-law) and come to me for that, you are mistaken. You need not come to me for these. These are not in my power. These (that is, birth of child and death of relatives) are dependent on Purva Karma. Even Parameshvar, the great God who has created the world, cannot alter these. Do you think He can tell the sun or the moon: Rise some 2 yards farther away from your usual or appointed place? No, He cannot and will not do that. That would produce disorder, chaos.[36]

Sai's words (that giving offspring and averting death were not in his power), were contradicted by other alleged statements of his, such as his comment to one Shinde of Harda: "What! Have you got puffed up? Where was there any male progeny in your destiny? I tore this body (pointing to Sai's body) and gave you one."[37]

In several other cases, such as that of Damodar Rasane, Baba was said to have overcome astrological obstacles for granting offspring.[38]

According to Hindu tradition, though the cosmic law of karma is inescapable, saints may intervene and alter a given situation. This is done not so much by transforming or eliminating the *pūrva-karma* of an individual (which would be neither possible nor desirable) but by modifying or ameliorating some of its effects, without affecting the overall karmic trajectory of the person involved.

If Baba thought it was impossible for him to act without strongly affecting one's karma, he would refuse to intervene in events, simply saying: "The Faqir will not let me do that" or "I can only do what the Faqir orders me to."[39]

On this issue, the following episode is illuminating:

> Sometime after Baba had revived a child who seemed to fall down dead in mid-day heat, a woman came and cried for Udhi to save her son who had been bitten by a cobra. It was not given, and the boy died. She came again and cried.
>
> H. S. Dikshit: "Baba, the woman's cries are heart-rending. For my sake, revive her dead son."
>
> Baba: "Bhav, do not get entangled in this. Bhav, what has happened is for his good. He has entered into a new body. In that body, he will do specially good work, which cannot be accomplished in this body, which is seen here.
>
> "If I draw him back into this body, then the new body he has taken will die and this body will live. I will do this for your sake. But have you considered the consequences? Have you any idea of the responsibility and are you prepared to take it?"
>
> H. S. Dikshit desisted from pressing his request.[40]

Coming back to the *upadeśa* given to Chandorkar and his family, Baba said:

> I do not do any chamatkars (miracles). You have your astrologers. They work 2 or 4 days ahead and give out their predictions, some of which come true.
>
> I look further ahead. What I say happens. My art also is a

> kind of astrology. But you people do not understand this. To you, my words look like chamatkars because you do not know the future. So you regard events as proof of my miracle-working power and you turn your reverence to me. I, in my turn, turn your reverence to God, and see that you are really benefitted.[41]

Sai Baba here distinguishes between prophecy and miracles (*camatkārs*): humbly giving all praise to God alone, Sai denies being able to operate *camatkārs*. He affirms, however, having a clear knowledge of the future, that is, of being clairvoyant.

This interesting utterance of Baba's ("my art also is a kind of astrology"), appears to contradict other sayings of his:

> Saints exist to give devotees temporal and spiritual benefits.[42]

> My business is to give blessings.[43]

> God has agents everywhere; they have vast powers. I have very great powers.[44]

> I can revive the dead boy and bring back his spirit from the new body it has entered, killing it and reviving the corpse. But that is marring the useful work the new body will do.[45]

> I am not confined to these three-and-a-half cubits.[46]

The episode in which Baba practiced *nāmasmaraṇa* in order to save the wife of Nigoj Patil from plague is noteworthy. Being disturbed by the noise of a *māmlātdār* party, he lost his concentration and was unable to effect the miraculous cure:

> Baba (to Mhalsapati, during the night): "I say, come on. Today we shall be on the watch. The rude Rohilla (death from plague) wants to take away the wife of Nigoj Patil. I am praying to Allah to prevent that by Nama Smaran. You better see that no one comes and disturbs me in my Nama Smaran."
>
> Accordingly, Mhalsapati kept awake.... But, unfortunately, in the middle of the night, the Nivas Mamlatdar came. He and his peons..., at midnight,...stating that Darsan and udhi were wanted, made noise. Mhalsapati tried to prevent it, but who could prevent official *hauteur*...? Mhalsapati tried to oblige the peons by getting them down the steps and giving them

> udhi, but the noise disturbed Baba's trance (contemplation).
>
> Baba sat up and hurled foul curses. He told Mhalsapati: "Arre Bhagat, you are a man with family! And don't you know what is taking place at Nigoj? This disturbance has caused a failure in my efforts. That Patil's wife is dead. Let that be. What has happened is for the best."
>
> In his anger, Baba threw away Mhalsapati's cloth, telling him that he should not allow disturbance to Baba's holy work of contemplation and prayer.[47]

It may be noted that Baba's last words to Chandorkar are ambiguous: "I, in my turn, turn your reverence to God, and see that you are really benefitted." In a sense, he appears to contradict his "claim" of being powerless.

Without any pretense at resolving contradictions concerning the sayings of a *pāgal* saint (!), this quotation, for its uniqueness, bears high value. Challenging the devotees' blind faith in his omnipotence, Baba implicitly gave an important lesson: one must constantly test one's own convictions in order to acquire spiritual maturity.

All devotees firmly believed and continue to believe in Sai's vast powers (*siddhis*, and so on). This is the reason why Muktananda placed Sai Baba in the realm of the perfect beings (*siddha-loka*). A dialogue between Muktananda and a devotee reports:

> Devotee: "You talk about superior planes and not about planets. Are these planes physical or spiritual?"
>
> Muktananda: "There are superior planes which are subtler than the physical one. The Pitru-loka, for instance, is the world of the ancestors, Svarga-loka is paradise, and there also exists a realm called Siddha-loka where very evolved beings such as Bhagavan Nityananda, Zipruanna, and Sai Baba of Shirdi dwell."[48]

The goal of *karma-yoga*, however, is not to attain higher planes of existence, be it even paradise (still within the *saṃsāric* realm) but to extinguish the ego, thus attaining freedom (*mukti*). The classic exposition of *naiśkarmya* (disinterested action), leading to the annihilation of ulterior karmic seeds (*bījas*) is found in chapter 5 of the *Bhagavadgītā*. As Krishna, the Blessed One, states in verse 11:

With the body, the thought-organ, the intelligence,
And also with the senses alone,
Disciplined men perform action,
Abandoning attachment, unto self-purification.[49]

Life is thus transmuted into a *mahā-yajña*, a supreme sacrifice. For the *karma-yogin*, action, to use a poignant simile, is like writing on water, that is, leaves no contaminating traces (*vāsanās*). God himself offers the highest example of *naiśkarmya* through the descent of his *avatāras*, incarnating for the welfare of humanity and the reestablishment of *dharma*: Krishna, Rama, and so on set the ideal of altruistic action for all people.

Once established in *naiśkarmya*, a person's activity becomes God's activity, thus transcending the law of karma.

In the absence of any specific references relative to Sai's "path of action" in the light of Sufism, no comparison can be attempted, though of course the idea of 'good works' (*a'māl-i-saliha*), as well as insistence on the fundamental ethical values of love, justice, and so forth are, as in all religions, a common refrain throughout Sufi literature.

With reference to Kabir, he, like most Indians, believed in *saṃsāra*, in the law of karma, and the traditional axiom of *avidyā-karma-saṃsāra*.

As he is reported saying in the *Ādi Granth, gauṛī* 13:

I was in immobile and mobile creatures,
In worms and in moths;
I passed through many births of various kinds.
In this way I occupied many bodies,
But when, O God, I assumed human birth,
I was a Yogī, a Jatī, a penitent, a Brahmacārī,
Sometimes a king, an emperor, and sometimes
A beggar.[50]

I bring this chapter to a close by quoting one of Kabir's poignant warnings:

The soul is inevitably tied by the solid ropes of its karma,
For this reason one keeps coming and going on this earth.
If, though being born with the privilege of human features,
One continues ignoring God's Name,
He will go back to the beginning of the painful cycle,
With repentance as the sole companion.[51]

Notes

1. Osborne, *Incredible Sai Baba,* 92–93.

2. Narasimhaswami, *Charters and Sayings,* 240.

3. Ibid., 241.

4. Ibid.

5. Ibid., 239–40. On Damodar Savalram Rasane of Ahmednagar, see Narasimhaswami, *Life of Sai Baba,* 3:48–57.

6. At Puttaparthi, where Satya Sai Baba was born and has his *āśram,* called Prashanti Nilayam ("Abode of Eternal Peace").

7. Swami Muktananda, *Le secret des Siddhas* (Paris, 1982), 55 (my translation).

8. Swami Muktananda, *En compagnie d'un Siddha* (Paris, 1981), 77 (my translation).

9. W. Halbfass, *India and Europe: An Essay in Understanding* (Albany, N.Y.: SUNY Press, 1988), 344.

10. Narasimhaswami, *Charters and Sayings,* 2.

11. Ibid., 214.

12. Ibid., 126.

13. Ibid., 81.

14. Ibid., 265.

15. Ibid., 80.

16. Ibid., 30n.

17. See ibid., 99.

18. Ibid., 114.

19. Ibid., 231.

20. Ibid.

21. Ibid., 118.

22. Ibid.

23. Ibid., 117–18.

24. Ibid., 118.

25. Ibid., 126.

26. Ibid., 78.

27. Ibid., 78–79.

28. Ibid., 80.

29. Ibid., 115.

30. Ibid., 107.

31. Ibid., 69.

32. Ibid., 125.

33. Ibid., 2.

34. Ibid., 126.

35. It may be remembered how Baba had helped Minatai at the moment of her delivery, by sending her *udī* through a Gosāvī.

36. Narasimhaswami, *Charters and Sayings,* 159.

37. Ibid., 171.

38. Ibid.

39. Osborne, *Incredible Sai Baba,* 40.

40. Narasimhaswami, *Charters and Sayings,* 130–31.

41. Ibid., 159–60.

42. Ibid., 8.

43. Ibid.

44. Ibid., 16.

45. Ibid.

46. Bharucha, *Sai Baba,* 95.

47. Narasimhaswami, *Life of Sai Baba,* 2:13–14.

48. Swami Muktananda, *En compagnie d'un Siddha,* 139 (my translation).

49. *kāyena manasā buddhyā kevalair indriyair api / yoginaḥ karma kurvanti saṅgaṃ tyaktvā 'tmaśuddhaye //* The translation is from Edgerton, *Bhagavadgītā,* 29.

50. Quoted from M. Hedayetullah, *Kabīr,* 219.

51. Mishra, *Mistici Indiani,* 538, *ramainī* 2.

12

Modes of Expression in Sai Baba's Teachings

Baba's typical ways of expressing his *upadeśa* form an important theme, the modes of communication between master and disciple bearing upon the nature and substance of the teaching itself.

In the first place, one must distinguish between nonverbal and verbal communication. Silent *upadeśa* was of utmost importance. It is known that Baba would often remain mute for long periods. Sometimes he passed days in silence or would simply mumble a few words: as always, there was no predetermined rule. It is not an overstatement to say that the silent *darśan* of Sai represented in and of itself the highest form of teaching: an intense communion based on love, devotion, and surrender to God.

On February 20, 1912, G. S. Khaparde wrote in his diary: "We attended the Kakad Arti and the remarkable part of it was that Sayin Saheb left the Chavadi and entered the Masjid without saying a single word except: 'God is the greatest of all.'"[1]

Sai Baba's enigmatic and bizarre personality profoundly affected his devotees, who at the same time loved and feared him. In nonverbal interaction the teacher's glances and smiles are what is most valued. Devotees prayed that Baba might just throw a look at them, so as to be purified and blessed by his sight. Sai Baba's "yogic" glances were apparently powerful. G. S. Khaparde wrote: "He looked exceedingly pleased and cast yogic glances at me. I passed the whole day in a sort of ecstasy."[2]

This silent communication between Baba and his devotees operated not only during *darśan* hours but also while a *bhakta* would be engaged in *pādasevana* (massaging Sai's legs and feet) or when Baba would invite people to partake of a smoke from his earthen pipe (*cilīm*).

Again quoting G. S. Khaparde in two episodes, dated December 20, 1911 and January 12, 1912:

> Today I pressed Baba's legs. The softness of his limbs is wonderful.[3]

> He was very gracious and repeatedly let me have smoke out of his pipe. It solved many of my doubts and I felt delighted.[4]

Sai Baba's presence (beyond his words and speech) often seemed so powerful as to produce a radical transformation in one's life. On the transformative force of *maunam* (silence), a passage taken from a dialogue between Ramana Maharshi and a devotee deserves mention:

> Devotee: "Why doesn't Sri Bhagavan go about preaching the truth to the people at large?"
>
> Bhagavan: "How do you know that I don't? Does preaching consist in mounting a platform and haranguing the people around? Preaching is simple communication of knowledge and can be done in silence too. What do you think of a man listening to a harangue for an hour and going away without being impressed by it so as to change his life? Compare him with another who sits in a holy presence and leaves after some time with his outlook on life totally changed. Which is better: to preach loudly without effect or to sit silently sending forth intuitive force to act on others?"[5]

The teaching of *advaita* through silence is effectively recalled by Shankara in his commentary on *Brahmasūtra* 3.2.17:

> Scriptures tell us how, when questioned by Baskalin, Badhva taught him Brahman through silence alone, as follows: Baskalin asked: "O Badhva, teach me Brahman." But he remained silent (*sa tūṣṇiṃbabhūva*). And, since he was asked a second and a third time in the same way, he answered: "Verily, I have told you; however, you understand not. This Self is in absolute calm" (*brūmaḥ khalu tvaṃ tu na vijānāsi / upaśānto 'yamātmā //*).

Aparokshānubhūti 107 also states: "Let the wise be always identified with that silence which is attainable by the yogin, and from which words and mind together retract, without attaining it."[6]

In Hindu iconography, Shiva Dakshinamurti stands as the paradigm of the sage expounding the truth of *ātman* through silence. Ramana Maharshi declared in the last stanza of his *Five Verses on the Self*: "The One Self, the Sole Reality, alone exists eternally. When even the Ancient Teacher, Dakshinamurti, revealed It through speechless eloquence, who else could convey it by speech?"[7]

Sai Baba must have indeed emanated what Ramana called an "intuitive force." His *maunam* reflected the conviction that only through the silencing of both speech and mind may the voice of God be heard.

Descending from the transcendent plane of ineffability to the ordinary everyday plane of language, it struck people how Baba's speech was frequently obscure and enigmatic.[8] According to his contemporaries, he spoke so on purpose, almost enjoying witnessing the devotees' puzzlement while listening to him. Sai did not use a clearer attitude with newcomers.

On the other hand, Baba never encouraged an atmosphere of secrecy, nor were there any "initiatic hierarchies" among his followers. Baba's teaching was expressed publicly, so that anyone present could hear and learn.

Often, to better elucidate a point, he would send a person to one of the village devotees, who were more accustomed to his symbolic parlance. For instance, Baba advised "Hemadpant" to go and see Shyama (known as Baba's intermediary), or he would direct someone else to go ask "Bhagat" Mhalsapati for clarifications.

But why did Sai Baba make his *upadeśa* deliberately so difficult to understand?

The use of apparently incomprehensible or paradoxical expressions has a long and rich tradition within mystical circles. In this regard, the use of *kōans* as a means of enlightenment (*satori*) in the Rinzai schools of Zen Buddhism immediately comes to mind.

Sai Baba seems to have had a clear awareness of the limitations and overall inadequacy of language in conveying metaphysical truths. The mystical approach is, after all, fundamentally speechless. If the truths of *ātman-Brahman* or of God's omnipresence are clearly beyond language, still, a need is felt to communicate those "discoveries" through the "screened" or veiled medium of conventional signs: the *upadeśa* of sublime silence thus cohabits with the spoken or written word.

Once on this plane, however, Baba usually avoided discursive talk, i.e., argumentation. He never gave speeches, nor did he ever address people as a preacher. His terse sayings and short *kathās* were a kind of "medicine for the spirit." If they bewildered the listener, on the other hand they brought about a "shaking up," an energetic call to "wake up" from religious torpor and the forgetfulness of the Self.[9]

Recall how Sai once defined even Krishna's teachings to Arjuna as mere *avidyā* (ignorance). The fact is that the sacred precept cannot escape the fundamental weakness of language: with its

Sai Baba seated on the stone inside the masjid in his typical posture.

"aporetic" character, it is ambiguous at best and subject to diverse interpretations. The radical dichotomy between what *is* (*ātman*), and what *becomes* (*māyā*), extends to the sphere of language, which is itself *mithyā* (unreal) and thus ultimately delusive.

This notwithstanding, Sai Baba rehabilitated the value and function of language: as a nail drives away another nail, the sacred *upadeśa,* though being *avidyā,* removes *avidyā,* opening to the ontological plane, that is, the awareness of the Self. All sacred literature is, at best, an instrument aiming at its own transcendence and must be abandoned once *mokṣa* has been achieved. Needless to say, such an understanding is Vedāntic through and through.[10]

The problem arises of how to make the best use of language, of how to surpass the shadowy realm of signs through the use of those very signs! Such a radical leap may be achieved only by prompting the subtler intellective organ of man presiding over the faculty of intuitive experience (*anubhava*). Through intuition, which may be understood as a condition of special clarity or "luminosity" of one's *buddhi,* man may connect himself to the divine plane in a supreme, "magical" élan.

According to devotional schools, however, such a leap is possible only through the intervention of divine grace (*kṛpā*). It cannot be the automatic result of an effort, that is, something which may be "naturally" induced. The luminosity of one's *buddhi* allows the *jīva* to open himself/herself to God and His grace, beyond the mediation of language.

The question next arises on how to favor or predispose the disciple's mind and heart towards this immediate, intuitive comprehension. It is at this point that the teaching of Baba, so often paradoxical and symbolic, comes to the fore.

The person confronted with Baba's obscure speech is forced to ponder over it, in an effort to decipher the message. Like an oracle, which does not reveal or conceal but rather hints, Sai most often gave an indication but did not offer the content of that indication.

This approach is clearly manifested in Baba's allegorical stories, in which one is confronted with a high degree of difficulty of interpretation. His numerical symbolism, on the other hand, followed a more or less regular pattern and could be understood more easily, as we have seen in the examples concerning *dakṣiṇā.*

Whenever Sai Baba narrated a story, there were four possible results: (1) the devotee wouldn't be able to make sense of it, though trying his best; (2) the devotee, unable to understand, would be sent by Baba to a villager from whom he would be given an explanation of the story; (3) the devotee would think he had understood, but had no confirmation of this fact; (4) the devotee would understand and Baba would approve of his interpretation.

Of course, more than one meaning could be attributed to each of Baba's stories, thus broadening the range of possible solutions. Though all of the four situations are attested to in the sources, the first one appears particularly interesting from a hermeneutic viewpoint. Not infrequently one or another of Sai's stories would be deemed incomprehensible by the public.

What may be hypothesized is that, in many instances, there was no logical answer: Baba would have purposely narrated nonsensical stories. The more the devotee tried to give coherence to the narrative through innumerable deductions, the more he found it to be an enigma.

Such a failure was perhaps not without positive consequences. I suggest that it encouraged an attitude of humility in the disciple while, at the same time, it favored a perception of the infinite mystery of existence.

In these cases, Sai Baba's prior aim might have been to stimulate the realization of the absolute unnecessity of coming up with any answer whatsoever! As in the *kōan* exercise, the giving up of all rationalistic efforts in search of an answer may open one's mind to an immediate and intuitive comprehension and self-discovery.

Baba's enigmatic sayings fall into four categories: (1) symbolic utterances relative to numbers, (2) allegorical utterances, (3) parables, and (4) paradoxical utterances. The distinction between allegory and parable, though admittedly somewhat artificial, serves the purpose of elucidating subtler nuances of approach.

Numerical symbolism was a constant theme in Sai's *upadeśa*. If a visitor did not catch the typical symbolism of number two (*niṣṭhā-saburī*), of number four (*manas, buddhi, citta,* and *ahaṃkāra*), of number six (the *ṣaḍripus*), and so on, Baba or one of the villagers would normally elucidate it for him.[11] We have no trace in Sai's teachings of letter symbolism, that is, speculations concerning the nature and exoteric meaning of vowels and consonants (a practice that is traditionally attested to within Tantric schools in relation to *maṇḍala* and *yantra* rituals).

Allegorical sayings are not easy to assess. Allegory may be defined as a metaphor prolonged into a continuous narrative, aiming at the presentation of an abstract truth. Every detail contained in it is significant and must be interpreted, since it often bears a hidden meaning.

An example of allegory is offered by this short story of Baba's: "A man had a very beautiful horse. In spite of all his efforts, it would not be yoked. A vidvan [learned person] suggested that it should be taken back to the place whence it came from (its source). That was done. Then it became controllable and useful."[12]

A possible interpretation may be the following: the beautiful horse symbolizes a *jīva* whose *indriyas* (senses) are uncontrolled. The man (perhaps that same *jīva*!) trying to discipline the horse is one who has realized the need of bringing the *indriyas* in check but, not knowing how to do it and where to go, finds himself unable to subdue his "horse." The *vidvān* is the sage, the guru offering the right advice. He suggests that the horse, that is, the *jīva* should be drawn back to his place of origin, that is, *Brahman*, the One, which is his true abode. The moment he is taken back to his source, his senses become pacified, calm. Having been reintegrated in the One, he becomes controllable and useful.

This is just one among the possible readings. Sai Baba's aim was precisely to spur the devotee so that, by giving a referent to each element of the allegory, he might come up with a sensible interpretation.

Baba's use of parables in his teachings is noteworthy. The etymology of the term *parable* implies the idea of collocating each element of a narrative next to another, in order to compare them. What is important is the lesson which may be derived from the story as a whole, where the details serve the function of evidencing the main point. The story, though an imagined one, must bear vivid, realistic tones.

Although the parable is ideally distinguishable from allegory, in Sai's accounts the two forms are generally inextricably fused. Consider one brief and, at first glance, bizarre tale in which the literal sense is clear, but devoid of religious significance:

> A person rode on a camel which passed excreta. I gathered all the excreta and ate them up. My belly was puffed up—swollen. I felt listless. Then the rider took pity upon me. He gave me four grains of Bengal gram (caṇā, Cicer arietinum) and I ate them and drank water. Thus my vehement turbulence ceased. My swollen belly subsided. Now hereafter it will be cured.[13]

It is clear that one must pass beyond the literal to find a possible meaning. Here is my interpretation:

The camel is God's grace. What he passes out is the "manure" of devotion, that is, divine love. The devotee (here Sai, setting himself as example) gathers it and "eats" it avidly—so avidly that he develops a kind of "spiritual indigestion" (the intoxication of love), which leaves him swollen and stupefied. The rider of the camel is the guru. All excesses are negative and must be avoided: he thus cures the indigestion of his pupil, bringing him back to his normal state by administering four grains of chickpeas. These four grains symbolize the four elements that make up one's individuality: the mind (*manas*), the intellect (*buddhi*), the reasoning faculties (*citta*), and the ego principle (*ahaṃkāra*). Once these have returned to their normal state, the ecstatic languor ceases. The pupil may then realize that his ordinary condition is itself perfect, divine.

The focal point of Baba's story would thus be the following: an intense love of God is the royal path leading towards liberation. One needs the guru's guidance, however, in order not to lose oneself in the intoxication of the wine of divine love and to realize the truth that God envelops everything, as the very heart of all beings.

Recall how, in a story previously mentioned, an animal represented God's grace and its nine balls of droppings represented *navāṅgāni* (the nine characteristic forms of *bhakti*).

In some of Baba's abstruse and paradoxical sayings he himself is the subject of the stories, which devotees interpreted as recollections of the master's previous lives:

> I sat near a post and then a great serpent woke up, and was very angry. It used to jump up and also fall from above.[14]

> I once changed the lower part of my body for that of a parrot, and after a year's experience, I discovered that it was a serious loss. I lost a lakh of Rupees.[15]

These sayings are impossible to evaluate. No rational, deductive parameter is applicable. Baba evidently enjoyed occupying the mind of his devotees with enigmas and riddles. He did so not only through speech, but also through his gestures. An entry in the diary of G. S. Khaparde, dated March 8, 1912, reports: "At the midday Arti Sayin Baba approached me and touched my left arm and held his hand waist high just as we do to indicate a young man, with the other hand he made a sign as we do to indicate a man passing away. He made a sign with his eyes. I did not understand the whole and puzzled over it all day."[16]

To the villagers' eyes, Baba's incomprehensible speech extended to the bizarre, extemporaneous "ritual acts" he performed. Here we may recall Sai's use of taking steps in the direction of the four cardinal points while absorbed in contemplation, murmuring sacred words. Baba would also sprinkle water in various directions.

Some devotees hypothesized that he used to perform these magical feats in order to avert evil forces or for reasons of purification. Sai Baba's action, symbolizing globality or fullness, bore a deeper significance: through it, the archaic practice of "ordering space" i.e. of creating harmony (cosmos) out of chaos, was enacted.

The cardinal points (*caturdiśa*), are a symbolic structure meant to order and encompass the whole of space. Starting with the north (*uttara*), considered the highest point, the direction of *brāhmaṇs*, and moving clockwise, that is, keeping *pradakṣiṇā*, we meet with the east (*pūrva*), the south (*dakṣiṇā*), and the west (*paścimā*), which pertain to *kṣatriyas, vaiśyas,* and *śūdras,* respectively. The West, being the realm of obscurity, is viewed as inauspicious.

Baba's steps were probably taken following this movement, that is, the course of the sun. The execution of such a ritual act is considered meritorious and may function as a magic, protective circle, delimiting a consecrated area, as in the case of *maṇḍalas*.

Pradakṣiṇā ritual is related to the archaic solar figure of Vishnu and his three steps, through which, according to myth, he encompassed the whole universe (earth, atmosphere, and sky).[17] Tantric treatises furnish detailed instructions for the correct execution of *pradakṣiṇā*. For instance, the *Liṅgārcanacandrikā* specifies the number of circumambulations to be done in the worship of each deity: one for Candi, one and a half for Shiva, three for Ganesha, four for Hari, seven for Surya, and so on.[18] *Pradakṣiṇā* is usually done an odd number of times, since odd numbers are generally viewed as more auspicious than even ones.[19] As Mircea Eliade observed, ritual circumambulation, as the entrance into a *maṇḍala* (*imago mundi*), indicates a march toward the center (*axis mundi*).[20]

If, on the other hand, someone walks counterclockwise, an act technically known as *prasavya*, it is believed that the result will be ominous: malediction and even death may befall the person.

Among Baba's bizarre acts, it is appropriate to recall two other rites by which the saint intended to protect his devotees: the grinding of wheat and the distribution of it along the village boundaries, to prevent the goddess of cholera or plague from entering the village, and the rubbing of coins while reciting the names of his *bhaktas*, apparently averting evil influences from them.

The paradoxicality of his sayings, gestures, and ritual acts increased in connection with Baba's frequent and unpredictable bad moods and rages. G. S. Khaparde, on February 18, 1912, wrote in his diary: "Madhavrao Deshpande woke me up in the morning and after prayer attended the Kakad Arti. Sayin Saheb took it very cooly, and hard words said as usual after it were of a very mild character.... The midday Arti passed off as usual except that towards the end of it Sayin Baba got a bit impatient and told the people to clear out fast."[21]

Khaparde appeared surprised when noticing that Sai Baba was in a good mood. On March 3, 1912, he noted: "I attended the Kakad Arti and Sayin Baba looked pleased and passed into the Masjid without any hard words. Abdulla, in trying to remove a hanging lamp, by accident let it drop on the ground and get shattered. I thought this might anger Sayin Baba but it did not. He took no notice of it."[22]

Moreover: "At Baba's Arati G. G. Narke found him in a rage without any apparent cause and wondered if Baba was mad. This was a passing thought. Later in the evening, when G. G. Narke massaged Baba's feet, Baba told him: 'I am not mad.'"[23]

It is well known that Sufi mystics made a wide use of symbolisms, allegories, and paradoxes in their teachings. Illustrious examples of intentional cryptic uses of language, are represented by the cases of Shibli of Baghdad (861–945), and the Iraqi Niffari (d. 865).[24]

The historical reason for this cryptic orientation can be found in what was, at the time, the ever-present danger of Sufis being faced with being accused of heresy by custodians of Islamic orthodoxy. In the course of time, the inclination towards enigmatic and eccentric behavior was not so much motivated by fear of heresy accusations but took the form of tradition, which the single mystic or teacher chose to either minimize or emphasize.

The symbolism of letters is certainly among the most characteristic forms of Sufi mysticism, whereas speculations on numbers are less frequent. The paradoxicality and meaninglessness of signs is well conveyed in this Sufi story, which has a kind of "Zen flavor":

> A man who had spent many years trying to puzzle out meanings, went to see a Sufi and told him about his search.
>
> The Sufi said:
>
> "Go away and ponder this—IHMN."
>
> The man went away. When he came back, the Sufi was dead. "Now I shall never know the Truth!" moaned the puzzler.
>
> At that moment the Sufi's chief disciple appeared.
>
> "If," he said, "You are worrying about the secret meaning of IHMN, I will tell you. It is the initials of the Persian phrase 'In huruf maani nadarand'—'These letters have no meaning.'"
>
> "But why should I have been given such a task?" cried the puzzled man.

> "Because, when a donkey comes to you, you give him cabbages. That is his nutrition, no matter what he calls it. Donkeys probably think that they are doing something far more significant than eating cabbages."[25]

In Sai Baba's stories the preeminence of a Hindu orientation versus a Sufi one seems undeniable: his references to his previous lives and especially his symbolism, both numerical as well as conceptual, are an important evidence of this.

Interestingly, Muktananda viewed Sai Baba's oddities as a typical feature of the perfect *siddha*: "The two great saints of whom you must have seen the pictures in our meditation hall, Sai Baba of Shirdi and Zipruanna, were also great renunciants and very powerful ones. Even nowadays, people regard the temples where they are buried as places of great holiness. Pilgrims come from far away just to touch the stones of those temples. All these saints were naked or wore rags and behaved in very strange ways."[26]

There are affinities between Sai Baba's stories and Kabir's poetic style, filled with cryptic, allusive imagery. A particularly intriguing aspect of Kabīrian literature is represented by the so-called *ulṭabāṁsī* poems, that is, poems with reversed language, patterned on the allusive speech (*sandhā-bhāṣā*) of the Nātha masters and the Tantric Sahajiyā schools.[27] As M. Eliade explains:

> The sandhā-bhāṣā...seeks to conceal the doctrine from the noninitiate, but chiefly to project the yogin into the "paradoxical situation" indispensable to his training. The semantic polyvalence of words finally substitutes ambiguity for the usual system of reference inherent in ordinary language. This destruction of language contributes, in its way, toward "breaking" the profane universe and replacing it by a universe of convertible and integrable planes. In general, symbolism brings about a universal "porousness," "opening" beings and things to transobjective meanings.[28]

The charm of Kabir's enigmatic poems, besides the beauty and vividness of their imagery, lies in their "urgency." From the "resonance" of the poetry, the listener perceives Kabir's burning appeal to conversion, even though the meaning of each word of the lyric often eludes comprehension. Such semantic ambiguity constitutes one of the major attractions of Kabir's poetry.[29]

A few examples of Kabir's allusive and paradoxical speech:

> In the sky there is an upside down well, and near it is a nice young lady who draws from it its magic water. Fortunate is he who knows how to reach that well and avidly gulps down its water![30]

> I skinned the fish, I washed it, and placed it on a high niche. Among so many fish, one alone has been able to see the sun! The others continue to swim in the slimy water of the pool.[31]

> I set fire to my house and abandoned it, taking only a stick with me. May only he who is ready to burn his house follow me![32]

> I've opened the shop of love, where to weigh my merchandise I use heads of decapitated people. Whoever wants the love which I sell, must come up with the price I request![33]

Finally, here is how Kabir describes the sad situation of man in prey of illusion:

> In this age of darkness, a thirsty man chases a mirage, coming close to it but without ever reaching it, till he falls to the ground, dying of thirst.
>
> The fountain was close, its crystalline waters gurgled, but the fool dragged himself behind a fairy,[34] and was not able to see his salvation.[35]

Notes

1. See the monthly publication *Shri Sai Leela,* Jan. 1986, 7.

2. Bharadwaja, *Sai Baba,* 56. Khaparde annotated this on January 7, 1912.

3. Ibid., 61.

4. Ibid., 58.

5. Osborne, *Teachings of Ramana Maharshi,* 90.

6. *yasmādvāco nivartante aprāpya manasā saha / yanmaunaṃ yogibhirgamyaṃ tadbhavet sarvadā budhaḥ //*

7. A. Osborne, *The Collected Works of Ramana Maharshi* (London: Rider, 1959), 97.

8. V. B. Kher suggests that Sai began speaking symbolically and in parables only from 1910 onwards, as the number of his visitors grew. See Kamath and Kher, *Sai Baba,* 9.

9. On the crucial role of folk narrative in Indian culture, with particular reference to Maharashtra, see the study of Kirin Narayan, *Storytellers, Saints, and Scoundrels: Folk Narrative in Hindu Religious Teaching* (Philadelphia: University of Pennsylvania Press), 1989.

10. Cf. Shankara's commentary *ad Bṛhadāraṇyaka Upanishad* 5.1.

11. For an overview of numerical symbolism within the Indian context, see Abbott, *Keys of Power,* 284–309.

12. Narasimhaswami, *Charters and Sayings,* 276.

13. Ibid.

14. Ibid.

15. Ibid., 275.

16. *Shri Sai Leela,* Feb. 1986, 10–11.

17. See *Rig Veda* 8.12.27. For an examination of Vishnu's three strides, see Jan Gonda, *Viṣṇuism and Śivaism,* 7f.

18. See A. Bharati, *The Tantric Tradition* (New York, 1975), 93.

19. See Abbott, *Keys of Power,* 309.

20. See Mircea Eliade, *Yoga: Immortality and Freedom* (Princeton: Princeton University Press, 1973), 224f.

21. *Shri Sai Leela,* Jan. 1986, 6.

22. *Shri Sai Leela,* Feb. 1986, 9.

23. Narasimhaswami, *Charters and Sayings,* 183.

24. On these two Sufi mystics, see Schimmel, *Mystical Dimensions of Islam,* 77–82.

25. Idries Shah, *Wisdom of the Idiots,* 158.

26. Swami Muktananda, *En compagnie d'un Siddha,* 155 (my translation).

27. See Vaudeville, *Kabīr,* 143f.

28. Eliade, *Yoga,* 250–51.

29. A fine presentation of Kabir's paradoxical *ulṭabāṁsī* language may be found in Linda Hess, *The Bījak of Kabīr,* trans. Linda Hess and

Shukdev Singh (San Francisco: North Point Press, 1983), appendix A, "Upside-Down Language," 135–61.

30. Mishra, *Mistici Indiani*, 247–48, *sākhī* 45.

31. Ibid., 262–63, *sākhī* 23.

32. Ibid., 304, *sākhī* 13.

33. Ibid., 307, *sākhī* 22.

34. *Māyā*.

35. Mishra, *Mistici Indiani*, 552, *ramainī* 4.

13

Sai Baba's Universalism

Perhaps the most significant element in Baba's *upadeśa* is his constant call to interreligious understanding and tolerance. Sai's approach, tending to maximize the aspects that unite religions (mysticism, ethics) and minimize those which divide them (doctrines, rituals), had its roots in the Hindu-Muslim syncretistic attitudes prevalent in the Deccan area. Typical of modern neo-Vedānta Hinduism, it makes syncretism and tolerance one of its most distinctive features. Truly, in the immense ocean of Indian spirituality, new religious influences are never totally rejected but are rather accepted and amalgamated under different guises.[1]

In this regard, it is noteworthy that N. Kasturi recognized the most important teaching of Sai Baba to be the message of unity or oneness (*ekatva*):

> Question: "What about the teaching? What do you think was the most important teaching which Shirdi Baba gave in his times, and which Satya Sai Baba nowadays carries on?"
>
> Kasturi: "It was the concept of unity. The unity of all creation."
>
> Q.: "Was this the most important?"
>
> Kasturi: "Yes. And here it is the same. Unity is divinity."

As we have seen, Baba during his lifetime succeeded in creating an atmosphere of reciprocal harmony between the Hindu and Muslim communities in Shirdi. He repeatedly admonished: "All Gods are one. There is no difference between a Hindu and a Mohammadan. Mosque and temple are the same."[2]

The fundamental idea orienting Baba's teaching, rooted in Hindu universalism, was that all religions are but paths (*mārgas*) leading to the same final goal, which different traditions call by different names: *mokṣa*, liberation, union with God, and so on. For this reason, Sai Baba disapproved of religious conversions, which he viewed as a sign of ignorance. As G. S. Khaparde remarked in 1933: "Sai Maharaj always impressed me as one who believed all religions to be true and helpful to those born into them, for their further evolution. So he insisted on each following his own ritual, without interfering with that of another."[3]

In the final experience of the ego's extinction or the absorption in the Self, all separations naturally disappear: names and forms, rituals and dogmas (as all superimposed, ideological structures), fade away.

Though the Hindus and Muslims probably made up around 98 percent of Baba's following (the Hindus figuring as the absolute majority), Sai's universalism ideally included all faiths. The few meetings which Baba had with Parsi and Christian visitors highlighted his equanimity towards all faiths.

Regarding the Parsis, the *Charters and Sayings* reports:

> Peston Jamas and his brother-in-law went in about 1915 to Shirdi, to see "Sai Maharaj." There at the Dikshit Vada, there was much crowding and rich people alone were accomodated upstairs and these two Parsis were left downstairs.
>
> "What sort of justice is here in this Darbar! Big people enjoying comforts above and poor people left downstairs to suffer inconvenience," thought these Parsis. They then went to Baba, at the Mosque.
>
> Baba (to someone present) said: "Take these people up."
>
> And thus they were given accommodation upstairs.[4]

Parsi devotees grew in number in the years following Sai Baba's death. During my visit to Shirdi in 1985 I met with several of them and interviewed one Homi Baba, a bizarre Parsi ascetic dressed in a white *kafnī* and wearing a band around his head (clearly imitating Sai's attire). In the village, he figures as a spiritual leader of sorts for the Parsi devotees of Sai Baba.

Regarding Baba's encounter with Christians or his opinion on the Christian religion, two passages have come down:

> When a Christian, Chakra Narayan by name, was appointed Police Fouzdar[5] at Kopergaon, a devotee said to Baba: "We have got a Christian for the Fouzdar."
>
> Baba: "What of that? He is my brother."[6]

Narasimhaswami observes that this Chakra Narayan: "Was perhaps the only one or one of the few Protestant Christians who had some appreciation for Baba.... He conceived a great regard for Baba because he found that Baba was not moved by kamini or kanchana (woman or wealth)."[7]

> Baba to H. S. Dikshit (who had been recently speaking ill of Christ and Christianity at his own lodgings): "Get away. Do not massage me."
>
> Again, when H. S. Dikshit repented and approached, Baba raised no objection to his massage.[8]

Within a theistic discourse, Sai Baba insisted on the adherence to universal ethical principles (love, righteousness, peace, truth, nonviolence), the practice of spiritual exercises valid for all (prayer, meditation, repetition of God's name, and so forth), and the faith in a supreme divine principle (called *Brahman*, Vishnu, or Shiva by the Hindus and Allah by the Muslims).[9]

In his teachings he never insisted on the adherence to particular ritual practices or dogmas or on the performance of any exterior ceremony. As we have seen, he also avoided theological speculations. Baba probably viewed all these as unnecessary and perhaps even useless and dangerous (see the "evils" of intellectualism, dogmatism, ritualism, and so forth).

For the *faqīr*, it wasn't so important what his devotees believed but rather how they lived. Religion, Baba implicitly affirmed, is genuine only insofar as it is a concrete, practical experience daily affecting one's existence. Above all, religion is orthopraxy.

The authority as well as the swiftness with which Sai Baba tackled this issue was due to the fact that he was a mystic, that is, what he said was the result of his own intuitive experience: having followed the path and having had experience of the goal, he disliked being entangled in abstract speculations.

The realization of the oneness of Being (*ekatva, waḥdat al-wujūd*) was impressed in his own flesh, through the example of his life, and represented an inextricable blend of Hindu and Sufi features.

An eclectic form of Sufism certainly contributed to molding Sai Baba's universalistic vision.

As early as the sixteenth century, two important Sufi literary works such as the *Bahr al-hayat* (Sea of Life) and the *Rushd-nama* of Abd al-Quddus (c. 1456–1537), a Chishtiyya saint, showed the influence of Nāthapanthī yogic circles upon Sufism.

The syncretistic mysticism of the Moghul Prince Muhammad Dārā Shikōh (1615–59) and of some of the religious circles immediately preceding and following his times offer the most vivid examples of Indo-Muslim universalism.

The great-grandson of Emperor Akbar (1542–1605), Dārā Shikōh was profoundly influenced by Sufis of the Qadiriyya school (Mir Muhammad, Mulla Shah Badakshi) as well as by Hindu mystics in the line of Kabir, such as Jagannath Mishra and especially Baba Lal Das.

In 1656 Prince Dārā Shikōh commissioned the Persian translation of the *Yogavasishtha* and he himself translated the *Bhagavadgītā* (1653–55) and fifty-two Upanishads, these latter published under the Persian title of *Sirr-ī Akbar* (The Great Secret).

In the introduction to the *Sirr-ī Akbar*, Dārā told of his religious search, begun in 1641. He expressed the idea that, since the Koran itself states that each race has its own prophet, the Indians must have theirs, as well as their own sacred books (Vedas and Upanishads). In his opinion, the Upanishads manifest that divine secret (*sirr*) which the Koran left unexplained. He actually viewed the Upanishads as being of the greatest antiquity and placed them as the ultimate scriptural source of monotheism (*tawḥīd*), which he deliberately equated with nondualism.

Dārā expressed the equation monotheism = monism more fully in his short treatise *Majma' al-Bahrayn* (The Mingling of the Oceans) of 1657. Here, Dārā articulated his thought through the homologization of different terms and divine figures taken from Hindu and Muslim traditions. Thus, the term *rūḥ* is said to be equivalent to the term *ātman*, *Ishrafil* to *Mahādeva*, *Mikail* to *Vishnu*, and so forth. Again and again Dārā defended the legitimacy of Indian ideas and theories (cosmic cycles, final release, and so on) by referring to allegorically interpreted passages taken from the Koran.[10]

Though he was condemned to death as a heretic by a committee of theologians (*ulamā*) organized by his brother and successor Aurangzeb, Dārā Shikōh remained, or thought he remained, true to his Muslim identity. His form of syncretism represented perhaps a borderline case, one that was not followed by most other Sufis.[11]

The ascendancy of Sufi circles upon Sai Baba, influenced by Marathi *advaita-bhakti* traditions, as well as by currents of Deccani *bhakti*-poets (both Hindu and Muslim), appears only natural. Syncretistic encounters, at a popular level, were indeed the most fertile ground for the formation of personalities such as that of Sai Baba.

On the other hand, it should be noted that "intellectual" attempts at religious exchange among the two traditions, such as those made by Akbar, Dārā Shikōh, and so forth, as well as the various forms of popular syncretism, were always regarded with suspicion and often condemned as heretical by Islamic orthodoxy.[12]

The poems of Kabir, who, together with Guru Nanak, was perhaps the most illustrious upholder of a form of "monotheistic *bhakti*," are pervaded by a universalistic awareness: in his vision, Rama is the same as Rahīm, Allah the same as Shiva. Thus Kabir sang in one of his *padas*:

> Do not dissociate Hari from Allah, if you don't want the emptiness of your faith to drag you towards the saddest epilogue.
>
> It is the same God Who created both Hell and Paradise, Who pervades us all with His Glory.
>
> Thus, give up all rivalry of creed and unite together to sing His Virtues in chorus.
>
> Warns Kabir: "If you wish to save yourself from the torrent of mundane afflictions, take refuge at His Divine Feet!"[13]

These same words could well have been spoken by Sai Baba. Like Kabir, Sai longed for the return to the One having a thousand names. He implicitly recognized the equality of all men and rejected the divisive notion of a "chosen religion," as if God could be the monopoly of a restricted circle, group, or race.

In this regard, consider one of Kabir's many admonishments: "I am the faqīr who has found his truth: One God only created Hindus and Muslims alike, and they, poor ignorants, fight each other in His Name!"[14]

Like Kabir, Sai Baba did not intend to found a new religion. Both saints wished to leave their disciples a clear religious message, to insist, as Giuseppe Tucci observed, "on those elements which religions have in common, on that indefinable experience which under different names enlivens all faiths, rather than to give importance to rituals, dogmas, and ceremonies."[15]

Cried Kabir:

> O Mullāh, why do you call your Allāh from the minaret? Can't you see that His presence fills the skies? He is certainly not deaf, nor mute, and His answer to your call is in all things. I sang the glory of Hari in silence, thus forgetting passions and desires.
>
> A liar is the Mullāh, if he dares contradict me. I have seen with my own eyes that Rāma and Allāh are but two names of the same God![16]

In conclusion, the close spiritual bond connecting Sai Baba to Kabir appears evident: on all major issues concerning their teachings there is an overall identity of views.

It is significant that Satya Sai Baba has extended Shirdi Baba's universalism to comprehend the five main religions present on Indian soil (Hinduism, Islam, Buddhism, Christianity, and Zoroastrianism). In his *Sarvadharma* emblem (a lotus flower whose five petals contain the symbols of the faiths), all the religions are viewed as different paths leading to the same destination, symbolized by the center of the lotus, that is, the God-head or the Absolute.

In the historico-religious continuity and expansion of this universalistic impulse we may recognize one of the most distinguishing features of the Sai Baba movement, in harmony with the modern neo-Vedāntic trend.

Notes

1. For a historical presentation and insightful critique of the notion of Hindu tolerance, see Halbfass, *India and Europe,* chap. 22 ("'Inclusivism' and 'Tolerance' in the Encounter Between India and the West"), 403–18.

2. Narasimhaswami, *Charters and Sayings,* 262.

3. From G. S. Khaparde's introduction to the first edition of M. V. Pradhan's book *Shri Sai Baba of Shirdi,* 7.

4. Narasimhaswami, *Charters and Sayings,* 261.

5. Subinspector.

6. Narasimhaswami, *Charters and Sayings,* 261.

7. Narasimhaswami, *Life of Sai Baba,* 3:204.

8. Narasimhaswami, *Charters and Sayings,* 262.

9. Of course, within a nontheistic or transtheistic religious dimension, such as that of Theravāda Buddhism, "faith in a supreme, divine principle" would be viewed as an erroneous or, at least, problematic notion! On this issue, see Ninian Smart, "Numen, Nirvāṇa, and the Definition of Religion," in *Concept and Empathy: Essays in the Study of Religion,* ed. Donald Weibe (New York: New York University Press, 1986), 40–48.

10. For an excellent study of the *Majma' al-Bahrayn,* see Daryush Shayegan, *Les relations de l'Hindouisme et du Soufisme d'après le Majma' al-Bahrayn de Dārā Shokūh* (Paris: Editions de la Différence, 1979).

11. On Dārā Shikōh, cf. the work of Bikrama Jit Hasrat, *Dārā Shikūh.* For an overview of Dārā's writings, see A. Schimmel, *Islamic Literatures of India* (Wiesbaden: Otto Harrassowitz, 1973), 39f.

12. For an overview of the Hindu-Muslim exchange, see Wilhelm Halbfass, *India and Europe,* chap. 2 ("Islamic Encounters with Indian Philosophy"), 24–35.

13. Mishra, *Mistici Indiani,* 451, *pada* 258.

14. Ibid., 353, *pada* 58.

15. Quoted in Stefano Piano, *Guru Nānak e il Sikhismo* (Fossano: Editrice Esperienze, 1971), 104 (my translation).

16. Mishra, *Mistici Indiani,* 354, *pada* 60.

Epilogue

This presentation of Sai Baba's life and teachings has aimed at offering a general introduction to the public of the saint's charismatic figure, highlighting the multiple influences which molded his personality.

The popularity of Shirdi Sai Baba in present-day India is quite extraordinary. All over the Subcontinent, more than 150 temples (*mandirs*) are consecrated to his cult. They are scattered throughout the country: from Delhi to Madras, from Gujarat to Bengal. Of course, most of these temples are found in Maharashtra, but many are also located in Andhra Pradesh and Tamil Nadu.

The devotees of our *faqīr* are estimated to be in the millions in Maharashtra alone. The village of Shirdi has become one of the most renowned pilgrimage places in the State, and tens of thousands of pilgrims crowd it during the major Hindu religious festivals (*Rāmanavamī, Dasserā, Gurupūrṇimā, mahāsamādhi* day, etc.).

Even outside India, temples have been erected in his name by Indian emigrants. We know of the existence of Sai *mandirs* in Kathmandu, Nepal, in Thimphu, Bhutan, in Accra, Ghana, and even in London.

The Sai Baba organization, that is, the Sansthan, is efficient and well organized, taking charge of the upkeep of Shirdi's "sacred places," ritual practices, publications, evangelization, and administration of funds and donations. Its two main centers are located in Shirdi and Bombay.

One must also keep in mind the activities that single groups of devotees carry on; activities that are, on one hand, devotional (*bhajan* groups, readings, etc.), and on the other hand, dedicated to service, such as assistance to the poor, the sick, and so on. One of these current groups, headed by the popular guru Narayana Baba, has organized periodic trips to Europe and the United States to make known the life, teachings, and mission of Sai Baba. On their 1981 tour, I had the opportunity of meeting with Narayana Baba and his group in Venice, Italy.

The spread of Sai Baba's fame during his lifetime and even more so after his death, is principally due to his reputation as a miracle worker. The monthly *Shri Sai Leela,* official organ of the Shirdi Sansthan, publishes (in addition to Baba's stories and teachings) testimony of people claiming to have been cured or variously blessed through their contact with the Shirdi saint. Indeed, Sai Baba's "eleven assurances," always quoted in devotional booklets, emphasize the saint's ever-present, protective and miraculous power. They are:

1. Whoever puts his feet on Shirdi soil, his sufferings will come to an end.
2. The wretched and miserable will rise to joy and happiness, as soon as they climb the steps of my mosque.
3. I shall be ever active and vigorous even after leaving this earthly body.
4. My tomb shall bless and speak to the needs of my devotees.
5. I shall be active and vigorous even from the tomb.
6. My mortal remains will speak from the tomb.
7. I am ever living, to help and guide all who come to me, who surrender to me and who seek refuge in me.
8. If you look to me, I look to you.
9. If you cast your burden on me, I shall surely bear it.
10. If you seek my advice and help, it shall be given to you at once.
11. There shall be no want in the house of my devotee.[1]

Within Maharashtra, Sai Baba images may be found a bit everywhere: in stores, taxis, temples, private *pūjā*-rooms, adorning walls, etc. Recently, a three-hour Hindi movie on the life and miracles of the saint (*Shirdi ke Sai Baba*) was produced in Bombay. The actors, all Sai *bhaktas,* are said to have refused any payment, performing their parts in a spirit of pure devotion.

These few sparse comments may suffice to account for Sai Baba's present renown. If, moreover, one relates Shirdi Baba to other gurus variously connected with him, such as Upasani Maharaj, Godavari Mataji, Meher Baba, and Satya Sai Baba, the significance of this Sai Baba movement increases remarkably.

The worldwide fame of the living saint Satya Sai Baba of Puttaparthi is, in itself, an amazing religious phenomenon: the total number of his devotees, in constant expansion, is currently estimated to be as high as ten million.[2]

In conclusion, further studies of the religious and sociological dimensions of the Sai Baba movement appear to be a necessary undertaking. From a standpoint of historico-religious evolution, the movement is particularly interesting for its eclectic origins, its gradual development, and its growing doctrinal and charismatic aspects. My own research has been intended as an introductory contribution to the study of this fascinating phenomenon of neo-Hinduism.

Notes

1. See the back-cover of Narasimhaswami's *Life of Sai Baba,* vol. 1.
2. See A. Bharati, *Religious Revival in Modern Times,* 348.

Appendix 1
Gods, Goddesses, Demons, and Religious Festivals

Akkabai	"The elder-sister lady." A female deity of disease particularly attested to in northern India.
Apasmarapurusha	The demon-dwarf of chaos and forgetfulness; it lies defeated under Shiva Nataraja's foot.
Ashvins	Two Vedic deities, twin sons of the sun or the sky, ever young and handsome.
Atri and Anasuya	The parents of Dattatreya.
Banai, Banabai	The *dhangar* wife of Khandoba.
Bhavani	One of the four major Maharashtrian goddesses.
Biroba	A *dhangar* Śaiva god, at times called brother to Vithoba.
Brahmā	The creator god. Together with Shiva and Vishnu, Brahmā constitutes the Hindu triad. To be distinguished from *Brahman* (the Absolute) and the *brāhmaṇ* caste.
Caturmāsya	The four months of rainy season, a time of fasting and other special religious observances. Not an auspicious time for marriages and other such ceremonies.

Dakshinamurti	A name of Shiva, facing the southern direction from which death comes.
Daśaharā/Dasserā	See Vijayā Daśamī.
Dattatreya	Lord of ascetics. In Maharashtra he is popular as an incarnation of the Hindu triad, Brahmā, Vishnu, and Shiva.
Deva/Devatā	God.
Devī	Goddess. The manifestation of *śakti,* divine potency and energy.
Dīpāvālī/Divālī	A major festival involving the worship of Lakshmi (goddess of wealth), the celebration of Vishnu's victories, and the expression of brotherly and sisterly affection.
Durdevatās	A class of evil deities.
Durga	"The unattainable one." An all-India terrible goddess, she is the wife of Shiva and is worshipped throughout India.
Ekādaśī	Eleventh day of each half-month, sacred to Vaiṣṇavas.
Ganesha/Ganapati	"Lord of the gaṇas." The elephant-headed god who is beloved throughout Maharashtra.
Ganesha Caturthī	The festival celebrating the birthday of Ganesha on the fourth day of the lunar bright half of Bhādrapada (August–September).
Gauri	A goddess of the harvest and protector of women. A name for Parvati before her marriage with Shiva.
Gopala, Govinda	Names of Krishna.
Gurupūrṇimā	This festival falls on the full moon day in the month of Āṣāḍh (July–August). On this day, sacred to the memory of the great sage Vyasa, Hindus honor and worship their teachers.
Hanuman	Also known as Maruti. The monkey devotee of Rama.

Hari	A name of Vishnu-Krishna.
Indra	A Vedic deity. The god of the firmament, the personified atmosphere. King of the gods.
Ishvara	A general name for god, though mostly attributed to Shiva. Often used in combination, as in Parameshvara (Supreme God).
Iṣṭadevatā	A god chosen as his/her special deity by an individual.
Janardana	A name of Vishnu. Also the name of Eknath's guru.
Janmāṣṭamī	Also known as *Gokulāṣṭamī*. This is the festival celebrating Krishna's birth. It falls on the eighth lunar day in the dark fortnight of the month of Bhādrapada (August–September) in northern India, and of Śrāvaṇa (July–August) in the South and Bombay.
Kal Bhairav	A terrible form of Shiva.
Kali	"The dark or black one." A terrible form of Shiva's wife.
Keshava	"Having much hair" or "Having fine hair." A name of Vishnu or Krishna.
Khandoba	A popular Maharashtrian god, *avatāra* of Shiva, whose home is the temple of Jejuri.
Krishna	The eighth and principal *avatāra* of Vishnu. A popular all-India god.
Lakshmi	The goddess of wealth and prosperity. Consort of Vishnu. See also Mahalakshmi.
Lakshmi-Narayana	The divine couple, Vishnu and his consort.
Mahadeva	"Great god." A name for Shiva.
Mahalakshmi	One of the four great goddesses of Maharashtra. Her home is the temple in Kolhapur.
Mahāshivarātri	The "great night of Shiva," during which worship of the *liṅga* with *bel* leaves, and recitation of Shiva's thousand names is carried on. The festival is celebrated on the

	fourteenth night of the new moon of the month of Māgha (January–February).
Makara Saṃkrānti	This festival marks the return of the sun to the northern hemisphere. It usually falls on the last day of the month of Pauṣa (December–January).
Mani and Malla	Two demons defeated by Khandoba.
Mari/Mariai/ Mariamma	A village goddess, formerly in the care of the untouchable *mahār* caste. Goddess of epidemic diseases (especially cholera).
Martanda	Also known as Martand Bhairav. Another name for Shiva Khandoba.
Maruti	The usual Marathi name for Hanuman. Every village has a temple dedicated to him.
Matsya	The fish incarnation of Vishnu.
Mhalsa	The first wife of the god Khandoba, from the Liṅgāyat community.
Mhaskoba	A Śaiva deity represented by a rock, with a major shrine at Vir, near Jejuri. Probably evolved from Mhasoba.
Mhasoba	The buffalo demon as a god. The deity of boundaries, represented by a stone covered with red.
Mrityuñjaya	"The victorious over death." An epithet often attributed to Shiva.
Muharram	The first ten days of the first month of the Muslim year; associated with the memory of the martyred Husain, the Prophet's grandson.
Murlidhar	"The bearer of the flute"; a name of Krishna.
Nāgapañcamī	A festival in which *nāgas* (serpents) are worshipped. Said to celebrate the return of Krishna from his triumph over the snake Kaliya.
Narasimha	The man-lion. Fourth incarnation of Vishnu who assumed this form to deliver the world from the tyranny of Hiranyakashipu, a

	demon who, by the favor of Brahmā, had become invulnerable.
Narayana	A name for Vishnu.
Nataraja	"King of dance"; a name of Shiva.
Navnāth	The nine legendary Nātha ascetics, worshipped as a group as well as under their individual names.
Paramātman	The soul encompassing all souls, a name for the abstract God.
Parashuram	Rama with the axe (*paraśu*). The *brāhmaṇ avatāra* of Vishnu.
Parvati	"The mountaineer." Consort of Shiva.
Prajapati	"Lord of creatures," a progenitor, creator. In the Vedas the term is applied to Indra, Savitri, Soma, Hiranyagarbha, and other deities.
Radha	The lover of Krishna.
Rama	The hero of the *Rāmāyaṇa,* seventh *avatāra* of Vishnu.
Rāmanavamī	The festival commmemorating Rama's birth, on the ninth lunar day in the light half of the month of Caitra (March–April).
Ravana	The demon king of Laṅkā whom Rama opposes in the great *Rāmāyaṇa* epic.
Sadashiva	"The always kind or auspicious one." A name of Shiva.
Saptashriṅgī Devī	One of Maharashtra's four major goddesses. Seven hills or horns on a hill near Nasik are her home.
Sarasvati	The classical Indian goddess of music and learning.
Satyanarayana	A form of Vishnu as the embodiment of truth. Though temples dedicated to Satyanarayana are relatively few, his worship has been popular since Purāṇic times.
Satyanārāyaṇa Pūjā	A popular rite performed when some new undertaking or journey is begun or to insure good fortune in the coming year.

Shani	The planet Saturn. His influence is an evil one.
Shankara	A name for Shiva, the auspicious one (when not referring to the eighth-century founder of Kevalādvaitavedānta).
Shesha	The cosmic thousand-headed snake that forms Vishnu's couch and canopy during his sleep between intervals of creation.
Shitala	"She who makes cold." The goddess of smallpox. She is represented as a golden-complexioned woman sitting on a lotus or riding in red clothes on an ass.
Shiva	"The auspicious one." The great god of destruction and of the reproductive power of nature; patron of all ascetics.
Sita	The virtuous wife of Rama.
Uma	A wife of Shiva. Another name for Parvati.
Vamana	The dwarf incarnation of Vishnu.
Varaha	The boar incarnation of Vishnu.
Venkateshvara	The lord of the Venkata hill (Tirupati) in southern India. A form of Vishnu.
Vijayā Daśamī	Also called *Dasserā*. Chiefly a men's festival involving worship of the implements of a trade or profession, including those of war. Formerly included buffalo sacrifice.
Vishnu	A great god, protector and preserver of the universe and of mankind, who descends on earth in various incarnations (*avatāras*).
Vitthala/Vithoba	Names of the god of Pandharpur, worshipped as an incarnation of Vishnu.
Yama	The god of death. He is represented with two insatiable dogs with four eyes and wide nostrils; the dogs guard the road to his abode.
Yashoda	Wife of the cowherd Nanda, and foster-mother of Krishna.

Appendix 2
The Hindu Calendar

Caitra	March–April
Vaiśākha	April–May
Jyaiṣṭha	May–June
Āṣādh	June–July
Śrāvaṇa	July–August
Bhādrapada	August–September
Āśvin	September–October
Kārttika	October–November
Mārgaśīrṣa	November–December
Pauṣa	December–January
Māgha	January–February
Phālguna	February–March

Glossary

abhaṅga: Literally, "unbroken, inviolable." A particular metrical composition used by the *Vārakarī* saint-poets.

abhaya: Fearlessness. In iconology, *abhaya mudrā* is the hand pose of a deity, inspiring confidence and trust.

abheda: Absence of difference or distinction.

Abhinavagupta: The great eleventh-century philosopher of Kashmir Śaivism.

abhyāsa: Exercise, practice, exertion.

ācārya: Master, teacher.

adharma: Unrighteousness, evil.

adhyāsa: Superimposition.

Adhyātma Rāmāyaṇa: A "philosophical" *Rāmāyaṇa,* probably composed in the fifteenth century, aiming at a synthesis of Rama *bhakti* with *advaita-vedānta* philosophy.

adhyāya: Chapter of a treatise.

advaita: Nondualism. Kevalādvaitavedānta is a prominent school of monistic philosophy.

ahaṃkāra: Principle of individuation; egotism.

ahiṁsā: Nonviolence.

aḥwāl: Plural of *ḥāl*. A transitory spiritual state of enlightenment or rapture, associated with passage along the Sufi path.

āī: Mother. Often appended to the name of a goddess seen as mother.

akiñcanya: The state of being utterly destitute.

Ālam al-Lāhūt: The world of divinity.

Ālam al-Malakūt: The world of sovereignty, or the world of intelligible substances.

Allāh Mālik: Sai Baba's favorite expression, meaning "Allah is the king or souverain."

Amritānubhava: An important philosophical treatise of Jñāndev.

amṛta: Literally, "nondeath." Nectar of immortality.

aṁśa: Part, fragment.

anahada: The mystical "unstruck sound or vibration."

ānanda: Divine joy, bliss.

ananyatā: Nonotherness.

angāt ālelī: One who is possessed.

angāt yeṇe: Literally, "to come into the body." Possession of a person by a god.

anna: Food.

anta: End.

antarajñāna: Inner knowledge, omniscience.

antarayāmin: The inner ruler, the Supreme Being as present in the region of the heart.

anubhava: Intuitive experience.

anuṣṭhāna: Religious practice, ritual performance.

Aparokshānubhūti: An *advaita-vedānta* treatise attributed to Shankara.

āratī/ārtī: The ceremony of circling a tray of lights before a deity or a holy man at the end of worship while chanting a hymn.

arcanā: Literally, "honoring, praising." The homage paid to a deity.

Arjuna: Proper name of the hero of the *Bhagavadgītā*.

artha: Object; meaning; wealth.

arūpa: Formless.

āsana: Yogic posture.

āśīrvāda: Ritual blessing.

āśram: The retreat of a guru and his disciples.

Ātmabodha: An *advaita-vedānta* work ascribed to Shankara.

ātman: The individual soul, identical with *Brahman*, the impersonal Absolute.

ātmanivedana: The offering of one's self to a deity.

ātmatyāga: Self-forgetfulness.

ātmavidyā: Knowledge of the self.

avadhūta: Literally, "shaken off." An ascetic who has abandoned all worldly ties.

Avadhūtagītā: "Song of the free." A Vedāntic text ascribed to Dattatreya.

avaliā/avliyā: A Muslim saint.

āvaraṇa: Covering up; the conceiling power of *māyā*.

avatāra: An incarnation of a god.

avidyā-karma-saṃsāra: The dreadful cycle of ignorance breeding actions breeding rebirth.

bābā: Holy man, father.

bābhūḷ: Gum arabic, an acacia tree.

baddhas: The bound or impeded ones (on the spiritual path).

bāī: Woman, lady. A respectful form of address.

bakūḷ: *Mimusops elengi*. A flowering tree and its flower.

balutedār: One of the twelve public servants from district castes of a village entitled to *balute*, which was a specific share of agricultural produce in return of some services.

banyan: *Ficus bengalensis*. A huge tree famous for its leafy branches and cool shadow. Some of its branches take roots in the soil and grow out as separate trees. The banyan is thus a symbol of immortality.

bāpū: Father.

baqā: Abiding eternally in God.

barakat: Blessing, holiness. The spiritual power inherent in a Sufi saint giving him his charisma, transferable after his death to his tomb and to his descendants.

ba-shar: Orthodox, conforming to Islamic law.

bel/bilva: *Aegle marmelos,* a tree sacred to Shiva. The bilva leaves are utilized in Shiva's worship.

Bhagavadgītā: Literally, "the song of the Lord." Often called simply the *Gītā*. Krishna's message to Arjuna in the *Mahābhārata* epic.

Bhagavan: Lord. Most general title of a god.

Bhāgavata: A theistic, devotional cult centered on the worship of Vishnu-Krishna.

Bhāgavata Purāṇa: A Purāṇa devoted to Krishna.

bhāī: Brother, most common appellation.

bhajan: Devotional group singing, usually accompanied by instruments. Also the devotional song sung by such a group.

bhākrī: Flat unleavened bread made of sorghum, millet, or maize flour. The staple food of rural Maharashtra.

bhakta: A devotee of a *bhakti* cult.

bhakti: Devotion, usually a personal devotional relationship to one particular god. The "Bhakti movement" refers to the historic presence of numerous schools of *bhakti* saint-poets and teachers in the various linguistic regions.

bhara: Burden, load, weight.

bhārūḍa: Allegorical story presented in dramatic form.

bhasman: Sacred ashes.

bhāū: Brother.

bhil: A hill tribe.

bhukti: Enjoyment through the senses.

bhūt/bhūt bādhā: Ghost; possession of a person by a ghost.

bibā: *Semecarpus anacardium,* often used as an aseptic alcaline.

bīja: seed.

Brahma-jijñāsā: Literally, "the desire to know Brahman."

brahmacārin: Student; celibate. *Brahmacarya* is the first stage in the life of a high-caste Hindu.

Brahmajñāna: Knowledge of *Brahman.*

Brahman: The impersonal Absolute.

brāhmaṇ: Member of the highest priestly caste.

Brahmāṇḍa: The cosmic egg of Brahmā.

Brahmarandhra: The place from which the soul departs at death, that is, the back of the cranium.

Brahmasūtra: The basic text of all Vedānta schools, ascribed to Bādarāyaṇa. Composed of 550 short *sūtras* purporting to summarize the teaching of the Upanishads, it is almost incomprehensible without a commentary.

buddhi: Intellect, intelligence. In the Sāṃkhya system, the first product of the union of Purusha and Prakriti.

caitanya: Consciousness. Also proper name for the supreme *Brahman*.

camatkār: Literally, "astonishment, surprise." A miracle.

caturdiśa: The four cardinal directions.

cāvaḍī: A rural assembly hall.

cetya-muktatā: Literally, "mental liberation."

chakkī: The grindstone found throughout the Deccan, used for grinding *javar* or other food grains.

chakkī-nāma: Any form of folk poetry sung by women to accompany their work at the grind-stone.

chattrā: Ceremonial umbrella.

chillā: Memorial to a Muslim saint. Also, a forty-day period of solitary seclusion, spent in fasting and prayer.

Chishti order: The most widespread of the Indian Sufi orders, it emphasizes the practice of *samā* (ritual dancing) in order to achieve states of ecstasy.

Chokamela: A fourteenth-century *mahār* saint-poet.

cilīm: Clay pipe.

cit: Consciousness.

citta: Thought.

dakṣiṇā: Sacrificial fees.

dama: Self-restraint.

dāna: Gift, charity.

daṇḍa: The ascetic's staff, emblem of spiritual power.

Dārā Shikōh: (1615–59) Moghul prince famous for his eclectic mysticism, a blending of Islamic doctrines and nondual Vedānta.

darbār: A royal court. Sai Baba's dilapidated mosque came to be known as his "darbār."

dargāh: Literally, "court." Tomb of a Muslim saint, often a center of healing.

darśan: Literally, "vision." Seeing an idol or a person with divine power.

Dāsabodha: The most important work of the Marathi saint-poet Ramdas.

daśāvatāras: The traditional list of the ten incarnations of Vishnu.

dāsya: A slave, servant.

dervish: Any Sufi. The anglicized word carries the connotation of the Sufi who stresses ecstasy over knowledge.

deśastha: One of the four most important *brāhmaṇ* castes in Maharashtra, living in the Desh region. Numerous and dominant until the rise of the Chitpavans.

Desh: A country or region; in Maharashtra, the area east of the Ghats from the Godāvarī River south to the Karnataka region.

deshmukh: The hereditary and principal revenue officer of a *pargaṇā* in the Desh area.

deshpānde: Hereditary accountant and record keeper of a *pargaṇā*.

dhangar: A shepherd caste.

dhāraṇā: Concentration.

dharma: Law, religion, support, righteousness, morality.

dhautī: A yogic cleansing exercise.

dhikr: The mentioning of God, sometimes in combination with other ritual activities or spiritual exercises, with the aim of bringing the Sufi closer to God.

dhunī: Sacred fire.

dhyāna: Contemplation, meditation.

dīkṣā: Initiation.

dīnabandhu: Literally, "friend of the poor."

dohā: A couplet form used by Hindi *bhakti*-poets such as Kabir.

Dvāpara-yuga: Second era of each age or *kalpa*.

Dvārakāmāī: "The many-gated mother." The Hindu name that Sai Baba gave to his mosque. Dvārakā, the capital of Krishna, was submerged by the sea (cf. *Mahābhārata* section 16).

ekāgratā: One-pointed concentration.

ekānta: Devotion to one single object.

Eknath: (1533–99) One of the major saint-poets of Maharashtra. He edited the *Jñāneshvarī* and prepared the way for later *bhaktas*.

Eknāth Bhāgavata: Eknath's famous Marathi commentary on the eleventh *skanda* of the *Bhāgavata Purāṇa*.

fanā: Literally, "passing away." Absorption of the individual self into the divine.

faqīr: Literally, a "poor man." A Muslim mendicant who wanders about subsisting on alms.

faqr: Poverty.

gādī: Mattress, seat of power (as of a king).

gaṇa: Multitude or troops. Ganesha, the elephant-headed god, is also known as the lord of the *gaṇas* (Ganapati).

Gangapur: One of the holiest places connected with Dattatreya worship.

gāon: Marathi word for village (Skt. *grāma*).

garbha-gṛha: Literally, "womb-house." The innermost sanctuary of a Hindu temple.

Ghazālī, Abū Hamīd al-: (1058–1111) Great Islamic theologian whose works have contributed to the acceptance of Sufism within the religious orthodoxy.

ghī: Clarified butter.

Godāvarī: The holiest river of the Deccan, revered as the Ganges of Maharashtra.

gopī: Milkmaid.

Gorakhnath: One of the luminaries of the Nātha yogic cult. He probably lived between the ninth century and the twelth century.

Gosāvī: An ascetic or a sect of ascetics.

Granthāvalī: An important collection of poems attributed to the saint-poet Kabir.

gṛhastha: House father. Male head of a household. The second stage in the life of a high caste Hindu.

guṇa: Quality.

gurav: Priest of local deities.

guru: Literally, "heavy," related to Sanskrit *giri* (mountain). Spiritual guide or religious teacher.

guru-paramparā: Tradition or lineage of teachers.

Gurucharitra: A religious text within the Dattatreya tradition, relating the life of Narasimha Sarasvati; written around 1538 by Sarasvati Gangadhara.

Hajj: The pilgrimage to Mecca, one of the five fundamental duties of all Muslims.

hakīm: The Muslim doctor.

haṭha-yoga: Literally, "forceful yoga," aiming at the cultivation of the body through the practice of physical postures (*āsanas*) and breathing exercises (*prāṇāyāma*, etc.).

Hazrat: A title given to Sufi saints and masters.

Hemadpant: The prime minister of the Yādava kings Mahadeva and Ramachandra (1271–1310). Composer of the *Chaturvargacintāmaṇi*, an encyclopaedic work on the *Dharmaśāstra*.

hṛdaya: Heart.

ḥulūl: Indwelling; infusion of God or the divine essence in a creature.

Huwa: "He," the great pronoun of divine ipseity. One of Allah's beautiful names.

ihāmutra-phala-bhoga-virāga: The renunciation of the pleasures one may derive from the fruits of his actions. An expression equivalent to the concept of *vairāgya* (dispassion).

ināmdār: Holder of *inām* (a grant in perpetuity without conditions).

indriyas: The sense organs.

īśitva: Literally, "superiority, supremacy."

ittiḥād: Identification of the divine and human natures.

jagat: The world.

jagir: Lands in which revenue collection was farmed out to a high-ranking noble, in return for which the noble owed military service to the government.

jagirdār: A holder of a *jagir*.

jāgṛīt: Wakeful; used for an especially potent, awake god.

jambu: The rose-apple tree.

janma: Birth, lifetime.

japa: The practice of repeating one of God's names or a mantra.

javar/javārī: *Holcus sorghum*. The staple grain of Maharashtra.

jhand/sami: *Prosopis spicigera*.

jholī: Also known as *cūpadarī*. A rectangular piece of cloth in which ascetics keep their begged food.

jihād: A Sufi's inward or spiritual struggle against the temptations of this world; war against non-Muslims.

jīva (jīvan): Life or individual soul.

jīvanmukta: Literally, "liberated while still living."

jīvātman: The individual soul or self.

jñāna: Knowledge.

Jñāndev: (1271?–1290) The founder of the *bhakti* movement and one of the greatest Marathi saint-poets.

Jñāneshvarī: Jñāndev's magnum opus. An interpretation of the *Bhagavadgītā* containing about nine thousand verses in the *ovī* meter. A unique combination of philosophy, poetry, and mysticism.

jñānin: Literally, "a knower." A sage who has attained perfect knowledge.

jośī: Astrologer.

julāhā: A weaver. Also the caste of weavers.

jyotir: Light.

Kabir: The fifteenth-century Muslim weaver of Benares, one of the greatest saint-poets of the northern Sant tradition.

Kabīrpanthī: The movement of Kabir's followers.

kafnī (kaphan): Shroud. Sai Baba's robe.

Kailāsa: The mythical Himalayan mountain which in Hindu mythology figures as Shiva's paradise. It is regarded as one of the loftiest peaks to the north of the Manasā lake.

kākā: Father's brother. An endearing term often used by Sai Baba.

Kali-yuga: The fourth age of the fourfold cycle of the universe; the "dark age" in which we presently live.

kāma: Sensual desire.

kāminī/kāñcana: Woman; gold. The two major dangers for men along the spiritual path.

Kāpālika: Literally, "bearers of the skull." A Śaivite sect.

karma (karman): Action, fate, destiny.

karma prarabdha: Karma accumulated in a previous birth.

karṇī: Black magic.

kārya: An effect.

kathā: A religious story.

kāya-sādhanā: Literally, "Body cultivation." The principal aim of the Nātha sect.

khaṇḍa-yoga: The discipline through which one is able to separate one's limbs; the verbal root *khaṇḍ* mean "to break, divide, destroy."

kīrtana: A religious discourse accompanied by *bhajan.*

kīrtankār: A storyteller.

kōan: An enigmatic, often paradoxical phrase, on which the Zen Buddhist monk must meditate in an effort to uncover the "meaning" of it.

kos: A measure of distance equivalent to about two miles.

krodha: Anger.

kṛpā: Grace.

Kṛta-yuga: The first age in each world era. The golden age.

kṣatriya: Literally, "warrior." The military caste.

kuḷkarṇi: Village accountant.

kumbhār: Potters.

Lāhūt: Divinity.

langoṭī: Strip of cloth covering the genitals.

lāvaṇī: A type of love song.

laya: Derived from verbal root *li*, the term means dissolution, extinction, but also rest, repose.

Leṇḍī: Literally, "a lump of dung." A streamlet, the locale of Shirdi's gardens.

līlā: Literally, "play, amusement." A divine miraculous act.

liṅga: The phallic symbol of Shiva.

Liṅgāyat: A person belonging to the Vīraśaiva faith.

lobha: Greed, covetousness.

mada: Intoxication.

Madārī order: The most prominent among Sufi heterodox orders.

Madhva: (1238–1317) The representative of Vedāntic dualism.

Mahābhārata: The great epic of the Pāṇḍava and Kaurava clans and the war at Kurukṣetra.

mahant: Head of a monastery.

mahār: The largest of the untouchable castes in Maharashtra. Chief participants in a movement for equality which culminated in a large Buddhist conversion.

mahārāja: A title used for royalty, some holy men, and some gods.

mahāsamādhi: The "great death" or casting off of the body by a Hindu saint.

mahimā: Greatness, might, power.

Mahipati: (1715–90) Author of the *Bhaktalīlāmrita* and other texts on the saint-poets.

majzūbs: Literally, "attracted." A Sufi drawn immediately to God without his/her own effort or guidance from a *pīr*.

Malakūt: Allah's incorruptible Kingdom; royalty.

Malik: The King. One of Allah's beautiful names.

Mālik al-Mulk: The Possessor of the Kingdom. One of Allah's beautiful names.

māmā: Maternal uncle, father-in-law.

māmlātdār: *Tālukā* revenue officer.

manana: Thoughtful reflection.

manas: Mind.

maṇḍala: The circular diagram that functions as a schematic map of the sacred universe.

mandir: Hindu temple.

maṅgalam: Auspicious.

mantra: A sacred and magic formula.

mantra-japa: The repetition of a sacred formula.

Manu: The traditional first man; the law giver.

maqām: A station on the Sufi path, differing from *ḥāl* (state) in that it can be attained through the Sufi's own efforts, while the latter is God-given.

Maratha kingdom: The kingdom ruled by Shivaji, and later his son and grandson and the *peśvās*, existing from 1660 to 1818.

mārga: Path.

mārvāḍī: Money lenders and businessmen, from Marvar originally.

masjid: Mosque.

mast: This term may be derived from a Sufi expression, or else from a Persian word meaning "overpowered." Meher Baba used this word to indicate someone who was "God-intoxicated," a mad ascetic.

maṭha: Hermitage, monastery.

matsara: Jealousy.

Matsyendranath: Traditionally regarded as the first human

teacher of *haṭha-yoga* and as the originator of the Nātha sect. Matsyendra is said to have had twelve disciples, the most famous being Gorakhnath.

maulānā: Literally, "our lord." Teacher of Islamic law.

maunam: Silence.

māyā: Illusion, the power to cause illusion.

mithyā: False.

moha: Delusion.

mokṣa/mukti: Final liberation, release.

mudrā: Literally, "seal." A particular way of holding the hands and fingers so as to indicate a particular meaning.

mullā: Muhammadan jurist or theologian, also a schoolteacher.

mumukṣus: The ones having desire for liberation.

muraḷī: A flute.

murīd: A novice, or pupil of a *pīr*.

murshid: A spiritual guide. The term can refer to a *pīr*.

mūrti: Literally, "form, likeness." An image of a deity as a focus for worship and *darśan*.

nāga: A snake.

naiśkarmya: Disinterested action.

naivedya: Food offered to a deity.

nāma-rūpa: Literally, "name and form." The body-mind complex.

namaskār/namaste: A greeting with the palms pressed together in the so called *añjali* gesture.

nāmasmaraṇa: The rammemoration or repetition of a divine name.

namāz: The Muslim ritual prayer, which must be recited five times a day.

Namdev: (1270–1350) A contemporary of Jñāndev; a saint-poet held to be the originator of many of the practices of the *Vārakarī* tradition.

Narada: The name of a mythical sage.

Nāth-pañcāyatan: A group of five teachers believed to be invisibly communicating with one another.

Nātha: Literally, "lord." Name of an important sect of Śaiva ascetics.

navāṅgāni: The nine "limbs" of *bhakti.*

navas: A vow to a god, often involving the promise of an offering in return for the granting of a request.

nididhyāsana: Profound and repeated meditation.

nīm: The margosa tree.

nirākāra: Without form.

nirguṇa: Without qualities or attributes.

niṣṭhā: Faith.

Nizām: The state with Hyderabad as capital; created in 1724 by the Muslim ruler Nizām ul-Mulk.

Oṃkāra: The syllable *Om,* the primeval vibration, ground of all creation.

ovī: A poetic stanza form often used for religious songs.

pādukās: Raised impression of the feet or the sandals of a saint or a god.

pāgal: A mad person.

pālkhī: A palanquin.

Pañcadashī: Ascribed to Vidyaranya, it is one of the most important post-Shankara *advaita-vedānta* treatises.

pañcāyata: The council of a caste or a village.

Pandhari: A religious name for the holy town of Pandharpur, home of the god Vitthala.

pānsupārī: A roll of betel leaf with areca nut; believed to be a powerful mouth-digestive.

panth: Literally, "road" or "way." A religious group or persuasion; often translated sect or cult.

pāramārthika-satya: The Supreme Truth or Reality.

parāyaṇa: Making anything one's chief object of devotion.

pargaṇā: A province.

Parsi: A member of the Zoroastrian faith; a small group of highly educated and successful people, originally from Persia, now concentrated in Bombay.

Pāśupata: Literally, "Lord of beasts." Earliest and most influential sect of Śaivism; founded by Lakulisha.

Patañjali: Author of the *Yogasūtras*, who probably lived in the second century C.E.

pati: Lord.

pāṭīl: The village headman.

peśvās: The rulers of the Maratha Empire from the early 1700s until 1818, when the *peśvā*'s armies were defeated by the British.

peṭh: A section of a city, originally demarcated by a market.

phala: Fruit, reward.

pipal: *Ficus religiosa*. The most sacred tree in India. Regarded as the dwelling place of the Hindu triad Brahmā, Vishnu, and Shiva and as a symbol of immortality.

pīr: Literally, "elder." A Muslim saint and master in the Sufi tradition.

pīṭha: Case, pedestal (especially of an idol).

pitṛs: Fathers, ancestors.

pothī: A holy text or a manuscript.

povāḍā: A ballad recounting heroic deeds.

pradakṣiṇā: Circumambulation of a god or a holy place.

prakāśa: Light.

Prakriti: The female principle of active energy in the Sāṃkhya system of philosophy. Nature.

prāṇa: Life-force, the breath of life.

prāṇāyāma: Breathing exercise.

prapatti: Perfect surrender. The acme of *bhakti-mārga*.

prāpti: The power of obtaining everything. One of the eight superhuman faculties.

prasād: Anything received as a gift from the deity. Often a portion of the offering a worshipper has made.

Prashanti Nilayam: Literally, "abode of peace." Name of Satya Sai Baba's *āśram* in Puttaparthi (Andhra Pradesh).

prātibhāsika-satya: Illusory truth or reality.

prema (preman): Pure love.

preta: Corpse, ghost.

pūjā: Ritual worship.

pujārī: Temple priest.

Pundarika: The saintly person to whom Vitthala appeared, impressed by his virtue and filial piety.

Purāṇas: The most voluminous body of all Sanskrit texts, composed chiefly in the first millennium of our era. Mythical histories of gods and kings.

pūrṇimā: Full moon day.

puruṣārthas: Any one of the four objects or aims of human existence: *kāma*, the gratification of desire; *artha*, acquirement of wealth; *dharma*, discharge of duty; *mokṣa*, final emancipation.

Purusha: The male principle of passive knowingness in Sāṃkhya philosophy. Universal soul.

Puttaparthi: Birthplace of the living saint Satya Sai Baba, where he has his *āśram*.

qavvālī: Music recital in the Sufi tradition.

qāzi: Muhammadan judge or administrator of law.

rāga-dveṣa: The pair of love and hatred, attraction and repulsion.

rākṣasa: A demon.

Ramananda: The Vaiṣṇava reformer traditionally believed to have been Kabir's teacher.

Ramanuja: (c. 1050–1137) An eleventh-century South Indian philosopher who gave a philosophical foundation to the Vaiṣṇava devotional movement, which became known as *Śrī Vaiṣṇavism*.

Rāmāyaṇa: Epic of the ideal king, Rama, and the ideal woman, Sita, his wife.

Ramdas: (1534–81) A *bhakta* of Rama who founded a religious order and began the "Maharashtra *dharma*," idea of a special ethos for a Hindu state.

riḍā: Conforming to divine will.

rīṇānubandha: Prenatal karmic ties.

roṭī: Bread.

ṛṣi: A seer, wise man.

rūpa: Form.

śabda: Sound; word; scriptural authority.

saburī: Patience.

sadguru: Literally, "good or true teacher." The supreme teacher who is identified with the qualityless Absolute, dwelling in one's own heart.

sādhanā: Practice, study toward a goal of release from bondage. A *sādhaka* is one engaged in religious exercises so as to obtain *mokṣa*.

sādhu: A Hindu mendicant leading a pious and ascetic life.

ṣaḍripus: The six enemies, that is, lust, anger, greed, hatred, pride, and envy or jealousy.

saguṇa: With qualities or attributes.

sāī: A term of Persian origin, usually attributed to Muslim saints and holy men.

sākṣātkār: Literally, "putting before the eyes, making evident to the senses." Vision.

Śākta: Name for the cult of the Devī and for her followers.

śakti: The principle of female power. Divine energy, potency.

Sakuri: The village where Upasani Baba founded his *āśram*, the *Upāsanī Kanyā Kumārī Sthān*, which is presently run by Upasani's successor, Sati Godavari Mataji.

śālagrāma: Smooth ammonite stone found in rivers, said to be a "natural form" (*svarūpa*) of Vishnu.

samā: Musical sessions held by Sufis, with the object of inducing a state of spiritual ecstasy.

samādhi: A monument built over the remains of a Hindu saint. Also entrance into a state of union with *Brahman*.

saṃkalpa: Divine will.

saṃnyāsa/saṃnyāsin: The ascetic life; one who lives the ascetic life.

saṃpradāya: Custom, practice; a system of religious doctrine; a systematized tradition.

saṃsāra: Passage. The term used to describe the ceaseless round of birth and death and rebirth. The changing world.

saṃskāra: Life-cycle rituals.

sanad: A document conveying a government order and bearing the royal seal.

sanātana dharma: The eternal law.

sant: Close to the English word saint in meaning, but with no etymological connection. Generally used for the *bhakti* saint-poets of the Marathi and Hindi speaking areas.

śānti: Peace.

śaraṇāgati: Seeking refuge, surrender.

sarvajña: Literally, "knower of all." An omniscient being.

śāstrin: A teacher knowing the scriptures.

sat: The real, the essential.

satka: Baton, staff.

satori: The Zen Buddhist enlightenment experience.

satpuruṣa: An enlightened being.

satsaṅga: Good company. A group of religious people.

sattva: Moral goodness, virtue. The purest of the three *guṇas*.

satya: Truth.

satyāgraha: Literally, "holding to truth." The technique of nonviolent endurance and action developed by Mahatma Gandhi.

sevā: Service.

Shankara, Shankaracharya: A philosopher who lived during the eighth or ninth century. Founder of the Dasanāmī order and chief formulator of the Kevalādvaitavedānta school of philosophy. A Śaiva *bhakta.*

sharī'at: The Law of God; the revealed and canonized body of Islamic Law.

Shāstra: A Hindu text or treatise, considered to be of divine origin.

Shivaji: (1630–80) The first *chhatrāpati* (king of the Marathas), founder of the Maratha empire and most important hero of the Marathi speaking people.

siddha: One who has attained extraordinary powers through ascetic practice.

siddha-loka: The world or realm of perfect beings.

siddhi: Attainment, extraordinary power.

sīmollanghan: The crossing of the borders.

sirr: Mystery; the "ground" of the soul.

śiṣya: A pupil, disciple.

smṛti: What has been committed to memory; tradition. Proper name for a certain class of scriptures.

sonār: Goldsmith. The caste of goldsmiths.

spanda: Vibration. Technical term within Kashmir Śaivism.

sparśa: Touch.

śraddhā: Faith.

śravaṇa: Hearing; audition.

śrī: An honorific term.

śruti: That which has been heard. Sacred knowledge orally transmitted by the *brāhmaṇs* from generation to generation; the Vedas.

strī-dharma: The code of conduct appropriate for women.

subhedār: Chief officer of a *subhā* (province).

Śuddha Brahman: The Pure Absolute.

Śuddha Caitanya: Pure Consciousness. A characterization of *Brahman* favored by Sai Baba.

śūdra: A person belonging to the fourth and lowest caste. His only business, according to Manu 1.91, is to serve the three higher classes.

sūtra: Literally, "thread." Aphoristic textbook.

Svāmin: Lord; today usually "Reverend."

svarga: Heaven.

svarūpa: Literally, "own form"; "very being."

svastika: A mystical cross or mark made on persons and things to denote good luck. A solar symbol.

svecchā-maraṇa: The power of averting death.

takiyā: A resting house for Muslim visitors.

tālukā: A division of a district.

tamas: One of the three *guṇas*. Darkness, dullness, inertia.

tapas: Literally, "heat." Especially the heat generated by ascetic practices.

ṭarīq: A road, path, or way. The system or doctrine associated with particular Sufis or a school of Sufis.

taṣawwuf: Mysticism, equivalent to the English Sufism.

tat: That; name of the supreme being.

tawājud: An induced ecstasy.

tawakkul: Trust in God. Mystic state of abandonment into God's hands.

telī: Oil pressers.

Tilak, Bal Gangadhar: (1856-1920) A fervant nationalist leader, founder of the public Ganapati festival, and an important politico-religious influence even today.

tīrtha: Fording place. Holy water; place of pilgrimage.

titikṣa: Patience, endurance.

tongā (tāṅgā): A two-wheeled cart drawn by a horse.

Tretā-yuga: Third world age.

trimūrti: The Hindu holy triad: Brahmā, Vishnu, Shiva.

Tukaram: (1608–49) A saint-poet of Dehu near Pune, one of the most beloved poets in the Marathi tradition.

tuḷśi: *Ocymum sanctum;* a plant sacred to Krishna. Holy basil.

udī: The sacred ash which Sai Baba got from his perpetually burning fire (*dhunī*).

ulamā: Plural of *ālim;* a man trained in the Islamic religious sciences.

ulṭabāṁsī: Upside-down, reverted language.

unmatta: Crazy, mad.

upadeśa: Teaching, religious instruction.

Upanishads: Philosophical and mystical texts, from around 650–200 B.C.E., very important in the development of Hindu thought.

upāsana: Worship.

upekṣā: Endurance, patience.

urs/urūs: Literally, "marriage with God." The festival commemorating the death date of a *pīr,* normally the most important festival at a *dargāh.*

vāḍā/wada: An area of residence, often by caste. A traditional joint family home.

Vaikunta: Name of Vishnu's heaven, variously described as being situated in the northern ocean or on the eastern peak of Mount Meru.

vairāgya: Dispassion, renunciation.

vaiśya: The merchant caste.

vanaprastha: Forest dweller; the third stage in a *brāhmaṇ*'s life.

Vārakarī: Literally, "one who keeps a regular time." The name for the pilgrims to Pandharpur.

varṇāśrama: The traditional four-fold division of castes (*varṇa*): *brāhmaṇ, kṣatriya, vaiśya,* and *śūdra.* Also, the four stages of life for the three higher castes.

vāsanās: The impression of anything remaining unconsciously in the mind; tendencies.

Vasudeva: Patronimic of Krishna, son of Vasudeva.

vatandār: Holder of *vatan* (a hereditary estate given by a government for certain services).

Vedānta: Literally, "the end of the Vedas." The philosophical systems based on the Upanishads. Kevalādvaitavedānta is dominant in Indian intellectual circles today.

Vedas: The four Vedas form the earliest literature of the Indo-European peoples, dating roughly 1200–1000 B.C.E. The *Rig Veda* is considered the holiest of texts by the orthodox.

vibhūti: Supernatural power. Also a name for sacred ash.

vicāra: Inquiry, examination, investigation.

vidvān: Literally, "possessed of learning, learned man."

vidyā: Knowledge.

vimarśa: Reflective awareness. A technical term within Kashmir Śaivism.

vināyaka: Remover (of obstacles). A name of Ganesha.

vīrya: Manly vigor, virility, strength, heroism.

Vishnusahasranāmastotra: *The Hymn of the Thousand Names of Vishnu.* The commentary on this text ascribed to Shankara is most probably his.

viśuddhi: Complete purification, purity.

viveka: Discrimination, discriminative power.

Vivekacūḍāmaṇi: The Crest-Jewel of Discrimination. An *advaitavedānta* work attributed to Shankara.

Vyasa: Literally, "arranger." Proper name of a Vedic sage credited with the compilation of the Vedas, the *Mahābhārata,* and the Purāṇas.

vyāvahārika-satya: Conventional or ordinary truth.

waḥdat al-wujūd: The doctrine of the Unity of Being, positing that all Reality is a borrowed fragment from the Being of God.

Yādava kingdom: Centered at Devgiri, near modern Aurangabad, the dynasty of the Yādavas in the eleventh and twelth centuries saw the beginnings of Marathi literature and the foundation of Mahānubhava and *Vārakarī* traditions.

yag: Sacrifice, oblation.

yajña: Vedic sacrifice.

yantra: A mystical diagram supposed to possess occult powers. A "device" for harnessing the mind in meditation or worship.

yātrā: Pilgrimage.

yoga; yogin: Discipline, spiritual endeavor in order to control the mind and the senses; a practicioner of yoga.

Yogavasishtha: It occupies the first place among the so-called philosophical *Rāmāyaṇas*. A didactic poetic work presented as a dialogue between prince Rama and his teacher Vasishtha.

yuga: An age. Classically, four ages form a cycle in the life of the universe.

zamindār: Holder of *zamin* (land). Landowner, peasant-proprietor.

Zen: An important school of Mahāyāna Buddhism in Japan.

Zoroastrianism: The religion of Zoroaster of sixth-century Persia, practiced in India by a small but influential group of Parsis.

zuhd: Renunciation.

General Bibliography

Abbott, John. *The Keys of Power: A Study of Indian Ritual and Belief.* Reprint; Seacaucus, N.J.: University Books, 1974 (1932).

Abbott, J. E. and Godbole, N. R., trans. *Stories of Indian Saints: Translation of Mahipati's Marathi Bhaktavijaya.* Reprint; Delhi: Motilal Banarsidass, 1982 (Pune, 1933).

Abhayananda, Swami. *Jnaneshvar: The Life and Works of the Celebrated Thirteenth Century Indian Mystic-Poet.* Naples, Fl: Atma Books, 1989.

Adhyātmarāmāyaṇa (with Hindi translation). Gorakhpur: Gita Press, 1958.

Advaita Ashram. *Life of Sri Ramakrishna.* Calcutta: Advaita Ashram, 1948.

Allah, Ibn Ata. *Traité sur le nom Allāh.* Paris, 1981.

Alper, Harvey P., ed. *Mantra.* Albany, N.Y.: SUNY Press, 1989.

Ananthakrishna Sastry, R., trans. *Viṣṇusahasranāma with the Bhāṣya of Śrī Saṁkarācārya.* Madras: Adyar, 1980.

Anawati, G. C. and Gardet, L. *Mistica islamica: Aspetti e tendenze, esperienze e tecnica.* Torino: Società Editrice Internazionale, 1960.

Ashokananda, Swami. *Avadhūta Gītā of Dattātreya.* Madras: Ramakrishna Math, 1988.

Atreya, B. L. *The Yogavāsiṣṭha and its Philosophy.* Benares: Indian Bookshop, 1939.

Avate, T. H. *Nāmadeva Gāthā.* Pune, 1923.

Ayyangar, Srinivasa T. R., trans. *Śaiva Upaniṣads.* Madras: Adyar, 1953.

Babb, Lawrence A. "Glancing: Visual Interaction in Hinduism." *Journal of Anthropological Research* 37(1981): 387–401.

Babu, Sarath R., ed. *Dattātreya: Glory of the Divine in Man.* Ongole, 1981.

Banerjea, Akshaya Kumar. *Philosophy of Gorakhnath with Goraksha-Vacana-Sangraha.* Gorakhpur: Mahant Dig Vijai Nath Trust, 1961.

Bapat, N. G. *Economic Development of Ahmednagar District 1881–1960.* Bombay: Progressive Corporation Private, 1973.

Bassuk, Daniel E. *Incarnation in Hinduism and Christianity: The Myth of the God-Man.* London: The Macmillan Press, 1987.

Bayrak, Tosun, comp. *The Most Beautiful Names.* Putney, Vt.: Threshold Books-Amana Books, 1985.

Bendre, V. S. *Sheikh Mahammadkṛta Kavitāsaṅgraha.* 1961.

Bharade, S. A. (Bharadvaja). *Jñānadeva va Jñāneśvara.* Pune, 1931.

Bharati, Agehananda. "Pilgrimage in the Indian Tradition." *History of Religions* 3, no. 1(1963): 135–67.

———. *The Ochre Robe.* New York: Doubleday, 1970.

———. *The Tantric Tradition.* New York: Samuel Weiser, 1975.

Bhardwaj, S. M. *Hindu Places of Pilgrimage in India.* Berkeley and Los Angeles: University of California Press, 1973.

Bhatkhande, S. M. *Nityasūtrāṇi: A Bouquet of Celestial Songs of the Cidākāśa.* Bombay: Nityananda Institute of Culture, 1986.

Briggs, G. W. *Gorakhnāth and the Kānphaṭa Yogīs.* Calcutta: Motilal Banarsidass, 1938.

Brown, Mackenzie D. "The Philosophy of Bāḷ Gaṅgādhar Ṭiḷak: Karma vs. Jñāna in the Gītā Rahasya." *Journal of Asian Studies* 17, no. 2(1958): 197–206.

Burnouf, M. E. "Sur les trente-deux signes caractéristiques d'un grand homme." In *Le Lotus de la Bonne Loi.* Traduit du Sanscrit, accompagné d'un commentaire et de vingt et un mémoires relatifs au Buddhisme, 553–647. Reprint; Paris: Adrien Maisonneuve, 1989.

Cashman, Richard I. "The Political Recruit of God Gaṇapati." *Indian Economic and Social History Review* 7, no. 3(1970): 347–73.

———. *The Myth of the Lokamanya: Tilak and Mass Politics in Maharashtra.* Berkeley and Los Angeles: University of California Press, 1975.

Census of India, 1961. Vol. 10. *Maharashtra*. Pt. 7–C, *Weekly Markets of Maharashtra*. Bombay. Printed in India by the Manager, Government Central Press, Bombay, and Published by the Manager of Publications, Delhi. 1968.

Chakravarti, Mahadev. *The Concept of Rudra-Śiva Through the Ages*. New Delhi: Motilal Banarsidass, 1986.

Coomaraswamy, A. K. *The Dance of Śiva*. Bombay, 1948.

Corbin, H. *L'Homme de lumière dans le soufisme iranien*. 2d ed. Paris, 1971.

———. *En Islam iranien*. Vol. 2, *Sohrawardi et les platoniciens de Perse*. Paris, 1971.

Courtright, P. B. *Gaṇeśa: Lord of Obstacles, Lord of Beginnings*. New York: Oxford University Press, 1985.

———. "The Ganesh Festival in Maharashtra: Some Observations." In *The Experience of Hinduism: Essays on Religion in Maharashtra*, edited by Eleanor Zelliot and Maxine Berntsen, 76–94. Albany, N.Y.: SUNY Press, 1988.

Crooke, William. *Things Indian: Being Discursive Notes on Various Subjects Connected with India*. London: John Murray, 1906.

———. *Natives of Northern India*. London: Archibald Constable, 1907.

———. *Religion and Folklore of Northern India*. London: Oxford University Press, 1926.

Dasganu. *Shree Gajanan Vijay* (an English adaptation by N. B. Patil). Shree Gajanan Maharaj Sansthan, 1980.

Dasgupta, G. *Obscure Religious Cults*. 2d ed. Calcutta: Firma K. L. Mukhopadhyay, 1962.

Date, V. H. *Spiritual Treasure of St. Rāmadāsa*. Delhi, 1975.

Deleury, G. A. *The Cult of Viṭhobā*. Pune: Deccan College Post-graduate and Research Institute, 1960.

Dev, S. S. *Dāsabodha*. Dhule, Ś. 1827.

Dhere, R. C. *Datta Sampradāyācā Itihāsa*. 2d ed. Pune, Ś. 1835.

———. *Musalmān Marāṭhī Santakavi*. Pune, 1967.

Dhol, N. *Pañcadaśī*. Calcutta, 1879.

Eaton, Richard Maxwell. "Sufi Folk Literature and the Expansion of Indian Islam." *History of Religions* 14, no. 2(1974): 117–27.

———. *Sufis of Bijapur, 1300–1700: Social Roles of Sufis in Medieval India.* Princeton: Princeton University Press, 1978.

Eck, Diana L. *Darśan: Seeing the Divine Image in India.* 2d ed. Chambersburg, Pa.: Anima Books, 1985.

Edgerton, Franklin, trans. *The Bhagavadgītā.* New York: Harper & Row, 1964.

Eliade, Mircea. *Yoga: Immortality and Freedom.* Bollingen Series, Princeton: Princeton University Press, 1973.

Enthoven, R. E. *The Folklore of Bombay.* Oxford, 1924.

Fani, Mohsan. *Dabistan or School of Manners.* Translated by D. Shea and A. Troyer. 3 vols., Paris, 1843.

Feldhaus, Anne. "God and Madman: Guṇḍam Rāuḷ." *School of Oriental and African Studies* 45(1982): 74–83.

———. *The Deeds of God in Ṛddhipur.* New York: Oxford University Press, 1984.

———. "The Image of the Forest in the Māhātmyas of the Rivers of the Deccan." In *Panels of the VIIth World Sanskrit Conference,* vol. 3, *The History of Sacred Places in India as Reflected in Traditional Literature: Papers on Pilgrimage in South Asia,* edited by Hans Bakker, 90–102. Leiden: E. J. Brill, 1990.

Frydman, Maurice. *I Am That.* Bombay: Chetana, 1973.

Gaborieau, Marc. "On Traditional Patterns of Dominance among South Asian Muslims." *Colloques Internationaux du C. N. R. S.,* no. 582 (*Asie du Sud: Traditions et Changements*): 189–95.

———. "Les ordres mystiques dans le sous-continent indien: Un point de vue ethnologique." In *Les ordres mystiques dans l'Islam: Cheminements et situation actuelle,* edited by A. Popovic and G. Veinstein, 105–34. Paris: Éditions de l'École des Hautes Études en Sciences Sociales, 1986.

Gambhirananda, Swami. *Eight Upaniṣads (with the commentary of Śaṅkarācārya).* 4th ed. Calcutta: Advaita Ashram, 1977.

Ghurye, G. S. *Indian Sādhus.* Bombay: Popular Prakashan, 1964.

Gimaret, Daniel. *Les noms divins en Islām: Exégèse lexicographique et théologique.* Paris: Éditions du Cerf, 1988.

Glucklich, A. "The Royal Scepter (Daṇḍa) as Legal Punishment and Sacred Symbol." *History of Religions* 28, no. 2(1988): 97–122.

Gode, P. K. "Studies in the History of Hindu Festivals: Some Notes on the History of Divālī Festival (between c. A.D. 50 and 1945)." Pune: *Annals of the Bhandarkar Oriental Research Institute* 26 (1946): 216–62.

Gokhale, V. D. ed. *Amṛtānubhava*. Pune, 1967.

Gonda, Jan. *Notes on Brahman*. Utrecht: J. L. Beyers, 1950.

———. *Eye and Gaze in the Veda*. Amsterdam: North-Holland, 1969.

———. *Triads in the Veda*. Amsterdam: North-Holland, 1973.

———. *Viṣṇuism and Śivaism: A Comparison*. New Delhi: Munshiram Manoharlal, 1976.

———. *Change and Continuity in Indian Religion*. New Delhi: Munshiram Manoharlal, 1985.

Halbfass, Wilhelm. *India and Europe: An Essay in Understanding*. Albany, N.Y.: SUNY Press, 1988.

Hariharānanda Āraṇya, Swāmi. *Yoga Philosophy of Patañjali*. Albany, N.Y.: SUNY Press, 1983.

Hasrat, Bikrama Jit. *Dārā Shikūh: Life and Works*. Calcutta, 1953.

Hassan Ali, Meer. *Observations on the Mussulmauns of India: Descriptive of their Manners, Customs, Habits and Religious Opinions made during a Twelve Years' Residence in their Immediate Society*. Reprint; Karachi: Oxford University Press, 1973 (1917).

Hatengdi, M. U. *Nityananda: The Divine Presence*. Cambridge, Mass.: Rudra, 1984.

Hatengdi, M. U. and Chetanananda, Swami. *Nitya Sutras: The Revelations of Nityananda from the Chidakash Gita*. Cambridge, Mass.: Rudra, 1985.

Hedayetullah, Muhammad. *Kabir: The Apostle of Hindu-Muslim Unity: Interaction of Hindu-Muslim Ideas in the Formation of the Bhakti Movement with Special Reference to Kabir, the Bhakta*. New Delhi: Motilal Banarsidass, 1977.

Heidegger, Martin. *Unterwegs zur Sprache*. Pfullingen, 1959.

Hess, Linda. *The Bijak of Kabir*. Trans. Linda Hess and Shukdev Singh. San Francisco: North Point Press, 1983.

Hohenberger, A. *Rāmānuja, ein Philosoph indischer Gottesmystik*. Bonn, 1960.

Hume, R. E. *The Thirteen Principal Upanishads*. Reprint; London: Oxford University Press, 1949 (1921).

The Imperial Gazetteer of India. 24 vols. Oxford: Clarendon Press, 1908.

Iyer, Raghavan. *The Moral and Political Thought of Mahatma Gandhi*. 2d ed. Santa Barbara: Concord Grove Press, 1983.

Joshi, Hariprasad Shivprasad. *Origin and Development of Dattātreya Worship in India*. Baroda: Maharaja Sayajirao University of Baroda, 1965.

Kalyana Kalpataru. *The Divine Name Number* (Gorakhpur). 5, no. 1(1938).

Kamat, R. K. *Śrī Gurucaritra*. 3d. ed. Bombay, 1966.

Kane, P. V. *History of Dharmaśāstra*. Government Oriental Series, class B, n. 6, 5 vols. Pune: Bhandarkar Oriental Research Institute, 1930–62.

Karve, Iravati. *Maharashtra State Gazetteer, Maharashtra: Land and Its People*. Bombay, 1968.

———. "The Indian Village." *Rural Sociology in India*, edited by A. R. Desai. Bombay: Popular Prakashan, 1969.

Kathāsaritsāgara, 2d ed. Vol. 2. Delhi, 1968.

Kinsley, David R. "Through the Looking Glass: Divine Madness in the Hindu Religious Tradition." *History of Religions*, 13, no. 1 (1974): 270–305.

Knipe, David M. "Night of the Growing Dead: A Cult of Vīrabhadra in Coastal Andhra." In *Criminal Gods and Demon Devotees: Essays on the Guardians of Popular Hinduism*, edited by Alf Hiltebeitel, 123–56. Albany, N.Y.: SUNY Press, 1989.

Kolenda, Pauline. "Pox and the Terror of Childlessness: Images and Ideas of the Smallpox Goddess in a North Indian Village." In *Caste, Cult and Hierarchy: Essays on the Culture of India*, edited by P. Kolenda, 198–221. New Delhi: Folklore Institute, 1983.

Kramrisch, Stella. *The Hindu Temple*. 2 vols. Reprint; Delhi: Motilal Banarsidass, 1977 (1946).

Kripananda, Swami, trans. *Jnaneshwar's Gita: A Rendering of the Jnaneshwari*. Albany, N.Y.: SUNY Press, 1989.

Kulkarnee, Narayan H. "Medieval Maharashtra and Muslim Saint-Poets." In *Medieval Bhakti Movements in India: Sri Caitanya Quincentenary Commemoration Volume*, edited by N. N. Bhattacharyya, 198–236. New Delhi: Munshiram Manoharlal, 1989.

Kulkarni, K. R. *The Saint of Shegaon: A Book of Poems on the Life of Shri Gajanan Maharaj*. Nagpur, 1969.

Lambert, H. M., ed., *Jñāneśvarī,* translated by V. G. Pradhan. 2 vols. London: Allen & Unwin, 1967.

Lawrence, B. B. "The Early Chishti Approach to Samā." In *Islamic Society and Culture: Essays in Honour of Professor Aziz Ahmad,* edited by M. Israel and N. K. Wagle, Manohar, 1983.

Lorenzen, David N. *The Kāpālikas and Kālāmukhas: Two Lost Śaivite Sects.* Berkeley and Los Angeles: University of California Press, 1972.

———. "Traditions of Non-caste Hinduism: The Kabīr Panth." *Contributions to Indian Sociology* n. s., 21, no. 2 (1987): 263–83.

———. "New Data on the Kāpālikas." In *Criminal Gods and Demon Devotees: Essays on the Guardians of Popular Hinduism,* edited by Alf Hiltebeitel, 231–38. Albany, N.Y.: SUNY Press, 1989.

M (Mahendra Nath Gupta). *The Gospel of Sri Ramakrishna.* Translated by Nikhilananda Swami. New York: Ramakrishna-Vivekananda Center, 1942.

Macdonnell, A. A. *Vedic Mythology.* Reprint; Delhi: Motilal Banarsidass, 1974 (1898).

Madhavananda, Swami, trans. *The Bṛhadāraṇyaka Upaniṣad (with the commentary of Śaṅkarācārya).* 5th ed. Calcutta: Advaita Ashram, 1975.

Mahadevan, T. M. P. *Rāmaṇa Maharṣi: The Sage of Aruṇācala.* London, 1977.

Maharashtra. *Śrī Ekanāthī Bhāgavata.* Bombay, 1971.

Massignon, L. *La Passion d'al-Husayn-ibn-Mansur al-Hallāj, martyr mystique de l'Islam, executé à Bagdad le 26 Mars 922.* 2 vols. Paris, 1922.

Mate, M. S. *Temples and Legends of Maharashtra.* Bombay: Bharatiya Vidya Bhavan, 1962.

McDaniel, June. *The Madness of the Saints: Ecstatic Religion in Bengal.* Chicago: University of Chicago Press, 1989.

Michell, George. *The Hindu Temple: An Introduction to Its Meaning and Forms.* 2d ed. Chicago: University of Chicago Press, 1988.

Mishra, Laxman Prasad. *Mistici Indiani Medievali.* Torino: Unione Tipografico-Editrice Torinese, 1971.

Molé, M. *La danse extatique en Islam.* Paris: Sources Orientales 6, 1963.

Moreno, M. M. *Antologia della mistica Arabo-Persiana.* Bari: Laterza, 1951.

Muktananda, Swami. *En Compagnie d'un Siddha.* Paris: La Maisnie, 1981.

———. *Le Secret des Siddhas*. Paris: La Maisnie, 1982.

Nair, Thankappan P. "Tree-Symbol Worship among the Nairs of Kerala." In *Tree Symbol Worship in India: A New Survey of a Pattern of Folk-Religion*, edited by Sankar Sen Gupta, 93–103. Calcutta: Indian Publications, 1965.

Narayan, Kirin. *Storytellers, Saints, and Scoundrels: Folk Narrative in Hindu Religious Teaching*. Philadelphia: University of Pennsylvania Press, 1989.

Nava, Regina. *Aspetti dell'Iconografia di Gaṇeśa*. Venezia: Arsenale Editrice, 1988.

Nisargadatta Maharaj. *Sois*! Paris: Les Deux Oceans, 1983.

Nizami, K. A. "Sufi Movement in the Deccan." In *History of Medieval Deccan (1295–1724)*, edited by H. K. Sherwani and P. M. Joshi, vol. 2, 173–99. Hyderabad: Government of Andhra Pradesh, 1974.

O'Flaherty, Wendy Doniger. *Karma and Rebirth in Classical Indian Traditions*. Berkeley and Los Angeles: University of California Press, 1980.

Olivelle, Patrick. *Renunciation in Hinduism: A Medieval Debate*. 2 vols. Publications of the De Nobili Research Library. Vienna, 1986.

Oppert, G. *On the Original Inhabitants of Bhāratavarśa or India*. Reprint; New York: Arno Press, 1978 (1893).

Orenstein, H. *Gaon: Conflict and Cohesion in an Indian Village*. Princeton: Princeton University Press, 1965.

Osborne, Arthur. *The Collected Works of Ramana Maharshi*. London: Rider, 1959.

———. *The Teachings of Ramana Maharshi*. London: Rider, 1971.

Pain, Charles, and Zelliot, Eleanor. "The God Dattātreya and the Datta Temples of Pune." In *The Experience of Hinduism: Essays on Religion in Maharashtra*, edited by Eleanor Zelliot and Maxine Berntsen, 95–108. Albany, N.Y.: SUNY Press, 1988.

Pangarkar, L. R., ed. *Dāsabodha*. Pune, 1923.

Panikkar, Raimundo. *Spiritualità Indù*. Brescia, 1975.

Pansikar, V. L. Sharma. *The Yogavāsiṣṭha of Valmiki: With the commentary Vāsiṣṭha mahārāmāyaṇa tatpāryaprakāśa*. 2 vols. Reprint; Delhi: Motilal Banarsidass, 1984.

Piano, Stefano. *Guru Nānak e il Sikhismo*. Fossano: Editrice Esperienze, 1971.

Piantelli, Mario. *Śaṅkara e la rinascita del Brāhmaṇesimo*. Fossano: Editrice Esperienze, 1974.

———. "L'autonomia umana e la libertà divina nell'ambito dell'Induismo." In *Peccato e riconciliazione nelle religioni*. Bologna, 1984.

Priyolkar, A. K. *Grānthika Marāṭhī bhāṣā āṇi Koṇkanī bolī*. Pune, 1966.

Pugh, Judy F. "Astrology and Fate: The Hindu and Muslim Experiences." In *Karma: An Anthropological Enquiry*, edited by C. F. Keyes and E. V. Daniel, 131–46. Berkeley and Los Angeles: University of California Press, 1983.

Purohit Swami. *Avadhoota Gita*. New Delhi: Munshiram Manoharlal, 1979.

Ramanujan, A. K. *Speaking of Śiva*. Hammondsworth: Penguin, 1973.

Ranade, R. D. *Mysticism in Maharashtra*. Reprint; Delhi: Motilal Banarsidass, 1982 (1933).

Ranade, R. D. and Belvalkar, S. K. *History of Indian Philosophy*. Vol. 7. Pune, 1933.

Renou, Louis and Filliozat, Jean. *L'Inde classique*. 2 vols. Paris: Imprimerie National, 1953.

Rizvi, S. A. A. *A History of Sufism in India*. 2 vols. New Delhi: Munshiram Manoharlal, 1983.

Rocher, Ludo. *The Purāṇas*. In *A History of Indian Literature*, edited by Jan Gonda, vol. 2, fasc. 3. Wiesbaden: Otto Harrassowitz, 1986.

Rolland, Romain. *The Life of Ramakrishna*. Calcutta: Advaita Ashram, 1960.

Rupkala, S. B. *Bhakta-mālā with Bhaktisudhāsvād ṭīkā*. 2d ed. Lukhnow, 1962.

Sadananda. *Vedānta-Sāra: A Work on Vedānta Philosophy*. Edited and translated by M. Hiriyanna. Pune: Oriental Book Agency, 1929.

Sakhare, Nanamaharaj. *Śrī sakal sant gāthā*. 2d ed. Vol. 1. Pune, 1967.

Sand, Erik Reenberg. "The Legend of Puṇḍarīka: The Founder of Pandharpur." In *Panels of the VIIth World Sanskrit Conference*, vol. 3, *The History of Sacred Places in India as Reflected in Traditional Literature: Papers on Pilgrimage in South Asia*, edited by Hans Bakker, 33–61. Leiden: E. J. Brill, 1990.

Sarasvati, B. "Notes on Kabir: A Non-literate Intellectual." In *Dissent Protest and Reform in Indian Civilization*, edited by S. C. Malik, 167–84. Simla: Indian Institute of Advanced Study, 1977.

Saunders, E. D. *Mudrā: A Study of Symbolic Gestures in Japanese Buddhist Sculpture.* Reprint; Bollingen Series, 58. Princeton: Princeton University Press, 1985 (1960).

Schimmel, Anne-Marie. *Islamic Literatures of India.* Wiesbaden: Otto Harrassowitz, 1973.

———. *Mystical Dimensions of Islām.* Chapel Hill: University of North Carolina Press, 1975.

———. *Islām in the Indian Subcontinent.* Leiden: E. J. Brill, 1980.

———. "Deccani Art and Culture." In *Vijayanagara—City and Empire: New Currents of Research,* edited by A. L. Dallapiccola, 177–87. Steiner Verlag Wiesbaden GMBH: Stuttagart, 1985.

Shah, Idries. *Wisdom of the Idiots.* 4th ed. London: Octagon Press, 1979.

Shankara Bhagavatpada, Sri. *Śrī Viṣṇusahasranāma Stotram* (with English translation of the commentary). Bhavan's Book University, 228. Bombay, 1978.

Sharif, Ja'far. *Islam in India or the Qanūn-I-Islām.* Composed under the direction of and translated by G. A. Herklots. Reprint; London: Curzon Press, 1972 (1921).

Shayegan, Daryush. *Les relations de l'Hindouisme et du Soufisme d'après le Majma 'al-Bahrayn de Dārā Shokūh.* Paris: Éditions de la Différence, 1979.

Siegel, Lee. *Laughing Matters: Comic Tradition in India.* Chicago: University of Chicago Press, 1987; Delhi: Motilal Banarsidass, 1989.

Silburn, Lilian, trans. *Mahārthamañjarī de Maheśvarānanda, avec des extraits du Parimala.* Paris: Éd. de Boccard, 1968.

———. *Kuṇḍalinī: The Energy of the Depths: A Comprehensive Study Based on the Scriptures of Nondualistic Kaśmīr Śaivism.* Albany, N.Y.: SUNY Press, 1988.

Sivananda, Swami. *Hindu Fasts and Festivals.* Shivanandanagar: Yoga-Vedanta Forest Academy Press, 1987.

Smart, Ninian. "Numen, Nirvāṇa, and the Definition of Religion. In *Concept and Empathy: Essays in the Study of Religion,* edited by Donald Wiebe, 40–48. New York: New York University Press, 1986.

Smith, Vincent A. *The Oxford History of India.* 4th ed. New York: Oxford University Press, 1985.

Sontheimer, Gunther D. *Pastoral Deities in Western India.* New York: Oxford University Press, 1989.

———. "Between Ghost and God: A Folk Deity of the Deccan." In *Criminal Gods and Demon Devotees: Essays on the Guardians of Popular Hinduism*, edited by Alf Hiltebeitel, 299–337. Albany, N.Y.: SUNY Press, 1989.

———. "God as the King for All: The Sanskrit Mallāri Māhātmya and its Context." In *Panels of the VIIth World Sanskrit Conference*, vol. 3, *The History of Sacred Places in India as Reflected in Traditional Literature: Papers on Pilgrimage in South Asia*, edited by Hans Bakker, 103–30. Leiden: E. J. Brill, 1990.

Stade, R. C. *Ninety-nine Names of God in Islam: A Translation of the Major Portion of al-Ghazali's Al-Maqsad Al-Asna*. Ibadan: Daystar Press, 1970.

Stanley, John M. "Gods, Ghosts, and Possession." In *The Experience of Hinduism: Essays on Religion in Maharashtra*, edited by Eleanor Zelliot and Maxine Berntsen, 26–59. Albany, N.Y.: SUNY Press, 1988.

———. 'The Capitulation of Maṇi: A Conversion Myth in the Cult of Khaṇḍobā." In *Criminal Gods and Demon Devotees: Essays on the Guardians of Popular Hinduism*, edited by Alf Hiltebeitel, 271–98. Albany, N.Y.: SUNY Press, 1989.

Svahananda, Swami, trans. *Pañcadaśī*, by Vidyāraṇya. Madras: Ramakrishna Math, 1975.

Syed, Mohammad Hafiz. *Suk-Sahela of Shah Burhan-uddin Janam*. Allahabad University Studies, 6, pt. 1. Allahabad, 1930.

Tacchi Venturi, P. *Storia delle Religioni*. Torino, 1971.

Tilak, Bal Gangadhar. *Śrī Bhagavad Gītā Rahasya or Karma-Yoga Śāstra*. Translated into English by A. S. Sukhankar. Pune, 1980.

Trimingham, Spencer J. *The Sufi Orders in Islam*. 2d ed. New York: Oxford University Press, 1973.

Tulpule, Shankar Gopal. *Classical Marāṭhī Literature: From the Beginning to A. D. 1818*. Wiesbaden: Otto Harrassowitz, 1979.

———. *Mysticism in Medieval India*. Wiesbaden: Otto Harrassowitz, 1984.

Tweedie, Irina. *The Chasm of Fire*. Shaftesbury, Dorset: Element Books, 1979.

Upadhyaya, K. D. "Indian Botanical Folklore." In *Tree Symbol Worship in India: A New Survey of a Pattern of Folk-Religion*, edited by Sankar Sen Gupta, 1–18. Calcutta: Indian Publications, 1965.

Valiuddin, Mir. *Contemplative Disciplines in Sufism*. London: East-West Publications, 1980.

Van Buitenen, J. A. B. "Rāmānuja on the Bhagavadgītā." Ph. D. diss. Utrecht, 1953.

Vatsyayan, K. *Kalātattvakośa: A Lexicon of Fundamental Concepts of the Indian Arts (Eight Selected Terms)*. Delhi: Indira Gandhi National Centre for the Arts; Motilal Banarsidass, 1988.

Vaudeville, Charlotte. *Kabīr Granthāvalī (Dohā)*. Pondichéry: Publications de l'Institut Français d'Indologie, 1957.

———. *L'Invocation: Le Haripāṭh de Dñyāndev*. Paris: École Française d'Extrême-Orient, 1969.

———. "Pandharpur: The City of Saints." In *Structural Approaches to South Asian Studies*, edited by Harry M. Buck and Glenn E. Yocum, 137–61. Chambersburg, Pa.: Wilson Books, 1974.

———. *Kabīr*. 2 vols. Oxford: Oxford University Press, 1974.

Verma, O. P. *A Survey of Hemadpanti Temples in Maharashtra*. Nagpur: Nagpur University, 1973.

Yogananda, Paramahansa. *Autobiography of a Yogi*. 12th ed. Los Angeles: Self-Realization Fellowship, 1981.

Yule, Henry and Burnell, A. C. *Hobson-Jobson: A Glossary of Colloquial Anglo-Indian Words and Phrases, and of Kindred Terms, Etymological, Historical, Geographical and Discursive*. Reprint; Delhi: Rupa, 1989 (1886).

Westcott, G. H. *Kabir and Kabir Panth*. 2d ed. Calcutta: Susil Gupta, 1953.

Wolpert, Stanley A. *Tilak and Gokhale: Revolution and Reform in the Making of Modern India*. Reprint; New Delhi: Oxford University Press, 1989 (1961).

Zelliot, Eleanor. "A Medieval Encounter Between Hindu and Muslim: Eknāth's Drama-Poem Hindu-Turk Saṃvād." In *Images of Man: Religion and Historical Process in South Asia*, edited by F. W. Clothey, 171–95. Madras: New Era Publications, 1982.

———. "Four Radical Saints." In *Religion and Society in Maharashtra*, edited by Milton Israel and N. K. Wagle, 131–44. Toronto: University of Toronto, Centre for South Asian Studies, 1987.

Selected Bibliography on the Sai Baba Movement

Studies on the Sai Baba Movement

Rao, Sham D. P. *Five Contemporary Gurus in the Shirdi (Sai Baba) Tradition.* Bangalore: Christian Institute for the Study of Religion and Society, 1972.

White, Charles S. J. "The Sai Baba Movement: Approaches to the Study of Indian Saints." *Journal of Asian Studies* 31, no. 4 (1972): 863–78.

———. "Structure and the History of Religions: Some Bhakti Examples." *History of Religions* 18, no. 1 (Aug. 1978): 77–94.

———. 'The Sai Baba Movement." In *The Sai Baba Movement: Study of a Unique Contemporary Moral and Spiritual Movement.* New Delhi: Arnold-Heinemann, 1985.

Sai Baba of Shirdi (d. 1918)

Bharadwaja, Acharya E. *Sai Baba the Master.* Ongole: Sai Master Publications, 1983.

Bharucha, Perin S. *Sai Baba of Shirdi.* Shirdi: Shri Sai Sansthan, 1980.

Das Ganu. *A Humble Tribute of Praise to Shri Sainath: Shri Sainath Stavanamanjari.* Translated into English by Zarine Taraporevala. Bombay: Sai Dhun Enterprises, 1987.

Ganguly, H. S. *Sai Baba of Shirdi.* New Delhi: Diamond Pocket Books.

Gunaji, Nagesh Vasudev. *Shri Sai Satcharita;* or *The Wonderful Life and*

Teachings of Shri Sai Baba (adapted from the original Marathi of Hemadpant). 10th ed. Bombay: Sri Sai Baba Sansthan, 1982.

Harper, Marvin Henry. "The Fakir: Sri Sai Baba of Shirdi." Chap. 2 in *Gurus, Swamis, and Avataras: Spiritual Masters and Their American Disciples*. Philadelphia: Westminster Press, 1972.

Hattiangadi, Shaila. *Sai's Story*. Bombay: India Book House, 1991.

Joshi, Hariprasad Shivprasad. *Origin and Development of Dattātreya Worship in India*. Chap. 12. Baroda: Maharaja Sayajirao University of Baroda, 1965.

Kamath, M. V. and Kher, V. B. *Sai Baba of Shirdi: A Unique Saint*. Bombay: Jaico Publishing House, 1991.

Khaparde, G. S. *Sources of Sai History*. Bangalore, 1956.

———. *Shirdi Diary*. Shirdi: Shri Sai Baba Sansthan.

Kher, V. B. "A Search for the Birth Place of Shri Sai Baba." *Shri Sai Leela* (Henceforth *SSL*), Jan. 1976.

———. "The Guru of Shri Sai Baba." Pts. 1 and 2. *SSL*, Apr. 1976 and May 1976.

———. "Shri Akkalkot Swami Maharaj and Shri Sai Baba." *SSL*, July 1976.

———. "The Miracle of the Mare." Pts. 1 and 2. *SSL*, March 1985 and April 1985.

———. "How K. J. Bhishma Composed 'Shri Sainath Sagunopasana.'" *SSL*, Sept. 1985.

———. "The Significance of Shri Sai Baba's Various Actions." Pts. 1 and 2. *SSL*, Oct. 1985 and Nov. 1985.

———. "Shri Sai Baba and His Devotee Khushalchand Seth of Rahata." *SSL*, July 1987.

———. "Sai Baba: The Nature of His Functions and Powers." *SSL* Aug. 1987.

———. "The Fakir whom Sai Baba Instructed for Twelve Years." *SSL*, Jan. 1990.

———. "Sai Baba and Sufis." *SSL*, Feb. 1990.

———. "Dincharya of Shri Sai Baba." *SSL*, March 1990.

Mehta, Rao Saheb H. B. *The Spiritual Symphony of Shree Sainath*. Bombay, 1952.

Munsiff, Abdul Ghani. "Hazrat Sai Baba." *The Meher Baba Journal* (Ahmednagar) 1(1938–39).

Murthy, Gopalakrishna S. *Understanding Shirdi Sai.* Hyderabad: Sri Shirdi Sai Prema Mandiramu, 1977.

Narasimhaswami, B. V. *Sri Sai Baba's Charters and Sayings.* Madras: All India Sai Samaj, 1942.

———. *Devotees' Experiences of Sai Baba.* 3d ed. 3 vols. Madras: All India Sai Samaj, 1965–67.

———. *Life of Sai Baba.* 3d ed. 4 vols. Madras: All India Sai Samaj, 1980–83.

Osborne, Arthur. *The Incredible Sai Baba.* Reprint; Delhi: Orient Longmans, 1970 (1957).

Parchure, D. D. *Children's Sai Baba: A Publication of Shirdi Sansthan of Sai Baba.* 3d ed. Bombay: Radharaman Printing Press, 1983.

Pradhan, M. V. *Sri Sai Baba of Shirdi.* 8th ed. Bombay: Sri Sai Baba Sansthan, 1982.

Ramalingaswami. *The Golden Words of Sri Sai Baba of Shirdi.* Shirdi, 1983.

———. *Ambrosia in Shirdi.* Shirdi: Shri Sai Baba Sansthan, 1984.

Sahukar, Mani. *Sai Baba: The Saint of Shirdi.* 3d ed. Bombay: Somaiya Publications, 1983.

Sai Sharan Anand. *Shri Sai the Superman.* Shirdi: Shri Sai Baba Sansthan.

Shepherd, Kevin. "Hazrat Sai Baba of Shirdi." In *Gurus Rediscovered: Biographies of Sai Baba of Shirdi and Upasni Maharaj of Sakori,* 1–80. Cambridge: Anthropographia Publications, 1985.

Shri Sai Leela. English ed. (Official organ of Shri Sai Baba Sansthan of Shirdi.)

Sri Sai Vani, no. 18–19 (July–Aug. 1981). Edited by Sri Narayana Baba. Thane, Maharashtra: Sri Bhagawati Sai Sansthan.

Tales of Sai Baba. Amar Chitra Kathā, no. 225. Bombay: India Book House.

Tanavde, S. V. *May Sai Baba Bless Us All.* Bombay: Tardeo Book Depot Publication, 1984.

Uban, Sujan Singh. "Sai Baba of Shirdi." Chap. 10 in *The Gurus of India.* London: Fine Books, 1977.

Upasani Baba of Sakuri (1870–1941)

Godamasuta, ed. *The Talks of Sadguru Upasani-Baba Maharaja.* 4 vols. Reprint; Sakuri: Shri Upasani Kanya Kumari Sthan, 1978 (1957).

Harper, Marvin Henry. "The Saint Who Suffered: Sri Upasani Baba Maharaj." Chap. 3 in *Gurus, Swamis, and Avataras: Spiritual Masters and Their American Disciples.* Philadelphia: Westminster Press, 1972.

Junnarkar, R. S. *A Pictorial Story of Shree Upasani Kanya Kumari Ashram, Sakuri.* Reprint; Sakuri: Shri Upasani Kanya Kumari Sthan, 1973 (1955).

Narasimhaswami, B. V. and Subbarao, S. *Sage of Sakuri: Life Story of Shree Upasani Maharaj.* 4th ed. Sakuri: Shri Upasani Kanya Kumari Sthan, 1966.

———. "Sri Upasani Baba." Chap. 6 in *Life of Sai Baba.* 3d ed. Vol. 2. Madras: All India Sai Samaj, 1983.

Sahukar, Mani. "Shri Upasani Baba." Pt. 2, chap. 3 in *Sai Baba: The Saint of Shirdi.* 3d ed. Bombay: Somaiya Publications, 1983.

Shashi, Ahluwalia. "Sai Baba of Shirdi." Chap. 15 in *Spiritual Masters from India.* Delhi: Manas Publications, 1987.

Shepherd, Kevin. "Upasni Maharaj of Sakori." In *Gurus Rediscovered: Biographies of Sai Baba of Shirdi and Upasni Maharaj of Sakori,* 83–142. Cambridge: Anthropographia Publications, 1985.

Tipnis, S. N. *Contributions of Upasani Baba to Indian Culture.* Sakuri: Shri Upasani Kanya Kumari Sthan, 1966.

Sati Godavari Mataji of Sakuri (b. 1914)

Harper, Marvin Henry. "Four 'Holy Mothers.'" In *Gurus, Swamis, and Avataras: Spiritual Masters and Their American Disciples,* 188–95. Philadelphia: Westminster Press, 1972.

Sahukar, Mani. *Sweetness and Light: An Exposition of Sati Godavari Mataji's Philosophy and Way of Life.* Bombay: Bharatiya Vidya Bhavan, 1966.

Tipnis, S. N. *Life of Shri Godavari Mataji.* Jabalpur: Aryan Press, 1983.

Meher Baba of Pune (1894–1969)

Abdullah, Abdul Kareem (Ramjoo). *Sobs and Throbs or Some Spiritual Highlights*. Reprint; Phoenix: Avatar Meher Baba Center, 1969 (1929).

Adriel, Jean. *Avatar: The Life Story of the Perfect Master Meher Baba; A Narrative of Spiritual Experience*. Santa Barbara, Calif.: J. F. Rowny Press, 1947.

Anzar, Naosherwan. *The Answer: Conversations with Meher Baba*. Bombay: Glow Publications, 1972.

———. *The Beloved: The Life and Work of Meher Baba*. North Myrtle Beach, S.C.: Sheriar, 1974.

Bharucha, H. P. *Meher Baba's Last Sahavas*. Navsari, India: Dr. H. P. Bharucha, 1969.

———. *Meher Baba: The Compassionate Father*. Navsari, India: Dr. H. P. Bharucha, 1972.

Brabazon, Francis. *Stay with God*. Sydney: Garuda, 1959.

———. *The East-West Gathering*. Sydney: Meher House, 1963.

———. *Journey with God and Messages of Meher Baba*. North Myrtle Beach, S.C.: Sheriar, 1971.

———. *The Silent Word: Being Some Chapters of the Life and Time of Avatar Meher Baba*. Bombay: Meher Baba Foundation, 1978.

Brunton, Paul. "I Meet a Messiah," "At the Parsee Messiah's Headquarters." Chaps. 4, 14 in *A Search in Secret India*. David McCay, 1934. London: Rider, 1970.

Cohen, Allan Y., ed. *The Mastery of Consciousness*. Middlesex: Eel Pie Publishing, 1977.

Donkin, William. *The Wayfarers: An Account of the Work of Meher Baba with the God-Intoxicated, and also with Advanced Souls, Sadhus and the Poor*. 2d printing; San Francisco: Sufism Reoriented, 1969.

Duce, Ivy Oneita. *How a Master Works*. Walnut Creek, Calif: Sufism Reoriented, 1975.

Harper, Marvin Henry. "The Highest of the High: Meher Baba." Chap. 4 in *Gurus, Swamis and Avataras: Spiritual Masters and Their American Disciples*. Philadelphia: Westminster Press, 1972.

Hopkinson, Tom, and Hopkinson, Dorothy. *Much Silence: Meher Baba, His Life and Work*. New York: Dodd, Mead, 1974.

Introvigne, Massimo. "Il dio che taceva." Chap. 5 in *I Nuovi Culti: dagli Hare Krishna alla Scientologia*. Milano: Arnoldo Mondadori, 1990.

Irani, Manija S. *Family Letters*. New York: Society for Avatar Meher Baba, 1969; North Myrtle Beach, S.C.: Sheriar, 1976.

Meher Baba. *Listen, Humanity*. Narrated and edited by D. E. Stevens. San Francisco: Sufism Reoriented, 1957; New York: Harper Colophon, 1971.

———. *Beams from Meher Baba on the Spiritual Panorama*. 2d ed. San Francisco: Sufism Reoriented, 1968 (1958).

———. *Sparks from Meher Baba*. North Myrtle Beach, S.C.: Friends of Meher Baba, 1962.

———. *Meher Baba on Love*. 5th ed. Pune: Meher Era, 1978 (1966).

———. *God in a Pill? Meher Baba on L.S.D. and the High Roads*. San Francisco: Sufism Reoriented, 1966.

———. *Discourses*. 6th ed. 3 vols. San Francisco: Sufism Reoriented, 1967.

———. *The Everything and the Nothing*. Berkeley: Beguine Library, 1971.

———. *Life at Its Best*. New York: Harper and Row, 1972.

———. *Darshan Hours*. Berkeley: Beguine Library, 1973.

———. *God Speaks*. New York: Dodd, Mead, 1973.

———. *The Path of Love*. New York: Samuel Weiser, 1976.

Natu, Bal. *Glimpses of the God-Man Meher Baba*. Vol. 1 (1943–1948). Walnut Creek, Calif.: Sufism Reoriented, 1977; Vol. 2 (1949–52). Bombay: Meher House, 1979.

Needleman, Jacob. "Meher Baba." Chap. 3 in *The New Religions*. New York: Doubleday, 1970.

Nigam, Keshav Narayan. *Meher Chalisa*. Hamirpur, India: K. N. Nigam, 1962.

Purdom, Charles B. *The Perfect Master: The Early Life of Meher Baba*. 2d ed. North Myrtle Beach, S.C.: Sheriar, 1976 (1937).

———. *The God-Man: The Life, Journeys and Work of Meher Baba with an Interpretation of His Silence and Spiritual Teaching*. London: Allen & Unwin, 1964.

———. *God to Man and Man to God: The Discourses of Meher Baba*. North Myrtle Beach, S.C.: Sheriar, 1975.

Tales from the New Life with Meher Baba. Narrated by Eruch [Jessawala], Mehera [Irani], Mani [Irani], and Maheru [Irani)]. Berkeley: Beguine Library, 1976.

Udasin, Satya Prakash Swami, ed. *The Life Circulars of Avatar Meher Baba.* Hyderabad: Meher Vihar Trust, 1968.

Satya Sai Baba of Puttaparthi (b. 1926)

Babb, Lawrence A. *Redemptive Encounters: Three Modern Styles in the Hindu Tradition.* Pt 3. Berkeley and Los Angeles: University of California Press, 1986.

———. "Sathya Sai Baba's Saintly Play." In *Saints and Virtues,* edited by John Stratton Hawley, 168–86. Berkeley and Los Angeles: University of California Press, 1987.

Balasingham, C. *Sai Baba and the Hindu Theory of Evolution.* Delhi: Macmillan Company of India, 1974.

Balse, Mayah. *Mystics and Men of Miracles in India.* New Delhi: Orient Paperbacks, 1978.

Balu, Shakuntala. *Living Divinity.* Bangalore: S. B. Publications, 1983.

Balu, V. *The Glory of Puttaparthi...* Bangalore: S. B. Publications, 1980.

Baskin, Diana. *Divine Memories of Sathya Sai Baba.* San Diego, Calif.: Birth Day Publishing Company, 1990.

Bharati, Agehananda. "So'hi Allah Wahi Rām? The Anthropology of the Hindu-Muslim Interface." Chap. 4 in *Hindu Views and Ways and the Hindu-Muslim Interface: An Anthropological Assessment.* Santa Barbara, Calif.: Ross-Erikson, 1982.

———. "Religious Revival in Modern Time." In *The Cambridge Encyclopedia of India, Pakistan, Bangladesh, Sri Lanka.* Edited by F. Robinson, 348–49. Cambridge: Cambridge University Press, 1989.

Bharvani, A. D. and Malhotra, V. *Shirdi Sai and Sathya Sai are One and the Same.* Bombay: Sai Sahitya Samithi, 1983.

Bhavan's Journal: Baba Shashtyabdapoorti Number. 32, no. 8 (Nov. 16–30, 1985).

Brooke, T. *Sai Baba, Lord of the Air.* Delhi: Vikas Publishing House, 1979.

Caffery, Susan. *Tales from Sai Wonder Land.* 2 vols. Bombay: Sri Sathya Sai Bal Vikas Magazine.

Craxi, Antonio e Sylvie. *L'Alba di una Nuova Era.* Modena: Libreria Internazionale Sathya Sai, 1982.

Devi, Indra. *Sai Baba and Sai Yoga.* Delhi: Macmillan Company of India, 1975.

Fanibunda, Eruch B. *Vision of the Divine.* Reprint; Prasanthi Nilayam: Sri Sathya Sai Books and Publications, 1987 (1976).

Gokak, V. K. *Bhagavan Sri Sathya Sai Baba: The Man and the Avatar: An Interpretation.* 2d ed. Delhi: Abhinav Publications, 1983.

———. *Sai Chandana.* Bangalore, 1985.

Haraldsson, Erlendur. *Modern Miracles: An Investigative Report on Psychic Phenomena Associated with Sathya Sai Baba.* New York: Fawcett Columbine, 1988.

Harper, Marvin Henry. "The Divine Magician: The Miraculous Life of Sathya Sai Baba." Chap. 5 in *Gurus, Swamis, and Avataras: Spiritual Masters and Their American Disciples.* Philadelphia: Westminster Press, 1972.

Hislop, John S. *Conversations with Bhagavan Sri Sathya Sai Baba.* 4th ed. Prasanthi Nilayam: Sri Sathya Sai Books and Publications, 1982.

———. *My Baba and I.* San Diego: Birth Day Publishing Company, 1985.

Introvigne, Massimo. "Sai Baba dei miracoli." Chap. 9 in *I Nuovi Culti: dagli Hare Krishna alla Scientologia.* Milano: Arnoldo Mondadori Editore, 1990.

Kakade, R. T. and Veerabhadra Rao, A. *Shirdi to Puttaparthi.* 4th ed. Hyderabad: Ira Publications, 1991.

Kanu, Victor. *Sai Baba: God Incarnate: An Introduction.* London: Sawbridge, 1981.

Kasturi, N. *Sathyam Sivam Sundaram: The Life of Bhagavan Sri Sathya Sai Baba.* 4 vols. Prasanthi Nilayam: Sri Sathya Sai Books and Publications, 1981.

———. *Loving God.* Prasanthi Nilayam: Sri Sathya Sai Books and Publications, 1982.

———. *Easwaramma: The Chosen Mother.* Prasanthi Nilayam: Sri Sathya Sai Books and Publications, 1984.

———. *Garland of 108 Precious Gems.* Prasanthi Nilayam: Sri Sathya Sai Books and Publications, 1984.

———. *Prasanthi: Pathway to Peace.* Prasanthi Nilayam: Sri Sathya Sai Books and Publications, 1985.

Kausalyarani, Raghavan. *Guide to Indian Culture and Spirituality: Based on the Divine Teachings of Bhagavan Sri Sathya Sai Baba.* 5th ed. Prasanthi Nilayam: Sri Sathya Sai Books and Publications, 1990.

Krystal, Phyllis. *Sai Baba: The Ultimate Experience.* London: Sawbridge, 1985.

Lee, Raymond L. M. "Sai Baba, Salvation and Syncretism: Religious Change in a Hindu Movement in Urban Malaysia." *Contributions to Indian Sociology,* 16, no. 1 (Jan.–June 1982): 125–40.

Levin, Howard. *Good Chances.* Tustin, Calif.: Sathya Sai Book Center of America, 1985.

Lowenberg, R. *At the Feet of Sai.* Bombay: India Book House, 1983.

Mangalwadi, Vishal. *The World of Gurus.* Chap. 8. Delhi: Vikas Publishing House, 1977.

Marwaha, Annemarie. *...and the Greatest is Love: My Experiences with Bhagavan Sri Sathya Sai Baba.* Prasanthi Nilayam: Sri Sathya Sai Books and Publications, 1986.

Mason, Peggy and Laing, Ron. *Sathya Sai Baba: The Embodiment of Love.* London: Sawbridge, 1982.

Mavinkurve, Brahmanand. *Namasmarana, a Universal Sadhana: A Garland of Extracts from Sri Sathya Sai Baba's Discourses.* Prasanthi Nilayam: Sri Sathya Sai Books and Publications.

Mazzoleni, Mario. *Un sacerdote incontra Sai Baba: Il maestro indiano è una incarnazione divina?* Milano: Armenia Editore, 1991.

Murphet, Howard. *Sai Baba: Man of Miracles.* 6th ed. York Beach, Maine: Samuel Weiser, 1987 (1971).

———. *Sai Baba Avatar: A New Journey into Power and Glory.* Reprint; Delhi: Macmillan India, 1980 (1978).

———. *Sai Baba: Invitation to Glory.* Delhi: Macmillan India, 1982.

Murthy, M. V. N. *The Greatest Adventure: With Sai to Sai. Essays on the Sai Avatar and His Message.* Prasanthi Nilayam: Sri Sathya Sai Books and Publications, 1983.

Narasappa, A. P., Narasappa, Radha, and Seethalakshmi, R. *Sahasradalakamala: 1008 Names of Bhagavan Sri Sathya Sai Baba with English Translation.* 2d ed. Bangalore: T. A. Appaji Gowda, 1985.

Page, V. S. *Dialogues with the Divine: Conversations with Bhagavan Sri Sathya Sai Baba.* Delhi: Gulab Printers, 1981.

Pavese, Armando. *Sai Baba. Anatomia del "nuovo Cristo" e dei suoi miracoli attraverso la psicologia del profondo, la parapsicologia e la fede cristiana.* Casale Monferrato: Editioni Piemme, 1992.

Penn, Charles. *My Beloved: The Love and Teachings of Bhagavan Sri Sathya Sai Baba.* Prasanthi Nilayam: Sri Sathya Sai Books and Publications, 1981.

Penn, Faith, and Penn, Charles. *Sai Ram: Experiencing the Love and Teachings of Bhagavan Sri Sathya Sai Baba.* Prasanthi Nilayam: Sri Sathya Sai Books and Publications, 1985.

Rai, Mohan R. *Satya Sai Avtar: Glimpses of Divinity.* New Delhi: Sterling Publishers, 1987.

Rao, Ganapati. *Baba: Satya Sai.* Rao Ganapati, 1985.

Rao, M. N. *Sathya Sai Baba: God as Man.* Tustin, Calif.: Sathya Sai Book Center of America, 1985.

Ruhela, Satya Pal, and Robinson, Duane. *Sai Baba and His Message: A Challenge to Behavioural Sciences.* 6th ed. Delhi: Vikas Publishing House, 1982.

Sahukar, Mani. "A Personal Reaction: The Charisma of Shri Satya Sai Baba." Pt. 2, chap. 3 in *Sai Baba: The Saint of Shirdi.* 3d ed. Bombay: Somaiya Publications, 1983.

Sanathana Sarathi. English ed.

Sandweiss, Samuel H. *Sai Baba: The Holy Man...and the Psychiatrist.* San Diego, Calif.: Birth Day Publishing, 1975.

———. *Spirit and the Mind.* San Diego, Calif.: Birth Day Publishing, 1985.

Satya Sai Baba. *Sathya Sai Speaks: Discourses given by Bhagavan Sri Sathya Sai Baba.* Compiled by N. Kasturi. 11 vols. Prasanthi Nilayam: Sri Sathya Sai Books and Publications.

———. *Chinna Katha: Stories and Parables.* Prasanthi Nilayam: Sri Sathya Sai Books and Publications, 1975.

———. *Sadhana: The Inward Path: Quotations from the Divine Discourses of Bhagavan Sri Sathya Sai Baba.* Prasanthi Nilayam: Sri Sathya Sai Education and Publication Foundation, 1976.

———. *Summer Roses on the Blue Mountains, 1976.* Prasanthi Nilayam: Sri Sathya Sai Education and Publication Foundation, 1977.

———. *Bhagavatha Vahini.* 3d ed. Prasanthi Nilayam: Sri Sathya Sai Education and Publication Foundation, 1979.

———. Upanishad Vahini. 4th ed. Prasanthi Nilayam: Sri Sathya Sai Books and Publications, 1980.

———. *Jnana Vahini.* 5th ed. Prasanthi Nilayam: Sri Sathya Sai Books and Publications, 1980.

———. *Dhyana Vahini.* 5th ed. Prasanthi Nilayam: Sri Sathya Sai Books and Publications, 1980.

———. *Sathya Sai Vahini.* Prasanthi Nilayam: Sri Sathya Sai Books and Publications, 1981.

———. *Prema Vahini.* 6th ed. Prasanthi Nilayam: Sri Sathya Sai Books and Publications, 1982.

———. *Geetha Vahini.* Reprint. Prasanthi Nilayam: Sri Sathya Sai Books and Publications, 1983.

———. *Vidya Vahini.* Prasanthi Nilayam: Sri Sathya Sai Books and Publications, 1984.

———. *Dharma Vahini.* 7th ed. Prasanthi Nilayam: Sri Sathya Sai Books and Publications, 1985.

———. *Leela Kaivalya Vahini.* Prasanthi Nilayam: Sri Sathya Sai Books and Publications, 1990.

———. *Summer Showers in Brindavan (1972, 1973, 1974, 1978, 1979).* 5 vols. Prasanthi Nilayam: Sri Sathya Sai Books and Publications, 1980.

———. *Summer Showers 1990: Indian Culture and Spirituality: Discourses by Bhagavan Sri Sathya Sai Baba.* Prasanthi Nilayam: Sri Sathya Sai Books and Publications, 1990.

———. *Voice of the Avatar: Extracts from the Divine Discourses of Bhagavan Sri Sathya Sai Baba.* 2 vols. Prasanthi Nilayam: Sri Sathya Sai Books and Publications, 1980.

———. *Ram Katha Rasavahini: The Rama Story: Stream of Sacred Sweetness.* 2d ed. Prasanthi Nilayam: Sri Sathya Sai Books and Publications, 1981–82.

———. *Sandeha Nivarini (Dissolving Doubts). Dialogues with Bhagavan Sri Sathya Sai Baba.* Prasanthi Nilayam: Sri Sathya Sai Books and Publications, 1985 (revised ed.).

———. *Discourses on the Bhagavad Gita.* Prasanthi Nilayam: Sri Satya Sai Books and Publications, 1988.

Shah, Indulal H. *Sixteen Spiritual Summers.* Prasanthi Nilayam: Sri Sathya Sai Books and Publications, 1980.

Sharma Arvind. "New Hindu Religious Movements in India." In *New Religious Movements and Rapid Social Change,* edited by James A. Beckford, 345–72. London: Sage Publications/Unesco, 1986.

Sholapurkar, G. R. *Foot-Prints at Shirdi and Puttaparthi.* 2d ed. Delhi: Bharatiya Vidya Prakashan, 1989.

Swallow, D. A. "Ashes and Powers: Myth, Rite and Miracle in an Indian God-Man's Cult." In *Modern Asian Studies* 16, no. 1 (1982):123–58.

Takyi, H. K., and Khubchandani, Kishin J. *Words of Jesus and Sathya Sai Baba.* Bombay: Prasanthi Printers, 1989 (1986).

Taylor, Donald. "Charismatic Authority in the Sathya Sai Baba Movement." In *Hinduism in Great Britain: The Perpetuation of Religion in an Alien Cultural Milieu,* edited by Richard Burghart, 119–33. London: Tavistock, 1987.

———. "The Community of the Many Names of God: A Saivite Ashram in Rural Wales." In *Hinduism in Great Britain: The Perpetuation of Religion in an Alien Cultural Milieu,* edited by Richard Burghart, 100–18. London: Tavistock, 1987.

Teachings of Sri Satya Sai Baba. Lakemont, Georgia: CSA Press, 1974.

Thomas, Joy. *Life is a Game. Play It!* Beaumont, Calif.: Ontic Book Publishers, 1989.

Tumuluru, Krishna Murty. *Digest: Collection of Sri Sathya Sai Baba's Sayings.* Pontevecchio Magenta, Milan: Fondazione Sathya Sai Seva Roveredo, 1985.

Uban, Sujan Singh. "Satya Sai Baba." Chap. 11 in *The Gurus of India.* London: Fine Books, 1977.

Unity is Divinity. Purity is Enlightenment. Modena: Libreria Internazionale Sathya Sai, 1983.

Warner, Judy. *Transformation of the Heart: Stories by Devotees of Sathya Sai Baba.* York Beach, Maine: Samuel Weiser, 1990.

Youngs, Homer S. *Translations by Baba.* Tustin, Calif.: Sathya Sai Book Center of America, 1975.

Index